Date Due

The Gods of Atheism

VINCENT P. MICELI, S.J.

THE

GODS

OF

ATHEISM

ARLINGTON HOUSE   *New Rochelle, N.Y.*

Library of Congress Catalog Card Number 76-115349

ISBN 0-87000-099-3

MANUFACTURED IN THE UNITED STATES OF AMERICA

TO HIS HOLINESS POPE PAUL VI
BY THE GOODNESS OF GOD
PRINCE OF PASTORS IN THE UNIVERSAL CHURCH
INFALLIBLE TEACHER OF THE CHRISTIAN FAITH
COURAGEOUS PROTECTOR OF HUMAN LIFE
WITH AFFECTION AND ADMIRATION
ON THE OCCASION OF
THE FIFTIETH ANNIVERSARY OF
HIS ORDINATION TO THE HOLY PRIESTHOOD

Contents

Acknowledgment

The research for this study on contemporary atheism began in the Spring of 1967 when WWL-TV, channel 4 of Loyola University of New Orleans, invited the author, then associate professor of philosophy at the university, to give a series of lectures on this subject as a part of its program in the public interest entitled: At The College Level. Ten half-hour lectures were taped and shown under the title of Adventures In Atheism. Audience response was good and so the city's educational channel WYES replayed the tapes at another time for the benefit of those who might have missed them. I am glad to render thanks to WWL-TV for goading me into this work.

At the end of that same academic year Loyola University presented me with a year's leave of absence and a grant of $3,300 to go to Europe and expand the lectures into a book-size study. I am deeply indebted to Loyola University for its initial interest and financial assistance towards the creation of the embryonic stages of this book.

After a year in Paris, where Part I of the book was researched, I was given another year's leave of absence, this time at Rome, but without a renewal of the grant, the university's fund for research grants having been discontinued. It was at this time of crisis that the Rev. Martin V. Jarreau, S. J., Vice-President of the University for Community Relations, persuaded the members of the Greater New Orleans Italian Cultural Society to finance the book to its completion. It was due to the sustaining vision and generosity of Fr. Jarreau, the Italian Cultural Society—under the leadership of Dr. Nicholas Accardo and Attorney Peter Compagno—along with many other benefactors, too numerous to mention here, that the period of gestation for this book was successfully completed. They deserve the greatest credit and my deepest thanks for insuring the book's development through its four parts to its birth in publication.

Preface

Father Vincent Miceli is the most recent of a valiant company within the Society of Jesus who clearly perceive that God is the heart of the matter no matter what aspect of reality or of illusion we seek to get straight. The question of God's existence runs, mercury-like, through the discussion and evaluation of all the other questions which stimulate or depress the minds of men.

Today, smack in the middle of the age of scientism, technology and the myth of progress, there is not a problem which can be put in perspective or given the hope of enduring resolution except in terms of our answer to the basic question posed briefly but definitely in the phrase of the scholastics: *Utrum Deus sit?*

Ultimately, the answer to that question and to the built-in question which follows from it—i.e., *What kind of a God is God, if He exists?* —is the beginning of the answer to any other questions worth asking. The master knots of human fate, the mysteries of life and death, the contradictions of good and evil, the history of nations and the destinies of persons, these, when all is said and done, have eternal significance or none at all according as we answer this first and basic question.

Whatever the merits of new methodologies in catechetics, none of these can compete with the quality of clarity, finality and basic importance which characterized the opening question of the very first catechism that introduced us, in something like formal terms, to the faith: *What is God?*

One need not be reminded that competent contemporary theologians and philosophers, who are exploring the multiple implications of this so fundamental question, have been forced to a vocabulary infinitely more complicated than that of the dreadful penny catechism. Indeed, the God Who was once understood, however dimly, as Pure Act, Sheer Intelligence, Untrammeled Truth and Love, has almost been lost in the rhetoric and the erudition of those who have sought to clarify by expanding the primitive, simple answers to the perennial, inescapable questions: *What is God? What are His claims upon us? What is His relevance to us? What part do we play in any providence, plan, purpose or design He (if He exists) may have? Moreover, if He does not exist, to whom or to what else shall we turn?*

I have mentioned that Father Miceli belongs to that perhaps small

With respect to the book's scholarly and spiritual formation, I would like to express my gratitude to some prominent scholars who cordially received me into their homes or studies and shared with me the wisdom of their reflections. Among such savants I wish to thank the Very Rev. Pedro Arrupe, General of the Society of Jesus, the Rev. Andrew Varga, S. J., Gabriel Marcel, Dr. E. L. Mascall, Jean Cardinal Daniélou, S. J., Sir Arnold Lunn, Mr. Garth Lean, Esq., Dr. Balduin Schwarz, Dr. and Mrs. Goetz Briefs, the Rev. Martin D'Arcy, S. J., Dr. John Crosby, Dr. Josef Seifert, Dr. Damian Fedoryka, the Rev. Anthony C. O'-Flynn, S. J., the Rev. Alfred J. Jolson, S. J. and the Rev. Vincenzo Miano, S. D. B., Secretary of the Vatican Secretariat for Non-Believers.

To two extraordinary scholars and friends—the Rev. Joseph F. Costanzo, S. J., Professor of Historical Jurisprudence and the Rev. Herbert A. Musurillo, S. J., Chairman of the Graduate Department of Classical Studies, both of Fordham University—I would like to pay a special tribute of gratitude. They studied the entire manuscript and raised it to a form of greater cogency by their sagacious criticisms. The scholars whom I have thanked here are, however, in no way responsible for the book's limitations.

Finally, I offer the tribute of cordial thanks to His Eminence John Cardinal Wright for his kindness in honoring this work with a preface of exceptional insight. An international teacher-witness and successor of the Apostles working in Rome, he is directly engaged in striving to cure modern society of its fascination for godless humanism. His mission is of the highest importance, for it puts full emphasis in the Christ-like training of young men destined for the priesthood, leaders destined to radiate the *Veritas* that liberates and the *Caritas* that elevates the community of men into the community of saints.

but God-sent group of Jesuits who have concentrated, with special and insistent attention, on these questions as their preoccupation in the midst of the riddles of the hour. It would be unjust and unfactual to pretend that these Jesuits are the only religious or other theologians concerned with the "problem of God" and the dialogue concerning whatever gods may be; it would, in fact, be depressing if such were the case. But those who love the Jesuit tradition rejoice in the work of those who see this as *the* central issue in our culture and our crises. One such is the incomparable Father Henri de Lubac, who brings such sensitivity, such gifts of intellect and love to the humanistic dialogue concerning the existence and nature of God. Another was our own Father John Courtney Murray, whom one often thinks God intended to be a great theologian rather than, as the pressures of the times turned him out to be, a somewhat specialized political philosopher. Father Murray's lectures at Yale on the existence and nature of God are the only evidence I need to bring in support of my argument in this regard.

Father Vincent Miceli is a third in this special company of contemporary Jesuits. His contribution is an analysis of the modern alternatives to God, the gods of present-day atheism, which those who answer the first question of the penny catechism in a negative fashion, however expensive their best sellers, are obliged sooner or later to worship.

The logical and psychological compulsion to choose some strange god, if the God of Abraham and of Jesus Christ be rejected, rests on needs deep in human nature. Man is a rational animal, as the Greeks taught us. He is also, it is pleasant to remember, a laughing animal. He is a social animal, an economic animal, a political animal and all the other kinds of animal that a score of anthropologies have proven him to be. But underneath it all and overriding all else, he is a mystical animal. He either prays or pouts; he either adores or anguishes. In moments of cultural crises, like our own, he may do all of these in varying proportions. But he remains unalterably God-centered. He cannot exist without a God, and if he rejects the true God he will invariably, instinctively, even perversely create his own false god.

Father Vincent Miceli brings unusual qualifications to his analysis of the gods of atheism and his consequent oblique defense of the God of our fathers. He is the son of a family that honored and cooperated with the God of Life. His vocation to the priesthood in the Society of Jesus was and remains a vocation to serve the God of Truth. His passion to share the truth unto the salvation of others, humble and exalted alike, identifies him as the servant of the God of Love. His academic background prepares him to bear his intellectual and apostolic witness with unusual preparation, skill and cogency. It is a privilege to commend *The Gods of Atheism* to all those who have found God, with whatever fragile hold, and to those who seek Him, with whatever reluctant fear lest having Him they must have naught besides.

JOHN CARDINAL WRIGHT
Prefect, Sacred Congregation for the Clergy

October 1970

Introduction

Atheists, like saints, are made not born. It is not easy to become a saint. The road to the summit of moral transfiguration is steep and treacherous. Left to himself, man cannot manage the climb; his sin-weakened nature is in absolute need of divine grace. Thus, God, Who is holiness Himself, alone can develop sanctity in man. But man, endowed with intelligence and freedom, must, of course, cooperate in his own sanctification. Now the perfect human formula for sainthood is found in Mary's response to God: "Behold, the servant of the Lord. Be it done unto me according to Thy word." Saints are, therefore, formed in the image of God's Word whose "food was to do the Will of Him Who sent me."

Paradoxically, it is not easy to be an atheist either. It is terrifying to attempt escape from the Divine Lover. The road leads down to violent serfdom. Here, however, unlike the quest for sanctity, the drive for atheism is a one-sided affair, demanded by man, contested by God. No one becomes an atheist unknowingly or unwillingly. Even so-called "born atheists" indoctrinated from childhood onward in the schools of Organized Atheism eventually, as adults, must make a decision for or against God. For that matter, the same is true of Christians drilled in the fundamentals of their faith as children. After all, how does one teach minors? According to their capacity, of course. Thus, early indoctrination in itself is a perfectly valid method for instructing minors in the faith of their fathers. The method is vitiated when employed in indoctrinating children, or adults for that matter, in known falsity or moral evil. When, however, minors become intellectual adults, indoctrination should cease. Faith bolstered by reason should be taught and practiced. The science of theology is taught to the intellectually advanced. Thus, in the adult the responsibility for belief calls for his ratification of his childhood faith by a decision for God and His revelation. St. Peter, the Apostles, the learned Fathers and Doctors of the Church exhorted Christians of all walks of life to be always ready to present any inquirer with reasonable answers for the faith that ruled their minds and hearts.

For their part, atheists are not backward in giving reason to their unbelief. And they do so with philosophic profoundity and literary virtuosity, as this study aims at demonstrating. Pascal recognized what Ronald Knox might have called "the enthusiasm," that is, the blazing zeal in the religion of humanistic atheism. His immortal statement on the subject declares: "Atheism is an indication of spiritual vigor but only to a certain degree."[1] We hope to show that atheism's vigor arises from its heroic will to create mythical gods in place of the true God. We hope to prove that its feebleness is demonstrated by its utter inability to cure the contradictory crisis it creates between man whom it would advance in freedom and its own New God whom it cannot restrain from devouring mankind.

Thus, this study will maintain that no atheist chooses merely to deny God. For the atheist's spiritual posture against God is at the same time his posture in preference for some other Being above God. As he dismisses the true God he is welcoming his New God. Why must this be so? Because every personal commitment of man presupposes, deep in the metaphysical core of his being, a hunger for being as truth and goodness. Man is intrinsically burdened with an incurable hunger for transcendence. If being abhors a vacuum, the vacuum it most violently shrinks from is the total absence of Infinite Being. And history demonstrates that man is inconsolable without the True God. Dostoyevsky who experienced this abhorrence in atheist Russia has one of his characters in *The Devils or The Possessed* express it thus: "If a man were to be deprived of the infinitely great, he would refuse to go on living and die of despair. The infinite and the immeasurable is as necessary to man as the little planet which he inhabits ... My friends, God is necessary to me if only because he is the only being whom one can love eternally."[2]

We have said that it is terrifying to attempt to live without God. Kirilov, one of the many atheists in *The Devils* testifies to

---

1. Blaise Pascal, *Penseés*, ed. Brunschvicg, III, p. 431.
2. Feodor Dostoyevsky, *The Devils or The Possessed* (London: Penguin), pp. 655–656.

this truth. "To realize that there is no God and not to realize at the same instant that you have become God yourself—is an absurdity, for else you would certainly kill yourself. I cannot understand how an atheist could know that there is no God and not kill himself at once!" Why then are so many atheists alive and flourishing? Because, according to Kirilov, they have accepted the role of being their own gods. "For three years I have been searching for the attribute of my divinity, and I've found it: the attribute of my divinity is—Self-Will! That's all I can do to prove in the main point my defiance and my new terrible freedom. For it is very terrible. I am killing myself to show my defiance and my new terrible freedom."[3]

Against the background of this truth, how can we explain the rapid advance of open and camouflaged atheism in our times? How can we evaluate Nicholas Hartmann's call for a "postulatory atheism" which teaches that God not only does not exist, but also that He ought not to exist? In studying some of the great intellectual atheists of our times, we will try to show that such atheists continued to exist and work laboriously, even though they deliberately denied the existence of God, because they had created for themselves a new, attractive god of their own. And they had dedicated themselves and their work to this new Transcendent Being. Far from despairing over the loss of the rejected God, these learned giants, with high *hubris,* threw themselves into the thrilling eschatological *divertissement* of planning and directing the temporal destiny of man in the service of their New God.

Eric Voegelin carefully concluded, after studying profoundly the new Gnostic gods espoused by our modern atheists, as follows: "The death of the spirit is the price of progress. Nietzsche revealed this mystery of the Western apocalypse when he announced that God was dead and that He had been murdered. This Gnostic murder is constantly committed by men who sacrifice God to civilization. The more fervently all human energies are thrown into the great enterprise of salvation through world-immanent action, the farther the human beings who engage in this enterprise move away from the life of the spirit. And since the life of the spirit is the source of order in man and society, the very success of a Gnostic civilization is the cause

3. *Ibid.,* pp. 614–615.

of its decline."[4] Humanistic atheism in the modern form of the idolatrous adoration of the new Gnostic gods is destroying the society of man.

The aim of this work is to indicate that the great sin of contemporary atheism is that it consists, through a sustained act of Supreme Self-Will, in a total preoccupation with the human. This atheism induces man to fall down before himself in narcissistic adoration and love. In one form or another, the systems of thought expounded in this work call man to a religious allegiance solely to Man-God. They reject the one True God and the God-Man whom He sent to divinize man in a valid way. "Not Thy Will but My or Our Human Will be done," is their sole creed, dedication and enterprise.

Pascal, recording the unutterable religious experience he had in an encounter with the true God on the night of November 23, 1654, indicates the only sure road back from the dreadful social ditch into which advancing atheism has tripped man. He wrote: "God of Abraham, God of Isaac, God of Jacob, not of the philosophers and scholars. God of Jesus Christ. God of Jesus Christ. *My God and Your God* ... He alone can be found by the ways taught in the Gospels ... He alone can be kept by the ways taught in the Gospels. Sweet and total submission to Jesus Christ ... "[5]

In this work we are not inspired with a spirit of animus. We are inspired with the spirit of Christian criticism of these atheistic philosophies that have brought and are still inflicting on man great tragedy. It must be remembered throughout this study that the scholars treated, almost to a man, were originally Christians who knew the ways and the message of the Gospels well. Early in their lives they knew Jesus Christ as the Son of God. Moreover, they even loved and lived the ways and message of the Gospels for some part of their lives. Why they went away from God and broke with Christ as His Divine Son they have recorded in many of their works with the hope of persuading others to follow their paths. From the testimony of their lives as atheists, from history's witness of the evil effects of their systems of thought and from long reflective research

4. Eric Voegelin, *The New Science Of Politics* (Chicago: University of Chicago Press, 1952), p. 131.
5. Blaise Pascal, *Pensés* (London: Penguin), pp. 309–310. Italics in original.

we have come to the conclusion that theirs are dangerously misleading and even at times degrading views that sap the spiritual substance of man. That is why we have undertaken to identify, analyze and evaluate their religious philosophies of life. It is hoped that this study may lead readers to reject the paths that run to the temples of the strange Gnostic Gods of humanistic atheism. For in these temples the masses are trapped in the millenium of temporality. On the positive side, it is hoped that those groping for the true God may be helped to find Him and hold Him where he can only be found and held —in Jesus Christ, the way, the truth and the life, in the sweet and total submission to the God-Man.

V.P.M.
Rome

Part One

Gods as Adventures of the Mind

With the blade of his criticism, his *Critique of Pure Reason,* Kant, the executioner, beheaded belief in God. God, therefore, became now nothing but fiction.

Werke IX
Heinrich Heine

The scene is hell. Friedrich Engels in his epic poem depicts Danton, Voltaire and Hegel welcoming Satan, just back from a fact-finding tour to earth where he had also been training freethinkers and atheists in their campaign to transform men into "Godless selfgods " Hegel is explaining what his strategy in this battle was:
"And Hegel, whose mouth until this moment grimness locked,
Suddenly rose up giant high and spoke:
'I consecrated all my life to Science,
Preached atheism with my whole strength:
I placed Self-Consciousness upon her throne,
Convinced I had already conquered God.' "

Friedrich Engels
Quoted by Georg Siegmund
in *God On Trial*

CHAPTER I

Mystery of Atheism

ATHEISM, THE THEME OF THIS STUDY, HAS FROM THE dawn of creation, been *the* great temptation for intelligent creatures. As a possible posture for free persons, atheism is rooted in a universe which, despite its magnificent luminosity, is yet incapable of introducing the free creature to a direct encounter of knowledge and love with his Creator. Ecstatic as he is over the immediate experience of his own splendor as discovered in the fascinating union with a universe resplendent and at his service, the creature tends to be drawn almost inevitably away from the invisible Presence toward an all-engrossing immersion into the visibly beautiful universe of matter and men. There arises a quasi-identification of the created person's project with the project of an ever-evolving universe. This identification often enough develops into the prolonged, permanent, spiritual separation of the creature from his transcendent Creator. Eventually, lost in the love of the ever-present and splendid universe, the creature comes to possess himself, his society and his world as if they were exclusively his own. The fact that he himself and all creatures are really the exclusive possession of a transcendent Lover is lost sight of, or if remembered, resented and rejected, as we shall see in the course of our study.

Thus atheism arises from a mentality and attitude which involves a flight from the invisible toward the visible, from the transcendent toward the immanent, from the spiritual toward the material in such a way that not only are the invisible, transcendent and spiritual rejected as dimensions of reality, but they are denied existence itself. Essentially negative in nature, as etymologically demonstrated from the two Greek words from which it arises, the negating alpha *A* and *Theos,* the word for God, atheism, nevertheless, makes its thrust from a negative-affirmative act of freedom. For atheism receives its true, full meaning from the reality it rejects—God. It represents a choice the creature makes of himself and his universe in preference to his Creator. For every temptation to deny God has as the necessary correlative of this denial the affirmation of the creature over God. All intelligent and free creatures are challenged during their lives to choose God. Another way of expressing this reality is to say that all intelligent and free creatures are tested to see if they will accept God above themselves and their universe by a love of preference. Even Christ, the God-Man, was not exempted from the temptation to atheism in this sense. When the devil led Christ up to a high mountain to show Him in an instant all the kingdoms of the world, he was testing Christ to find out if He were more than man and, if he discovered that Christ was merely man, this same test was calculated to seduce Christ into a denial of God. Here are the devils words: "I will give you all this power and their splendor, for it has been turned over to me, and I can give it to anyone I please. If you will do homage before me, it shall all be yours." But Christ instantly rejected the proposed infidelity: "It is written, 'The Lord thy God shalt thou worship, and Him only shalt thou serve.' "[1]

The person, therefore, who now professes to be and is an atheist did not become such overnight. It is important to realize that atheism, like any other hardened position and prejudice,

1. Luke 4 : 5–8.

normally begins with relatively light, willful stands of rejection. Often enough the beginnings of atheism can be traced to intellectual doubts about the existence or goodness of God. The person is being tested in a *crise de foi,* crisis of faith. There is nothing unnatural or evil in such tests, tormenting though they may be. For God allows these tests in order to give man the opportunity to grow up into a mature, seasoned fellowship of love with Himself. Indeed St. Peter could exhort the early Christians to rejoice "though now for a little while, if need be, you are made sorrowful by various trials, that the temper of your faith—more precious by far than gold which is tried in fire —may be found unto praise and glory and honor at the revelation of Jesus Christ."[2]

Clearly, then, it is seen that the first shoots of atheism arise from the ground of man's infidelity toward God. In the beginning these infidelities may be regretted and resisted, for the mind and will of man, unlike those of the angels, do not ordinarily harden immediately into irrevocable irreconciliation against God. Somewhere along the line, however, a person permits more frequent infidelities, settles down at peace with them and finally abandons the fight for fidelity to God altogether. A decision is firmly made against God. Once the individual's denials of God become mentally and volitionally habitualized, once these denials are incarnated into his goals, motives, enthusiasms—into his project for life, however naturally noble or humanitarian it may be—once, in a word, his rejection of God has become *universalized,* then the unbeliever has raised his particular atheism to the level of a doctrine as well as of a practice. For such a person atheism becomes a theory, a principle, as well as a practical way of life, that justifies metaphysically, theologically and morally all human thought and endeavor as being necessarily opposed to the very idea of God.

The fact that men live in a world in which God is neither visible nor immediately encountered reveals merely the cosmic conditions that make atheism a possible human choice. The causes of atheism, however, always remain within man himself. In the course of history there have always been atheists, but compared to the overwhelming increase of contempo-

2. 1 Peter 1 : 6–8.

rary unbelievers atheists in the past were relatively few in number. Moreover, their atheism was for the most part a purely private affair. As individuals they usually expressed a definite, deliberate, dogmatic denial of God's existence and, since the coming of Christ, specifically rejected the God of the Christians' religious consciousness.

Today, however, the new atheism has attracted millions of souls throughout the world. In the East the new atheism is organized, politicalized; its leaders hold the reins of political, economic and spiritual power. The new atheism refuses to be treated as an abstract system of thought alongside other interesting bookish systems. Atheism in the East identifies itself as the most important historical event of all times; it is dynamic, apostolic, dramatic and demands heroic sacrifices of its adherents; it is scientific, messianic, militant. It has organized and dominates over a billion people willy nilly in its crusade to eradicate God from the hearts and minds of men. And in its mission to make the world totally safe for atheism, it is continually attacking, plotting, propagandizing so that the sun never sets on its activities and there is never any time out from its mission.

At this point we ask ourselves about the state of atheism in the Christian West. Unfortunately, the West is also seriously ill with the disease of bland atheism that is rapidly becoming virulent. Many of its loves are repulsively materialistic; its morals decadent; its crime rates soaring; quantity has replaced quality as one of its ideals; its new god is science and technology; its new allies and alliances are expedient agreements made with tyrannical regimes at the expense of honesty and fidelity to the true God and its true friends. Its goal seems to be peace and prosperity at any price, even the price of changing its true God for an idol. Thus atheism is widespread today in the East and West both as a personal and a social disease. Pope Paul VI, in a speech given at a General Audience on June 14, 1967, faced with anguish these unpalatable facts: "It would be interesting to make a synthesis of the characteristic objections to faith in our times. We could observe the way in which many of these objections proceed from the *'forma mentis,'* that is, from the manner of using our knowing faculty which school, science and the modern mentality have educated into us almost without our knowing it . . . In the world of thought everything is doubted today, and consequently, religion too: It seems as if the mind of modern man finds no peace except in total negation, in abandoning any kind of certainty and any kind of faith. He is like a person with infected eyes who finds no rest except in obscurity, in darkness. Is the realm of darkness to be the final end of human thinking, of man's unquenchable thirst for truth and of his encounter with the living and true God?"[3]

Recently an event of world-wide significance took place and the West's ignoble response to the significance of this event only emphasized the West's contamination with the disease of the new atheism. On November 7, 1967, Moscow celebrated the fiftieth anniversary of the rise of Red atheism to tyrannical power over unhappy, Holy Russia. There was nothing *golden* about this anniversary for the people of Russia, for the people of Christian Eastern Europe, for the Christian people of Cuba, for the hundreds of millions of Chinese or for the people of the rest of the world. Yet how did the West for the most part respond to the commemoration and celebration of the fifty-year advance of triumphant tyranny? Speeches, tributes, cablegrams poured into Moscow extending glowing congratulations to that headquarters of hell on earth for having successfully created a concentration camp of many countries for one billion souls, a "workers' paradise lost," in the title of Eugene Lyons' recent book.[4]

Why were there no statesmen of the free world who dared recall to their subjects the tremendous cost in millions of bodies, minds, souls who were, and are presently still being, tortured, degraded, murdered that the revolution may continue to advance? Was it the magnitude and frequency of the crimes that developed callosities on the Christian consciousness? Why has the Christian consciousness lost its Christ-like compassion and sensibility at the afflictions unjustly imposed upon millions? Moral indifference is the disease of the diluted Christian. Can it be that Christians of the West have become cold to their suffering brethren behind iron and bamboo curtains because

3. Pope Paul VI, "Faith and the Modern Mentality" (Chicago: Scepter Publishers, 1967).
4. Eugene Lyons, *Workers' Paradise Lost* (New York: Funk & Wagnalls, 1967).

they have become cold to Christ? Dull in themselves, have they become dead to others?

In 1949, on the 23rd of November, Dr. Charles Malik, Chairman of the Delegation of Lebanon to the Fourth Session of the General Assembly of the United Nations made a statement before the Political Committee of the General Assembly, assessing the malignant evils that the Godless regime in Moscow had inflicted upon the world and its own people up to that time. Here is part of that statement:

> ... Rights that are absolute and unconditional, rights that are natural and inalienable, rights that inhere in the very nature and dignity of man as a person are rejected by Communism and trampled upon by Communist states in practice ... The Communist state ... necessarily suffocates spontaneity, inner dynamism, freedom and diversity. The spirit of man, which can be itself and its best self only in freedom and love and genuine communion is choked and annihilated by totalitarianism ... Man is not respected by being declared 'the most precious capital'; for man *is* only when he is viewed as destiny-bearing and a destiny-burdened being, and when his relation to himself and to others and to God springs freely and responsibly from the inner depths of his soul.

And Dr. Malik went on to unmask the pious pretensions to peace which the Soviet Union was forever propagandizing:

> Communism in general and the Soviet Union in particular do not really wish peace. Every peace offensive on the part of the Soviet Union is but a strategic or tactical device determined by the particular stage in the development of Communism. It is, in reality, just a phase of an overall war plan.[5]

On November 7, 1967 very few voices in the press and communications media of the free world had the courage to remind the atheist tyrants, even timidly, of the crimes they have perpetrated upon the peoples of the whole world. The tragic fate of millions of peasants, intellectuals, scientists, poets, musicians and churchmen under atheist domination is not surprising.

5. Charles Malik, "War and Peace," speech before UN, (New York: National Committee for a Free Europe, 1950).

Where heaven is obliterated the earth becomes a jungle. But what is surprising is that so few in the Christian West, known as the haven of religious liberty, spoke up to break the eternal silence of the millions of victims, living and dead, whose voices should have been heard to challenge the lies that poured forth from the throat of the Premier of the Red Tyranny in his four-hour, dithyrambic orgy of self-praise.[6]

Recalling the immediate liquidation of thousands by the tyrants when they took over the reins of government in Russia in 1917 is nightmare enough; far more frightful is the realization of the slow assassination of millions of others through these fifty years; unspeakably ghastly has been the prolonged crucifixion of Holy Russia; the steady strangulation of liturgy, literature, art and prayer has been a sacrilege of a heinous sort. But perhaps the most satanic project of the fifty years of the Revolution is its program to extinguish Christian hope or the hope of any transcendent life hereafter in the hearts of all men. This is an especially demonic program because hope in an after-life is all that is left to men, already condemned to death as all are, a hope that alone can sustain and inspire men to make something worthwhile of the present life.

When we realize how silent religious leaders of the West have been in the face of this project for despair, we cannot fail to ask, "Why has this attack on Christian hope raised such little counter-attack in the West? Why have even the Catholic communication media—press, radio, TV—been so paralyzed before this anti-theistic assault?" One had hardly grown reluctantly accustomed to this apathetic scandal of silence, when a new and far more detestable scandal was enacted in the West. One is rendered speechless with astonishment at this new perversion. Attaining the same end as the Communist project to extinguish Christian hope, the horror of this new crime arises from

6. In reading many periodicals of European and American origin, the only organ of eloquent, hopeful protest against the fifty years of Soviet tyranny I was able to find was that of *National Review,* a fortnightly published in New York City. In its lest-we-forget October 31, 1967, issue entitled "50 Years of Soviet Communism," NR looks at the half-century Red Revolution through the minds and hearts of some twenty artist-witnesses whose literary masterpieces so vividly recount the evil news of this godless aggression that the reader is shaken with compassion for the millions of captives behind the iron and bamboo curtains. In contrast, all other accounts seemed fascinated with the success of the Red aggression and implied it was here to stay.

the fact that the project to destroy hope is now undertaken and carried through not by professional atheists but by men who, through special training, positions and duties, are supposed to be dedicated Christian leaders. Priests and bishops, whose vocation it is to sustain and foster faith and hope in themselves and among the faithful, have become the advocates for the prostitution of religion to the purposes of atheism. When ordained ministers and consecrated bishops tell the faithful that "God is dead," when these teachers of the Gospels declare their inability to accept any longer the Virgin Birth, the Divinity of Christ, the Resurrection, the Ascension, the Real Presence, the immortality of the soul, hell, heaven, sin, grace, redemption, when, under the guise of *re-interpreting* Holy Scripture, these teachers *repudiate* Christianity, then has the spirit of Anti-Christ become incarnate in men and the most demonic form of atheism is attacking the Mystical Body of Christ. For then a most grotesque drama is being enacted before the eyes of horrified Christendom in that its anointed ones have become atheists and, still vested as angels of light, they "disown the Lord" in His own house, cause truth to be maligned, introduce destructive sects into the Church, exploit the faithful with specious arguments and lead many to follow their ungodly ways.

Is it any wonder then that Dr. Charles Malik, towards the end of his statement on War and Peace, speaking as a sympathetic friend who loves Christianity and all that the Christian West stands for in its ideals, could yet, nevertheless, honestly set forth the decadence of the West in these words:

> There are many phases of Western life which are repulsively materialistic. The spirit of business and gain, the maddening variety of things exciting your concupiscence, the utter selfishness of uncoordinated activity, all this is not something to attract and inspire . . . To the superficial observer who is unable to penetrate to the core of love and truth which is still at the heart of the West, there is little to choose between the soulless materialism of the West and the militant materialism of the East . . . There is a general weakening of moral fibre. One gains the impression that the great fund of moral strength which has been handed down from the tears and labours of the ages is not being creatively replenished . . . I must say in all humility that the leadership of the West in general does not seem

to be adequate to the unprecedented challenges of the age.[7]

From what has been said so far, atheism is seen as perhaps the most serious spiritual affliction of modern man. There is no dimension of man's activities that has not withered under the destructive voracity of this parasite. Earlier in this chapter we merely indicated some of the stunting effects this blight has had on theological thought, political practice and morals. These will be developed further as our study progresses. But first a closer scrutiny must be given to the roots and forms of atheism.

We have already indicated that atheism is not a blind, innate, untaught, instinctive posture for intelligent creatures. Rather it is a conscious, voluntary, even premeditated development in man. To be sure it stems from a variety of causes and is animated by any number of powerful motives. However, none of these motives, taken singly or all together, for that matter, produces or can explain the atheistic man. In the final analysis, therefore, the phenomenon of atheism will have to be seen as the choice of a free person, influenced by certain circumstances, to be sure, some under and some beyond his control, and driven on by certain motives, all freely fostered however, to break off communion with God irrevocably. A man becomes an atheist because he wants to be an atheist; he wills to be an atheist. Looked at under this light of self-determination against, of self-alienation from God, atheism appears to be much more than a problem; it is a mystery in the meaning given this word by Gabriel Marcel. A look into this creative, classic distinction will prove most fruitful and enable us to understand the nature of atheism more profoundly.

A *problem* is a mental investigation undertaken with respect to an object. A problem bears on something completely outside the investigator. Man becomes an observer before a problem, scrutinizing the object from all sides. And there exists a complete answer to the problem which, given enough time and developing enough know-how, man will eventually obtain. Objectified thought solves problems. But man as a person, as a subject, is not involved in the solution or make-up of a problem.

7. Dr. Charles Malik, "War and Peace."

Scientific knowledge embodies, *par excellence,* the problematic approach to things, to objects.

However, when a man is dealing with realities which cannot be objectified, he cannot use effectively the problematic approach to these realities if he would grow in a valid understanding of them. Why? Because such realities do not exist solely outside the knower; such realities necessarily include and involve the knower as a subject. For example, I cannot regard freedom as outside myself, nor myself as outside freedom. Freedom, as such, is not an object for it includes me and it includes me as a subject who is quite concerned about my freedom and the freedom of my fellow man. Here we have a vision of the greater, the infinite range of the mystery of being. Every question bearing on a mystery recoils upon the questioning subject who will never be able to give a perfect answer or produce a perfect solution to the question. The reason is that the area of the mystery being investigated is ontologically infinite, too profoundly fruitful to be fully comprehended by the limited mind of man. Love, participation in being, hope, freedom and their contraries hate, alienation, despair, serfdom are not merely problems; they are inexhaustible mysteries in this non-theological sense of the word. For these realities involve each human subject in his ontological, intellectual, psychological and historical developments.

If we look at man as he really is known in our concrete experience, we see that his reality is built on the metaphysical fact that his being has its origin in participation in being. His nature craves further participation in being and all his activities are a driving toward a goal which consists in perfect participation in being, in communion with his fellowmen and with the Transcendent. We see that each person's dynamic, physical and metaphysical nature, from its very conception, grows up automatically, spontaneously reaching out for more being, for the plenitude of being. At the moment when the person dramatically breaks the barrier of the womb and appears on the stage of world history, he is caught in the acts of crying, clutching, straining to grasp, to be with other persons and things, to attain greater degrees of being. This spontaneous language of cries and gestures revealing the hunger for greater being testifies to man's innate drive to transcend himself, not merely horizontally to men and things but also vertically to God. Thus, 'to be' means 'to be with'; for man especially, *esse est co-esse.* Human existence, if it is to be authentically human, must be existence in communion. Isolation and alienation are the death of hum an persons. In a metaphysical depth far below the sociological surface, "No man is an island."

As a man grows up through physical to intellectual aware- ness, he is called upon to translate the natural, spontaneous at- traction of his nature for greater being into a reasonable, conscious, free, loving decision to be with the other; he is called upon to donate himself to the other—to things, his fellowmen, God. Only in giving himself in this reasonable manner does man discover and develop his full person, his subjecthood, his *I.* Now the fact that man is free and able to refuse to be with the other renders the future of man ambiguous. Sooner or later, and in- deed quite frequently in his life, the great crisis and challenge comes to every man: Shall I say Yes or No to the Thou? And this brings us full circle to our explanation of atheism. Communion is a form of freedom, of love; it is not a problem; it is a mystery in which every man is involved. Communion is the free gift of the self offered and accepted between an *I* and a *Thou;* it is mutual surrender of love. No matter how often experienced, commun- ion is an inexhaustible mystery of love; it will always be the cause of eternal wonderment. Now atheism is the contrary of communion vis à vis the Absolute Thou; it is the mystery of the great refusal. Yet man's greatest dignity consists in this: His metaphysical need and hunger for greater being, for the pleni- tude of being, testifies to the infinite goal to which he is called. He is called to consummate conversation and communion with the Absolute Thou. The atheist deliberately attempts to break his vital, intimate bond of communion with God. He refuses to transcend, to go up higher at the invitation of his nature and the Author of his nature. The atheist says: "I will not ascend."

To the believer the atheist is a mystery; to the atheist the believer is a mystery. Somehow man must try to understand both to the best of his ability. What the atheist does not see is that in rejecting God he rejects himself. In refusing to give himself in spirit to God, he refuses to transcend himself in the experience of a felt and lived communion with God. In effect he banishes God from his own horizon and exiles himself from the infinite visibility of God. He determines to contract his vision within the blinders of time. God no longer influences his life or his world because God, by man's decree, no longer lives or indeed exists anywhere.

What the believer must somehow demonstrate to the atheist is that when man chooses God he simultaneously chooses the spiritual plenitude of his own person; he decides to achieve full subjecthood, to reject retiring into the shell of objecthood. When man chooses God, he witnesses before his fellow man to the vivid, vital presence of God to all men. A man in communion with God testifies wherever he may be to God's omnipresence. If, as has been demonstrated on the merely human level, the fullness of the *I* is achieved only in its self-donation to the *Thou,* then, *a fortiori* on the level of the divine, the *I*-creature's surrender to the *Thou*-God will not only achieve the perfection of the creature's person, but will also vivify the intimate, encompassing presence of God to all men, a presence that summons all men to find themselves in Him.

But, it may be asked, how does the hardened sinner who still believes in God's existence differ from the professional atheist? Does not such a believer, who is deliberately attached to sin without any intention of immediately rejecting sin, break the bond of communion with God as irrevocably as does the hardened atheist? Of course he does, for such a sinner, steeped in immorality, is in revolt against God. His practical atheism is not so much a denial of God's existence and His moral law as a declaration in deeds that he will honor neither God nor His law by submission to them. Such a believer still clings to the cadaver of faith as a last, tenuous link with God. He acknowledges in word God's existence and the validity of His moral law. Like the Pharisees of Christ's time, such practical atheists are often eloquent in their words about God, delinquent in their practice of these teachings and in their service to God and men. Of them the Lord complained to His prophet and Christ repeated the complaint: "This people honors me with its lips, but its heart is far from me."

Practical atheists are a scandal to their fellowmen, encouraging religious indifference, even, at times, complete unbelief in those they scandalize.[8] Again, as evidenced in the

8. Etienne Borne, *Atheism* (New York: Hawthorn Publishers, 1961).

Pharisees, practical atheism is usually a form of soft material- ism. Such pseudo-followers of God try to reduce the true God to their own image and likeness, one favorable to their own worldly ambitions, planning to put this God, His Messiah and His people in the service of their earthly kingdom. It was just such a perversion of His Father's kingdom that Christ fled when his earth-bound people attempted to make Him king of their earth-bound kingdom. Thus the practical atheism of bad Christians is often made the excuse for the total rejection of God by real atheists. In this sense, then, practical atheism is the stone of scandal that trips others into the ditch of godlessness.

The greatest evil the practical atheist perpetrates against his fellow men is that by his adherence to sin he witnesses against God. His revolt blurs, obscures, obliterates the vision of God for others. And when men lose the vision of God, who is the meaning and reason for everything, they lose themselves, for nothing makes sense any longer and nothing directs one anywhere. Régis Jolivet has perceptively expressed another aspect of this truth, "When the spiritual element in us grows weak, the presence of God loses its evidence and vividness."[9] The practical atheist testifies that for him, in the matter of his adherence to certain injustices and wickedness, God might just as well be non-existent for all the influence He has in bringing about his conversion. In leaving this subject of practical atheism aside, we should stress that often the hardened practical atheist is a much greater criminal in the eyes of God and a more pernicious scandal to his fellow men than the professional atheist. For the practical atheist, especially of the Pharisee type, sins against the light and, as an especially despicable form of perversion, he hypocritically presents immorality as though it were religious righteousness.

So far we have indicated from a negative viewpoint how it is possible to deny God. Man has the desire to know God the way he knows science, creatures, his fellow man; that is, directly, with evidence that is compelling. But this desire is impossible, unrealizable in this time of trial. For God, as Pure Absolute Spirit, cannot now be met in effortless encounter, nor can He be made the *object* discovered at the end of mere abstract reasoning, nor the conclusion of an experimental process. For God

9. Régis Jolivet, *The God of Reason* (New York: Hawthorn Publishers, 1958).

is not an idea, nor the conclusion of a syllogism, nor the conquest of a positivistic process. He is mystery, presence, gift; not problem, idea or object.

Moreover, we saw how the possibility of choosing atheism is simultaneously the opportunity of choosing God. Atheism is possible in order that man may accept the challenge to choose God and make that choice of God with the same qualitative love of preference with which God chose to love, create and dwell with man. In other words, atheism is possible in order that the whole man, knowing and loving, may attain the moral heights of being with God through his free cooperation. If God could be accepted with the same ease as we accept the law of gravity, faith and love of preference as priceless moral values would no longer be existent. And man could no longer follow his noblest vocation—his struggle to participate in God's moral goodness. God has to be won, to be achieved as the result of a long struggle that overcomes many difficulties. Only the violent bear Him away or, to be more correct, are borne away by Him. There is no easy way to God. The person who sulks in atheism because he has no sensible evidence, no solid physical facts for God's existence opens himself to the critique of being petulantly unreasonable in demanding what is impossible.

But there has to be some form of evidence of God's existence if the acceptance of God is to be reasonable. And, of course, there is. There exists the evidence of spiritual experience, evidence which is of a meta-problematic order, different from but complementary to the objective evidence of facts found in the universe of physical things. Man, in encountering his universe, experiences the facts of an infinite multiplicity and apparent chaos of being. Entering into these facts with what Gabriel Marcel calls "secondary reflection," that is, with a personalized recollection and intimate reflection, the whole man—the rational, affective, moral being—experiences the presence of the Transcendent in the intelligibility, beauty, order—physical and moral—encountered in men and things. Man obtains a secure knowledge of God's existence as the Necessary implied by the contingent, the Absolute Truth supposed by his own growing truth, the Perfect Good commanding his own moral maturity. Thus the Transcendent becomes present and communes with man *from within* as well as from without. Now the universe of things and men appeal to and seize not merely the knower's abstract reason, but the whole man, sense and soul. True, as Daniélou has demonstrated, God's cosmic covenant with man, as read in the book of creation, does not lead the religiously pagan soul unerringly "to that living God who is so near at hand and yet so far." In the darkness of his fallen nature, the religious pagan misunderstands the message of "the cosmos, the conscience and the spirit" and falls into idolatry. But at least he maintains his quest for that unknown God about whom Denys truly said: "We know well that He is, and what He is not. But what He is remains for us entirely unknown."[10]

Only God's positive revelation of Himself—initially through Abraham and the Jews, finally in its splendid fullness in Jesus Christ—could bring fallen man to a realization of the truth enunciated by St. Paul: "In Him we live and move and have our being . . . And in Him all things hold together." Thus, atheism is possible because man can reject this living, personal experience of the presence of the Transcendent even after he has sifted the event by reason and found it was not an illusion but a solid conviction based on and arrived at through a consistent relationship with the objective data of reality. Man may reject this living event as being unscientific, too subjective and, therefore, lacking the rigor of perfect proof. Atheism is possible because there exists a human attitude that demands that God be proven like the correct answer to a problem, or the discovery of a new law of physics. The rigidity of the scientific method denies that anyone who is invisible can be validly discovered as a presence, accepted as a person or lived with as a friend.

We mentioned obstacles that must be overcome by man if he is to know and accept God. It is the seriousness of these very obstacles that gives atheism a positive value, that gives it the appealing appearance of possessing some truth. Pascal caught this value in his pithy critique: "Atheism is an indication of spiritual vigor, but only to a certain degree."[11] Viewing atheism from the Christian's position, de Lubac wisely asserted that the more we believe in God, the more we are atheists as to false gods.[12]

We might express some of the difficulties that make atheism

10. Jean Daniélou, *God And The Ways Of Knowing* (Cleveland, Ohio: World Publishing Company, Meridian Books, 1965).

11. Blaise Pascal, *Pensées,* ed. Brunschvicg, III, 225; p. 431.

12. Henri de Lubac, S.J., *The Drama of Atheist Humanism* (New York and Cleveland: Meridian Books, World Publishing Company, 1965).

not only possible but also plausible in the form of a metaphor.
Every man is beckoned to ascend the mountain of the universe
for a rendezvous with God at the summit. But the climb that
leads to God is studded with desolate steeps where death stalks
to claim the headlong and the foolhardy. The prudent climber
humbly prepares himself to scale the peaks, crags, rocks; to
cross the chasms; to maneuver successfully the weight of his
supplies; to provide beforehand for the density and debility of
the senses, the dizziness of heights and the frigidity of the
atmosphere. Applied to real life, the believer patiently and pru-
dently scales the peaks of pain, the crags of evil, the chasm of
death; he overcomes the hardships and obscurities of the climb;
the debilities of his body and the treachery of his surroundings
do not deter him from his goal. Aided by light from the summit,
for which he has prayed, he avoids blind alleys and eventually
attains God, albeit, like Moses, shrouded and protected in the
clouds of creation, he attains God in the brilliant darkness of
reason and faith. Nevertheless, he is certain that God is in
those clouds, beyond them, nay more, in himself, nearer to himself than he is to his own being. Passage through the last portal
of suffering—death—will alone usher him into face to face
communion with God.

Now the atheist objects to the difficulties of the climb. How
can an all-good God obstruct the ascent to Himself with such
abominable barriers—death, sin, evil, pain, poverty, ignorance,
slavery? Only a cruel, a despotic God could arrange such an
inhuman situation, such utter absurdity. The truth is that such
a God is an illusion, a convenient human projection whereby
man hopes to make this life bearable by putting his hopes in a
future life of happiness guaranteed by his own God. The atheist
cries that there is no one beyond his marvelous senses, his
brilliant mind. There is no one in or beyond the spinning planets, the billions of gallaxies. As he studies the universe, under
the glow of his declaration of his independence from God, the
atheist sees that the universe seems stable enough in itself and
has no need of a God. The universe beckons him, godless, liberated, with wondrous powers of body and mind, to scale its
heights on his own, and harness its limitless, secret resources
for his own health and wealth. As he views the misery of the
masses in poverty, ignorance and disease, he is fired to purify

society with violence if need be, of its avaricious establishment, built upon the myths and morals of organized religion; he
vows to enthrone man at the summit as his own God.

Thus modern atheism is no longer merely a speculative system aimed at proving in a rational manner that the existence
of God is neither actual nor possible. The modern atheist is not
an atheist because he is incapable of finding and using the
means to encounter God. Indeed, his denial of God is his choice
of a crusade against God. Dostoyevsky, that brilliant prophet
and fearless judge of our times, demonstrated in his novels,
which are full of all types of atheists, that the contemporary,
learned, liberalistic, collectivist humanist is far less an atheist
than he is an anti-atheist.[13] The contemporary atheist does not
love God, rather he hates God. That is the secret of his orgy of
anti-atheism. In the final analysis of our tortured era, the supreme reason for its darkness of despair is the word that arises
from the depths of its being. Out of the bitter abundance of its
heart our embittered age screams at God: "No! We will not
serve you! We will not love you! We will love and serve man
without you!"

What contemporary adventurers in atheism have failed to
see, as de Lubac so soberly observes, is that "man cannot organize the world for himself without God; without God he can only
organize the world *against* man. Exclusive humanism is inhuman humanism."[14] Consequently the orgy of antitheism is infinitely more heinous than the mere mental revolt of atheism.
Indeed modern atheists are activists against God; they proudly
participate in the madman's delirium over the assassination of
God, with this difference, that their's is a joyful while the madman's was a sorrowful delirium. "We have killed him [God]—
you and I!—Shall we not ourselves have to become Gods, merely
to seem worthy of it? There never was a greater event!"[15]

Thus the secular humanists, exulting in this "crime of
crimes," this "heroism of heroisms," admit that they did not
bring about the "murder of God" in an accidental manner. They
planned the deed; they knew what they were doing. First they

13. Feodor Dostoyevsky, *The Brothers Karamazov; The Possessed; Journal of
an Author; A Raw Youth* and others.
14. de Lubac, *op. cit*, p. ix.
15. Friedrich Nietzsche, *The Joyful Wisdom*, trans. T. Common; English
translation, ed. O. Levy (New York: Macmillan, 1910) Vol. 10, p. 125.

cleverly dissolved God and religion as a myth, using the acidly erosive power of scientific rationalism. Man, in his adolescent fears and insecurities, had built up this myth over the centuries by projecting his own aspirations for permanency, peace and happiness into an Absolute Good and an eternal heaven. The here was horrible; the hereafter would be heavenly. But our learned athesits, the avant-garde of humanity-come-of-age, illumined with scientific vision and animated with prophetic zeal, irrevocably erased the horizon of a heavenly hereafter. Dutifully they accepted the responsibility of creating heaven here on earth; they accepted the role of being the creators of history and of history's destiny. Presently they are at work feverishly founding the opulent, cultural, Secular City. Tomorrow, as atheism advances, will dawn a universally desacralized civilization. Eventually, when atheism is fully triumphant, a celebration is planned for the advent of the Christless Cosmos by the first world-wide Godless generation.

It would be a mistake to take today's atheists as mere dreamers. They know what they want; they have drawn up plans about how they are going to get it; their books are everywhere to be read, their actions everywhere to be witnessed. They know the obstacles that stand in the way of their Christless Cosmos. They are forever developing and improving techniques to eradicate these obstacles. They are at total war with the religious consciousness of men. They rightly see as their most deadly enemy the religious consciousness of Christians. Thus, contemporary atheism, in its messianic drive to bring all men into the fold of its religionless utopia, is quick to use all forms of spiritual coercion and physical violence. It is fanatically determined to eradicate the religious consciousness of man. In order that it may successfully implant an alien secularized consciousness in men, modern atheism has developed a fixed, rigid philosophy of human nature and of the cosmos; in the West it is organized into an Establishment through a kinship of humanism and progressivism; in the East and in Cuba it is organized into a political monolith; everywhere it has adopted an arbitrary code of ethics; it employs flexible, conspiratorial tactics and in its messianic imperialism it excludes no man or thing from insertion, forcible or otherwise, into its "great, uniform ant-hill" hegemony.

Dostoyevsky has delineated the principal types of pernicious atheism in modern times under the symbolism of three images. These images represent the ideals of atheism for mankind. De Lubac points out the meaning of these images. "The ideal of the 'man-God,' the ideal of the 'Tower of Babel' and the ideal of the 'palace of glass'—these three images are ready to hand, respectively denoting the spiritual ideal of the individual who is a law unto himself, the social ideal of the revolutionary who proposes to insure, without God, the happiness of mankind, and the rational ideal of the philosopher who rejects every kind of mystery. In the concrete reality of the Dostoevskian universe, these three types—types of inverted faith rather than of pure disbelief—are intermingled in a variety of permutations and combinations."[16]

Dostoevsky brilliantly unmasks these forms of ideal atheistic humanism so as to reveal them for what they are in their metaphysical, moral and theological nakedness—the most efficiently ruthless systems ever devised for inflicting upon society man's inhumanity to man. And he relentlessly demonstrates the bankruptcy of these systems, predicts the triumph of the God-Man over the man-God in the soul of society and man's resurrection beyond the Stygian stable of atheistic humanism.

The plan in this book is to demonstrate how every form of atheism, even the initially well intentioned, constricts, shrinks, enslaves the individual atheist within and against himself and, eventually, as atheism reaches plague proportions among men, goes on to enslave and murder society. I hope to justify this study by showing how organized atheism is the greatest social engineer of falsehood and human degradation in our times. Finally, I hope to suggest means whereby man can successfully thwart these adventures in atheism and invite him to go beyond atheism, to ascend to the infinitely expansive level of self-donation in being, the level of friendship with God where God and men share all gifts in the Gift of the God-Man. Man must go beyond atheism or be driven on by his own stubborn pride and hate to the void of social and spiritual suicide.

16. Henri de Lubac, *op. cit.*, p. 188.

CHAPTER II

Feuerbach: Humanity Becomes God

LUDWIG FEUERBACH (1804–1872) PUBLISHED HIS BOOK *The Essence of Christianity* in 1841. Immediately he was hailed as a new Prometheus. Why? His spiritual training and development will give us the answer.

Ludwig Feuerbach, raised in a solidly Christian family, went to Heidelberg University, because he wanted to become a Protestant minister. God was his first love, theology his all-consuming interest. On campus, however, he ran smack into a students' revolt against religious authorities. He was shocked at the brutal suppression of the revolt by the State police who were called in by the spiritual powers. He was enraged and embittered at the punishment inflicted upon his two brothers who at Erlangen were leaders in a secret organization that directed the revolt there. Young Feuerbach, shaken in his allegiance to the Church, began to move away from theology toward philosophy. He left Heidelberg and enrolled at the University of Berlin where the great Hegel was lecturing.

Meeting Hegel completely revolutionized his life. In Feuerbach's own words Hegel became his "second father," Berlin the place of his "spiritual rebirth." For two years he attended Hegel's lectures. Moreover, he was on intimate terms with Hegel —more so than with any of his other professors. Hegel liberated him from "the clutches of the dirty clerics." His very dissertation was on the basic doctrine of Hegel's philosophy, "on reason, the one, the universal, the infinite," where he developed reason as the supreme metaphysical principle, the first cause of all things, "the all-embracing, universal, true abode of all things and subjects." Thus, Feuerbach now saw as unquestionably situated solely in Reason perfections, such as unity, universality and infinity, which were formerly and normally attributed solely to God. Under Hegel's influence Feuerbach broke with theology, considering it merely as a past phase in man's intellectual progression. He now advanced beyond Christianity, passionately demanded the total divorce of philosophy from theology, called for a "new religion of action" and insisted on man's undivided concentration on this world so that an "efficient, spiritually and physically sound people" could be formed from this revolutionizing liberation from the Absolutist God.

De Lubac tells us that "in the years that followed Hegel's death in 1831, the focus of philosophical debates was the problem of God, and it was on this subject, and not primarily on political and social matters, that the split occurred between the right and left wings of Hegelianism."[1]

Now Hegel, the progenitor of a famous brood that split into two factions at war with each other, was far from being an atheist himself. Nevertheless, he set the stage for the assault upon God. It was generally agreed that God was the object of both philosophy and theology; of the former by the light of reason, of the latter by the light of revelation. But Hegel questioned whether the philosophers or the theologians had succeeded in attaining the real God. He protested that the God of Christian experience was an inadequate, a premature, not-yet-developed God. Hegel set himself the task of completing the good news of the Gospels; he would go beyond Christianity by demonstrating that the only valid God was dialectically evolving Thought or Spirit Which gradually, inevitably attains and

1. Henri de lubac, *op. cit.,* p. 8.

reveals Itself in conceptual clarity and complete self-consciousness through the entire scope of cosmic and human history. Hegel set himself the mission of rescuing the God of Christianity from the vagueness of imagery, the symbolism of myths, the simplistic charm of parables.

Moreover, Hegel had a bill of particulars against the Christian God. The trouble with the Christian God is that He is only experienced and remembered when the human conscience is sick or in trouble. But this Jewish-Christian God, Who is unapproachable and inscrutable in His aloof transcendence and unattainable by the imagination, mind or heart of man, arouses in man resentment against the only choice he is offered by this mysterious God—obedience or revolt. Frustrated by the demoralizing experience of failing futilely to satisfy his hunger for communion with the transcendent God, humbled by the degrading knowledge of his abject powerlessness, man resents the situation that equates God's glorification with his own depreciation. The transcendent God of the Old and New Testaments thus succeeds in enslaving and alienating His worshippers. He sets before them the face-to-face eternal embrace of Himself as a goal that is actually beyond man's personal achievement. Yet He continually tortures man's metaphysical hunger as if this human aspiration for complete communion were actually attainable. In effect, says Hegel, the Judaeo-Christian God is a cruel tyrant Who fosters between Himself and men the infamous dialectical relationship of master and slave.

Despite the apparent liberation of the spirit found in the New Testament, the apparent snapping of the bonds of Fate, the seemingly magnificent release from the master-slave degradation, Hegel brands Judaeo-Christianity as a backward religion, a religion of endless, hopeless waiting whose devotees are either wandering in a desert looking for a land flowing with milk and honey or sighing in a vale of tears scanning the horizon for the advent of the new heaven and earth beyond time. Idle Christians, it turns out, are only more sickly replicas of wandering Jews, the former incurably looking for the second coming, the latter still alerted for the first, of the Messiah. Both suffer from "unhappy consciences" which beget not true religion but sentimental religiosity. Both are forever hoping for the unreal, the impossible. Both are always away in another world, unemployed and sterile in this world of great affairs and challenges. Christianity is the old slavery under a milder regime. The New Testament demands the rejection of this world even as the Old did. Both insist God is apart, beyond, divorced from this world which at best is a sinners' prison, an exiles' passing and dying city.

Hegel's basic opposition to the Jewish and Christian religions is that they create men who can be witnesses and martyrs for the next world, but never "heroes of action" in this. These religions forever forbid their faithful to aspire to the glory of the Titans, the heroism of Lucifer, the adventure of Faust.

Hegel concluded that Christianity was a social and historical failure. For souls who are withdrawn by religious conviction from their age can never create a great civilization; they can only produce a spiritless era in which men reluctantly endure the happenings of time for the happiness of eternity. The Judaeo-Christian God is all too purely transcendent, so far out of this world as to be irrelevant.

In one sense this failure of the God of Revelation was unavoidable. After all, was not this God a mere antithesis of the dialectical evolution of Spirit? Hellenism, with its serene gods of immanence and order, was the thesis of evolving Thought. Christianity, with its tragically crucified God, was the antithesis. Hegel's God and Hegel's religion is the synthesis of these two—the reformed, the mature, the complete God. The Christian God had to die, to pass into its opposite—the absolute into the relative, the infinite into the finite, the eternal into the temporal, the transcendent into the immanent—in order that the valid God might lose and find himself again on a higher level of self-consciousness in the unfolding drama of cosmic history which is the drama of the self-achievement of the total, conscious being of God. By participating in this world-drama and committing himself to the development of this history, man will fulfill his authentic role as a hero of action and expand his liberty to meaningful dimensions. His greatest glory is to cooperate willingly in the achievement of the fullness of the being of the immanent God of perfect self-Consciousness.

Hegel succeeded in paganizing Christianity, demythologizing the Gospels and creating a religion of the cosmic, integrat-

ing, evolutionary Absolute in cooperation with whose dialectical maturation to perfect self-consciousness man would find
his own greatness, even though man himself is a mere dialectical moment destined to personal obliteration on that dialectical journey. All modern atheism will thus be seen to be rooted
in Hegel's rejection of the God of the master-slave relationship,
the God who begets an "unhappy conscience" in man, the God
who reduces man from being a hero to being a "beautiful soul."

Now Feuerbach, leader of the left-wing Hegelians, was profoundly influenced by Hegel's challenge to the God of Christianity. He was especially impressed with Hegel's doctrine of
the religious alienation of man in the master-slave relationship
with the Christian God. But he disagreed radically with what
had been done by Hegel to correct this unhappy relationship.
The God of Christian experience did not need to be reformed;
man himself needed to be reformed; man did not need to be
rescued from the Christian God; he needed to be rescued from
his own illusions about God. If there was one truth the noble
soul and the "unhappy conscience" of man pointed to it was
that the whole idea of God as the Absolute Other was sheer
illusion.

Feuerbach saw the inevitable outcome of Hegel's reduction
of God from the God of Abraham, Isaac, Jacob and Jesus to the
God of the philosophers and scientists. He saw that the God of
the fifth Gospel—the gospel of reason according to Hegel—was
merely a man-made God, sprung full-blown from the Hegelian
head. Taking his inspiration, however, from Hegel's work as a
beginning which was going in the right direction, Feuerbach
set himself to account psychologically for the illusion of all
religion. He realized that Hegel had already demolished God
without even suspecting his own great accomplishment. Feuerbach successfully drew the logical conclusions of Hegel's work
in his book *The Essence of Christianity.* In an heroic manner
he continued the process of the reduction of God to the being
of man and, indeed, of all theology to anthropology.

It was quite understandable, then, that the left-wing Hegelians, upon seeing God falling from heaven under the assault of
this new Titan, were filled with enthusiasm and rallied round
him as a leader more courageous than Hegel himself, a leader
who dared the ultimate act—the annihilation of God. Feuer-

bach was seen as having ascended above the throne of God and
having brought down to earth not only new fire, but heaven and
the God of heaven's fire himself. Feuerbach was acclaimed for
having swept the heavens clean of the phantom of God, exor-
cised this sacred sorcerer from the consciousness of his age,
broken forever this theological tyrant's fatalistic, master-slave
domination of men, restored divinity to its rightful owner—
liberated Humanity—and rendered the thousands of years' discussions about God henceforth pointless.

In the words of Karl Barth, "Feuerbach's teaching was essentially a summons, an appeal, a proclamation."[2] He wrote in
order to restore man to his innate dignity. It was Feuerbach's
contention that the Christian idea of man, far from liberating
man, actually succeeded in enslaving him to an illusory absolute. How did Feuerbach arrive at this conclusion? Was he the
victim of the slow secularization of Christianity which
preceded his times and how much does he contribute by his own
writings to the loss of the Christian mind that plagues our
times? These are the questions we hope to explore and answer
in this chapter.

Feuerbach was a modern philosopher who, by his own admission, was totally preoccupied with the problem of theology. "All
my writings," he wrote, "have had, strictly speaking, one purpose, one intention, one theme. This is nothing else than religion and theology and whatever is connected with them."[3] As
one conversant with the history of theology, Feuerbach knew
that Christianity broke upon an ancient, pagan world, burdened down with countless gods, spirits, demons and controlled
implacably by the tyrannical stars and Fates above, as the great
Liberator. For Christianity emancipated man from the metaphysical matrix of Fatalism. Its good news proclaimed that
man is the effect of infinite, creative Love. A divine seal within
man's nature reflects, however dimly yet unmistakably, the
ineffable nature of his Absolute Creator. Reason, liberty, immortality, providence over cosmos and community are divine
endowments which God shares with man, His favorite image.
No longer caught on the wheel of irrational and eternal recur-

2. Karl Barth, Introductory Essay to *The Essence of Christianity,* p. xi.
3. Ludwig Feuerbach, *Das Wesen Der Religion,* (Leipzig: Alfred Kroner Verlag), p. 3.

rence, no longer the historical plaything of blind chance, no longer a mere spark from the world-soul that moves within the iron circle of cosmopolitan necessitarianism, man, liberated by Christianity, rejoiced in a world expanded with newly revealed horizons for intelligence, freedom, love. Each man, one by one, was now seen to be the known, the chosen, the person individually embraced by the Absolute Lover. "I have loved you with an everlasting love, therefore have I chosen you, taking pity on you."

The initial emotions that Christianity released in a converted world that was formerly pagan and idolatrous were those of intense, exhilarating gladness, radiant joy, triumphant applause, inexpressibly peaceful relief at the deliverance from fatalism and the reception of new human life in the divine family of the Holy Trinity. At last the true Transcendent was really known as the One, True God in three distinct Lovers—the Father of Men, the Saviour of men, the Advocate of men. From now on man's greatness was to consist in his grateful recognition of his divine origins and in his enthusiastic cooperation for the attainment of his divine destiny—eternal, supernatural communion within the unveiled family of God.

It was true that Christianity reminded man that he was and would ever remain during his life on earth wounded by sin. As a result of his sin and its consequent ravages in his mind, will and whole being, Christianity incessantly warned man that he would have to combat daily until the moment of his death the assaults of the world, the flesh, the devil and, above all, his own inordinate nature, if he seriously hoped to attain his sublime destiny. But Christianity assured man that in Christ, the Redeemer, and in His message and mission entrusted to His Living Church man would find all the power needed to overcome his debilities and the superabundant graces needed for his sanctification.

Here was a message and mission capable of keeping man young in spirit, vital, free, creative and, above all, joyously striving to grow up in Christ, despite the rampant ravages of sin in history all around him. Here was a message and mission that would develop man and his cosmos to divine greatness, while it overthrew the powers of evil in the visible and invisible worlds.

But when Feuerbach looked at the world of his times, he discovered an astonishing phenomenon. Illusion, indecision, immorality were rampant in a supposedly Christian civilization. The fact was, however, that Europe was no longer Christian; it had cut itself adrift from its Christian moorings in the revolts and apostasies of the seventeenth and eighteenth centuries. Most men still professed Christianity in word, but lived atheism in deed. Feuerbach was already witnessing the fulfillment of Renan's sagacious prophecy. Philosopher-historian who lost his faith in the seminary of St. Sulpice, Renan, a contemporary of Feuerbach, wrote: "It is possible that the collapse of supernatural belief will be followed by the collapse of moral convictions and that the moment when humanity sees the reality of things will mark a real moral decline. We are living on the perfume of an empty vase."[4] Yet, even though men were no longer moved by the Christian ideal and no longer strove for supernatural greatness, they were, nevertheless, still haunted by the perfume of that vase. Feuerbach himself testified that "because of its indecisive half-heartedness and lack of character . . . the superhuman and supernatural essence of ancient Christianity still haunts the minds of men—at least as a ghost."[5] He planned to dissolve the ghost, dispel the perfume. He made it his sacred mission to restore man's spiritual coherency by "erasing this most rotten stain, the stain of our present history."[6] He would break man's ties to both God and Christianity, myths that held a guilt-ridden society in total bondage.

All the young fellow-Hegelians of the left applauded Feuerbach's "world-moving step" which "with unrouged truth demasks Christian and philosophical hypocrisy," as Rouge so enthusiastically described this mission. Indeed the adventure for atheism thrilled the young Hegelians. Marx and Bauer projected the publication of an *Archive For Atheists* aimed at being more brazenly atheist than Rouge's *German Yearbooks*. Thus by 1841 the "religious mask" was thrown to the winds and Rouge could write: "Bruno Bauer (and Marx) . . . and Feuerbach have already reached the summit and planted the flag of athe-

4. Quoted by Arnold Lunn and Garth Lean in *Christian Counter-attack*, Blandford Press, (London: 1969) p. 18.
5. Ludwig Feuerbach, *The Essence of Christianity*, translated by George Eliot (New York: Harper Torchbooks, 1957), p. 15.
6. *Ibid.*, p. 15.

ism and mortality; God, religion and immortality are hereby
deposed, and the philosophers' Republic, Man, and the new gods
of Man proclaimed."[7] Without Hegel, therefore, Feuerbach
might never have formulated so precisely the nature of modern
humanistic atheism. Yet he was also influenced by his friend
Friedrich David Strauss, who specialized in interpreting the
origins of Christianity. Strauss claimed he had accounted for
the Christian illusion through his study of the Jewish people.
Feuerbach, paralleling his friend's effort, claimed he could account for the Christian illusion in particular, and for the illusion of religion in general, through psychological and
anthropological causes. In his Life of Jesus, Strauss developed
the theory that the gospels were the myths embodying the aspirations of the Jewish people. In his Essence of Religion, Feuerbach reached a similar conclusion in his field of endeavor,
proclaiming that God is merely a myth which embodies the
highest aspirations of the human consciousness. "Those who
have no desires," he wrote, "have no Gods . . . Gods are men's
wishes in corporeal form."[8]

Thus, according to Karl Barth, "Feuerbach worked with an
energy surpassed by few contemporaries of his stamp precisely
in order to displace religion."[9] Now two theses control the development of Feuerbach's atheistic humanism. The first, a
negative thesis, develops Hegal's idea of alienation. However,
Feuerbach does not apply this concept as Hegel had done, to
dialectically evolving Mind, but to man—that flesh and blood
creature who exists only in community, whose being is found
only in the unity of man with man—the unity of I and Thou.
Now this man with man—the unity of I and Thou—this being
of man in community—this is God. The true dialectic is no
monologue of lonely Thinker with Himself, but a dialogue between I and Thou.[10] Alienation, in Feuerbach's sense, arises in
man when man discovers that, in his struggle for a better life,
his existence is dependent, limited, threatened; he is agitated
by needs, ideals, desires, fears; he is buffetted by loves and
hates, attractions and abhorrences, values and disvalues; he is

7. Quoted by Georg Siegmund in God On Trial (New York: Desclée Co., 1967),
p. 257.
8. Ludwig Feuerbach, The Essence of Religion, p. 115, 117.
9. Karl Barth, Introductory Essay to Ludwig Feuerbach's The Essence of
Christianity, p. x.
10. Ludwig Feuerbach, The Philosophy of the Future, p. 41.

forced to sift the good from the evil, all the time realizing from distressing experience that he finds in himself unstableness and weakness yet, at the same time, an attraction for noble virtues and deeds. In his desire to stabilize the noble qualities he finds in his nature, man hypostasizes, idolizes, absolutizes them outside his own changeable being into an Absolute Other who is unchangeable. This Other is endowed with wisdom, will, justice, love, all the noble feelings and virtues which man himself experiences from time to time, both in himself and in his fellowmen. Thus the absolutized attributes appear to man as if they were the exclusive ornaments of another, an infinitely more perfect being then himself. Spontaneously, religiously, man projects and objectifies his own goodness and greatness in the fantastic being he calls God. God is thus the product of pure human imagination. Feuerbach writes:

> God is for man the commonplace book where he registers his highest feelings and thoughts, the genealogical album into which he enters the names of the things most dear and sacred to him.[11]

In this way man simultaneously dispossesses himself and enriches his God; in affirming God he denies himself; the poorer he becomes, the richer his God becomes; nothing really exists in God except what belongs and actually really still is in man's heart. Karl Barth records Feuerbach's reaction to this process of expoiliation:

> Feuerbach honors those feelings and sacred things, but he wants it understood that in the album there stands only what first was in the heart of man. He only wants the honest confession that the alleged mystery of religion is of man; that man is dreaming when he imagines that a Something Other, objectively confronting him, is that ground, that Whence, that Necessity and that Law; is the source from which his wishes and ideals flow and is the sea of fulfillment toward which they tend. Man is dreaming instead of recognizing that it is his own being, his desire and duty to live as man, which he, as a religious man, quite rightly equates with God.[12]

11. Ludwig Feuerbach, *The Essence of Christianity*, p. 132.
12. Ludwig Feuerbach, *The Essence of Christianity*, Introductory Essay by Karl Barth, p. xvi.

Who, then, and what really is the nature of this God? Feuerbach answers more comprehensively thus:

> God as the epitome of all realities or perfections is nothing
> other than a compendious summary devised for the be-
> nefit of the limited individual, an epitome of the generic
> human qualities distributed among men, in the self-reali-
> zation of the species in the course of world history.[13]

Thus man strips himself and the human species of his highest attributes and creates with these virtues the essence of his
own God. Man must die that God may be born. As Spenlé so
aptly formulates what happens in this process of alienation,
"Religion is thus transformed into a vampire which feeds upon
the substance of mankind, its flesh and its blood."[14]

While tearing down the Absolute Spirit of Hegel, Feuerbach
remained Hegelian enough to accept this process of human
alienation as a justified process on the dialectical timetable of
man's ascent to perfect self-consciousness. Religion as a product of human alienation, God as the idol of man's self-annihilation were necessary phenomena if the human species were to
progress towards intenser, maturer self-realization. After all,
consciousness thrives on man's ability to project himself, to
objectify himself and his species. Only in the milieu of duality
can man know himself, achieve his person in full—an action
reminiscent of the adage that one must lose oneself in order to
find oneself.

But eventually, in dialectical history, every antithesis must
rise to the synthesis; every rejection must move to a higher
reception; every alienation become a more perfect repos-
session. In his positive thesis, then, Feuerbach contends that
man has reached that point in his historical development
where he has to take back from religion and God that nature
which he had rejected in their favor. Feuerbach saw himself
as the prophet and the expediter of this process of reclama-
tion and the herald of the advent of the kingdom of man. He
set out to destroy the vampire of God, to dispel the phantom
of religion, to liberate man from the mighty myth of the

13. *Ibid.*, p. xvi.
14. Jean-Edouard Spenlé *La pensée allemande de Luther à Nietzsche*, p. 122.

Absolute Other, to restore man to man and hence to his own greatness. He indicates that the principal aim of his mission is to present mankind to the greatness of his own essence and thereby to inspire men to have faith in their humanity.

But the chief obstacle to man's faith in himself and his own greatness is the Christian God. It was necessary, therefore, to dethrone the God of the Christian conscience, to dissolve the religion of Christianity. For Feuerbach realized that God, as the sum of the attributes which make up the greatness of man, had never been more sublimely nor attractively created than in the ineffable, Christian vision of the triune fellowship of divine persons, each endlessly active on a special mission of love and service to fallen humanity. Moreover, no other religion so convincingly revealed the infinite contrast that existed between this inacessible, hidden God of love and the abysmally impoverished, totally dependent, all-but-annihilated, wounded nature of man, mired hopelessly as it was in an existence of suffering and sin. For Feuerbach here was a classic case of *corruptio optimi pessima!* Christianity was the sublimest, the religion of religions, for it alone fully revealed the glory of God. Yet, paradoxically, by the very fact that it was the highest of religions, Christianity was simultaneously the most pernicious of religions, for no other religious system ever succeeded so thoroughly, in the very name of its perfect God, in extinguishing so adequately the greatness of man in the fires of alienation.

Thus Feuerbach, speaking of the one, passionate aim of his life and work—the mission to give man his due, to rescue him from a God-ridden existence, to reveal to mankind its great essence, its great value, its great vocation in history—could write in *The Essence Of Christianity:* "God was my first thought, reason my second and man my third and last."[15] Elsewhere he insists that his intentions are positive, though his method may be negative: "I deny only in order to affirm. I deny the fantastic projection of theology and religion in order to affirm the real essence of man."[16] "Certainly my work is negative, but, be it observed, only in relation to the inhuman, not to

15. Ludwig Feuerbach, *The Essence Of Religion.*
16. *Ibid.,* p. 4.

the human elements in religion."[17] "While I do reduce theology to anthropology, I exalt anthropology to theology; very much as Christianity while lowering God into man, made man into God."[18]

At the conclusion of his Heidelberg lectures delivered in 1848 and later published as The Essence of Religion, Feuerbach crystallized the purpose of all his teaching thus: I aim to change "the friends of God into friends of man, believers into thinkers, worshippers into workers, candidates for the other world into students of this world, Christians, who on their own confession, are half-animal and half-angel, into men—whole men."[19] Earlier he had indicated this direction for his improvements when he said that he would transform "theologians into anthropologians . . . religious and political footmen of a celestial and terrestrial monarchy and aristocracy into free, self-reliant citizens of earth."[20]

Here was an atheistic humanism that destroyed God as the Absolute Other; yet simultaneously here was a theistic humanism that divinized man. "The divine essence is the glorified human essence transfigured from the death of abstraction. In religion man frees himself from the limitations of life; here he throws off what oppresses, impedes or adversely affects him; God is man's self-awareness, emancipated from all actuality; man feels himself free, happy, blessed only in his religion because here only does he live in his true genius; here he celebrates his Sunday."[21]

It must be observed that Feuerbach does not divinize individual man in his particularity, but he identifies God with the essence of man, with humanity. His is a religion of Humanity, the apotheosis of man though the apotheosis of mankind. In this he differs from that other left-wing Hegelian, Max Stirner, who rejected Feuerbach's "essence of man" as being too abstract, too ideal, too far from concrete reality. Stirner identified God with the "unique individual." *Ego mihi deus!* (I am my own God!) Feuerbach, on the other hand, wrote: "It is the essence of man that is the supreme being . . . If the divinity of nature is

17. Ludwig Feuerbach, *The Essence Of Christianity,* p. 40.
18. *Ibid.,* p. 43.
19. Ludwig Feuerbach, *The Essence Of Religion,* p. 170.
20. Ludwig Feuerbach, *The Essence Of Religion,* p. 14.
21. Ludwig Feuerbach, *The Essence Of Christianity,* p. 173.

the basis of all religions, including Christianity, the divinity of man is its final aim . . . The turning point in history will be the moment when man becomes aware that the only God of man is man himself. *Homo homini Deus!"* [22] He goes on to delineate his altruistic humanism more in detail, thus: "Man spontaneously conceives of his own essence as individual in himself and generic in God; as limited in himself and infinite in God." But when he finally sheds this mythical view and accepts personal participation in his common humanity, man finally realizes the divine dimension of his own being. In so doing he breaks the bonds of auto-eroticism, goes forth in deeds of love to his fellow men and establishes a community of love in the fellowship of his own species. It is at such a time that he clearly sees and experiences the truth that "the distinction between human and divine is neither more nor less than the distinction between the individual and mankind."[23]

Does Feuerbach calmly accept the inevitable accusation that his doctrine reduces him to the status of being an atheist? His answer is quite forthright:

> I have only found the key to the cipher of the Christian religion, only extricated its true meaning from the web of contradictions and delusions called theology;—but in doing so I have certainly committed sacrilege. If therefore my work is negative, irreligious, atheistic, let it be remembered that atheism—at least in the sense in this work—is the secret of religion itself; that religion itself, not indeed on the surface, but fundamentally, not in intention or according to its own supposition, but in its heart, in its essence, believes in nothing else than the truth and divinity of human nature.[24]

Later on, somewhat sensitive about the charge of teaching atheism, Feuerbach makes a distinction between the atheist who denies God as a self-subsistent subject and the atheist who denies the attributes of divinity as belonging exclusively to mankind. The former, in Feuerbach's mind, is not really an atheist; the latter is the only true atheist.

22. Ludwig Feuerbach, *The Essence Of Christianity,* p. 159.
23. *Ibid.*
24. Ludwig Feuerbach, *The Essence Of Christianity,* Author's Preface, p. xxxvi.

Thus what theology and philosophy have held to be God, the Absolute, the Infinite, is not God; but that which they have held not to be God is God: namely, the attribute, the quality, whatever has reality. Hence he alone is the true atheist to whom the predicates of the Divine Being—for example, love, wisdom, justice—are nothing; not he to whom merely the subject of these predicates is nothing. And in no wise is the negation of the subject necessarily also a negation of the predicates considered in themselves. These have an intrinsic, independent reality; they force their recognition upon man by their very nature; they are self-evident truths to him; they prove, they attest themselves. It does not follow that goodness, justice, wisdom are chimaeras because the existence of God is a chimaera ... The fact is not that a quality is divine because God has it, but that God has it because it is in itself divine: because without it God would be a defective being ... But if God as subject is the determined, while the quality, the predicate, is the determining, then in truth the rank of the godhead is due not to the subject, but to the predicate.[25]

It becomes a logical conclusion from the above that the man who, like Feuerbach, denies the existence of the illusory subject God in favor of affirming the reality of the divine-human attributes of love, wisdom, justice—this man comes to terms with reality and chooses to make the object of his worship and reverence not the chimerical God of the Christians, but the essence of humanity. In doing this, such a man reveals, even as Feuerbach before him, the secret splendor of humanity; he also performs the first, essential act of true religion, embracing in thought, love and deed the inexhaustible mysteries and goodness of human nature.

The most important thesis of all Feuerbach's work and especially of *The Essence Of Christianity* is the positive one. It is his view that the essential message of all religion and of the Gospels of Christianity is that they are treating fundamentally about man and human greatness under the myth-symbols of God and supernaturalism. Using Hegel's razor of negation in the role of removing imaginary *entia*, Feuerbach reduces the Christian God to his only possible realization in the conscious progress of man and humanity. He reduces Christianity to the religion of humanity. Under the action of this levelling blade,

25. *Ibid.*, pp. 21–22.

the whole countenance of Christianity is radically changed.

What is the meaning of the Incarnation of the Son of God? God is a tear, an unutterable sigh in the depths of the human heart; he is an altogether human being. The Incarnation is the advent of a human being possessing human compassion for the whole species. Christ is the consciousness of that species; we are one in him; he is the unity of our consciousness, the focused consciousness of our unity. Thus, whoever loves man for the sake of man, whoever loves the human species for the sake of the species, he is the universal, the adequate, the divine man; he is the true Christian; he is Christ himself.[26] Miracles are merely the magical creations of a fervent fantasy which works ceaselessly to satisfy the longings of the human heart.[27] The Resurrection of Christ is "the fulfilled longing of man for an immediate certainty of his continued personal existence after death."[28] All supernatural significance exists only in man's imagination and thus when man receives the sacrament of Baptism, he merely receives the physical, curative, cleansing power of natural water and of nature in general. As for partaking of the Lord's Supper, we have here the sublimest self-enjoyment of human subjectivity. Men transform God into an objective, external thing in order to subject him to themselves as a repast of sensuous delight.[29] The Word of God is actually —when it speaks what is true—the word of man; its divinity is man's divinity, the essence of man imparted to all men.[30] And who is the Holy Spirit? Why, he is the "representation of the religious sentiment to itself, the representation of the religious emotion, enthusiasm; the personification of religion in religion. The Holy Spirit is, therefore, the sighing creature, the longing of the creature for God."[31]

And so it goes on and on. It is always the same negating process under which these demythologizations of God and Christianity are made. But Feuerbach protests that he has no intention of being merely negative. He emphasises that in reality, far from wishing to deprive man of his most sacred truths,

26. *Ibid.*, p. 388.
27. *Ibid.*, p. 219.
28. *Ibid.*, p. 220.
29. *Ibid.*, p. 392.
30. *Ibid.*, p. 153.
31. *Ibid.*, p. 132.

he is really liberating him from inhibiting idols. The new
knowledge about God, religion and man actually frees man by
giving him the opportunity to grasp the full greatness he has
longed and fought for through thousands of years of violence
and bloodshed. Moreover, Feuerbach observes, for a long time
now it has been evident that theology, the Church and religion
have been denying God in favor of man. Ever since Luther the
interest in God has focused more on what God means for man
than on what God means in himself. Is it any wonder, then,
muses Feuerbach, justifying his demolition tactics against theology, that theology has become anthropology? Christianity in
its theological form "has long ago disappeared not only from
reason but also from the life of humanity." It is now a scandalous fact that Christianity "is nothing more than a fixed idea
that stands in the most glaring contradiction to our fire and
life-insurance companies, our railroads and steam engines, our
picture galleries, our military and industrial schools, our
theatres and scientific museums."[32] Therefore, today "man is
the beginning, the middle and the end of religion."[33]

We have briefly considered the atheistic humanism of Feuerbach. What strikes us forcefully is the completeness of his process of reductionism. E. L. Mascall in his Secularization of
Christianity calls Feuerbach's achievement "an even more heroic example" of reductionist theology than that accomplished
by Kant, Schleiermacher and Hegel.[34] By merely interchanging
subject and predicate in any theological statement, theology is
transformed into anthropology, religious myth is dissolved and
the truth about man's identity as God is revealed. The simplicity
of this truth-finding device is appealing and Feuerbach's universal application of it in his reductionist ritual is quite ingenious. Yet whoever intelligently listens to Feuerbach's new rule
for truth and alertly follows the creation of his full-blown humanism will have to concur whole-heartedly in the judgment
passed upon it by Karl Barth: "We have heard Feuerbach. We
have heard something quite extraordinarily, almost nauseat-
ingly, trivial."[35]

32. *Ibid.,* p. xliv.
33. *Ibid.,* p. 282.
34. R. L. Mascall, *The Secularization Of Christianity,* footnote, p. 7.
35. Karl Barth, Introductory Essay to *Essence Of Christianity,* p. xix.

Critique

Feuerbach was truly a child of his generation. To understand his atheistic humanism, it will be important to see him within his historical milieu. This should help us to come to an appreciation of the currents of thought and spiritual effort that flowed together in his pen and person. In the year 1842 Feuerbach published The Essence of Christianity. It was the very year in which Auguste Comte completed the publication of his voluminous *Cours de philosophie positive.* As de Lubac observes, "this coincidence of dates emphasises the convergence of the two designs." He goes on to record the perceptive remark of a witness of these events. "Shortly afterwards, Emile Saisset wrote: 'Herr Feuerbach in Berlin like Monsieur Comte in Paris, offers Christian Europe a new God to worship—the human race.' "[36]

Protestant theology in Feuerbach's day contributed to the rise of a self-sufficient, pretentious humanity. This self-glorification had seized *les philosophes* of the eighteenth-century Enlightenment, children of the French Revolution, who put their faith in Reason, gave an impetus to profane learning and developed a widespread spirit of skepticism and empiricism hostile to Christianity. The ascent of humanity was in the air and Feuerbach was happily perfumed with its sweet aroma. Thus the religion of Reason apotheosized the mind of man as his sole source of greatness and salvation. The concept, the judgment, the philosophical treatise were the keys to self-mastery, to God-mastery. With inspiration from nineteenth-century Romanticism, whose emphasis was feeling, the heart, the mystical, the religion of the human heart was said to deify man; the human heart was now the sole locus of divine wisdom. Scientism rejected God as an explanation of the cosmos; the universe seemed to it self-sufficient, if not always self-explanatory. As man—his mind, his heart, his feeling, his freedom, his science—increased, God decreased. Even the theologian, following Luther, overstressed religion as being the seeking of God not in Himself and for Himself but rather the seeking of God in man and for man. God was discovered not everywhere, not in heaven, but solely on earth and in men. Some theologians

36. Henri de Lubac S. J., *The Drama Of A Theist Humanism,* p. 77.

went so far as to identify the Godhead with the humanity of Jesus. Feuerbach found no difficulty in shifting this identity from the humanity of the individual to the human species. The climate of overweening self-assurance created the mentality in Feuerbach to found a new religion whose dominant mark would be humanistic and whose heaven would be this world. Indeed, he admits, as Karl Barth recalls, that "Schleiermacher's Berlin Church of the Trinity, remained holy ground throughout his entire life. There he learned that man is not only the measure of all things, but also the epitome, the origin and end of all values—the view that gives justification and assurance to human existence and its needs, wishes and ideals."[37]

Because he was nurtured on a theology that had long neglected hope in favor of human self-reliance, Feuerbach was blinded to the real, transcendent needs of man—his hunger for a Transcendent God, a personal Saviour and Sanctifier who could really justify men and restore them to moral wholeness, who, though always transcendent, would yet always be present to men. Feuerbach's God was all too human and, as such, was suspected by many of being the illusion of illusions. Nor could Feuerbach justify his God on the grounds of his concern for human greatness, for the human heart, for the emancipation of man from slavery. These very same ideals have been incarnated in movements of messianic importance that have been led by human devils, as history has so often demonstrated.

In fact, Feuerbach's humanist atheism was immediately pressed into service by his star pupil, Karl Marx, as the foundation for the erection of the monolith of communism. Purged of abstraction and plunged into the social, economic alienation that smoldered between capital and labor, Feuerbach's cult of "abstract man" became Marx's "science of real men and their historical development." The halo of divinity was shifted from the head of abstract man to the brow of the proletariat. Scientific socialism became the new humanist religion. The new alienation led to the negation of the negators, the unmasking of the hidden powers who manipulated the impoverished masses, the expropriation of the expropriators. And foremost among the expropriators, of course, was the Christian God who

37. Karl Barth, Introductory Essay to *The Essence Of Christianity*, p. xxviii.

was suspected and, some said was caught in the act of being, in the words of Jean Lacroix, "an artifice which the rulers used in the past to keep the majority in unending political adolescence, and thus to prevent their reaching full development."[38] God, the Church, Christianity—along of course with property, the State and all bourgeois institutions—were the monstrous myths, the ideological, sociological, theological stumbling blocks that had to be cleared from the path of man's progress to the realization of his own divinity. Thus Feuerbach's humanism was transformed into the militant atheism of social democracy. And of its vigorous program for saving the world Karl Barth wrote: "Regarding all this, there were three principal things to be attempted in the name of truth: rebellion, desertion and war against the Church."[39]

Assessing Feuerbach's thought, Copleston writes: "Feuerbach's philosophy is certainly not outstanding. For example, his attempt to dispose of theism by the account of the genesis of the idea of God is superficial. But from the historical viewpoint his philosophy possesses real significance . . . In particular, the philosophy of Feuerbach is a stage in the movement which culminated in the dialectical materialism and the economic theory of Marx and Engels."[40]

From the theological viewpoint, Feuerbach's "theory is a platitude," says Karl Barth.[41] Hans Ehrenberg pinpointed the cause of its shallowness. Feuerbach, "true child of his century, was a non-knower of death and a mis-knower of evil." He refused to address himself to the reality of death and misunderstood the nature of moral evil. His is the master illusion presented by the Arch-liar to man in the Garden of Eden: Man experienced in good *and evil* is a better man, is like God, nay, is God himself. The acceptance of this illusion is the foundation of all tragedy in history, the foundation of all enslavement. Faith in the creature—in the tempter's word, in man's self-sufficiency—to the exclusion of faith in the true Word of God is the root of the bankruptcy of Feuerbach's atheistic humanism. Any edifice of thought or program of action founded on

38. Jean Lacroix, *The Meaning Of Modern Atheism*, p. 32.
39. Karl Barth, Introductory Essay to *The Essence Of Christianity*, p. xxvii.
40. Frederick Copleston, S.J., *A History Of Philosophy*, Vol. 7, Part II, p. 67.
41. Karl Barth, Introductory Essay to *The Essence Of Christianity*, pp. xxvii-xxviii.

this illusion is bound to become a form of rigid dogmatism and
cruel aggression inflicted upon humanity. And, of course,
Feuerbach's is no exception. His edifice of thought is founded
on the myth of an abstract, non-personal, merely mentally existing humanity; he equates this non-being with God and calls
on all men to worship it; this is mental and religious chicanery.
Truth, religion, divinity are incarnated in persons—divine and
human individuals. Idolatry to the concept humanity results in
intellectual and religious suicide.

Probing into the psychological depths of Feuerbach's flight
from transcendence, Karl Barth sees there a spirit of imperti-
nence that bespeaks the total absence of the light that comes
from the virtue of humility. This arrogance is spoken of not so
much with the intention of castigating it as a moral fault as to
spotlighting it as a tragic, self-inflicted posture leading to metaphysical and theological blindness. For the sun of humility performs a double function in the life of every man who opens
himself to receive its rays. First, it reveals the natural ground
upon which man stands in relation to all being and especially
to Transcendent Being. It makes brilliantly clear to man his
radical, ontological, existential condition before God, attract-
ing him to go out of himself with confidence and to accept the
Absolute Other with love and himself with gratitude, as a creature always related through total dependence upon God, for his
being and his life. Secondly, and even more importantly, on the
higher ground of revealed religion, the sun of humility floods
man with the truth of his radically tragic, existential posture
before a God who would save him, namely that he is always a
sinner destined to die, yet eternally related to the God-Man
through absolute dependence upon Him for the grace of salvation.

In conclusion, can it be honestly said that Feuerbach succeeded in attaining the goals of his work? He wanted to liberate
man from the degradation of enslavement to the tyranny of the
Absolute Other; he wanted to help man secure his own greatness in the fellowship of sharing the divinity and religion of
humanity. Actually what did he do to man and for man?

Inwardly, within the individual, he cut the vision of man
down from its inexhaustibly fruitful speculations on the eternal life and marvellous missions of the Blessed Trinity, down

from its thrilling perusal of the supernatural elevation and sublime destiny of glorified man, back to the limited, transitory, confining conceptions of man the animal and worker. Here is a myopic mind that has drained reality of its exalted mysteries and thus inhibited and thwarted the infinite thrust of the free intellect. Instead of increasing and broadening man's opportunities for intellectual inquiry into nature, supernature, the transcendent and transitory purposes of human life, Feuerbach enprisons the mind of man in the repressive, occult, irrational *mysteries* of an anti-Christian religion of humanism. Whereas Christ demonstrated in His teaching and life that the truth would make men free, history has demonstrated that the myths of Feuerbach make men slaves.

We have in Feuerbach the expression of an inordinate itch to contract the inexhaustible plenitude of transcendent Being into a kind of cosmic, social solipsism. History is a cruel, incorruptible witness to the crimes atheistic humanism has perpetrated against human beings. Its theological *"reductio ad humanum,"* sprung from a hateful negation has, delivered many nations and over a billion souls in a span of fifty years into slavery at the hands of a Party of inhuman dogmatists, and their totalitarian States, in a living tomb of universally deadening moral, intellectual and political conformism. Atheism is always a movement from freedom to servitude; it always produces the excess of tyranny. If the individual enthrones himself against God, he simultaneously isolates himself in the prison of egoism and the sterile desert of auto-eroticism. When atheism takes the form of a social conspiracy to dethrone God, it takes as its communal mission the messianic goal of secularizing every cell of society until the whole body is militantly atheistic. And, in the words of de Lubac, this community in cosmic captivity, animated with the Feuerbachian animus against God and Christianity, "takes its outward course in disorder, begets tyrannies and collective crimes, and finds its expression in blood, fire and ruin."[42]

42. Henri de Lubac, S.J., *The Drama Of Atheist Humanism*, p. 7.

CHAPTER III

Nietzsche: God Becomes Superman

THE VIOLENT HATRED BEHIND NIETZSCHE'S ATTACK upon God, specifically the Christian God, rages from his resentment against that God's malignant effect upon man. The God of the Christians is convicted for creating out of man a community of intellectual and moral cretins. We read in Antichrist:

> The Christian conception of God—God as god of the sick, God as a spider, God as a spirit—is one of the most corrupt conceptions of the divine ever attained on earth. It may even represent the low-water mark in the descending development of divine types. God degenerated into the *contradiction* of life, instead of being its transfiguration and eternal Yes! God as the declaration of war against life, against nature, against the will to live! God—the formula for every slander against "this world," for every lie about the "beyond!" God—the deification of nothingness, the will to nothingness pronounced holy![1]

1. Friedrich Nietzsche, *The Antichrist,* translated by Walter Kaufmann, in *The Portable Nietzsche* (New York: The Viking Press), pp. 585–586.

In his crusade to develop an elite of supermen, Nietzsche proclaimed the "death of God," not merely the God of the metaphysicians but of the theologians as well. And he opposed this God with an absolute, shouting No! A No that became more savage and frantic the closer he approached his collapse into madness. Co-heir of an atheism that was taken for granted as already scientifically proven, Nietzsche, like Feuerbach, Comte, Marx and a host of other *fin de siècle* intellectuals, took no pains to refute God philosophically. God and Christianity were simply passé and done with. There was no longer any need for a theoretical attack on what was annihilated. Moreover, Christianity itself was *in articulo mortis,* its scriptural fables faded, its dogmas drained of divinity, its philosophy discredited, its sacraments unmasked as efficient power symbols in the sacerdotal subjection of every phase of man's life.

But Christianity dies hard. It has been under assault for two thousand years. Wave after wave of heresy has been shattered against its rock of truth; sword after sword of oppression has been snapped against the breastplate of its fidelity. Yet it always survived the ravages of time—political intrigues, religious wars, schisms, internal corruptions, the treason of the intellectuals, the plots of under and over worlds. Nevertheless, in modern times, as Nietzsche read them, Christians themselves had finally tired of their theological mythology; they no longer believed in God. They were in the process of discarding Him for being irrelevant in an age of enlightenment, unnecessary in the new centuries of science, embarrassing in a time of psychological maturity, old in an era of modernity, cruel toward the gentle generations of fresh humanists, rigid in the face of evolutionary progress and politically implicated against the liberation of the masses. Nietzsche's madman shouted to the whole world the treason against their God and Church which the Christians were trying to ignore. Leaping into the midst of a crowd in the market place and transfixing his astonished listeners with piercing glances, he cried: "God is dead. God remains dead. And we have killed him. How shall we, the murderers of all murderers, comfort ourselves?"[2]

2. Friedrich Nietzsche, *The Gay Science (Joyful Wisdom),* trans. by Walter Kaufmann, in *The Portable Nietzsche* (New York: The Viking Press, 1967), p. 95.

But the counterfeit Christians had devised a way to comfort themselves. They insulated themselves from the tragedies of life behind the last bastion of Christianity. They defended themselves behind the rampart of Christian moral standards. They naively strove to maintain the practice of Christian morals, without their theological foundations. They deluded themselves into thinking that secularized forms of Christianity, such as democracy, socialism, welfarism, which had severed their lifelines with the Christian faith, could manage to prosper on their own. Nietzsche saw the futility of this subterfuge. If there was one reality this supreme skeptic never doubted, it was that "the murder of an absolute God" inevitably demanded the rejection of that God's set of absolute moral values. He knew that Christian conduct was not possible for any length of time without the underpinning of Christian convictions. And so if the time for metaphysical attacks against God and Christianity was past, the time for the technique of psychological analysis and the tactics of corrosive ridicule had arrived. Nietzsche moved in for the kill against a Christianity tottering on rotted foundations. Where hatred and violence had failed to bring down Christianity, mockery and laughter would succeed. Derision would now be the test for its truth and integrity. And Nietzsche was convinced that its farcical facade of objective ethics would crumble under the test of his acidulous cynicism. The tactic was simple. All one had to do was to demonstrate that Christian morals were a monstrous swindle against humanity, a capital crime against life. Aghast at the ferocity of this attack, Karl Jaspers wrote that "Nietzsche became the new fountainhead of anti-Christianity, which had perhaps never before been so radical and so aware of its ultimate implications."[3]

Nietzsche's family background was strongly Christian. He was born into a family of Lutheran clergymen. His father and both grandfathers were Lutheran ministers. As a youth Nietzsche was deeply religious and one must not be fooled by his own later, manic-depressive falsifications of this side of his nature. In *Ecce Homo,* where he gives a sarcastically pungent review of his life and works, we read: "Atheism is not for me the consequence of something else; still less is it a thing which has

3. Karl Jaspers, *Nietzsche And Christianity,* translated by E.B. Ashton (Chicago: Henry Regnery, Gateway Edition, 1961), p. 1.

befallen men; in my case it is, something that goes without saying, a matter of instinct."[4] Karl Jaspers seems to have been put off by this exaggeration, for he writes: "Christian contents, literal Christian teaching, Christian authority lacked real meaning for him. He had nothing to shake off later, not even a childish attachment to myths."[5] However, Nietzsche's early autobiographical notes written when he was nineteen reveal his deep religious faith. It is true that even then he was often painfully locked in a tormenting struggle with the Angel of Doubt. The boy was already agonizing over the problem "whether a mirage had not led mankind astray for two thousand years." Again, as a young prophet, he was predicting that "great upheavals are still in the offing, once the masses will have grasped that all Christianity rests on exceptions. The existence of God, immortality, biblical authority, inspiration— these will always remain problematical. I have tried to deny everything: Oh, tearing down is easy, but building up!"

In one deeply moving passage, however, the youthful Nietzsche seems to have banished the tempting angel and regained religious peace. He wrote:

I have already experienced many things, joy as well as sadness, lightness of heart as well as depression, but in all these things God has certainly led me as a father might lead his helpless little child. He has already imposed much suffering on me, but in all this I recognize with reverence His majestic power which has everything turn out for the best. I have firmly resolved to devote myself to His service forever. May the dear Lord give me the power and strength I need for this resolution. And may He protect me on my way through life. As a child I trust in His grace. He will protect us all so that no evil will befall us. But may His holy will be done! I will accept with joy whatever He sends me, whether happiness or unhappiness, whether poverty or riches. And I will boldly look death itself in the eye. Death will one day unite us all in eternal joy and blessedness. Yes, dear Lord, let the light of your countenance shine upon us forever! Amen![6]

4. Nietzsche, *Ecce Homo, Gesammelte Werke,* Vol. II, p. 1.
5. Jaspers, *op. cit.,* p. 9.
6. Nietzsche, *Werke in Drei Bande,* edited by Carl Hauser (Munich: Hauser Verlag, 1956), Vol. 3, pp. 7–155.

But, as he does to all men, the Angel of Darkness returned to buffet the soul of Nietzsche, seeing in this young genius what his mentor, Professor Ritschl, saw, a "future frontrank German philosopher" who would shake the world with his brilliance. In a famous youthful poem, "To An Unknown God," we can witness Nietzsche attempting to decide his future. He is at the crossroads of life. Will he give himself to God or will he break forever with Him? The poem reveals the weakening faith of Nietzsche and his mysterious fascination for revolt against God. The decision to break away is all but taken, yet the poem reveals a deep religious nostalgia to remain with God:

> Once more before I go my way,
> Before I fix my gaze ahead,
> I lift my trembling hands to thee
> To whom in solitude I pray.
> To thee in my heart's depth
> Sacred altars reverently
> I consecrate,
> Imploring that thy voice should keep
> Summoning me; altars whereon
> The words glow: TO AN UNKNOWN GOD.
> His I am, though to this hour
> I trot with the apostates' throng.
> I am his! I feel his net,
> Still fight its closing in on me;
> Were I to flee,
> I would return to serve him yet.
> I will to know thee, unknown one!
> Thou deep into my soul reaching,
> Storm swift through my life sweeping,
> Unknowable, like-to-me one,
> I would know, *Lord, I would serve thee!*[7]

In a letter to his sister Elisabeth on June 11, 1865, from Bonn, where he was attending the university, Nietzsche revealed he could no longer imitate her fidelity to the Christian faith. He had decided against God because faith in God left people effete with a "feeling of greatest smugness." As for himself, he longs for the virile thrills and dangers of "striking out on new paths in conflict with custom" where one is "uncertain of one's step

7. Nietzsche, *Gedichte,* (Leipzig: Insel Verley, n.d.) See also the Translation by Elinor Gastendyle Briefs in *God on Trial* by Georg Siegmund, p. 285–286.

when walking independently, shifting one's moods frequently, indeed, one's conscience, lacking often all comfort but always having the eternal goal of the True, the Beautiful and the Good in view . . . Should you long for peace of soul and happiness? Then by all means believe. Should you want to become a disciple of truth? Then search."[8]

Thus, in the cause of the perilous adventure for truth, Nietzsche abandons the Christian God. What is more, with Spartan discipline and barbaric ferocity, he mounts an offensive which culminates in a crusade against God. This Godless Crusade proclaims that God is dead and that man, that is Superman, is the New God who dwells on earth. Secondly, the Godless Movement proclaims that the New God Superman is immanentized in time, preparing for man a heaven here, not one in the nonexistent hereafter. The hereafter is really the here; the transcendent is nothing more than the immanent; God is really man, albeit elite man, Superman.

Perhaps one of Nietzsche's greatest contributions to humanity is his psychological and historical critique of the creative impotency and even degeneracy of his own generation, which unabashedly characterized itself as an "age of decadence." His appalling picture of its sterile positivism, bourgeois, hypocritical orthodoxy, trivial certainties, pedantic pretentions was begun in his first major work, *The Birth Of Tragedy*. With aroused ire he opens here his mission to persuade his generation to take itself seriously and to conclude courageously to the consequences of its basic assumptions. These qualities of honesty and fearlessness are splendid adornments of Nietzsche's work.

The major theme of *The Birth Of Tragedy*, worked out through a fantastic and now famous symbolism, deplores the decline of culture in the modern world. Nietzsche was nauseated by an educational system that had replaced cultural vitality with dull informational accretions; he despised the play-acting used to cover up the loss of spiritual substance, man's way of living "as if;" he fled the thickening boredom that enveloped a society of uninhibited sensations where everyone talked, no one listened and all moved with insatiable curiosity

---

8. Nietzsche, *Unpublished Letters,* translated by Kurt F. Leidecker (London: Peter Owen, Ltd., 1960), pp. 33–34.

behind masks of duplicity. "Art," wrote the author, "owes its continuous evolution to the Apollonian-Dionysiac duality, even as propagation of the species depends on the duality of the sexes, their constant conflicts and periodic acts of reconciliation."[9] Handsome Apollo, the god of plastic arts, symbolizes the creative luminosity and order of being; his highest achievement is breathing forms of Titan heroes into chaos. Dionysos, the god of music and bacchanalian delirium, symbolizes universal, unharnessed energy whose invisible surge constructs and destroys universes. From the stormy communion of these Olympian parents, Attic tragedy was born, the apex of human cultural achievement, an offspring whose marvelous features blend the serenity of Apollo with the enthusiasm of Dionysos. But artistic beauty has its fearful price and the Greeks willingly paid it. Their creation of beauty grew out of their fearlessness in facing the terrors and horrors of existence. Triumph over suffering, conflict, sickness, fate produces beauty. A race so hypersensitive, so emotionally intense, so sensitized to suffering could only live by developing the tragedies of the Titans into "the shining fantasy of the Olympians." And the work ends on the admiring cry of the author: "What suffering must this race have endured in order to achieve such beauty!"[10]

But along came notorious Euripides who devalued tragedy to comedy, reducing the Titan protagonists to common-herd pygmies and throwing the stage open to the stampede of the spectators. But though the vulgarizing dramatist was Euripides, the daemon who drove him and formed his message was the agitator Socrates. Greek culture succumbed because Socrates supplanted Apollo in his conflict with Dionysos and submerged Dionysos himself under the tide of his rationalistic dialectic. Rationalist fever consumes myths and mysteries and, with these obliterated, renders civilization rootless. Since Socrates' advent generation after generation has substituted theoretical for tragic, rationalist for aesthetic man. The substitute is a pallid fraud of the Greek ideal. Rationalism saps the beautiful by reducing it to the sensible, subjecting it to "the mechanism of concepts, judgments and syllogisms" and calling the end

9. Friedrich Nietzsche, *The Birth of Tragedy,* translated by Francis Golffing (Garden City, N.Y.: Doubleday, Anchor Books, 1956), p. 19.
10. *Ibid.,* p. 146.

product man's masterpiece.[11] And the truth is, as Nietzsche insists, that "only as an aesthetic product can the world be justified to all eternity."[12]

But modern society is sick with Socratism and scientific optimism. Its scientism demands an aristocracy of learned pedants. Yet its leveling optimism prepares the barbaric masses for a revolt that will avenge the injustices of the centuries. If men are to cure the blight that already corrodes their culture, Dionysos must be chosen over Socrates. With Socrates banished, there will be a rebirth of tragedy. Nietzsche himself will be the precursor of this renaissance. He appeals to his friends to abandon the learned of the day; they are merely the "precursors of senility." If they join him in preparing for the second coming of Dionysos, the new artists will experience triumphant joy while participating in the rejuvenation of tragedy and the "fire-magic," Dionysiac music. But they must be strong in their faith and steeled for hardship. In the end, the wand of Dionysos will recreate the cultural wasteland of their era by means of a whirlwind that cleanses the land of waste and renders it lush with the golden glow and verdant richness of new life. Only let them grasp the thyrsus in hand and follow Dionysos and his herald, prepared for a struggle that will eventuate in miracles.

When he finished *The Birth of Tragedy,* Nietzsche did not yet see explicitly that he and his Dionysos, his tragic ideal, would encounter on their return to the struggle for men's souls not Socrates, the irreconcilable Rationalist, but Christ, the unconquerable Redeemer. De Lubac, posing the question, "Did Nietzsche see at this time his tragic, Dionysiac ideal as the merciless antagonist to Christianity?" answers the question thus: "At the time of *The Birth of Tragedy,* he did not yet see in Dionysos—as he did later in *The Will To Power* and *Ecce Homo*—the symbol of a pagan type of religion to be set up against Christ. His way of looking at things was not primarily anti-Christian at that time. It was anti-Socratic."[13] There is, however, in the historico-psychological mechanism of critique in this work an explanation pregnant with the embryo that will one day ma-

11. *Ibid.,* p. 94.
12. *Ibid.,* p. 42.
13. Henri Lubac, S.J., *op. cit.,* p. 39.

ture into a violent transvaluation of all Christian values into the values of a new and godless paganism. It reads:

> It is the sure sign of the death of a religion when its mythic presuppositions become systematized, under the severe, rational eyes of an orthodox dogmatism, into a ready sum of historical events, and when people begin timidly defending the veracity of myth but at the same time resist its natural continuance—when the feeling for myth withers and its place is taken by a religion claiming historical foundations.[14]

Attack on the Christian Ideal

In *The Gay Science (Joyful Wisdom)*, Nietzsche proclaimed "God is dead!" But his listeners, apathetic in an age of bourgeois complacency, were struck speechless with incomprehension, evidently totally unaware of the event. "I come too early," cries Nietzsche's mad herald, dashing his lantern to pieces upon the pavement. "This tremendous event is still on its way . . . it has not yet reached the ears of man . . . the light of stars requires time, deeds require time even after they are done."[15] The "dreadful news" will take hold of minds in about two centuries and, when it does, men will be lost in giddiness and the weightlessness of all things.

Yet for "free spirits" and philosophers the demise of God should not be a cause of sorrow. Rather it should be the occasion for happiness, relief, exhilaration, dawn. The root of cheerfulness for such elite souls will be "that the Christian God has ceased to be believable . . . that the 'old god is dead.' " How can the death of such a divine Person be the cause of rejoicing? Very simple, argues Nietzsche. Questioners and thinkers no longer have to put up with God as "the rough-fisted answer" and indelicate obstacle to the adventures of their minds. Dawn has at last broken on an infinitely free, if hazy, horizon. Gratitude, amazement, anticipation, independence should swell our hearts. Now our world may be completely reevaluated *ad majorem hominis gloriam.* Man's ships may now venture forth unfettered, seek danger anywhere. Now is he challenged to work

14. Friedrich Nietzsche, *The Birth of Tragedy,* p. 68.
15. Friedrich Nietzsche, *The Gay Science,* p. 96.

his wonderful will to surpass himself. With God gone, the sea, *our* sea, was never more open, never more alluring, never more demanding.[16]

In other words, the demise of God and the dissolution of faith in Him has promoted man to the overlordship of the universe. Man's creative energies are now released to develop themselves to their unimaginable fullness. The Christian God, who had set limits to man's greatness, could now no longer shackle the thrust of his genius with commands and prohibitions. Man now needed no longer to sigh for an unreal, supernatural world in the great beyond; his soaring, wings unclipped, was to be done in time; his high adventure was not sainthood, but superhumanity. At last, two thousand years of frustrating nature are ended forever. In modern times it is essential for man to be an atheist.

How had humanity been so successfully doomed to degradation during the past twenty centuries? Nietzsche accused Christianity of destroying all the truth by which men had lived in pagan, classical times. Tragic truth, as understood and lived before Socrates, was undermined by Christian mythology. To be sure, Antiquity is convicted of the most monstrous crime against mankind in that it prepared the way for the conquest of Christianity. Socrates and Plato, founders of an anti-paganism—a sort of pre-existing Christianity with its God of absolute Beauty and Morality—prepared the ground for the advent of Christianity. With the work of its vanguard accomplices done so well, Christianity moved in to counter pagan truth with its own fiction. Such myths as a Triune God, moral world-order, sin, grace, redemption, immortality, resurrection, hell, heaven thoroughly destroyed the appeal of paganism for the masses. How could Christianity have ever duped so many ages of the learned and especially the modern age which is proud of its historical prowess?

Christianity developed an especially effective technique for proclaiming and spreading its doctrine and morals. Its principle of policy was "not whether a thing is true, but how it will serve." Its lack of intellectual integrity permitted resorting to any lie and manipulating the emotional thermostat of men until it reached the temperature of belief. It produced a veritable arse-

16. *Ibid.,* p. 448.

nal, educational arsenal, of the means for seduction to faith. The spirit that motivated the use of these means was the calculated denigration of its enemies or possible sources of opposition. It debased reason, philosophy, science, methodical doubt, even prudent caution. On the other hand, it heaped triumphant praise on all its doctrines and morals, referring them to the Creator as their source and to the Redeemer as their Promulgator, foreclosing thereby any criticism or reassessment of them and demanding, as the sole spiritual posture before its creed, acceptance of the whole with profound gratitude and humility. Christianity shrewdly nurtured the resentments of the hero-masses against the honors of the mighty; she attracted outcasts and failures of every sort by persuading them they were the equal before God and the Redeemer of any other man. Such doctrines swelled the weak, the ignorant, the foolish into fanatical folly so that they imagined themselves the light of the world and the salt of the earth. There was the magnetic power of paradox in her doctrine—life through death, honor through humiliation, mastery through slavery, power through impotence, ascendence through descent. The doctrine perplexed, outraged, incited to abuse and persecution. And wonder of wonders, it attracted the noble and strong as well as the lowly and ignoble. Nietzsche especially resented Christianity's power over the noble, whom he wanted to enlist in his elite of supermen for the remaking of humanity. Thus he invidiously assigns Christianity's success with the noble to its appeal to every cowardice and vanity of their fatigued souls as well as to their trust, guilelessness, forbearance, patience, resignation, neighborly love, submission to God. Christianity caught the noble in its nets when they were exhausted, unharnessed and in moods of depressing abdication of their entire selves.

What was humanity fighting in Christianity? A movement that aimed at conquering the strong, discouraging the noble, exploiting the miseries of men, eroding their self-assurance, poisoning their natural instincts, rendering them sick, weak until their will to power is reversed and turned against them— until they perish from the excesses of self-abasement, self-affliction, disintegrating in that most pitiable deformity whose most famous victim is the brilliant genius Pascal.[17]

17. Friedrich Nietzsche, *The Antichrist,* translated by Walter Kaufman in *The Portable Nietzsche,* p. 572.

Christianity, its doctrine and morals are founded on an historical distortion. And Nietzsche develops the following cohesive (in his mind) story of how Christianity was born and progressed. Christianity, using as its origin "the crude fable of the miracle worker and Redeemer," managed to hoodwink the world about the historical truth of its beginnings. Actually, Christianity began with the event of Jesus' death on the cross; it does not have roots in His life or teachings or any of His actions preceding His crucifixion. We have in Christianity the history of a subterfuge and misunderstanding that grew cruder as time went on. The original symbolism of Christianity developed through its swallowing up of the doctrines and rites of all the subterranean cults of the Roman empire as well as the nonsense of all kinds of diseased reason. Christianity's destiny lay in the necessity that its faith had to become as diseased, as base and vulgar, as the needs it was meant to satisfy were diseased, base and vulgar.[18]

Thus, a grand hoax from the beginning, Christianity was not founded as a way of life by Christ. "There was only one Christian and he died on the cross."[19] Jesus had nothing consciously to do with the founding of Christianity as a creed or community. Although he made a sharp distinction between the message of Jesus and the creed of Christianity, Nietzsche rejected both with contempt. He is against Jesus whose truthfulness, nevertheless, he defends. He is against the Apostles, the Church, the Fathers and all priests whose deception and dishonesty he abhors and condemns. Moreover, he is against both Jesus and Christianity because both advocate a type of life that reeks with the symptoms of decadence. With total antagonism against Christ and Christianity understood, we can proceed to relate Nietzsche's history of the lie of Christianity:

Jesus did not bring a new knowledge or a new faith; He merely achieved in Himself a new way of life. He transformed His individual life by evoking "a profound instinct for the way one must live so as to feel in heaven, to feel eternal." The heavenly bliss Jesus experienced was His "psychological reality of redemption." But all that is meant when one says that Jesus achieved beatitude is that He felt "at home in a world no longer touched by reality, in an inner world." Jesus' message

18. *Ibid.*, p. 610.
19. *Ibid.*, p. 612.

when He used the words light or life referred merely to this inner world. Parables, words, nature, everything, all reality are merely symbols of His inner world. Jesus was, thus, an anti-realist. Hence none of His words must be taken literally, for He could have no doctrine, no faith to formulate, nor morality to hand down to His disciples. He was neither a conscious nor unconscious founder of a religion.

But how did Jesus manifest His inner realization of true, eternal life in His outward words and actions? His good tidings consisted in erasing all contrasts, all distinctions. Nietzsche has Jesus speak as if the objective world of sensation and perception were non-existent to him because this world was full of contrasts, definiteness, distinctions. Jesus calls on the blessed to pass the world by, to go through it without interest. Here, then, is a Jesus who is non-resistance personified; He denies nothing, affirms everything, excludes nothing, no one from His love. Natives, strangers, Jews, non-Jews, enemies, friends, relatives—all are non-selectively loved and never depreciated. Therefore, no one is to be resisted; neither the heretic nor the persecutor, the tormentor nor the aggressor. Courts of law are to be shunned for no one ought to take an oath. If this conduct represents the inner life of Jesus, then Jesus is the acme of pure simplicity, untouched by history, culture, politics, war, good or evil. And, in fact, Nietzsche says that with no more contrasts existing for Jesus, there no longer existed for Him the concepts of sin, guilt, punishment, estrangement between God and man. Indeed, time, physical life, crises of any manner, even death itself have no reality for Jesus. They are all part of an absent, quite different world from the inner bliss of the life of Jesus.

To be sure, Jesus sealed His blissful life in His inner world by dying on the cross in the world of reality. "This bringer of glad tidings died as he had lived—not to redeem mankind, but to show one how to live."[20] Not to resist, not to be angry, not to hold responsiblity, not even to resist the evil one, but to love him also.

Now what manner of man could live such a life as is here depicted? Nietzsche says that here is a man who loathes reality, who was insensible to suffering in the real world, who aban-

20. *Ibid.,* pp. 608–609.

doned all resistance and fell back on love as the only way of life. Nietzsche finds in such a person "the moving charm of quite a mixture of the sublime, the sick, the childlike."[21] But the two most inappropriate concepts possible in the explanation of the Jesus type were misused by Renan when he called Jesus a genius and a hero. Nietzsche laughs this explanation to scorn. For him, Jesus is the exact opposite of these grand concepts. The apt term to be applied to Jesus would be the title idiot, in the sense in which Dostoevsky called his Prince Myshkin an idiot.[22]

But Nietzsche tells us that the perfections he found in the personality and life of Jesus actually belong to the category of decadence. To be sure, Jesus was a shining example of honesty itself, but He advocated a life "just the opposite of all wrestling, of all feeling-oneself-in-a-struggle." Such a physiological habit of shrinking from any contact with the concrete world represents an instinctive hatred of every reality, a flight into the untouchable, the incomprehensible, beyond time and space. Did not Jesus' way of living instinctively arouse the mighty to destroy Him? Did not the unnatural and sick world into which Jesus led His followers breed His own executioners? "This bringer of glad tidings" makes everyone a child of God and, as such, the equal of everyone else. But a man's worth, according to Nietzsche, is measured by the power of his will, by how wholeheartedly he will endure pain and torture and turn them to his own advantage. Without doubt, Jesus was a paragon of endurance, the soul of serenity. But He lacked self-control in Nietzsche's meaning of the term. There was nothing to be controlled in the life of Jesus. Was He not indifferent to all personal advantages and disadvantages? He was "blessed in peace, in gentleness, in not being able to be inimical."[23] "He died too early; he himself would have recanted his teaching, had he reached my age. Noble enough was he to recant."[24]

21. *Ibid.,* p. 603.
22. In Dostoevsky's *Idiot,* Prince Myshkin, embodied the Christ-like ideal. Loving, forgiving, utterly self-effacing, he both crushingly testified against current moral depravity and sparked criminal reprisals that drove him back to idiocy. Nietzsche loved Dostoevsky the psychologist, shunned him as ardent Christian. He saw the idiot Christian as the acme of decadence.
23. Dostoevsky, *The Idiot,* pp. 600–601.
24. Friedrich Nietzsche, *Thus Spake Zarathustra,* translated by Walter Kaufmann, in *The Portable Nietzsche,* p. 185.

Nietzsche was aware that his picture of Jesus was open to serious doubt and questioning. The Gospels give a quite different portrait of Jesus as Redeemer. Nietzsche admits that there exists "a gaping contradiction between the sermonizer on the mount, lake and meadow, whose appearance seems like that of a Buddha on soil that is not at all Indian, and that fanatic of aggression, that mortal enemy of theologians and priests."[25] Despite this radical contrast, Nietzsche insists that the peaceful Jesus of the mount and meadows is the genuine Jesus. The judging Jesus is the creation of his followers, a false interpretation by the primitive Christian community, striving desperately to survive in a hostile pagan world. "I myself have no doubt that the generous dose of gall (and even of *esprit*) first flowed into the type of the Master from the excited state of Christian propaganda; after all, the unscrupulousness of all sectarians, when it comes to constructing their own *apology* out of their master, is only too well known."[26]

Apparently in order to survive, the small Christian community, far from forgiving their enemies for killing their master, revived the feeling of resentment which their Master had repudiated by His death. They predicted that the kingdom of God would come as a judgment over the murderers of their Master. And Jesus Himself as "a judging, quarreling, angry, malignantly sophistical theologian" would continue to oppose His mighty enemies, the Scribes and Pharisees, and eventually conquer the all-powerful enemy, the Roman empire. Thus the fanatic and the militant was introduced into Jesus, the great, peaceful symbolist. Christianity completely distorted both the personality of Jesus and what He accepted as truth. Using Jesus the Judge as their instrument to press forth their own truth and mission, the Apostles appealed to the masses at the bottom of society, to outcasts and sinners. Christianity has been a false conspiracy from its inception; the whole New Testament is the book of distortions with which the world was to be trapped. The life of Jesus was first reduced to the screen of a faith; all seriously minded followers were bound absolutely to accept every article of this faith. A legend of salvation now replaced all of Jesus' symbols, parables. Formulae, rites, dogmas, a special

25. Friedrich Nietzsche, *The Antichrist,* p. 604.
26. *Ibid.,* p. 614.

history were universally imposed and substituted for the symbolic way in which Jesus lived. Out of the withdrawn, narrow,
wholly unworldly life of Jesus, the apostles "fabricated" a
world history, a personal immortality, a kingdom of God here,
present, militant and yet to come up to glory in a kingdom of
heaven in the beyond. They forged a personal Savior, Son of
God, the second person of the Trinity who founded this small
community for all times and for all eternity on Peter the Rock.
"All this is cynicism, unmatched in history, a mockery of symbol."[27] "In the Christian world of ideas there is nothing that has
the least contact with reality—and it is in the instinctive hatred
of reality that we have recognized the only motivating force at
the root of Christianity."[28]

Who among that little flock could have had the genius to
think up such a successful swindle? It was the genius Paul.
With rabbinical fire and impudence, he created the battle cry
that moved the millions. It was obscene; it was contemptible,
but it was eminently successful, for it offered a challenge and
promised a reward. "If Christ is not risen from the dead, then
our faith is vain." Paul, the greatest fabricator among the
Christians, produced the "malignant counterfeit" of a savior
figure in whom death and resurrection were the supreme realities.

What of the progress of Christianity after Paul and the Apostles had left the earthly scene? It had certainly spread like
wildfire even up to modern times. Nietzsche attributes this
phenomenal conquest of souls by the Christian movement to its
original falsification of moral values. He explains this re-
evaluation of values from an historical and a psychological
aspect:

Historically, the Jews were a brilliant but violently oppressed
people. They shrewdly realized that to survive with some kind
of decent existence against the powerful and great nations that
surrounded and often enveloped them, they had to attack the
values of the mighty in some subtle way. Keeping their raging
hatred and vindictiveness deeply hidden within their souls, this
priestly people, with frightening consistence, inverted the aristocratic value equation—"good/noble/powerful/beautiful/-

27. *Ibid.*, p. 608.
28. *Ibid.*, p. 613.

happy/favored-of-the-gods, maintaining . . . that only the poor, the powerless are good; only the suffering, sick, and ugly truly blessed. But you noble and mighty ones of the earth will be, to all eternity, the evil, the cruel, the avaricious, the godless, and thus the cursed and damned! We know who has fallen heir to this Jewish inversion of values . . ."[29] Christianity took up this technique of its parent religion. It appealed to the furious hatred and resentment felt by the millions of slaves, misfits and mediocre against the mighty. Looking deeper into the psychology of this shrewd ruse in human relations, Nietzsche claims that the resentment, the frustration of impotence drew the herd to Christianity by a very hidden attraction. What was happening was that the will to power, struggling even in impotence, created new evaluating ideals and moral interpretations. The masses, driven on by a fanatical hunger for justice, by their secret rancor against their overlords, by a madness to somehow control their rulers, saw in Christian spirituality, backed up by its dogmas, the perfect means for undermining the high, noble and strong. They said No to everything representing ascending power in life.

Christianity has conquered for twenty centuries because it has collected, organized, taught and disciplined the vast, numerically superior dregs of society against the few mighty. With a resiliency that is astonishing, it has adapted the mysteries, salvational aspirations, modes of sacrifice, asceticisms, rituals, philosophies, accusations against worldliness culled from paganism and Judaism to the needs of its faithful. In outbidding its competitors, it has brazenly stolen their brightest treasures, added her own creations and driven many religions from the market for souls. Nietzsche taught that "not Jesus but Christianity" is the fulfillment of Judaism. Christianity inherited Judaism's art of lying in the cause of holy survival and raised this art to consummate perfection in her New Testament. Omnipotent Yaweh, a promised land, a priesthood of sacrifice, a morality of sin and punishment were excellent Jewish fabrications. But they did not compare with the Christian creations of Trinity, God-Man, Pope, heaven, hell. In a sum-

29. Friedrich Nietzsche, *The Genealogy of Morals*, translated by Francis Golffing (Garden City, N.Y.: Doubleday, Anchor Books, 1956), p. 167.

mary account of what Christianity accomplished, Nietzsche writes:

> ... Then Paul appeared ... What he guessed was how one could use the little sectarian Christian movement apart from Judaism to kindle a "world fire"; how with the sumbol of "God on the cross" one could unite all who lay at the bottom, all who were secretly rebellious, the whole inheritance of anarchistic agitation in the Empire, into a tremendous power. "Salvation is of the Jews." Christianity as a formula with which to outbid the subterranean cults of all kinds, those of Osiris, of the Great Mother, of Mithras, for example—*and* to unite them: in this insight lies the genius of Paul. His instinct was so sure in this that he took the ideas with which these chandala religions fascinated, and, with ruthless violence, he put them into the mouth of the "Savior" whom he had invented, and not only into his mouth—he *made* something out of him that a priest of Mithras too could understand.
> This was his moment at Damascus: he comprehended that he *needed* the belief in immortality to deprive "the world" of value, that the concept of "hell" would become master even over Rome—that with the "beyond" one *kills life.* Nihilism and Christianism: that rhymes, that does not only rhyme.[30]

Ascent to Ideal Man

Nietzsche's notes for his *magnum opus,* the great synthesis of his philosophical thought, which he never completed but which appeared posthumously as *The Will To Power,* reveal an animosity to God for practically the same reasons that moved Feuerbach to embrace anti-theism. The Nietzschean thesis on God and religion is as follows. God is man's *alter ego,* sublimated, of course; he is the mirror of man, the psychological duplication and personification of the intense love, power and goodness that man surprisingly finds in himself at rare intervals. Knowing his own weakness and ambiguity, man does not dare attribute such marvelous virtues to himself, but concludes they must be the gifts and adornments of some super-creature, some superhuman being. Thus the strongest in man belongs beyond man, while the weakest in man belongs to man alone.

30. Friedrich Nietzsche, *The Antichrist,* pp. 649–650.

Religion, therefore, consists in this process by which man un-
clothes, defrauds and debases himself before an idol. The creation of God is the product of the diminution of man.

The very heart, therefore, of the human adventure is to be a
spiritual revolution whereby man will regain his greatness by
pitting the recreation of himself against the dissolution of that
"God who is a conjecture." The Nietzschean exposé of the un-
reality of God and of the conspiracy of Christianity to debase
man is merely the negative side of his adventure in humanism.
His fierce assault on God and Christianity is complemented by
an ardent passion for the rediscovery and transformation of
man. Listen to his glad tidings to his new men as spoken
through Zarathustra:

> Remain faithful to the earth, my brothers, with the power
> of your virtue. Let your gift-giving love and your knowl-
> edge serve the meaning of the earth. Thus I beg and be-
> seech you. Do not let them fly away from earthly things
> and beat their wings against eternal walls. Alas, there has
> always been so much virtue that has flown away. Lead
> back to earth the virtue that flew away, as I do—back to the
> body, back to life, that it may give the earth a meaning, a
> human meaning.[31]

Thus the splendid decision that effects the rejection of God
and the complete renunciation of religion is a necessary first
step in man's self-conquest. Only through this decision will the
earth begin to become a site of recovery, exuding a new fragrance and bringing salvation and hope. If man clings to God
and religion, he shall have to pay dearly for his cowardice. Let
him move up to become something more than man. The time
has come to shed his God-skin and Christian clothing; history
is presently ordering him to come up higher or suffer sinking
into nihilism. This is his great moment of transition. Will man
ascend or descend? Again Zarathustra exhorts his followers
upward:

> *Behold, I teach you the Superman.* Man is something that
> shall be overcome. What have you done to overcome him?
> All beings so far have created something beyond them-

31. Friedrich Nietzsche, *Thus Spake Zarathustra*, p. 188.

selves; and do you want to be the ebb of this great flood and
even go back to the beasts rather than overcome man?
What is the ape to man? A laughingstock or a painful
embarrassment. And man shall be just that for the Superman: a laughingstock or a painful embarrassment. You
have made your way from worm to man, and much in you
is still worm. Once you were apes, and even now too, man
is more ape than any ape.
Whoever is wisest among you is also a mere conflict and
cross between plant and ghost. But do I bid you become
ghosts or plants?
Behold, I teach you the Superman. The Superman is the
meaning of the earth. Let your will say: The Superman
shall be the meaning of the earth![32]

As long as God was on the human scene, man had a *dolce far
niente* existence. Addicted to appealing for everything to the
Almighty, his created powers had atrophied and he had become
a miserable beggar, unable to bestir himself to rise or advance.
But now there lay before him a life of challenge, of hardship,
of suffering and, yes, of loneliness. For, bereft of God, man was
alone, on his own; bleak loneliness has enveloped him and rendered his new condition almost intolerable. He must now create out of himself, out of nothingness. Without any outside aid
he was attempting perhaps the impossible—the creation of Superman.

In expounding his revolutionary philosophy of human nature
Nietzsche gives us a rather sketchy and curious account of
man's place in the cosmos. Of course, with the myth of God
erased, man could hardly be represented any longer as the
metaphysical or spiritual *imago Dei.* That would be calling for
an *imago nihilis,* the image of nothingness. Then, too, Nietzsche despised those who philosophize as metaphysicians. He
would evaluate man empirically, as he finds him in history.
Thus Nietzsche accepts Darwin's findings on man up to a point,
the point being man's evolving origin from lower forms of life
up through the ape to his present form. Nietzsche agrees that
men are merely animals, essentially the same as apes. However, unlike Darwin, he refuses to believe that all men occupy
a unique position in the cosmos and that the race is inevitably
evolving, through a blind, on-going progress, to the perfection

32. *Ibid.,* Prologue, No. 3, Part 1, pp. 124–125.

of the millenium. Millions of facts contradict that naive optimism. Witness the decadence in every phase of nineteenth-century cultural life.

The truth is that men are distinguished from chimpanzees only by a *potentiality* that *can* raise them above animals in cultural performance. History demonstrates, however, that the masses will never better themselves. Because of fear and laziness they will never become human, but remain animals forever. The weak are numerous and will ever remain decadent. On the other hand, Nietzsche disagrees with the pessimism of his master, Schopenhauer. The human predicament, bad as it is, is not all darkness. History shows that there has ever been the living testimony of a few stronger spirits among men who have managed to rise above being mere primates and to make themselves "truly human beings." Nietzsche, a fervent believer in the "great man" theory, explains that these molders of the universe, imbued with spirit and the willingness to suffer, learned how to "organize the chaos" within themselves and the cosmos. A Plato, Phidias, Michelangelo, Shakespeare, Leonardo, Napoleon, Paul, Jesus brought about major changes in humanity not by the quantity of their work, but by their art of improving, organizing and beautifying the chaotic in the flood of human experience; these men of genius integrated, disciplined, focused into harmony the inexhaustible powers of life. They improved nature interiorly and exteriorly. Such examples of greatness emphasized the real meaning of humanity. "The goal of humanity cannot lie in the end but only *in its highest specimens.*" Only such men attain man's true nature; the vast majority of men remain animals, never realizing themselves or achieving true existence. For true existence rejects the temptation to allow one's life to be but a mere accidental flow of events. True existence is lived when man has "a high and transfiguring total aim," a deliberately chosen goal which is attainable and which gives one's whole human activity a powerful thrust upward to the more than human.

Rousseau, Nietzsche felt, by stressing a romantic return to nature, was insisting that man remain an animal, agitated by the lowest and cheapest feelings, becoming a beast of prey or a Catilinian criminal. Rousseau's reductionism fathered all the most ignoble modern, social heresies—democracy, socialism, humanitarianism, pacifism. His collectivities so easily degenerate into revolutionary mobs thirsting for blood, once the restraints of culture, artistic tradition and reason are removed. Instead of urging men to return to nature, Nietzsche challenges them to "cultivate," "improve," "transfigure" and re-create human nature.

Since the leveling of the vast majority of men is inevitable and their improvement impossible, Nietzsche takes comfort in the fact that thousands of years of human degeneration were really necessary as prelude for better times to come. Plowing under is a necessary preparation if the ground is to produce a superior harvest. Therefore, let the leveling of mankind continue, nay, let it be accelerated, for only thus will Superman arrive, the elite Titans who will be the architects of a new civilization, a new morality, a new eschatology.

> . . . While, in other words, the democratization of Europe will amount to the creation of a type prepared in the subtlest sense for *slavery*—the individual, meanwhile, the exceptional case, the *strong* man, will turn out to be stronger and richer than he has probably ever been, thanks to the lack of prejudice in his schooling, thanks to the enormous varied practice he can get in skills and disguises. I meant to say that the democratization of Europe is at the same time an involuntary arrangement for the training of tyrants—taking the word in every sense, including its most intellectual.[33]

Brinton shrewdly remarks that "Nietzsche has achieved the philosopher's favorite task, the reconciliation of the irreconcilable. Hegel could have found no better example for the benign workings of the dialectic; out of democracy, dictatorship; out of the rule of the herd-men, the rule of the Supermen."[34] We shall now see how Nietzsche's discovery of the philosopher's stone— the handy ultimate which reveals the meaning of all human experience—influenced his final evaluation of man, his society and his destiny.

---

33. Friedrich Nietzsche, *Beyond Good And Evil*, translated by Marianne Cowan (Chicago: Henry Regnery Co., 1966), III, p. 175.
34. Crane Brinton, *Nietzsche*, (New York: Harper, Torchbooks, 1965), p. 130.

The Will to Power

Nietzsche had been profoundly impressed by Schopenhauer's interpretation that Will is the prime principle and mover of the universe. Schopenhauer had taught that the Will to Existence or the Will to Live was basically evil. Thus, his pessimism consisted in teaching that human life and human Will, as evils, must be blunted by living as anemically as possible. The greatest evil one could do another was to grant the tragedy of life to another through procreation. Now Nietzsche had read Schopenhauer's *The World As Will And Idea* when he was a youth and, though deeply impressed, he did not agree wholeheartedly nor jump immediately into print to correct his master's interpretation of the role of the Will in the universe. In his early writings Nietzsche used the will to power to explain behavior and did not approve of it. In his work, *The Dawn,* Nietzsche admits that he is experimenting with moral evaluations and prejudices: "With this book begins my campaign against morality." He attempts to prove that all psychological phenomena can be traced back to two fundamental sources: fear and power. There is yet no sign here that he sees the will to power as the unifying force of all reality. Kaufmann records Nietzsche's journey to his discovery thus:

> In his next work, *The Gay Science,* Nietzsche still experimented with the notion of power and did not yet expound any monism nor any systematic psychological theory. The book also contains the first tentative consideration of the conception of the eternal recurrence of all events. Then, suddenly, the implications of both the will to power and the eternal recurrence struck Nietzsche's mind at once, like a flash of lightning, and in a frenzied feeling of inspiration he wrote his *Zarathustra*—the first published work to contain any mention of the will to power by that name —and there expounded both concepts. From then on he considered it his task to work out the details of the insight which had been offered in the "dithyrambs" of *Zarathustra:* the universality of both the will to power and the eternal recurrence.[35]

35. Walter Kaufmann, *Nietzsche: Philosopher, Psychologist, Antichrist* (New York and Cleveland: World, Meridian Books, 1966), p. 162.

Thus the development of Nietzsche's interpretation of the Will and its function and goal in the universe was a slow process, the result of years of discernment of the workings of the will in human psychical histories.

Yet Nietzsche had decided early in life to say Yes to the human adventure, despite its endlessly harsh trials, indeed, *because* of these very hardships he agreed to accept life cheerfully. Not for him the Nay-saying of Schopenhauer, nor the near-death quietism of contempt and calm that this philosopher advocated. At first, as we have seen, Nietzsche found life livable because of its enhancement through Grecian tragic art. But since both Socratism and Christianity had once again degraded life and reduced it to chaos and decadence, Nietzsche realized that tragic art needed the aid of violence or at least of some more powerful force, if man and his culture were to be raised from the "slough of despond" to new humanistic heights. Nietzsche found his philosopher's stone in the Will to Power; in his healing hands it would be the panacea for sick society.

Thus Schopenhauer's Will to Live, an evil thing, was transformed by Nietzsche into his own Will to Power, a very good reality.

> What is good? Everything that heightens the feeling of power in man, the will to power, power itself. What is bad? Everything that is born of weakness. What is happiness? The feeling that power is *growing*, that resistance is overcome.
> Not contentedness but more power; not peace but war; not virtue but fitness (Renaissance virtue, *virtù*, virtue that is moraline-free).
> The weak and the failures shall perish: first principle of *our* love of man. And they shall even be given every possible assistance to perish. What is more harmful than any vice? Active pity for all the failures and all the weak: Christianity.[36]

The world, then, is the Will to Power, nothing more. Man himself is also this Will to Power, nothing else. Life, its instinct for growth, its durability are all Will to Power. "Where the Will

36. Friedrich Nietzsche, *The Antichrist*, translated by Walter Kaufmann; in *The Portable Nietzsche* (New York: Viking Press, 1967), p. 57.

to Power is lacking, there is decline. It is my contention that all the supreme values of mankind *lack* this will—the values which are symptomatic of decline, *nihilistic* values, are lording it under the holiest names."[37]

Nietzsche's Will to Power must not be seen as a metaphysical ideal transcending this world like Plato's pure ideas. On the contrary, Nietzsche is forever defending this phenomenal world against the fraud of the transcendent universe. The Will to Power is wholly terrestrial. In a world which is a unity in an eternal evolving process of development and becoming, the Will to Power is manifested everywhere. Every phase of this process of becoming can be interpreted as the Will to Power. Thus, the inner guiding of this universe is this Will to Power; it exists and directs every phase of organic life. This sweeping empirical hypothesis for the explanation of whatever happens in the universe and its diverse forms of evolving life gives unity to cosmic and human phenomena. The development of high Greek culture is now explained as an effect of the will to power. In developing his culture, man wills to outstrip, surpass, submerge and extinguish his rivals. The doubtful outcome of the struggle stresses the ambiguous nature of the Will to Power. It is a two-edged sword, capable of producing good or evil, depending on whether it is wielded by the powerful few, the elite or by the petty many, the masses. As indicated in the notes which he left for his projected *magnum opus,* Nietzsche planned to trace the lines of influence between the Will to Power and the many phenomena of the human adventure. In a work such as this, which is focused on the Nietzschean adventure in atheism, we will restrict our study to Nietzsche's reflections on the relationship of the Will to Power to the human activities of knowledge, religion and morality.

Power and Knowledge

The thirst for knowledge is a manifestation of the drive of the Will for Power. The intellect is a weapon in the Will's campaign to seize more power. For Bacon, "knowledge is power," in the sense that knowledge dispels darkness concerning the nature of reality, reveals truth and thereby liberates man to make

37. *Ibid.,* p. 572.

use of both nature and truth to attain higher culture and more truth. For Nietzsche knowledge is power for the sake of more power. Power is its own ultimate, absolute end, the essential aspect of all being. Man wants power more than life; he continually risks his life to ascend in power. The aim of knowledge is not to know or love but to dominate. Each man wants to master, organize, order the flood of impressions, thoughts, feelings, sensations that sweep in and through him in his process of becoming. He must do this for the practical needs of his life. Reality is not stable; it is becoming. Men transform becoming into being by imposing patterns of stability, unity, familiarity on the deluge of their experiences. This is the action of the Will to Power. Knowledge is the Will to Power interpreting the flux of reality. It follows that all truth is a matter of reading meaning into reality, not of discovering meaning in myself and in reality. It further follows that for Nietzsche there is no absolute truth. The idea of absolute truth was, anyway, a hoax, the first and worst of all deceptions perpetrated by philosophers and priests who planned to dominate man by entangling him in the web of religion. These creators of holy illusions were dissatisfied with the real world of becoming because it guaranteed them no security. They, therefore, created a new world where an Absolute Being, established Truth, and stable positions of power assured them positions of eternal mastery. As a matter of fact, contemplation of the real in order to discover its essence and its unchangeable Origin is in today's modern world a sterile, passive and impossible activity, now that God is really dead. "We have abolished the world of truth with our Will to Power." Nothing is true. The very idea of truth is merely God's shade. What place has God's ghost at the Banquet of Becoming? Away with the cult of truth! The time has come for the cult of lucidity. Let us be courageously consistent in our choice of power over truth. Since God is really dead, then that "reason," that "truth," that "morality" which were rooted in him have become mere idols, specters of a non-existent world. Today is the twilight of these idols. One can admit, of course, that truth is a species of error, a sort of wraith of God, necessary for the existence of a special type of mentality. Philosophers and theologians suffer from this diseased mentality; their everlasting activity is to tyrannize over nature. Full of faith in themselves, these hunters after shadows repeat the age-old error. This error, in the words of Nietzsche, "always creates the world in its own image; it cannot do otherwise, for philosophy *is* this tyrannical desire; it is the most spiritual will to power, to "creation of the world," to the *causa prima.*"[38] But what is a special cause of resentment to Nietzsche is that these philosophers, besides tyrannizing over themselves, succeed, as the poet Milton expressed it, in persuading the multitudes that "millions of spiritual creatures walk the earth, unseen both when we wake and when we sleep." Such teachers are ghouls, robbing the grave of God and feeding themselves and their followers on His dead body.

Now Nietzsche admits that some "fictions" are necessary and useful for controlling the business of human living. Plato's noble lie was intended to be used for the betterment of the Athenian citizens. The danger is that arbitrary myths tend to become, in the course of time, unchallenged assumptions, taking on the aspect of eternal truth. To give but a few examples, such myths as the existence of enduring essences, of equal natures, of the law of causality are not really true. They have achieved their durability in the minds of men because men have imposed these myths on the chaos of Becoming in order to preserve humanity from being swept into annihilation. Myths less useful to the survival or advancement of the human race have been discarded as "errors." Useful myths are retained as "truths." Language, therefore, does not mirror reality, but merely masks a philosophical and theological mythology. Hence all truths are fictions, subjective interpretations of reality. Now these interpretations are perspectives, points of view, from which one imposes on reality what he wills to be there. Perspectives necessary for the welfare of mankind, Nietzsche accepts not as true but as useful and good. Perspectives harmful to mankind, Nietzsche rejects not as untrue but as evil. The religious, God-oriented perspectival view of the universe and mankind is evil because such a view places a negative evaluation on this world and on man's mission within it. The Will to Power view preserves the dynamism of Becoming for the world and promotes man to the status of Superman, opening up an infinite horizon

38. Friedrich Nietzsche, *Beyond Good And Evil,* translated by Marianne Cowan (Chicago: Henry Regnery Company, Gateway Edition, 1966), p. 9.

and future for man's unending advancement in power.

Nietzsche has made knowledge the handmaiden of power; he has made art the serf of power. Thus both knowledge and art have become propaganda for power. His utilitarian, exploitative theory of knowledge and truth anticipates the pragmatism of William James and the instrumentalism of John Dewey. Already William James' crass statement about truth being "the cash value of the idea" is prefigured in Nietzsche's teaching that truth is the power value of the idea. When the only reason for knowledge becomes the hotter pursuit for more power, then truly philosophizing has become a violent hammering activity that smashes old idols and chisels new ones. Then truly philosophy has become a way of war. And Nietzsche is honest enough to admit this. He has his new oracle, Zarathustra, drunk with power, predict for the world a future of fire and slaughter, a necessary purge for the advent of pitiless Superman. In *Ecce Homo,* Nietzsche, the prophet en route to madness, proclaims: "I herald the coming of a tragic era. We must be prepared for a long succession of demolitions, devastations and upheavals . . . There will be wars such as the world has never yet seen . . . Europe will soon be enveloped in darkness . . . We . . . waiting on the mountain . . . even look forward without any real compassion to this darkening . . . our heart overflows with gratitude, amazement, anticipation, expectation."[39] "Thanks to me," writes Nietzsche in *The Will To Power,* "a catastrophe is at hand. A catastrophe whose name I know, whose name I shall not tell. Then all the earth will writhe in convulsions." It will be the advent of nihilism.

Nietzsche proved to be a seer who had a deep insight into the decadence of his age and a prophet with accurate foresight as to the tragedies this decadence would engender. Two twentieth-century world wars and the threat of a third establish Nietzsche as an accurate, far-seeing thinker. His prediction of a world agonizing from crisis to crisis was a wish come true. "Thanks to me, a catastrophe!" His Will to Power, his philosophy of aggression, taken seriously by his intellectual heirs and pushed to their logical, demoniacal limits, have acted as catalysts to the modern cataclysms. All that man holds dear—the

39. Friedrich Nietzsche, *The Gay Science (Joyful Wisdom)* in *The Portable Nietzsche,* pp. 447–448.

act of creation, the act of knowledge, the act of loving—all are acts of the Will to Power, manifestations of aggression. In a world where aggression is the supreme, nay the only activity, where the dethronement of God, truth and love are the highest expressions of the will to power, the acme of aggression, men are abandoned to endure the hell they have willingly created.

Power, Rank and Religion

Among the stronger spirits who contend for power, it is convenient to distinguish between two broadly hostile groups. Both groups are elites, molders of history whose leaders are intellectually well trained and volitionally well disciplined. Yet each group is oriented in a direction opposed to the other. One group is aflame over this world and its thrilling possibilities; the other is zealous for the world beyond and its glory. The former group embodies the Will to Power as represented by the highter type of human—the Warrior for this World of Becoming; the latter incarnates the Will to Power as represented by the lowly Priest —the Advocate for the World of the Absolute. Both groups are in an endless struggle for the control of the mediocre majority, each hoping to found its own high culture on the necessary, broad base of a strong, solidly consolidated collectivity. The Warriors for this world represent a truly ascending form of human life. On the contrary, the Priests and the mediocre masses represent decadence, decomposition, weakness. Unlike the Priests, who pose as shepherds of the herds, it is not the mission of the elite of this world to lead the masses to greener pastures or to minister to their needs. The masters of this world are not servants; they are creators. The miserable masses exist merely to serve their natural masters as a solid foundation upon which these lords of the earth can lead their isolated, superior lives and build for the coming of yet higher types of man and eventually for Superman. What are the human characteristics that distinguish Warriors from Priests? How may one distinguish the one from the other?

The Warrior, as master of the earth, is noble by nature. A lover of this world, he is naturally good as opposed to the unnaturalness of the despiser of this world. Open, honest, secure in his exercise of the Will to Power, he has no need to prove his

might by deeds of cruelty or oppression. Should he harm anyone, he does so incidentally, unintentionally in the creative use
of his power. Goethe, breaking Friederike's heart by loving her
tenderly but refusing to marry her, had no wish to hurt this
darling creature. But acting out of his own creative, overflow-
ing power, he could not be expected to restrict his genius by
concern for others. The truly powerful master must concentrate on self-discipline, self-creation. Thus, the warrior is
strong, healthy, handsome, noble in bearing; he delights in the
harshness of bodily combat. And he heartily, regularly enjoys
the indulgences of his healthy sense appetites. He is a shining,
physical paragon of Dionysos. He is motivated by honor, not by
selfish interests. He is the acme of finesse and gentility with a
keen appreciation for Order and Rank. He is, in a word, aristocratic with an aristocracy of excellence in taste and performance. Yet he hates with the same enthusiasm as he loves,
loathing demagogism, enlightenment, romanticism, pity,
plebeian familiarity, religion and God, especially the Christian
God and religion.

The Priest, on the other hand, is intrinsically ignoble, unnatural, evil. Physically weak, diseased in mind and, at times, in
body, he is a "professional negator, slanderer and poisoner of
life."[40] He is unable to enjoy clean sensuousness; he lacks the
honor, pride, forthright honesty of the Warrior. He reaches for
power through control of the consciences of princes and pau-
pers. This will for power, perversely strong, is abetted by an
intensely sharpened intellect. His craftiness compensates for
his puniness; his virtuosity with concepts and words conquers
the crowds and his physically superior warriors. He employs by
instinct "the most wide-spread, really *subterranean*, form of
falsehood on the earth."[41] Through the ages priests and warriors have battled for the soul of society and civilization, but the
priests have always won the victory. The Warrior, the elite of
this world, has never yet been appreciated nor given his rightful place of power in society.

Even in the past this higher type has appeared often–but
as a fortunate accident, as an exception, never as some-

40. Friedrich Nietzsche, *The Antichrist*, in *The Portable Nietzsche*, p. 575.
41. *Ibid.*, pp. 575–576.

thing *willed*. In fact, this has been the type most dreaded–
almost *the* dreadful–and from dread the opposite type was
willed, bred and *attained;* the domestic animal, the herd
animal, the sick animal–the Christian.[42]

We have seen, earlier in this chapter how the shrewd, degenerate priests won over the masses to their side, enlisting them
as enemies against their natural masters. The priests established themselves as lords of the masses over the opposition of
their naturally superior foe, the warriors, by inventing God,
morality and religion. And their greatest, secret weapon was
the creation of Christian dogma and ethics. Both these sopo-
rifics silently soothed and satisfied the yearnings for salvation
of the millions—that organized collectivity which outnum-
bered and overwhelmed the elite power cells of this world.
Then this organized Christian multitude, under the versatile
direction of a disciplined hierarchy, adapted itself to meet the
rising expectations of a modern society that had turned democratic progress into a new religion. This fraudulent accomodation has had the effect of rendering the Christian religion so far
impregnable. What is to be done? Are we to concede final victory and give up the fight to work for superior men? Not at all!
The time has come for the new barbarism which will break the
chains of priestly domination. The new immoralists have as
their mission to liberate the priest-ridden masses and open the
way for the free development of superior individuals.

A new pride my ego taught me, and this I teach men: no
longer to bury one's head in the sand of heavenly things,
but to bear it freely, an earthly head, which creates a
meaning for the earth.[43]

The time has come to oppose morality with immorality, to call
what priests call good, evil and what they call evil, good. The
time has come for the transvaluation of all values.

Power and Values

The way to destroy Christianity, that blight which degraded
man by ruining Greek beauty, demolishing the Roman Empire,

42. *Ibid.,* pp. 570–571.
43. Friedrich Nietzsche, *Thus Spake Zarathustra,* p. 144.

thwarting Islam and, thanks to the vengeance of Luther, transfiguring the Renaissance, is for the highest few of this world, imitating their master Nietzsche, "to condemn Christianity as the highest of all conceivable corruptions." And then to set their hearts on the creation of the potentially higher man, the Superman, by jettisoning the insufferable burden of Christian morality. Unlike Feuerbach, who chose humanity as the object and goal of his transforming ministrations, Nietzsche despised humanity and chose only the highest caste—the *fewest*—for his process of glorification. "Man is something which must be surpassed; man is a bridge and not a goal." Nevertheless, Superman will not be achieved through the blind process of inevitable evolution toward the perfect. Reality is not that benign. Only the Will to Power activated intensely in superior individuals will incarnate Superman from a myth to a man. History testifies that man is quite willing to remain mired in gross animality. Without the aid of great individuals, he will sink back into the wriggling anonymity of the worm.

> Man is a rope, tied between beast and overman—a rope over an abyss. A dangerous across, a dangerous on-the-way, a dangerous looking-back, a dangerous shuddering and stopping. And what is great in man is that he is a bridge and not an end.[44]

Thus Superman is the meaning of the earth and, unless the elite of this world work hard for his coming, man, as "a rope tied between beast and Overman," will certainly plunge into the abyss of animality. The elite must continually repeat the following Zarathustrian battle cry: "Let your Will say: Superman *is to be* the meaning of the earth." Here the Will to Power is identified with the Will to Being, imitating in its own fashion the God of the Christians Will to Creation: *Fiat lux.* And in relation to man the Christian God had said: *Faciamus hominem ad imaginem et similitudinem nostram.* But Nietzsche and his followers proclaim in defiance of the Christian God's creative edict an opposing one of their own: Let us make Superman to our own image and likeness. For we are now at a point in history when we noble ones can, for the first time, plan on a grand scale for human nature. We are ready to put into prac-

44. *Ibid.,* pp. 126–127.

tice our design for breeding the Superman.

But the new nobles, the Supermen, will never make an appearance in history until the elite of this world have the courage to transvalue all values. They must have the audacity to smash the Judaeo-Christian tablets of the moral law and to proclaim, like a new Moses from a mountain top of thunder and lightning, a new code of values, a code which arises out of the superabundance of the elite's surging vitality and Will to Power. Superman is the Warrior for the World *par excellence.* He and his followers will overthrow the rule of the Church and her priest-directed slaves. Superman will restore the strong to power. By personifying in himself the new values, Superman will rescue the earth from "the despisers of life" who poison themselves and others with the arsenic of other-worldliness.

Superman and his followers will be cruel, hard, ruthless, pitiless, unscrupulous, deceitful, boastful, truculent, sensual and frivolous. Their motto will be: "Evil, be thou my good!" But sometimes Nietzsche seems to be logically and defiantly inconsistent. For besides practicing all the above-mentioned "virtues," the new nobles will also be brave, honorable, strong, serious, lofty and ascetical. Superman and his elite are clearly enigmas, moral paradoxes, men "beyond good and evil." This dilemma will not be understood unless one realizes that the new elite neither professes nor practices any uniform, universal, absolute moral code. The reason is that such an absolutist moral code is the fruit of religious resentment and arises from an attitude of nay-saying to life in this world. The absolutist moral code, called by Nietzsche a slave-morality, represents a form of descending, degenerate life. The virtues that slave-morality extols, such as kindness and humility, are beneficial to the society of the weak and the powerless, but regarded by strong, independent individuals as dangerous and evil.

> The most spiritual men, as the *strongest,* find their happiness where others would find their destruction: in the labyrinth, in hardness against themselves and others, in experiments; their joy is self-conquest; asceticism becomes in them nature, need, instinct. Difficult tasks are a privilege to them; to play with burdens which crush others, a recreation. Knowledge—a form of asceticism. They

are the most venerable kind of man; that does not preclude their being the most cheerful and kindliest. They rule not because they want to but because they *are;* they are not free to be second.[45]

Superman's morality represents the highest grade of morality among different standards of morality. The standards of slave-morality condemn the "good" men of master-morality as evil. Since slave-morality is the morality of the masses, its moral evaluations fulfill the needs of the herd. Hence the herd is expected to practice its degenerate morality, since its utility is found in promoting the existence, survival and welfare of the herd community. There can actually be a peaceful co-existence between slave- and master-moralities, provided the slaves control their Will to Power for forcing their own low values upon the elite of this world, provided they give up their ambition to dominate the masters and remain content to keep their values to themselves. But, of course, the herd is not content to do this and, therefore, Superman is needed to curb the masses.

The new nobility of this world, on the other hand, are called upon to accept the values of Superman, values which alone will enable man to transcend his present position of decadence. Superman and his followers, therefore, must stand beyond good and evil in the sense that they are far superior to the good and evil of herd morality. Under no circumstances are they to be obligated to follow the common level of morality. For this low code reduces all men to egalitarian mediocrity, prevents the development of the master class and destroys the quality of human art and culture. It is clear, then, that Nietzsche does not free his elite from all moral restraint or encourage it to moral libertinism. Such license would beget personal and social chaos and suicide. Yet only the elite can safely live "beyond good and evil" in the sense that they alone can transcend the decadent Christian morality of resentment which endeavors to impose its own values universally. Living beyond these decadent values, the higher type of man creates new values that express an ever ascending life toward the perfection of this world in Superman. Therefore, let slave-morality be for slaves and master-

45. Friedrich Nietzsche, *The Antichrist*, pp. 645–646.

morality for masters. But let the former keep to itself, far below
the latter in a spirit of peaceful coexistence.

Power, History and Eternal Recurrence

But Superman, driven on by a superior Will to Power, courageously transvaluing all values and audaciously living by the
higher standards of the new immoralism, is not yet Nietzsche's
highest honor for this world and life. There remains the glory
of immortalization. For if all life, and especially the higher
type of culture and morality, are irrevocably annihilated by
death, what does it profit the higher men to live with a yea-
saying attitude to this world? It would seem senseless to build
up what is doomed to utter extinction. Since he had already
rejected the Christian view of world history, Nietzsche had to
solve this dilemma with some hopeful doctrine of his own. It
would scarcely be wise for Nietzsche to place himself in the
psychologically awkward position of exhorting his master type
to work mightily now merely for personal and social obliteration in a little while. Psychologist Nietzsche met this problem
by making Zarathustra, prophet of Superman, the herald of the
doctrine of eternal recurrence as well. But a brief résumé of
Nietsche's view of world history is needed to place his theory
of eternal recurrence into proper perspective.

Christianity gave birth to a total, unified view of world history founded on such doctrines as: creation, the fall, the Incarnation, Redemption, Sanctification, the Parousia and the final
Judgment. Christ, the God-Man, is the beginning, center and
end of human and cosmic history. Because of Him, mankind
has developed the Will to Absolute Truthfulness and Absolute
Morality. But this Will to Absolute Truth and Morality, like a
two-edged sword, divided mankind into two violently hostile
camps, those accepting and those rejecting the Christian view
of history. The Christian view of history is thrilling, tragic,
exalting yet crushing; it is simultaneously fearful and paradoxically peaceful. The Christian is sure of the meaning of history.
For him the historical process is not arbitrary, not a mere,
evolutionary, blind changing upward. The profound metaphysical and theological meaning behind empirical events, al-

though not traced by the Christian in all or even most of its details, is, nevertheless, known to be fundamentally about decisions made by God and men concerning the salvation of each individual soul and the advent of the final kingdoms of Satan and God. The Christian views the past, present and future as integrally important in God's plan to redeem society and the cosmos. Events are oriented to the restoration of all things in Christ.

Nietzsche, on the other hand, looked back to the Greek tragic era before Socrates as the pinnacle of man's glory in history. At present man has fallen very low from that high stature. If he is to ascend again those lofty heights of Antiquity, he will have to re-create his society and, through the high standards of the new immoralism, effect a *rapprochement* with the Greek world of tragedy. It was Christianity that poisoned and killed the grandeur of Antiquity. The time has come to reject the Christian view of history which brought man so low. Nietzsche taught, therefore, that there is a valid total view of history. Man creates meaning in empirical events; he does not discover a meaning that is there nor an intelligent, transcendent, absolute Director of these events. That way lies superstition. Reality is beyond meaning, beyond lack of meaning. Moreover, this is not a singular universe. History, far from being a single course of decisive events under the guidance of divine and human intelligence, is in reality "fragmented into an experimental laboratory for coining men." History is "the great testing plant." "Mankind does not advance; it does not even exist. The total aspect is that of a huge experimental station, where some tests succeed . . . and countless others fail." Here is a complete reversal of a total view of history, a repudiation of the idea of unity in history. Nietzsche erases the idea of unity in history and writes in his own idea of eternal recurrence. Naturally, the emphasis in history now shifts from a unified theme and goal of history to ways of trying to understand history and guide it toward a man-imposed ideal. This process is to be determined by the Will to Power of the higher men. The superior type of man will now replace God, the Christian Creator and guiding Spirit of history, and plan and manage history as a whole himself. This conscious realization of cosmic power fills the higher men with joy. But all joy wants eternity. And eternal recurrence is the only guarantee of eternal joy in the possession of power in time and in this world. Eternal recurrence in Nietzsche is the antithesis of any faith which looks to another world for eternal joy. In *Zarathustra* we read:

> . . . If ever you wanted one thing twice, if ever you said, "You please me, happiness! Abide, moment!" Then you wanted back *all.* All anew, all eternally, all entangled, ensnared, enamored—oh, then you loved the world . . . I beseech you, my brothers, *remain faithful to the earth* and do not believe those who speak to you of other-worldly hopes.[46]

Thus, the doctrine of eternal recurrence is fundamental to Nietzsche's philosophy of man, the cosmos and history. He admits that the idea is rather dismal, even oppressive. But just as the Christian faces death as the severest test of his ability to say Yes to God so the higher men use the eternal recurrence as the supreme test of their willingness to say Yes to the world and life as they are. Nietzsche, in *The Gay Science,* imagines a demon appearing to one of the loneliest of the higher types— one is reminded of Satan tempting Christ in the desert—and putting the ultimate temptation, in the sense of a trial and test, before this soul. "This life as you now live it and have lived it, you will have to live once more and innumerable times more, and there will be no things new in it . . . all in the same succession and sequence."[47] Will you curse and gnash your teeth at this dismal destiny, thereby becoming a nay-sayer to life? Or will you *"crave nothing more fervently* than this ultimate, eternal confirmation and seal," thereby becoming a yea-sayer to the world of eternal Becoming? The world-approving elite, in so far as they are actors in this life, want to act the play over and over again forever. In so far as they are spectators, their eternal cry is *encore! encore!* They gladly follow their master Zarathustra whose destiny it is to be the teacher of the eternal recurrence. Their highest courage and Will to Power is to accept gladly "the eternal recurrence even of the smallest" people who cause in the elite "disgust with all existence." And "Alas, nausea! nausea! nausea!" Even so, despite this meta-

46. Friedrich Nietzsche, *Thus Spake Zarathustra,* p. 435.
47. Friedrich Nietzsche, *The Gay Science,* pp. 101–102.

physical sickness, the elite welcome the recurrence of every last detail of this life. "Oh, how should I not lust after eternity and after the nuptial ring of rings—the ring of the recurrence!"[48]

Besides being a theory, eternal recurrence is presented as an empirical hypothesis by Nietzsche. Energy, once thought to be unlimited, is now known to be limited. This being so, "the principle of the conservation of energy" appeared to Nietzsche to be both a demand and a proof of eternal recurrence. Energy that is eternally active cannot create eternally new forms. It must, therefore, return under the same forms. Everything has returned, will return again; occurrences are but recurrences; present history was once past and past history will again be future. There is nothing new anywhere, neither on the sun, beyond the sun nor under the sun. Nothing is beginning or arriving on the closed, revolving wheel of eternal recurrence. The cosmos is locked up against penetration from above and barred in against escape to the beyond. We are back on the wheel of fate forged by the Stoics, yoked forever to the treadmill of cosmopolitan necessitarianism. Our monotonous round of duties is confined world without end to the compound of cosmic captivity.

Critique

Gabriel Marcel, outstanding French dramatist-philosopher, in a lecture given at Loyola University in New Orleans, March 25, 1965, entitled "Man Before the Death of God," said of Nietzsche:

> Without a doubt, there can be no greater mistake than to say Nietzsche belongs to the past, for it is the contrary that is true. Even, and above all, for those who regard themselves as his opponents, Nietzsche is the most modern of the moderns.

Stephen Tonsor, writing in *National Review,* January 18, 1968, has this to say of Nietzsche: "During the 1870s and 1880s when the new physics, the new symbolic art and literature, the new psychology, new social theories and the new philosophy

48. Friedrich Nietzsche, *Thus Spake Zarathustra,* p. 340.

were being formulated, the German-speaking lands were the cuttingedge of revolutionary society and radical thought. Of those German thinkers none was more characteristic than the prophet of modernity, Friedrich Nietzsche . . . the great philosophical poet of the late nineteenth century."

Nietzsche, therefore, is still very much with us. However shall we evaluate him, this philosopher whose thought runs over in all directions? In his manner of living and his manner of thinking and writing, Nietzsche was a man of extremes. The good-willed reader who opens his soul to Nietzsche cannot fail to come to this conclusion. And Nietzsche would agree with him. "We immoralists do not even need to lie . . . We would come into power even without the truth . . . The magic which fights for us is the magic of extremism."[49] And in answer to a letter from his friend Georg Brandes, Nietzsche exclaims: "The expression 'aristocratic radicalism' which you are using is very good. If you permit me, this is the most intelligent word I have thus far read about myself."[50] Then too, Nietzsche foresaw the public victory of the extreme side of his thinking and it gave him the experience of triumphant power. His letter to Paul Deussen states, speaking of his latest manuscript at the publishers: "When I am done, much of what was debatable till now is *no longer debatable.* The realm of *tolerance* has been reduced by means of value judgments of the first order to mere cowardice and weakness of character. To be a *Christian*—to name but one result—will henceforth be considered indecent. Much of this most revolutionary conversion (transvaluation of all values) of which the world shall know, is already going on and progressing inside me."[51] Or again, in a letter to his friend Brandes concerning his autobiography, *Ecce Homo,* which Marcel thinks was written in a state of delirium, Nietzsche boasts:

> With a cynicism which is destined to become world historical, I have now related myself. The book is called *Ecce Homo* and is an assassination without the least respect for the crucified one. It ends with thunder and lightning

49. Quoted by Jaspers, *op. cit.,* p. 94.
50. Friedrich Nietzsche, *Unpublished Letters,* p. 125.
51. *Ibid.,* pp. 142–143.

against everything Christian or infected by Christianity so that you won't know any more where to turn or what to do. At last I am the first psychologist of Christianity and, old artillerist that I am, can move up heavy guns the existence of which not even any opponent of Christianity had suspected in the least. The whole is the prelude to the *Transvaluation of All Values*, the work which lies before me, finished. I swear to you, in two years we shall have the whole earth in convulsion. I am a destiny.[52]

Indeed Nietzsche was destined to be the true prophet of the madness of modernity. His prophecies of doom were accurate to a ghastly degree. His new barbarians swept the world into two volcanic wars in the first half of the twentieth century. This same barbarism, structured on the backs of a billion slaves, advancing through terrorism, is presently probing the earth's free hegemony in so-called skirmishes of national liberation as preliminary warm-ups to what may be the ultimate atomic blow-up of civilization on the earth. Nietzsche's books have been successful because of their high voltage shock value. There is a hypnotizing fascination in Dionysian fanaticism. But besides the chaotic excesses, there are the gifts of this writer. These have attracted millions, like moths, to fly into his incandescent madness. The style is sharp, violent, petulant, poetic, epigrammatic, declamatory, clear, ambiguous through sudden and surprising changes. Nietzsche is always straining to say what no one else had ever said, to be unique, to be supreme in his writing and in his ideas. "I am not a man: I am dynamite," says Nietzsche in *Ecce Homo*.

Philologist Nietzsche was an early pioneer among the expeditions to demythologize the Gospels. His virulent attacks on everything divine or supernatural in the New Testament make his modern death-of-God heirs appear as "backward Christian exegetes" in comparison. "For as a philologist one sees behind the holy books . . . the philologist [says] swindle."[53] "One should read the Gospels as books of seduction by means of *morality* . . . What follows from this? That one does well to put on gloves when reading the New Testament. The proximity of so much

52. *Ibid.*, pp. 147–148.
53. Friedrich Nietzsche, *The Antichrist*, p. 628.

uncleanness almost forces one to do this . . . Need I add that in
the whole New Testament there is only a *single* figure who
commands respect? Pilate, the Roman governor."[54]

Copleston has this to say of Nietzsche's manic eruptions
against the Gospel and Christianity: "As for Nietzsche's attitude to Christianity, his increasingly shrill attack on it is ac-
companied by an increasing inability to do justice to his foe.
And it is arguable that the vehemence of his attack was partly
an expression of an inner tension and uncertainty which he
endeavored to stifle."[55]

Despite Heidegger's efforts to make him one at all costs,
Nietzsche was no metaphysician. His work has stimulated others to think in one direction or another. But as for himself,
given to "philosophizing with a hammer," Nietzsche smashed
all dialogue and dialectic with other philosophers. He isolated
himself and his thought from the rays of dialectic scrutiny so
that his meaning of life might triumph unopposed. Jaspers tells
us that Nietzsche's attitude to being suffered from universal
negativity, from unending dissatisfaction with all aspects of
being. Rather than reason carefully, Nietzsche oscillated from
desperate denials to boundless assertions. His philosophy often
slipped into the fanaticism of pronunciamento. "Nothing is
true, all is permitted." Even his terms are words of will rather
than products of the intellect: Life, Strength, Will to Power,
Superman, Breeding, Eternal Recurrence, Dionysos. All such
expressions, though packed with dynamite, suffered from extraordinary vagueness and ambiguity, even changing meaning
to suit their author's volatile moods. Contradictions are the
curse of Nietzsche's writings. But since Nietzsche holds truth
to be relative, it never bothered him to be inconsistent. From
within the dynamic process of Becoming, of which he admitted
he was a blind, integral part, Nietzsche himself decides what
is ascending and descending life, who is master and who is
slave, what is the intelligible structure and meaning of the
Becoming process, what are slave and what are master morals.
Such sheer subjectivism by a subject himself caught up as a
blind part of an inevitable recurring Becoming sucked Nietz-

54. *Ibid.*, p. 626.
55. Frederick Copleston, S.J., *History of Philosophy* (New York: Doubleday
and Co., Image Books, 1965), Part II, Vol. 7, p. 193.

sche's thought into a whirlpool of absurdities. From this vortex of chaotic contradictions, the blackest human urges have been released; a veritable legion of human devils have made use of Nietzsche's intoxicating excesses to scourge the human race.

We know enough from his books and letters to be able to say categorically that Nietzsche would have shrunk in horror from the dogmatism of Nazism and anti-semitism. He loathed the power of the collective State and condemned his brother-in-law's militant anti-semitism. Yet the fact remains that these plagues against humanity were spawned from the misrepresentations and applications arising from Nietzsche's philosophy of nihilism. His arbitrary doctrines of Will to Power, Superman, Blond Beast, racial purity, anti-theistic atheism, inflamed and fed to militant madness such ugly, egotistic monsters as Hitler, Stalin, Mussolini who, with their millions hypnotized by these extremisms, strove to devour each other in an orgy of cannibalistic fury. Nietzsche, the immoralist, gave such tyrants the moral code they needed to justify their pogroms—the secular religion of Superman and the dominating morality of the masters.

Now what shall we say of Nietzsche, who admits that "his whole philosophy has theologians' blood in its veins?" Nietzsche, the anti-theistic theologian who is proud to be kin to priests! Though fascinated by the attractive personality of Jesus, Nietzsche, nevertheless, passionately refused to welcome this supreme exister. Christ represented an obstacle to Nietzsche's vocation to love this world and give it himself and all his meaning. Christ was so clearly from above, a witness against the pure, immanent meaning of this world. Christ was an invitation, an invocation to come up higher, to leave the world for the transcendent, tri-Personal Truth and Love. Nietzsche, Dionysos-Zarathustra, shrank from this easy escapism. That way the herd stampeded in wild fear into heaven. But not Zarathustra-Nietzsche. Infected with the spiritual infantilism of frenzied envy, Nietzsche determined to walk alone, stranded if need be in a world of golden ice and azure sky, where he need no longer encounter man, but commune solely with himself. Nietzsche, bursting with envy, wrote his own Gospels, modeled on the New Testament, but carefully calculated to be contradictions to the teaching of Jesus:

It is true that if you do not become as little children again, you will not be able to enter into *that* kingdom of heaven (and Zarathustra pointed to the sky). But we have no wish to enter the kingdom of heaven; we have become men— that is why we want the kingdom of the earth.[56]

It was André Gide who shrewdly analyzed the sickness of Nietzsche's spirit. Nietzsche was insanely jealous of Jesus. Gide writes: "In the presence of the Gospel, Nietzsche's immediate and profound reaction was—it must be admitted— jealousy. It does not seem to me that Nietzsche's work can be really understood without allowing for that feeling. Nietzsche was jealous of Christ, jealous to the point of madness. In writing his Zarathustra, Nietzsche was continually tormented with the desire to contradict the Gospel. Often he adopted the actual form of the Beatitudes in order to reverse them. He wrote *Antichrist* and in his last work, *Ecce Homo,* set himself up as the victorious rival of Him whose teaching he proposed to supplant."[57] Nietzsche, then, suffered from a God-complex, from an obsession to be the Savior of mankind. And he fumed in envy and hatred that Jesus had pre-empted this role two thousand years before him. Yet when he was under the appealing spell of Jesus, he everywhere likened himself and his doctrine to that of the Savior. Jesus, like Nietzsche, was "beyond good and evil." They both sided against those who judge; both wanted to be the destroyers of morality. "Jesus said: 'What do we sons of God care for morality'?"[58] Nietzsche, like Jesus, had to fight the Pharisees of his day, to challenge the apathy and stupidity of the masses, to denounce the decadence and arrogance of the learned. Nietzsche, like Jesus, scandalized everyone; both were set for the rise and fall of many. When he finally went mad, Nietzsche's fascination with Jesus attained the illusion of identity. He signed his last letters to Gast and Brandes, "The Crucified One." But when he was under the influence of his jealousy, his hatred of his arch rival poured like fiery, molten lava from his resentful heart:

That holy anarchist who summoned the people at the bottom, the outcasts and "sinners," the chandalas within Ju-

56. Friedrich Nietzsche, *Thus Spake Zarathustra,* p. 428.
57. André Gide, *Oeuvres Completes.*
58. Friedrich Nietzsche, *Beyond Good and Evil,* 164, p. 87.

daism, to opposition against the dominant order—using language, if the Gospels were to be trusted, which would lead to Siberia today too—was a political criminal in so far as political criminals were possible at all in an absurdly unpolitical community. This brought him to the cross: the proof for this is the inscription on the cross. He died for *his* guilt. All evidence is lacking, however often it has been claimed, that he died for the guilt of others.[59]

Nietzsche never forgave Jesus for taking the side of the lowly and poor against the mighty. Thousands of years before Nietzsche, Jesus had already revealed the decrepitude of master-morality. That Christ should have preferred "howling and gnashing of teeth" to "those who laugh here," that was the greatest sin on earth.

"Poor Nietzsche," writes de Lubac, "reproaching Christianity with being found on resentment!" His whole life and thought are steeped in resentment. The petulant childishness of enthroning man in the place of his dethroned God. The shallow trick of blaming the existence of evil on Socrates, St. Paul and the Christians is too absurd to merit serious refutation. Nietzsche does not write with historical accuracy. His doctrine that Christianity began as a Jewish conspiracy is an example of how he often substituted creative writing for historical scholarship. His naive substitution of secularized Superman for sanctified sons of God as the fulfillment of the serpent's seduction: *Eritis sicut dii* is another mythical transposition of Christian truth to a philosophy of immanent egotism. The dreary, pseudo-scientific, oriental promise of eternal recurrence is a diseased approximation of Christian immortality in eternal mansions. Nietzsche was forever knocking things down, taking delight in destruction:

O my brothers, am I cruel? But I say: what is falling, we should still push. Everything today falls and decays: who would check it? But I—I even want to push it. Do you know the voluptuous delight which rolls stones into steep depths? These human beings of today—look at them, how they roll into my depth! I am a prelude of better players, O my brothers! A precedent! Follow my precedent! And he whom you cannot teach to fly, teach to fall faster![60]

59. Friedrich Nietzsche, *The Antichrist*, p. 599.
60. Friedrich Nietzsche, *Thus Spake Zarathustra*, p. 321.

All of these extreme doctrines are thus seen to be the products of a serious but sick man. The reference to his sickness is not meant to be a personal attack, but merely to put Nietzsche's thought within its human, historical context. Nietzsche's letters are replete with reports of his illnesses—migraine headaches, insomnia, extreme tensions. He wrote under great excitement and exaltation which took a terrible toll of his health. His letters reveal him as being in constant quest of vigorous health, preoccupied with diet, climate, sedatives, disease and castration. Physically and spiritually Nietzsche was a sick man writing in and against a sick age.

Conclusion

Why does Nietzsche remain, even today, the apostle to the Moderns? Because he continues to fulfill a prophecy about what he would do to modern mankind. And that prophecy is enunciated in the form of a curse. Speaking of his "irksome admirers," of the "apes of Zarathustra," of "the unwarranted and wholly unfit who will some day cite my authority," Nietzsche fulminates:

> To this mankind of today, I will not be a light, nor be called a light. Those I will blind! Put out their eyes, O flash of my wisdom![61]

The "magic of extremism" has triumphed, as Nietzsche predicted. It has extinguished the light in millions of minds. In the realm of religion this prophet of atheism prepared the human spirit for its arrogant adventure of incarnating absolutist antitheism into a world-organized, armed, militant movement which has for the past fifty years been waging war on many fronts for the exclusive possession of the cosmos and human community. In the realm of morals, the magic of Nietzsche's exaggerated subjectivism has shattered his merely two codes of slave- and master-morality into millions of relativistic, situational standards egotistically lived by infallible private consciences.

This excess of moral individualism has also had the effect of undermining civil law and opening the flood gates to social

---

61. Quoted by Jaspers, *op. cit.*, pp. 106–107.

chaos and suicide in the forms of soaring individual crimes against citizens and spreading organized wars against large city communities. How faithfully the modern mind is fulfilling Nietzsche's exhortation: "O my brothers . . . Follow my precedent!"

Has not Nietzsche's preposterous willing backwards in the fatalistic acceptance of eternal recurrence been reversed by the communists' equally fanatical willing forwards in the fatalistic acceptance of the classless society? Extremes beget extremes and here is a classic example of that verity. Both wilfully blind faiths in a fanatical Future, though posing as liberators of mankind, actually torture man by stretching and pulling him apart on the rack of the lust for power. Yes, Nietzsche is modern because his anti-Christian humanism is slowly but surely convincing even free societies that the fullfillment of human existence is to be attained solely in terms of secularized power rather than in terms of fidelity to God and man. Nietzsche is modern because he has taught man how to use effectively, against God and his fellow man, the tactic of revolt. His magic of extremism, when carefully scrutinized, is seen to be the magic of revolt. His revolutionary craze was highly contagious and has spread like wildfire through almost every phase of human endeavor. We have indicated a few examples of this craze above. Let us try to analyze this tactic more extensively in the area that is directly pertinent to this book—God and religion, especially Christianity.

Even within the Catholic Church Nietzsche has his followers. Many of these would be shocked to be confronted with this fact, for they certainly are not conscious of being off-spring of Nietzsche. Nevertheless, some of their doctrines and, above all, their dialectical tactics are infected with the canker of Nietzschean resentment. We saw earlier in this chapter that Nietzsche replaced logical discussion with vigor, intenseness and energy of assertion. This technique is calculated to win over the majority of minds who crave instant, emotional certainty, freed from the hardship of patiently sifting assertion from performance, fact from fiction. Rhetoric succeeds through the magic of extremely ardent speech; revolution through the magic of extremely shocking deeds. These are Nietzschean tactics *par excellence*.

Now within the Catholic Church many are experiencing, as

Nietzsche suggested men should, in imitation of himself, "the voluptuous delight which rolls stones into depths." Some theologians, priests, journalists and professors are swelling their egos with the thrills of making shocking doctrinal pronunciamentos. Out of breath with excitement at advocating dangerous heresies, they deny the physical resurrection of Christ, the Virgin Birth, the Real Presence, faith and good works as necessary for salvation and the infallibility of the Church. Others, hastening to be up-to-date in the magical Secular City of Harvey Cox, advocate pre-marital sex, birth control through artificial means, homosexuality for some and the abolition of the ten commandments in favor of the law of Love governed by situation ethics. Nietzsche would certainly recognize his heirs in these secularized solons for the transvaluation of all values. Here is a frenzy for revolutionary innovation that borders on madness. In the realm of religious discipline, rhetorical ranting against the authority of the Church, against the policies of this group of bishops as opposed to that, against the policies and pronouncements even of the Pope testify to the magic of resentment that shakes priests and faithful. Certainly some of the Christian ranters have put a Nietzschean interpretation on the alleged opposition between the Institutional Church and the Faithful, the former, of course, being the masters and the latter the slaves. There is a thrill in this "coming of age" superiority that allows one to sit in judgment over the powers that be. When we scan the field of liturgy, we are shocked to find some bohemian liturgists eager to try anything for the thrill of novelty. They arrogantly contemn all the great creations of former geniuses—art, music, poetry, language. They think nothing of desacralizing these and desecrating the Holy Sacrifice for the sake of the magic of modernity. Like Nietzsche, they are dissatisfied with everything in the Temple of God.

In the field of Catholic journalism, ah, there Nietzsche's advice is followed with a vengeance. "What is falling, we should still push." Do two cardinals disagree on some point of doctrinal emphasis or policy of the Church? The media sensationalize it into a religious and even political feud! Is a priest disciplined? Authoritarianism is running rampant! Does a priest defect? He is loaded with invitations, interviews, glamorized, lionized on Catholic campuses, commercial TV and radio, in the slick magazines—publicized for the national and international millions to gape and gulp. Many Catholic journalists, professors and lesser lights, suffering from intellectual inferiority and moral mediocrity, experience voluptuous joy in tearing down their Church, liberally infecting with their own resentment the millions who are avaricious for the new, the bizarre, the unnatural. The same mania for pushing human beings into depths has now been discovered by faculty and students on Catholic campuses. Waving banners which read "academic freedom" or "students' rights" but which demand academic license and student control, thrilling demonstration after thrilling demonstration pushes and pushes until heads do roll into the depths of abject surrender of authority and craven abandonment of moral and academic standards. If there is any place where Nietzsche's tactics of intimidation have been successful, that place today is the Catholic college and university. There the triumph of extremism has become identified with the triumph of mediocrity.

We have no intention of leaving the reader with the false impression that the phenomenon of Nietzschean resentment is restricted to the Catholic Church. It flows over into and tortures Christianity throughout the world. For example, who does not see that Protestantism today is being reduced from a form of Christianity to a form of social service, through the mania for exclusive concern over civil rights? Yet the maddening lust for wild and "way-out" speculations, for advancing from shock to shock to new, extreme activities has permeated all human activities, leading to the crisis of chaos in art, music, theatre, cinema, literature, philosophy and politics. And Nietzsche remains on the podium, directing this cacophony of chaos. He predicted and willed it all. "For the hour has come, you know it, for the great, bad, long, slow revolt of the mob and slaves: it grows and grows . . . Lascivious greed, galled envy, aggrieved vengefulness, mob pride: all that leaped into my face."[62]

There it is, the magic of progressive modernity! Following Nietzsche, "the prelude of better players," those who have come in his spirit have not done badly. Outrageously denying the true and rejecting the traditional, they have accelerated the process of pushing persons and society into the steep depths of

62. Friedrich Nietzsche, *Thus Spake Zarathustra*, p. 382.

confusion. It is true that, upon examination, the wonderful deeds of the Nietzschean enthusiasts are discovered to be inferior products of posturing and bluffing would-be Saviors who —like their resentful master—are insanely jealous of the great minds in history whose achievements reveal the nakedness of these present-day mediocrities. It is not surprising, therefore, that under the spell of Nietzschean derangement the world has been scandalized at the hatred and violence of the Nietzschean aggressions. In the fifty or rather almost seventy years since Nietzsche's death, the world has been victimized by two major world wars, scourged by many political, religious, philosophical, sociological and psychological tyrants who experimented with man's soul and body in an unending series of techniques of degradation. And the new techniques being developed to remake man bode far greater doom for the future.

What is the remedy against the Nietzschean curse? How can mankind be liberated from the legion of Nietzsche's devils? Oddly enough and by implication only, Nietzsche suggests the remedy. A noble youth is meditating sadly in the forest, when Nietzsche's Zarathustra comes upon him. In the ensuing conversation, the youth breaks down and confesses with violent gestures and bitter tears the sickness that tortures his soul: "It is the *envy* of you that has destroyed me." But Zarathustra-Nietzsche embraces the youth and leads him away towards love. It was his envy of Jesus that destroyed Nietzsche. It is its envy of Jesus that is destroying a world that is following Nietzsche. The daring, resentful refusal of Christ must end in the madness of chaos. The remedy is for man to be led back to the love of Christ. To embrace Jesus is to embrace sanity and sanctity. Dostoevsky, prophet and contemporary of Nietzsche, proves to be a herald of healing to mankind. He analysed the sickness of modernity so well that he was capable of prescribing its only effective remedy. "We continually go astray, if we have not Christ and His Faith to guide us." "Repudiate Christ and the human mind can arrive at the most astounding conclusions."[63] "The West has lost Christ, that is why it is dying; that is the only reason."[64]

Salvation, peace, truth, freedom and love lie far above and

63. Feodor Dostoevsky, Notebooks 1879, *Journal Of An Author,* 1873.
64. Feodor Dostoevsky, Notebooks, 1871.

beyond Nietzschean madness. They can be experienced only in Christian mystery, beyond atheism which is the narrowest auto-erotic imprisonment, in Faith which is the self-donating openness to the infinite Love of the Absolute Thou. And Dostoevsky directs us to the most unerring way to that Faith:

> This profession of faith is very simple. This is what it is: to believe that there is nothing finer, deeper, more lovable, more reasonable, braver and more perfect than Christ; and, not only there is nothing, but, I tell myself with a jealous love, there cannot be anything.[65]

What a strange paradox! Nietzsche's jealous love which rejected Christ, led on to madness. Dostoevsky's jealous love which embraced Christ led on to gladness.

65. Henri Troyat, *Dostoievski* (1940), pp. 235–236.

CHAPTER IV

Marx: Cosmic Classless Society Becomes God

ON OCTOBER 25, 1967, ATHEISTIC COMMUNISM CELE-brated the fiftieth anniversary of its revolution and coming to power in Russia. From a handful of Bolsheviks who in 1917 toppled the Kerensky Provisional Government and seized control of the Russian State, led by Lenin and Trotsky, a colossal hegemony had evolved through five decades to that moment of the golden jubilee. From Russia, where the great Marxist experiment began, communism spread quickly everywhere, penetrating into every advanced nation and backward region, acquiring the reins of government in many nations and leavening with the spirit of revolt every major social organization. No political, academic, religious, economic or major professional movement has escaped its attentions and influence.

Indeed, today more than one billion persons are ruled by governments that openly profess and practice the doctrine of Marx. And millions of other persons are ruled by governments that fearfully sway to the winds of communist policies. In an age of unprecedented and proliferating crises, there is scarcely a turmoil anywhere in the world in which the catalyzing power of communism may not be discovered. Atheistic communism is a sword of division; it cuts asunder families, communities, nations, empires. It has, indeed, succeeded, directly or indirectly, by action or example, in keeping the world in a state of military conflict since its seizure of power in 1917.

Fifty years of continuous international drama! Fifty years of sustained, national and international, barbaric terrorism! Fifty years of civil wars in all parts of the world! Fifty years of internal and international intrigue and conspiracy! Fifty years of now charging, now creeping—but always advancing—totalitarian tyranny!

As we view today this recent calamitous milestone, a reflection on the future seems appropriate. What will be the destiny of ravished Holy Mother Russia in the next fifty years? What the future of the submerged Christian nations of Eastern Europe? Will China fight free from the twisting, crushing coils of the communist serpent? Will communist Cuba metastasize its cancer and infect the whole of Latin America? Will atheistic communism continue its triumphant march through humanity and history, branding permanently with hammer and sickle the Middle East, Europe, America and the whole world? Or ought we predict the collapse of communism from within? From an explosion of the unbearable pressures below? From a silent, gentle erosion of bureaucratic rigidity into pluralistic pliability? Or will this monstrous monolith have to be demolished from without? *Delendus est Communismus!*

The leaders of communism give a dogmatic answer to all these questions. Their system of thought and power is here to stay; it is guaranteed irreversible and final victory by the necessary, one-directional process of dialectical history. This is the main article of incontrovertible faith for all communists. Men will necessarily—some even willingly—continue to liberate themselves from non-communist exploitation through revolution and evolution until they arrive at the promised land of the classless society. The Party, headquartered in Moscow, will lead the world through its fighting proletariat to the communist messianic millenium. And in order to spur History on in its mission to the classless millennium, the Party has assembled and trained the world's greatest, most awesome military machine, assuring all men inevitable passage by land, sea and space to its earthly Jerusalem.

What is the secret of this most successful of revolutions? What inner, vital dynamism has driven it beyond merely Russian boundaries, or even European borders, to its world-wide dimensions? How has this unique revolution, conceived in the West, spawned its progeny so explosively in all sections of the world and in such widely diverse civilizations? How has this revolutionary humanism, cradled in Christianity, developed into the most terrifying, efficient, heartless Movement for Atheism the world has ever seen? A study of its spiritual origins and historical growth is essential for all believers—especially Christians—who will have to become seriously eager to understand the causes, nature and goals of this contemporary monster, if they are to fulfill their mission to lead their society in these times through Christ to God. This chapter will focus on the spiritual beginnings of communism with a concentration on *how* and *why* this crusading movement insists on being atheist in a militantly practical way and on forcing all men into its godless program.

German Philosophy: Cradle of Communism

Since the way things develop is greatly determined by the way they began, a study of Karl Marx's early life and family milieu will enlighten us as to the forces that helped mold his person and inspire his profession. Marx was born on May 5, 1818, in the little Rhenish town of Trier, distinguished as a Roman outpost in early times. He was bilaterally descended from a long line of Jewish rabbis. His father, Hirschel, in order to be able to pursue his legal profession successfully and his family life peacefully, had himself and his family baptized Christian. The family lived as very liberal Protestants, that is, without any profound religious beliefs. Thus, Karl grew up without any inhibiting consciousness of himself as being Jewish. In changing his credal allegiance, of course, the father, newly baptized Heinrich, experienced the alienation of turning his back on his religious family traditions. Thus, though politically emancipated and socially liberated from the ghetto, the experience of being uprooted and not completely at home in the Germany of the nineteenth century did affect the Marx family. Calvez, commenting on the situation of alienation, writes:

> One must be on one's guard against wishing to explain Marx wholly by his Jewish origins, as some recent anti-semites and philo-semites have actually attempted. If Marx was not ignorant of the problem of the emancipation of the Jews, he, nevertheless, did not attach any importance to it as an isolated problem. Quite simply, he related it to the more general and more fundamental problem of the emancipation of *man*. [Italics in original.] However, his Jewish origins, which made him an uprooted person, did predispose Marx to perceive with a very lively consciousness the alienations of man. Moreover, the universalism and radicalism of his solutions can be tied in with these origins.[1]

Thus, in a family atmosphere that was avowedly rationalist and Kantian, where Voltaire and Rousseau were staple reading, the young Marx grew up in a climate of freedom from religion as naturally as he grew up in his physical body. Thus, in the beginning at least, he was, in a manner of speaking, a natural born atheist. There was no hostility or ostentatiousness about his atheism, such as will certainly be present later in the militant atheism of Lenin. Marx was simply another verification of the well-known aphorism: *Tel père, tel fils.* After a brilliant career at school, Marx briefly attended the University of Bonn and then the University of Berlin where his intellectual enthusiasms were concentrated on law, philosophy and theology. After he earned a doctoral degree on the basis of a thesis on the Greek philosophers Democritus and Epicurus, Marx turned towards political journalism. He was made editor of the *Rheinische Zeitung,* which was quickly suppressed because of its advanced, revolutionary views. Marx and the other "Young Hegelians" whom he had met in Berlin were agreed that philosophy, if it were to achieve its ends, must realize itself in the practical sphere of politics and the reform of the state. Marx, therefore, belonged to that generation of great, intellectual,

1. Jean-Yves Calvez, *La Pensée de Karl Marx* (Paris: Éditions du Seuil, 1965), p. 21. Translation from the French by the author.

cosmopolitan, rationalist Jews whose company boasted such geniuses as Heine and Borne.

Karl Marx received the keys to his communist kingdom from his German masters Hegel and Feuerbach. Hegel gave him the keys of the unhappy conscience and the dialectical method of analyzing history. History, according to Hegel, is the contradictory unfolding of Reason itself from less to more rational forms, to the utmost rational form of existence—fully self-conscious Thought—God Himself. Here was a comprehensive system of philosophy which set the dialectical method to work explaining the whole gamut of cosmic and communitarian problems. The philosopher, hitherto a passive contemplative, was now challenged by the Hegelian enterprise to become an active participant in history. His new task was to discover truth in events rather than in theories. In his own philosophy Marx called this new process the principle of the "unity of theory and practice." Abstract speculation yielded to active participation in the "progressive development" of the "entire human race" as the source of "real positive knowledge about the world."[2] Knowledge was thus linked inseparably to historical action by Hegel's followers. But Marx, his most famous follower, interpreted this action to be revolutionary action, the sole way of development for matter and man. Thus the Hegelian philosophical impulse to give a scientific analysis of history became the Marxian revolutionary action to create history. The philosopher was now called upon to be not only more than a thinker, that is, a doer; he was also called upon to be a revolutionary. "The philosophers," wrote Marx, "have only *interpreted* the world in various ways; the point, however, is to *change* it."[3]

Ludwig Feuerbach, with the publication of his *The Essence Of Christianity,* supplied Marx with the key of a humanist, materialistic humanism. By revealing God to be the "fictitious" creation of man's sick conscience, Feuerbach denied the reality of God, of any transcendent, of spirit. He argued that God did not create man but that man created God out of his warped imagination. Hence only matter, nature and man exist. And man is to regain his own glory by knowing and controlling

2. Friedrich Engels, "Ludwig Feuerbach and the End of Classical German Philosophy" (1886), in *Marx And Engels: Selected Works* (Moscow: Foreign Languages Publishing House, 1955), Vol. II, p. 364.

3. Karl Marx, "Theses on Feuerbach" (1845) *op. cit*, p. 404.

matter, of which he himself is the highest product. Marx eagerly accepted Feuerbach's proposition that everything is ultimately nothing but matter. He thereby rejected Hegel's interpretation of history as the unfolding of the Absolute Mind, the ultimate spiritual reality. Combining Hegel's progressive dialectic with Feuerbach's radical materialism, Marx concluded that man, himself the real supreme being, was capable of discovering the laws of history in the unfolding material conditions of society. Truth is the process of material change. Consequently, the thinking man must seek to revolutionize the entire economic order of society. Thus the human enterprise began to take on the thrilling aspects of a social crusade for the Young Hegelians of the Left with the inspiration sparked by the reading of Feuerbach's thesis. On the liberating effect of Feuerbach's thesis, Engels writes:

> Then came Feuerbach's *Essence Of Christianity*. With one blow it pulverized the contradiction, in that without circumlocution it placed materialism on the throne again . . . Nothing exists outside nature and man, and the higher beings our religious fantasies have created are only the fantastic reflection of our own essence . . . One must have himself experienced the liberating effect of this book to get an idea of it. Enthusiasm was general; we all became at once Feuerbachians.[4] . . . With irresistible force Feuerbach is finally driven to the realization . . . that our consciousness and thinking, however suprasensuous they may seem, are the product of a material, bodily organ, the brain. Matter is not a product of mind, but mind itself is merely the highest product of matter.[5]

A genius in his own right, Marx minted a few keys to his own kingdom. He was dissatisfied with the cult of abstract man as found in his otherwise acceptable Feuerbachian materialism. Humanity, Feuerbach's new abstract deity for man, Marx replaced with the science of real men and their historical development. From now on the new social philosophy would concentrate on the materialism of economic problems and sociological situations. Socialism was the necessary outcome of the

4. Engels, "Ludwig Feuerbach and the End of Classical German Philosophy," *op. cit.,* Vol. II, pp. 366, 367.
5. Engels, *loc. cit.,* p. 371.

conflict between two classes—the powerful bourgeoisie and the rising proletariat. At the heart of every antagonism, matter, the sole reality in the universe, was essentially in motion, progressing inevitably upward in a spiralling direction and constituting man's evolution and history. Man by his work eventually will resolve the conflict in the millenium of communist society. While engaging in this process, man becomes the creator of his world, his history, himself. Marx's materialism, in speaking about the origin and nature of all existing things, claims that things have not been created, but everything is in essence matter and matter-in-motion. Applied to history and human affairs, materialism means that the basis of all human endeavors is found in man's material existence. Society is the social production of material life solely, an economic production. Thus Marx's application of this theory to the explanation of history is called "historical materialism."

On Marx's rejection of God as creator of the world and acceptance of the primacy of evolutionary matter, Engels, Lenin and even Stalin grafted Hegel's dialectical method. For Marx himself did not go beyond historical materialism. He does not give us in his writings a complete exposition of his theory of knowledge, that is, of the dialectical method as such. For the nature of the dialectical method and its function in history we must go back to Hegel, Engels and Lenin. Now what is dialectic? The term in its modern meaning originates in Hegel. It is a philosophy stating that all reality is in continuous flux; that there are no immutable eternal truths and consequently no science of metaphysics that studies stable essences and eternal things. Rather, change is eternal and proceeds by opposites opposing each other. Progress is impossible without struggle. Dialectic is the struggle that leads to the enrichment of reality, for in every clash of beings there is hidden the meaning of a unity on a higher level of being. Dialectical struggle, therefore, is far more fruitful than a static metaphysics because it allows for an unlimited progress in knowledge, in being, in history. Now the dialectic process is not merely an exterior technique for manipulating being; it is intrinsic to being, thinking, evolving reality. It is the unity of the content and the form of being. Whatever exists is essentially challenged by its opposite; the world moves ahead in this necessary clash of negations. Thus dialectics is equated to the science of the general laws of motion, both of the external world and of human thought. Engels clearly reveals the nature of the Marxian dialectic in the following passage:

> . . . The old metaphysics . . . accepted things as finished objects . . . this dialectical philosophy dissolves all conceptions of final, absolute truth and of absolute states of humanity corresponding to it. For it (dialectical philosophy) nothing is final, absolute, sacred. It reveals the transitory character of everything and in everything: nothing can endure before it except the uninterrupted process of becoming and of passing away, of endless ascendency from the lower to the higher. And dialectical philosophy itself is nothing more than the mere reflection of this process in the thinking brain.[6]

Dr. Gerhart Niemeyer, professor of political science at the University of Notre Dame, gives the following useful summary of the nature and function of the dialectic. "In considering everything a *connected and integral whole,* dialectics places the emphasis entirely on society as a whole matter than on the individual person. In stressing the *changeability of everything,* dialectics considers as more real that which is expected to come than that which now exists. In insisting on the *rapid and abrupt nature of change,* dialectics points to the inevitability of violent revolutions. And the concept of *contradictions* puts forward the idea of struggle."[7]

Thus, dialectical materialism is seen as the essential union between materialism and dialectics. Material conditions, social conditions, historical conditions are conceived as incessantly changing according to the dialectical laws. Marx and Engels eradicated from their materialism the limitations of all previous materialism. Dialectical materialism was free from being "predominantly mechanical," non-historical, non-dialectical, i.e., metaphysical in the static sense. Moreover, dialectical materialism, unlike its antique species, adhered consistently and comprehensively to the viewpoint of develop-

6. *Ibid.,* Vol. II, p. 362.
7. Gerhart Niemeyer, *Facts On Communism,* Vol. I: *The Communist Ideology,* United States Government Printing Office, Washington: 1960), p. 130. (Italics in original)

ment. It no longer regarded the human essence abstractly but as an "ensemble" of concretely defined historical, social relations. Old materialism merely interpreted the world from one static viewpoint; dialectical materialism changed and improved the world by its "revolutionary, practical-critical, activity."[8]

Claiming to be able to know all reality through the key of dialectical materialism, communism asserts that it is, therefore, a true "science." Perhaps Marx's central doctrine in what he called "scientific socialism" is the idea that the laws of the change of social conditions can be fully known and even accurately predicted through the materialistic analysis of society. As a prophet, therefore, Marx predicted that capitalism, with its bourgeois superstructured society, would inevitably disappear and be replaced by a Communist Utopia founded on proletarian rule. Subsequent and modern history have proved Marx an unreliable prophet. Moreover, since it is founded on *a priori* dogmas which it steadfastly refuses to subject to scientific experimentation and analysis, communism fails to meet the valid criteria of a science; it proceeds by unscientific methods. Its overweening claim to eventual omniscience can, therefore, be interpreted solely as a blind faith in the infinite powers of the human mind.

Atheism and Communist Humanism

As we have seen, Marx enthusiastically accepted Feuerbach's criticism that God is man's own invention and that nothing lies beyond matter. After Feuerbach, "the criticism of religion is substantially complete,"[9] claimed Marx. His "inspired demonstration" is irrefutable. For Marx and his followers atheism became henceforth an established dogma. Marx himself never bothered proving it theoretically again. Henceforth, his main concern was persuading men to undertake a life of practical, scientific atheism. Though rejecting his master's abstract man, Marx applied his godless, materialistic criticism

8. Lenin, "Karl Marx" (1914), *Selected Works* (London: Lawrence & Wishart, Ltd., 1939), Vol. XI, pp. 15, 16.

9. Karl Marx, *Toward The Critique Of Hegel's Philosophy Of Right* in *Marx & Engels: Basic Writings,* edited by Lewis S. Feuer (New York: Doubleday, Anchor Books, 1959), p. 262.

to concrete, individual man who is engaged in changing the world, creating industry, building society and making history.

With God effectively obliterated from reality through that "inspired demonstration," the critique of religious alienation, the highest being then enthroned in the universe becomes man. For Marx, man fills the vacuum created by the absence of God. Man becomes the only reality, the only meaning of the universe, of evolution, of history. Man, liberated from the divine shackle, is now free to create himself fully in solidarity with his fellow men. Not abstract man, not the man of the philosophers, but the existential individual, nay, to be more precise, the worker. The whole being of the individual man exists in his work. By his work man raises himself above his natural state of animality. By his work man conquers raw nature and adapts the cosmos to himself. By his work man creates the conditions he needs for self-advancement. Man is the creation of man by man; man is the producer of maturing man; man is his own savior. The essence of man consists in his being a worker. And his work not only snaps the divine shackle, but also breaks the cosmic chains that have hitherto held him back and down in utter frustration. For it is to his work that man owes his own origin; it is the principle of all creative power, the cause of history and whatever is human in the world. To be sure, this human omnipotence and creativity can be achieved only in a communist society. For there alone will one find the total process of activity radiating solely from the proletariat and directed by the fullest exercise of liberty.

We have here a practical humanism which is at once pure atheism, a quasi-divine naturalism and total revolutionism. Work, the essence of man's being, rips man suddenly, violently, irrevocably from God, from the transcendent and from the existing bourgeois world with all its forms of self-alienation. Work, man's greatest form of revolution, seeks to restore the divinity of man. The condition of slavery imposed by the three tyrants mentioned above—God, supernaturalism and capitalism—is vividly described by Marx:

> The basis of irreligious criticism is: *Man makes religion,* religion does not make man. In other words, religion is the self-consciousness and self-feeling of man, who either has

not yet found himself or has already lost himself again. But *man* is no abstract being, squatting outside the world. Man is *the world of* man, the state, society. This state, this society produce religion, *a perverted world consciousness,* because they are *a perverted world.* Religion is the general theory of that world, its encyclopedic compendium, its logic in a popular form, its spiritualistic *point d'honneur,* its enthusiasm, its moral sanction, its solemn completion, its universal ground for consolation and justification. It is *the fantastic realization* of the human essence because the *human essence* has no true reality. The struggle against religion is therefore mediately the fight against *the other world,* of which religion is the spiritual *aroma.*
Religious distress is at the same time the *expression* of real distress and the *protest* against real distress. Religion is the sigh of the oppressed creature, the heart of a heartless world, just as it is the spirit of an unspiritual situation. It is the *opium* of the people. The abolition of religion as the *illusory* happiness of the people is required for their *real* happiness. The demand to give up the illusions about its condition *is the demand to give up a condition which needs illusions.* The criticism of religion is therefore *in embryo the criticism of the vale of woe,* the *halo* of which is religion.[10] (Italics in the original).

If, according to Marx, "the criticism of religion is the premise of all criticism,"[11] then atheism is established by him as the major premise, the seminal proposition for a communist humanism. And if in the beginning is the revolution against God as man's first creative work, then the communist program must progress from this initial liberation to the final self-glorification of man. This ultimate victory over a hitherto hostile cosmos and community will inevitably be attained and celebrated only through man's dedication to revolutionary work. It becomes evident, then, that precisely because and, in as much as it is a humanism, communism is necessarily an atheism. Atheism is not an accidental accretion to communist humanism. It is intrinsic and essential to both its creed and conduct. Atheism is as inseparable from a vital communism as the soul is inseparable from a living man. Atheism is the reverse side of communist humanism.

10. *Ibid.,* pp. 262–263.
11. *Ibid.,* p. 262.

Marx gives us another indication of his radical atheism when he writes: "The profane existence of error is discredited after its heavenly *oratio pro aris et locis* has been rejected."[12] Even so it follows that the profane existence of injustice, exploitation, classes, governed, owners, ignorant, guilty, sick will likewise be destroyed after their heavenly refuge has been rejected. The first act of human amelioration, because it is the first act of human liberation, must always be the cry: "There is no God!" Yet the denial and dissolution of religious myths are mere sterile abstractions in themselves. They must be rendered fruitful by their incarnation into a positive program of work that will be enacted by the proletarian revolution for the establishment of all men in the solidarity of the communist society. Work is the complementary, creative power that makes the religious revolution meaningful. Work is the emancipating force that creates a society in the future in which man will no longer be subordinate, as a despised inferior, to an exterior, superior community. Work transforms the isolated individual of bourgeois society into the social man of communist humanism. Work renders man capable of developing all his powers to their fullest capacities; it perfects his whole nature; it inserts him organically, as equal among equals, into the classless community of concord.

But the attainment of this millenium will be the work of ages. It will have to be achieved through much suffering, after many set-backs; it will be the product of dialectical disasters and achievements on the way to certain revolutionary success. After all, Prometheus, the Titan and model of Marxist man, succeeded in discovering the arts and crafts for man's salvation only after he revolted against the gods crying: "I hate all the gods." And when he was punished by Father Zeus, Prometheus, far from being repentent and subordinate, answered Hermes, the servant of the gods, in these defiant words: "Be assured of this, I will never exchange my miserable lot for your servitude. I prefer to be riveted to this rock than to be the servile valet or errand boy of Father Zeus."[13] "Prometheus," says Marx in his doctoral thesis where he utilizes this myth of human greatness,

12. *Ibid.,* p. 262 (Prayer for the altars and hearths.)
13. *Aus Dem Literarischen Nachlass Von K. Marx, F. Engels Und F. Lassalle, (From The Literary Heritage of K. Marx, F. Engels und F. Lassalle),* compiled by F. Mehring (Stuttgart: Dietz, 1902), Vol. 1, p. 68.

"is the first saint, the first martyr on the calendar of philosophy."[14] Earlier, in 1837, he had written his father, "A curtain has fallen; my sanctuary has been demolished and it has become necessary to set up new gods there." In the same letter Marx indicated the new horizon for his vision: "Abandoning the idealism which I had met and cherished in Kant and Fichte, I discovered that the idea existed in the real itself. If the gods had formerly lived above the earth, they now became its center."[15] The whole Marxian project has been the verification of this new humanism.

Only the Promethean adventure with its audacious style could overthrow the oppressive society, already for ages deeply entrenched in power. Idealist, optimist solutions were powerless against feudalism, religion and capitalism which, aided by the connivance of religious and political powers, had buried the true nature of man under a gigantic superstructure, of economic and political tyranny. It will be the task of organized workers in this period of man's pre-history—the time before the advent of communist society—to tear down these prehistoric empires. The act of religious revolution is the first act of human history. It gives meaning to the history of man because it restores man to his greatness and to himself. Whatever events preceded the revolution against God and the reigning oppressive societies were not the history of man; they were the records of branded herds of animals, the pre-history of preman. History begins, therefore, with the denial of God and advances through the revolutionary destruction of bourgeois society to the enthronment of man as his own god in the communist community. Man is born and projected into history by his act of revolt against God, his "I will not serve!"

We indicated earlier that Marx's communism was the philosophical child of Hegel's dialectic and Feuerbach's humanistic materialism. Engels, close associate of Marx for many years, joined these two in a metaphysical marriage. Following Hegel's lead, he contended that being moves in history only by virtue of the contradiction that sets being against itself, against other being and against the threat of non-being. For Marx, be-

14. *Ibid.,* p. 68.
15. *Écrits De Marx Et De Engels À L'exception Du Capital,* edited by V. Adoratsky, (Moscow: 1931), Vol. 1, section ii, p. 213.

ing is matter; being is godless. These propositions are convertible. Now dialectical materialism advances unconsciously up through inanimate nature, through plant and animal kingdoms, into the resentfully conscious stage of master-slave dichotomy. It conquers the primitive, feudalistic, capitalistic alienations of pre-history man and culminates with final victory in the solidarity of social man in the communist society.

In this dialectical adventure the new meaning of man eradicates man's previous lust for possessing things. Being, creating, producing replaces having. Indeed, man divests himself of the exclusive relationship of having by a dialectical act of self-denial. His passion now is to be involved in community and communion with things and other men solely for the sake of his fellow man, as a member of the social solidarity of communist humanism. In his *Holy Family* Marx describes the new human meaning and relationship thus:

> Each of his human connections with the world: seeing, listening, feeling, tasting, touching, thinking, reflecting, being moved, willing, being active, loving, in summary, all the organs of his individuality, all, as organs which are immediately and formally communitarian, are in their objective productiveness or in their intercourse with the object the assimilation of it.[16]

Such is the Marxist high ground for human achievement. In his dialectical intercourse with the other—be it nature or other men—man creates and discovers himself as a social being within this dynamic intercourse. His history, his being, his society are created in the evolutionary process and social commerce which now constitute his reality. There is no such reality as an already established, static, universal human essence to which man ought to aspire. Each individual human essence is created and forged in the fires of dialectical materialism. Each individual becomes by his own efforts an existential, phenomenological essence. Man is not given a definition. Each man achieves his substantive meaning. No other being can define man. Nothing beyond him, for the transcendent has already been proven to be non-existent. Nothing below him, for man is

16. Karl Marx, *Sainte Famille*, translation Molitor, *Oeuvres Philosophiques*, (Paris: 1927), Éditions Costes, Vol. 1, p. 51.

the apotheosis of evolving matter and the work of his own
efforts. Man is, therefore, his own immanent, dialectic movement and definition. He is his own goal and god. This glorification of man is the goal of Marxist, atheistic humanism.

From another viewpoint, perhaps the major impact of Hegel's thought on Marx was its insight into the essentially active,
essentially contradictory and hostile relation between thought
and matter, between man and the world, between man and
man. As we have already seen, the vision of man as a finite
being in the process of becoming somehow infinite through his
struggle against nature and society led Marx to develop what
he called "scientific socialism," his science of society and historical development. Marx had great respect for the agonizing
process of genesis. From the crucible of this process, Marx
contended, feeble man draws a degree of infinite power, knowledge, action, love, even spirit, all purely human achievements,
harvested from his Promethean labors. A mere fragment, a
biologically nude scrap of nature in his origins, man, nevertheless, manages to raise himself above natural, animal existence
by his defiant feats. Powerful over, yet ever vulnerable to, nature, separated from, yet ever subordinated to and created by
nature, man finds in this paradoxical conflict the scourge of
both his freedom to create himself and his world and his necessity to submit to a social determinism that sweeps him along
through many uncontrollable tragedies to his final humanism.

Little by little man dominates nature; conversely and simultaneously, nature gradually determines him and his destiny.
The concrete realization of his humanity is forged by the determinism of the dialectical process. Yet man himself is not that
determinism. Man becomes human only by first having suffered and passed through what is inhuman. Subjected to the
brutality of biological nature, man responds with his own
forms of brutality against nature—his systems of law, morality, economics, religion. Each contradiction resolved, each
class struggle synthesized—be it between master and slave,
lord and serf, capitalist and worker—sees man advance to a
higher degree of human maturity. The laws of history that
govern the evolution of human society demand that man be
created, not out of the slime of the earth, but out of the brutality
of man's inhumanity to man. Out of the fires of his cosmic and

class struggles, man, the creator of his own history, will inexorably bring forth his future utopia—communist humanism. Yet this integral humanism will be real, not ideal, for it has already been conceived, it is presently being gestated and will eventually be born from the womb of the proletarians' tragedies. Writing of the spiritual nature of this integral humanism, de Lubac gives this perceptive analysis:

> Marx's doctrine, never plain naturalism, always paid as much attention to man's spiritual life as to his material existence. His communism offered itself as the only concrete realization of humanism; it quite deliberately claimed to be a total solution for the whole human problem; moving to the plane of reality, it did not propose to figure there only as a social phenomenon but as a spiritual phenomenon also. This is what gives it greatness, but this is also the radical flaw in it; it is this that bathes even its sound elements in a baneful atmosphere and it is this that chiefly arouses Christian opposition. "The religion of the workers has no God," Marx wrote in a letter to Hardmann, "because it seeks to restore the divinity of man."[17]

Communist Ethics

Marx's statement on the religion of the workers can be paraphrased by a parallel proposition on their ethics. The morality of the workers has no transcendent standard because it seeks to foster their class struggle. Engels had already stated: "For it (dialectical philosophy) nothing is final, absolute, sacred."[18] From this eternal flux of reality, he went on to conclude that all morality is but the practical struggle, the prolongation into conduct of each class's quest for its own interests, "... In reality every class, every profession has its own morality."[19]

Now if nothing is objectively absolute except "the struggle of mutually exclusive opposites" within the context of historical materialism, then communist humanisn, in order to justify its conduct, must discover within this struggle some absolute moral standard of its own. This it does, making historical expe-

---

17. Henri de Lubac, S.J., *op. cit.*, p. 17.
18. Engels, *op. cit.*, Vol. II, p. 362.
19. *Ibid.*, p. 383.

rience the absolute standard of its morality. At first sight this standard would seem to be very relativistic. But, theoretically at least, it is not so. Why? Because communist morality imposes tasks that are absolute, compulsory and enduring throughout history. Each moral task arises suddenly and is conditioned by the historical process and the possibility of the task's fulfillment against the opposition of superstructured society. Thus within the turbulent bosom of unfolding history the communist conscience is endowed with certain rights and burdened with important duties.

But what of the problem of freedom in the communist enterprises? Is deliberately free activity possible in a humanism seemingly so deterministic? Does the dialectical process develop itself in such a manner as to be ineluctably indifferent to human action? Is the law of communism such that its automatic working will inevitably destroy capitalism without the cooperation of man? Or is this doctrine just an ideal proposed for the contemplation of man's conscience and the inspiration of his liberty? May man merely fold his arms and eagerly await the Eden that historical materialism is inevitably preparing for him? If the answer to these questions is yes, then both freedom and morality are suppressed in communist humanism because impossible of expression in its radical determinism.

Communist teaching rejects the contradictory dilemma of ideal versus imperturbable determinism. Marx had written in his *The German Ideology:* "Communism is for us not a stable state which is to be established, an *ideal* to which reality will have to adjust itself. We call communism the *real* movement which abolishes the present state of things. The conditions of this movement result from the premises now in existence ..."[20] Thus communist humanism admits of no ideal outside the real, beckoning man to transcend historical experience. Moreover, it rejects an imperturbable determinism as this contradicts the eternal, dialectical flux of its process. What then is the nature of communism's ethics? We can probably understand its essence best by comparing it with traditionally accepted morality in civilized countries.

Western thinkers represent ethics as rooted intrinsically in

20. Karl Marx, *The German Ideology,* (London: Lawrence & Wishart, 1963), New World Paperback edition, p. 26.

human nature, which is oriented metaphysically toward an absolute order of values. Both human nature and the absolute order of values are grounded on the ultimate transcendent Nature and Order—God. As he knowingly and willingly accepts or rejects this order and its Author, man renders himself morally good or evil. Now communist humanism rejects the very conception of absolute transcendent standards of morality or unconditioned moral actions and obligations. It contends that there is no eternal truth, values or even beauty. Only that is true, valued and beautiful which the test of historical experience designates as so. Again to call this doctrinal and moral relativism is to say too little against this ethics and to say it falsely. For communists do not doubt nor are they eclectic about their moral principles. They know and state apodictically that neither truth, goodness nor beauty exists beyond human experience and history. Every attempt to escape the real, historical, human condition towards some form of transcendence is but an expression of man's alienation from himself. Traditional morality is just such a flight and illusory self-alienation from one's self. Thus, there are no immutable, transcendent values for communist humanists. There exist only values and judgments that are immersed in historical reality. Since historical reality is in constant flux, values are in constant flux; good and evil are in flux. Lenin writes:

> In what sense do we repudiate ethics and morality? In the sense that they were preached by the bourgeoisie, who declared that ethics were God's commandments. We, of course, say that we do not believe in God . . .
> We repudiate all morality that is taken outside of human, class concepts . . .
> We say that our morality is entirely subordinated to the interests of the class struggle of the proletariat.[21]

Therefore, morally, is not the Supreme Good for communist humanism this real world which man ought to possess and dominate fully? Is not the Supreme Good man's real, concrete life which he ought to elucidate, organize, suffuse with reason

21. Lenin, "The Tasks of the Youth League," (Speech Delivered at the Third All-Russian Congress of the Russian Young Communist League, Oct. 2, 1920), in *Selected Works* (New York: International Publishers, 1943), Vol. IX, pp. 474, 475, 477.

and social universality? Thus in communist humanism man has a very important moral mission, an absolute crusade. He must enter upon an enterprise which is always new, a challenge ceaselessly repeated by the dialectic of history. His task is to resolve contradictions between economic and social forces, to strike against capitalism, the ruling classes, the superstructured, bourgeoisie society. This is his absolute task, limited solely by the exigencies of history, to advance the social revolution. Through work men are to achieve the supremacy of man over blind chance and exterior cosmic conditions. History without man's cooperation is impotent. Marx had written:

> *History* does *nothing;* it "possesses *no* immense wealth;" it "wages *no* battles." It is *man,* real living man, that does all that, that possesses and fights; "history" is not a person apart, using man as a means for *its own* particular aims; history is *nothing but* the activity of man pursuing his aims . . .[22]

Moreover, men are not to be selfishly interested in their own personal development. Rather they are to be dedicated to liberating man from every self-alienation, thereby ushering in the communist society. Hence all ethical actions are subordinated to these historical, social goals. To communist humanism, man's value is conditional, not absolute; derivative, not ultimate. Hence, individuals, families, particular societies, whole nations exist for the communist society, not for themselves. Communist society exists for the production of material goods. Man is a physical, social part of a greater whole; he is an instrument to an impersonal, material end. Every worker is bound to dedicate his efforts to this end. No reward or punishment as such is promised for service or disservice to this cause. But history threatens man with a fatal alternative: Either communist society or barbarism. Thus Marx imperiously demands that man address himself to the moral tasks of subverting the existing contradiction of capitalism and erecting scientific socialism in its place. Here is the field in which man may vigorously exercise his liberty. The noblest use of human freedom is its

22. Karl Marx, *The Holy Family* (1845) (London: Lawrence & Wishart, 1956), p. 125.

cooperation with the historical process in transforming the world, in creating man, in revealing man to himself, in promoting man from being an object and animal to being a social, mature subject. So much for the scientific theory of communist morality. Commenting on Marx's imperious demand that this ethic be followed and his unscientific justification of it David Caute remarks:

> When writing of actual revolutions, Marx discarded all pretensions to scientific impartiality. There was no inconsistency in this; according to Marx, subjective revolutionary passion is at every stage an agent of the historical process. But one is entitled to ask whether in the mind of a single man—Marx's—subjective passion and scientific analysis can at any point be separated entirely.[23]

What about communist morality as an art? In practice communist ethics is quite a relative reality. Workers are to respond to commands that require their conduct to conform instantaneously to the shifting, often contradictory, policies of party strategy. Human virtue is identified with fidelity to the dictates of the class struggle. Virtue is deduced from the facts and needs of this struggle. Vice is a failure to adhere to the commands from above that set the daily strategy. One day an action, e.g. opposition to Nazi Germany, may be deemed in the interest of the socialist revolution. It is to be pursued as morally good. Suddenly, due to the flux of historical events and tensions, a pact with Nazi Germany may be dictated as the morally good action. Never mind that the same action is good on one day and evil on another. The historical necessities of the moment for the cause of communism are the determining factors of morality. And since these change rapidly, continually, the communist faithful must be ready to change suddenly with the shifting morality, even though these changes may cause severe psychological shocks in the souls of the comrades. The future of communism, decided by the events of the present and looking to its progression in history, is the only standard for moral judgements and actions. Morality is to serve the class struggle, which is another way of saying that ethics is to serve the ceaseless

23. *Essential Writings of Karl Marx* with an Introduction and Notes by David Caute, (London: 1967), A London Panther, p. 229.

pursuit of power by communist humanism. Here is the only cause that justifies human action. With God rejected, with transcendent standards and goals for morality denied, only what fosters a communist future and a capitalist failure has any moral value. Wherever they are not in power communists favor violent change as a forward and "good" movement against stability as a backward and "evil" condition. Wherever they are in power communists favor a stable fidelity to the true doctrine of Marx as a morally "good" policy against the treasonous revisionism of the "evil" liberalizers. Since man's future, according to communist humanism, is identified inevitably with the classless society, then the struggle for a communist victory justifies any means and any actions taken to further this absolute, historical cause. In the exercise of his freedom man is to enjoy unlimited dimensions so long as he observes this "law of laws," this first, this greatest, this only moral commandment. Whatever you do in thought, word or deed, do all for a communist victory under the leadership of the Communist Party.

In this connection the leadership of the Party, fearing the spiritual strength of nations whose traditional and Christian morality is practiced both in private and public life, works round the clock as silently and surreptitiously as the law of gravity to break down the moral integrity of the free nations of the world. Mr. Garth Lean, in his inspiring book *Brave Men Choose,* records the Party's machinations in this matter:

> To whose advantage, in this ideological age, is the maxim that private and public morality have no connection—or its extension that morality is impractical, even dangerous, in a democratic statesman? Lenin made it clear years ago that the preliminary to Communist take-over is the undermining of moral standards in the democracies. "Postpone operations until the moral disintegration of the enemy makes delivery of the mortal blow inevitable and easy," he said, while his friend and Ambassador in Sweden, Mme. Kollontai, reported: "Immorality in the schools is progressing satisfactorily."
>
> Such was the normal and successful strategy of world Communism between the wars. A bishop's son, who had become a Communist agent in Scandinavia, told the present author and his friends in 1934 that his instructions

were not to mention Marxism to the youth for some years, but to encourage heterosexual and homosexual looseness among them. "When they can no longer say 'No' to themselves, they will be unable to say 'No' to Communism," he was told.[24]

The relationship between moral depravity and espionage is today generally admitted. Communist spies are especially trained, according to the Australian Royal Commission on Espionage, "to detect weakness in character, weakness for drink, blondes, drugs and homosexuality."[25] In London, *The Sunday Telegraph,* March 25, 1962, reports that "a finishing school for girl spies" has been set up in East Berlin; the girls are taught every form of perversion and told they must not hesitate to use their knowledge to the full. Failure to "fix" important victims often involves reprisals on their families.[26]

Perhaps the classic work on the communist plan to exploit moral depravity as a sure road to conquest of non-communist nations is *The Yenan Way.* Written by South American ex-communist Eudocio Ravines, founder of the Communist Party in Peru, the work leaves the reader flabbergasted at the thoroughness and depravity of the leaders of the Communist conspiracy. Ravines organized the Popular Front in Chile in the thirties, he acted as one of the Comintern directors of the second phase of the Spanish Civil War; he had been a Professor at the Leninist Academy in Moscow. While he was on a visit to Moscow in 1935, Stalin personally sent him to be trained by Mao Tse-tung in methods of infiltration. His book narrates the steps of his training and how he later used the Yenan method in South America. In a sort of oral final exam conducted by Mao himself, Ravines reports what he had learned:

> I think the Yenan Way envisages a completely new kind of politics for us. If I understand you, it goes beyond the strict limits of the working class and poor peasants and the poor-

24. Garth Lean, *Brave Men Choose* (London: Blandford Press, 1961), Introduction, pp. xii, xiii.
25. *The Report of the Royal Australian Commission On Espionage:* presented September 14, 1955, printed October 1955, pp. 35, 111.
26. An excellent chapter on this matter is to be found in the work co-authored by Sir Arnold Lunn and Garth Lean, *The New Morality,* revised and enlarged, (London: Blandford Press, fifth impression 1965). I am gratefully indebted to these authors for the matter used here.

est of the middle class. We must go daringly into other fields, keep our eyes on the positions we want to win, and forget everything else; at any price, win friends, sympathizers and servants.

"That, especially that—servants," screamed Mao. "People who serve us, through greed, through fear, inferiority, vengeance, what have you, but who serve us. Serve the party, serve the designs of the Comintern, serve the cause of the revolution. Congratulations, my boy, you have caught the very essence of the Yenan Way. Now apply it."[27]

Mao confided to Ravines that already by 1935 the Communist Party of China had "won in this way hundreds of officers of Chiang Kaishek's army," snaring them with money, promotion, power, whatever it took to break their characters. General Ho Ying-Chin, former Premier of China, ruefully testified to the effectiveness of the Yenan technique when he reported of the Kuomintang leaders: "We all loved our country, but many of us loved our mistresses too; and we never realized until too late that they were Communists."[28]

Marx founded communist ethics on his pseudo-science of historical materialism. Lenin added an emotional fanaticism as another source of communist morality by following the radical immoralism of Nechayev. Eugene Lyons, reviewing five decades of Communist immorality in his book *Workers' Paradise Lost,* writes: "Lenin, it is important to recall, had found Sergei Nechayev, the apostle of absolute immoralism, even before he found Marx. In 1868, Nechayev wrote his celebrated *Catechism Of A Revolutionist,* in which he renounced all norms of civilized behavior and prescribed every imaginable depravity in the pursuit of the *ideal.* It is as fanatic, hate-packed a document as the human brain has ever produced. The revolutionist, he wrote, 'knows only one science, the science of destruction,' which does not stop at lying, robbery, betrayal and torture of friends, murder of his own family. His central dictum, that 'everything that contributes to the triumph of the revolution' is moral, has been echoed by Lenin and his disciples to this day and, indeed, figures in every communist pronounce-

27. Eudocio Ravines, *The Yenan Way* (New York: Scribner's, 1951), pp. 113–163.

28. Garth Lean, *Brave Men Choose,* Introduction, p. xiv.

ment on morality."[29] Max Eastman writes that "the confluence of these two streams of thought (Nechayev and Marx) is one of the greatest disasters that ever befell mankind."[30]

Communist Atheism Versus Religion

It has been observed by sages throughout the ages that man's calloused heartlessness toward his fellow man increases in proportion to his unconcern about God. Where, therefore, one would find a militant hatred of God, one should expect to find an aggressive malevolence against man. History has proven this dictum to be frightfully true. In the case of anti-theistic communism, whose hatred of God is well-nigh pathological, we discover, accompanying its malice, a virtually satanic ferocity against man. The movement is powered by and runs on the vehemence of its feud with God. Frustrated at being unable to attack God directly, the communists savagely, barbarically strike at Him in believers. Persecution of religion, "the war on superstition," as it is euphemistically called, is pressed inexorably in word and deed. Marx's contempt for religion was incarnated into a delirium of violent sadism by Lenin, Stalin and their modern successors. "Every religious idea," wrote Lenin to Gorky, "every idea of god, every flirtation with the idea of god is unutterable vileness . . . Any person who engages in building a *god,* or who even tolerates the idea of god-building, *disparages himself* in the worst possible fashion . . ."[31] The Godless Society in Russia has launched five-year plans for the liquidation of religion. Churches by the thousands have been closed; church bells melted down for military purposes, icons burned, religious leaders of every denomination herded into slave camps and prisons. What little religious practice is still allowed, exists for propaganda purposes, dominated by patriarchs and priests picked by the Party, preaching Party doctrine under the guise of the Gospel and responsible solely to the Party.

29. Eugene Lyons, *Workers' Paradise Lost* (New York: Paperback Library Inc., 1967), pp. 376–377.
30. *Ibid.,* Paperback Library, p. 377.
31. Lenin, "Letter from Lenin to A. M. Gorky," Nov. 14, 1913, in *Selected Works,* (London: Lawrence & Wishart, Ltd., 1939), Vol. XI, pp. 675, 676.

The cynical exploitation of religion of which Communism is capable was demonstrated by Stalin during the Second World War. When Hitler's armies invaded Russia and more than a million Russian soldiers defected, donning German uniforms in the hope of overthrowing their own hated, Godless regime, Stalin, realizing that communist humanism could never move his armies to defeat the Germans, shrewdly made religion legal and respectable again. Crusades against God ceased and were prohibited; church bells, silent these many years, rang out again. Holy Mother Russia was appealed to as the only ideal for which to fight and die. Not Communism! Indeed, the Communist International was formally dissolved. Far from having any longer a messianic mission, Communism, Socialism, Bolshevism, recognized as being positive menaces to the very survival of the nation, were disowned and discarded. Even with these cynical moves it is doubtful if the Russians would have rallied to defeat the invader, had not Hitler aided the Stalin ploy on religion with a colossal, arrogant blunder of his own. With violent stupidity he frustrated the eager yearning of the Russian millions for freedom from their ruthless regime and turned their intense hatred of that regime against the Germans. Hitler's racist cruelties against the Russian prisoners alerted the Russian people that there was to be no salvation from communism in the Nazi camps. Thus, what Stalin and communism could not effect among the Russian people, Hitler's cruelty accomplished. Shocked by his barbarities and fooled by Stalin's machinations about religion, the Russian people stiffened and fought back, for their homes and Holy Mother Russia, to defeat the Nazis and, alas, unbeknown to them, to solidify the communist regime for more than twenty additional years of tyranny over themselves.

And what is communist humanism's position on religion today? Its old position, once again openly hostile and thorough persecution of it. The Reverend Richard Wurmbrand, Evangelical Minister and refugee from Rumania who spent fourteen years in communist prisons after World War II for religious reasons, in testimony before a United States Subcommittee of the Committee on the Judiciary testified as follows on the question of communist exploitation of religion. The date was May 6, 1966.

Mr. Sourwine: . . . What has been the policy and practice of the Communists with respect to religion in the countries where they have come to power?

Reverend Wurmbrand: They used three great instruments. First of all, the persecution, to make everybody afraid. They never accepted that they have put anybody in prison for religious motives. They found always political motives . . . [There follow two incidents of Christian pastors whose Sunday sermons were twisted into political crimes. One received a 7, the other a 15 years prison sentence. The testimony continues thus:]
. . . There has been, secondly, the method of corruption . . . For the first time in church history the leadership of churches is dominated by the central committee of an avowed atheistic power. The central committee of the party decides who must be patriarch, who must be Baptist preacher, Pentacostal preacher, and so on. Everywhere they have found weak men or men with some sin. Those they have put in the leadership of churches and so you could hear in our theological seminary in Bucharest the theology that God has given three revelations—once through Moses, second through Jesus, and third through Karl Marx, and so on.
Religion is corrupted from within. Religion has been widely used, and is still, as the tool of Communist politics. The priests everywhere had to propagate the collectivization of agriculture and everywhere when Communists have something important to do, knowing the influence of religion, priests and pastors are put to preach these things.

Mr. Sourwine: Have the Communists shown themselves to be opposed only to Christianity, or to all religions?

Reverend Wurmbrand: To all religions. The Jewish religion has been persecuted just as the Christian religion. In the prison of Gherla we had a whole room with rabbis who were in prisons. We had in prison the Moslem priests and so on.[32]

32. *Communist Exploitation Of Religion,* Hearing Before the Subcommittee to Investigate the Administration of the Internal Security Act and Other Internal Security Laws of the Committee on The Judiciary, United States Senate, Eighty-Ninth Congress, Second Session. Testimony of Rev. Richard Wurmbrand. May 6, 1966. (Washington: U.S. Government Printing Office), pp. 12, 13.

Communist Atheism Versus The Catholic Church

It has been wisely perceived that communist humanism, as a commitment to godlessness, could only have taken root and flourished in the enfeebled body of a mankind that had once been vigorous but became venal in the profession and practice of Christianity. Indeed the record shows that Marx, with intense bitterness and total dedication, took up his world-shattering mission in resentful hatred of the heartless Christians around him whose pagan lives and policies he rejected. He started from the false premise that wicked Christians are the fruit of wicked Christianity. His conclusion that Christianity had been tried for eighteen hundred years and had failed only compounded his original error.[33] Nevertheless, the decadent Christian nations, whose national and international lives were truly scandalous, gave Marx in 1847 the weapon he needed to attack Christianity and organize a movement of his own to replace it. It seems quite accurate to state that communist humanism has deliberately formed itself into an anti-Christian humanism, that is to say, into an anti-religion religion, an anti-Church Church, an anti-Catholic catholicity, an anti-Messiah messianism. And communist humanism rightly sees in the Catholic Church—whose dogma, zeal and unity it imitates in transposed, secularized forms—the ultimate enemy it must destroy, if its ideology and Eden are to prevail in the end.

On her part, the Catholic Church, especially in her leadership, the Popes, has certainly recognized clearly the nature and aims of this militant humanism, even if many of her intellectuals have not. For more than one hundred years Popes have been analyzing and rejecting communism from the viewpoint of philosophy and Faith, warning not merely their own faithful but the whole world of the falsity of doctrine and the incredibly inhuman practices of this pseudo-humanism. As far back as

33. Marx had written in 1847: "The social principles of Christianity have now had eighteen hundred years to develop and need no further development by the Prussian consistorial councillors. The social principles of Christianity justified the slavery of Antiquity, glorified the serfdom of the Middle Ages and equally know, when necessary now to defend the oppression of the proletariat, although they make a pitiful face over it . . . The social principles of Christianity are sneakish and the proletariat is revolutionary." (Karl Marx, *On Religion*, London: Lawrence & Wishart, pp. 83–84.)

December 28, 1878, while Marx was still alive, Leo XIII stigmatized communism as "a deadly pestilence which attacks the essentials of society and would annihilate it."[34]

The Pope, however, who most often strategically and incisively made onslaughts on communism was Pius XI. In a salvo of documents which were appeals to the entire world, he seems to have made it his special service to man to unmask the movement's drive to dominate mankind and to challenge men to a renewed Christian commitment as the only efficacious remedy against the magic of evolutionary materialism. Although treated in particular sections of documents which were directly concerned with other social-spiritual problems, communist humanism is made the sole subject of special analysis and condemnation in the classic encyclical on its nature, tactics and goal—*Divini Redemptoris* (titled in English *Atheistic Communism*) published on March 19, 1937.[35] We will concentrate on this papal document which discusses the prevailing communism of that day, known as Bolshevism, and which, still in the ascendency, celebrated its fiftieth anniversary just recently.

As regards Bolshevism's philosophical theories on reality the Catholic Church has this critique to make: In maintaining that matter and its blind, evolutionary forces alone exist and that society is merely a higher, more complicated form of matter, formed ineluctably by the necessary laws of nature, Pius XI declares that this doctrine degrades the intrinsic sociality of man to being a mere external accretion added to man by the determinism of the historical process. Moreover, such a doctrine reduces man and society, in the infamous phrase of Stalin, to being at best "the most precious capital." Atheistic, anti-creationistic, it denies the specific difference between matter and spirit, body and soul. Dialectical differences alone exist in the diverse stages of developing matter. Then too, the survival of the soul after death and the hope of an eternal life are swept away by this radical materialism. Pius XI continues: "Communism is by its nature anti-religious and considers religion to be "the opium of the people" because the religious principles which speak of a life beyond the grave prevent the

34. *Acta Apostolicae Sedis, Leonis XIII,* Vol. I, p. 46.
35. See *La Pensée de Karl Marx,* p. 578, footnote.

proletariat from pursuing the realization of the Soviet paradise in this world."[36] Thus, communism denies the reality that man as a creature is naturally religious, that is, metaphysically dependent totally and always on his creator. It rejects with specious reasoning the experience that man throughout the ages is attracted morally and psychologically to God.

As he addresses himself to the doctrine of violent revolution which derives from the evolutionary, dialectical aspect of materialism, the Pope condemns it as being unfounded in reality and used as a pretext to justify violent crimes the world over, but especially in Russia, Mexico and Spain. Admitting that class differences exist, sometimes too based on resentment to real injustice, what the Pope condemns communism for in this matter is that it makes of all differences, good as well as evil, a principle for setting class against class permanently in violent hatred. Communism pushes to the point of irrational frenzy whatever conflicts exist between groups. Its messianic mission is seized with an all-pervading drive to rot every personal and social relationship of man. As a result of this metastatic fury communism perverts the whole of creation, transforming realism into materialism, economics into socialism, humanism into animalism, politics into militarism, religion into diabolism.

When Pius XI compares the Christian conception of liberty with that of the communist conception, he boldly asserts that communism "despoils man of his liberty, the spiritual principle of moral conduct." This despoliation is a consequence of its radical, dialectical materialism which, as we have seen earlier, rejects Christian morality. For communism denies the dignity of the individual, his transcendence before the collectivity. The person has no private, human rights; he is merely a cog, on a wheel serving the machine of the collectivity. Radical collectivism swallows up the individual and smothers his rights while suffocating his liberty. Man is a material instrument subjected totally to the purposes of an equally material collectivity. Though matter is important to man and society, the person is a spiritual whole and may not be reduced to his quantitative aspects. Moreover, the denial of man's right to private property and the resources of nature with its means of production is

36. *Acta Apostolicae Sedis, Pius XI,* Vol. XXIX, pp. 65–106, 1937.

another assault on the liberty and dignity of man. The fact that abuses in the exercise of this right have led to the unjust accumulation of massive wealth and the exploitation of the many by the few is no reason for depriving all men of a fundamental dimension of dignity and freedom. The solution to malnutrition is not starvation nor, for that matter, is starvation the solution to gluttony. Failing to make the clear and happy distinction, made by Leo XIII, between the right to possess private property which is personal and the obligation of how to use private property which is social, communism would reduce all men to the nudity of non-ownership. The fundamental trouble is that being blindly materialistic and narrowly economic, communism sees in private property the "original sin" of mankind. Such narrowness extinguishes in man the creative incentive to work matter into new, resplendent forms and to administer these forms for the expansion of man's liberty and welfare.

Finally, in reassessing the communist social doctrine, Pius XI rejects its teachings on the state and the family. The dictatorship of the proletariat is a regime of violence justified by its end, which is to subdue all organizations and groups which are not classless. Here is raw political power put inhumanly at the service of an impossibility—the illusionary abstraction called the classless society. This power undermines all societies, civic, business, social, family. For in communist social doctrine the primary value is placed on economics. All natural and conventional societies are seen merely as emanations of an evolving economic history. Such societies are to survive or disappear as they prove useful to the coming economic system of full-blown communist humanism. As an emanation of economics, the family exists for the production of goods; there is nothing sacred about it; it has no rights above or against the dictatorship of the proletariat; all societies derive their existences and functions from the economic level of their historical age. Pius XI condemns this inhuman, unnatural, pan-economic atheism. Every communist thesis put forth on the nature and purpose of creation, man and society is proven to be false not only under the light of true philosophy but also under the light of Divine Revelation. Mankind is, therefore, exhorted to refuse adherence to communist humanism and never to cooperate with specifically communist programs, for their intentions, means and ends are evil. Perhaps the most famous and well-known statement of this whole encyclical that sums up succinctly what a Catholic or any God-fearing person should know and do about communist atheism is this: "Communism is intrinsically evil and no one who would save Christian civilization may collaborate with it in any undertaking whatsoever. Those who permit themselves to be deceived into lending their aid towards the triumph of communism in their own country, will be the first to fall victims of this error."[37]

Communist humanism sees in the Catholic Church its archenemy. And it is engaged in an inevitable, unconditional fight to the death against her. The very essence of the Catholic Church, her absolute faith in God and total mission to humanity, is the cause of communism's enraged attack upon her. The Catholic Church professes the same truths that dominated the entire consciousness of her founder, Jesus Christ. She works zealously as the incarnate prolongation of his presence and sacramental succession, or rather, application of His salvation until the end of time. Her faith comprises, in the words of her founder, "all things that I have heard from my Father which I have made known to you."[38] Her mission in His words is: "My meat is to do the will of him who sent me."[39] "I am come that they may have life and may have it more abundantly." As did her founder, so too the Catholic Church claims absolutely the whole man—motives, thinking, loving, dying—for God. She challenges every man to enlist in Christ's society here and to work now for his own and his neighbor's salvation in that society hereafter.

Communist society lives by an equally radical but contra-Catholic faith and mission. Its faith and enterprise are the same as that which blazed in the lives of its founders, Marx and Lenin. They professed wholeheartedly Feuerbach's basic dogma: *Homo homini Deus:* Man is his own God. Moreover, their equally absolute mission demands the allegiance of the entire man. Communist humanism invites every man to dedicate his whole life to a crusade which is intensely anti-God in its negative thrust. In its positive work, the communist crusade

37. Pius XI, *Atheistic Communism* (Rome: 1937).
38. John 15 : 15.
39. John 4 : 34.

divinizes man through its revolutionary attainment of economic freedom in its classless society—a utopia that is forever locked securely in a time-space-matter evolution. Thus, it is clear that an implacable impasse exists between the Catholic Church and Communist Humanism. On essential doctrines concerning God, man, human society an unbridgeable chasm yawns between them. We are reminded of the deadlock that existed between Christ and His contemporary enemies, since the reasons expressed by Christ for that stand-off are identical here. "You are from below, I am from above. You are of this world, I am not of this world."[40] "My kingdom is not of this world."[41] The Catholic Church, therefore, sees communist humanism as a contra-truth, a contra-society, a quasi contra-church fighting against her relentlessly in a total war for the allegiance of each human person.

Unless communist humanism is recognized to be essentially and irrevocably anti-Catholic, not merely anti-religious or even anti-Christian, it will never be profoundly understood. This humanism proposes a directly opposite dogma for each doctrine the Catholic Church teaches. For whatever solutions the Catholic Church advances to various problems, communism proposes diametrically contrary remedies. The Catholic Church teaches that she can be recognized by her distinguishing marks; she is one, holy, catholic and apostolic. The communist quasi contra-church claims as her distinctive qualities that she is one, anti-theistic, universal and Marxist. Both organizations arouse heroic zeal in their finest faithful; both pursue messianic goals—secularized classless society for communism in time, divinized, sacramental society for the Catholic Church in time and into eternity. The direct opposition between the two societies runs from the dogma to dogma confrontation, through the diametrically opposed moralities and final ends. Yet, communist humanism, as the upstart newcomer, apes the Catholic Church with the calculated intention of transposing the Church's sacred doctrines and practices into its own atheistic teachings and profane rules for conduct.

We will, for the most part, restrict ourselves here to the doctrinal confrontation between the two societies. Communist hu-

40. John 8 : 23.
41. John 18 : 36.

manism teaches that man is his own origin; the Church teaches that God alone is His own non-causal origin. Communism creates man in socialist society as a "passion for his fellow man;" communist social man identifies himself with others in the strict meaning of that word, for he conquers the differences of alienation, objectification and personality by raising himself to the solidarity of revolutionary socialist society. Catholicism, however, teaches that such an identity of nature across differences is possible only in the Holy Trinity where each divine Person possesses the identically same divine nature while preserving His unique personality. Communism succumbs to the tempation to be like God, desiring to know all things, good and evil. For it claims that communist man, by suppressing all differences, attains perfect self-knowledge and perfect equality with all men. But Catholicism insists that perfect, transparent self-knowledge, perfect equality with other persons is found, once again, only in the Blessed Trinity. And man cannot be equated with God, claim the Christians. For how explain the chilling limitation of death and man's inability to escape it? Indeed, man's desire to know all and his enterprise to become God on his own terms is what introduced death by way of punishment into the human family.

Only in the Trinity is it possible for perfect identity to exist simultaneously with perfect otherness. The Father is eternally begetting the Son in perfect self-knowledge; the Father and Son are eternally breathing forth the Spirit in mutually infinite love. One identical divine nature is possessed by three perfectly diverse yet equal persons. Communist humanism teaches that the identity with man in perfect self-knowledge and perfect mutual love is fulfilled in socialist society through its perfection of man's passion for man. It is man, then, who confers upon himself infinite lucidity concerning himself and his society while also exercising absolute liberty in loving himself and this society. Now the Catholic Church teaches that metaphysically man is unable to confer anything upon himself; he is created gratuitously by God out of pure love. Being, existence, powers of activity, all is conferred upon him as gift; a creature, man is totally at every instant dependent on his creator. Certainly, he is obliged to know, love and be grateful for himself and others in whom he will fulfill his noblest aspirations. "What do you have, O Man, that you have not received? And if you have received it, why do you glory as if you received it not?"[42]

The Catholic Church realizes that man, faced with the radical dependence of his creaturehood, yet challenged to chose himself and his fellow man as final goals would experience the spiritual dizziness of a tempted creature. Would he humbly, gratefully acknowledge his creaturehood and choose God in preference to himself? The tragedy is that he chose himself, opting to become God without God, thus falling into sin. Sin is his self-alienation, not the projection from himself of an illusory God, as Feuerbach taught Marx. The attempt to become God in himself, by himself, is his self-alientation, a personal, subjective, self-inflicted alienation. The Catholic Church teaches that all alienations are founded on the source of alienations—sin. Sin corrupts, disrupts man who then corrupts and disrupts human conditions and relationships. Hence arise culpable and inculpable alienations. Spiritual schizophrenia severs man from himself because it severs him from his source—God. Once fractured within, man fractures the world about him which, in cosmic protest at man's sin, has already hardened itself against him. Dante expressed the sound relationship that alone can cure the restless, internal hostility of man: *"In la sua voluntate è nostra pace.* [In His Will is our peace.]"[43]

Thus alienated, man is unhappy, not because he imagined and projected an alien God, but because he imagined he himself could become God. Enamoured of his own beauty, brilliance, liberty, he decided to ascend the throne of God. Like Lucifer he fell; his fall is his alienation. A reconciliation between what he is and what he arrogantly tried to be is impossible on his own terms. Marx makes the fundamental mistake of equating the alienation of private property, his source for all alienations, with original sin; sin is an economic evil for him; it calls for an economic saviour. The Catholic Church teaches that sin is a spiritual evil, an insult by man against God; it calls for a divine saviour, since a limited creature cannot atone for an infinite offense against an infinite Being. Yet it also calls for a human savior, if humanity is to atone for its own offense against both God and man. Communist humanism holds that

42. St. Paul, I Cor. 4:7.
43. Dante Alighieri, *Divina Commedia,* "Paradiso," canto 3.

the redemption of man is achieved by the sufferings of the sacrificial lamb and economic saviour, the proletariat, whose crucifixion and resurrection in rebellion emancipates all men into the socialist heaven. Man is, therefore, his own saviour as well as being his own God. The truth of the matter is, as the Church teaches, that man is reconciled to God, his fellow man and himself by One who is at once fully Man and fully God. He is the only Sacrificial Lamb capable of destroying the alienation of sin and of establishing friendship between God and man. The sufferings of proletarians are the sufferings of mere creatures; the sufferings of Christ "knock down the wall of separation" that sin erected.

Moreover, no man has ever suffered alienation to the extent that the God-Man has. He has drunk its dregs. Emptied of divine glory, appearing as a slave, he was infinitely humiliated and, though innocence and holiness itself, was "made sin" in order to destroy it and thus raise man with Himself above the clouds. Then too, His work, His service is the primary efficacious work for man's salvation; proletarian deeds in themselves are absolutely sterile for salvation. "Without me you can do nothing."[44] Christ made His work man's work because He performed it in the name and behalf of His brethren; proletarian work is neither salvific, infinite nor divine; by itself it destroys rather than improves man. Christ is the universal man, not the proletarian as Marx claims. Christ identifies Himself and His mission with the destiny of every man that comes into the world; He comes and works to save all. The Christian partakes of this universal life and mission through sacramental union with Christ. Proletarian man, on the other hand, hates millions, divides men and fosters class wars of extinction. Christ and His Christians love, reconcile, promote communion of all men in their Saviour and their God.

And as for proletarian poverty and rejection by society, no worker-victims have ever been subjected to the humiliating experiences of the God-Man. Descended from a dynasty fallen from power, living and working like the poorest of the poor, rejected by His own nation and by the world, crucified by the religious leaders of His people and put to death by the Roman rulers of the world, Christ was buried as an executed criminal, perhaps the greatest failure history has ever seen. His life and

44. John 15 : 6.

death were alienation intensified to an infinite degree. In Him Christians defeat sin and death. "Death is swallowed up in victory! O death, where is thy victory? O death, where is thy sting? Now the sting of death is sin ... But thanks be to God who has given us the victory through Our Lord Jesus Christ."[45] Communist proletarian society recoils before the experience of death. Allegiance to their humanistic heaven on earth renders death more horrible than ever. For death ushers in the eternal loss of their earthly utopia, eternal personal annihilation for every man. But Christ, the Prince of proletarians, experiences lowly man's miseries in a most universal as well as individual way. As God He knows perfectly every suffering of each man. As man He compassionately takes into His own flesh and soul the intimate, intense experience of suffering that is known to the least of humans. Christ is the universal and the personal sufferer. Identified with Him as her head, the Church participates in this paradoxical and mysterious experience. She suffers in each of her members, dies in them, but continues in history as the universal sufferer, the extension until the end of the world of Christ crucified. No Marxist leader, no communist humanism can ever achieve this identity of suffering between the individual and the universal family of sufferers. Moreover, freely accepted, gladly submitted to, Christ's sufferings are a service to man and God. A man like His brethren in everything except sin, Christ alienated Himself from Himself, emptying Himself to become a slave. He then alienated Himself from His Father, consenting to become the target of divine vengeance against sin. He thus identified Himself with sinful man and died to save him from eternal death. Thus the mystery of iniquity, the mystery of alienation, is solved only in the mystery of Christ's infinite love—His divine-human love for His Father and His brethren. The dialectical history of divine-human love saves man, not the dialectical history of matter. "He who loves his life loses it; and he who hates his life in this world, keeps it unto life everlasting."[46] Here is the greatest genuine revolution! The revolution of love against sin! The revolution that topples the regime of Satan, breaks the chains of sin and returns man to God! Christ, the God-Man, is the passion of God for God; He is equally the passion of God for man. And He is the

45. 1 Cor. 15 : 54–55.
46. John 12: 25.

perfect human exemplar of what the passion of man for man should be. In His love all men are reconciled to God and to each other in the one truly perfect society, the Mystical Body of Christ.

How paltry, then, is the temporal glorification of man in socialist society! Compared to the temporal and eternal divinization of man in the Mystical Body of Christ it is a process of degradation! Marx glorifies men as "that most precious capital" in a classless humanity. Christ glorifies men as "sons of God" for whom he has prepared mansions in His Father's kingdom. Marx leaves the body of man as dust forever in the grave. Christ raises the bodies of His members to eternal companionship with Himself in glory at the right hand of the Father. Marx's revolution promised to establish a perfect, harmonious society in time; it has shattered the world in dissension and confusion. The Catholic Church, following her founder, seeks a reconciled society; she serves and cures the world. She is the only society that can effect permanent reconciliation between man and God and among men. Within this society all members become one with each other in their solidarity with Christ, the Head. All live the same doctrine, eat the same food, offer the same sacrifice of reconciliation, strive for the same heroic quality of service to God and man and are called to the same destiny—high sanctity through communion with each other in Christ. In this sense the Catholic Church is classless because all are made one in Christ.

The Catholic Church is seen, then, as the perfect human society for imperfect man. In her alone the apotheosis of men and mankind can be realized. Infinitely perfect in her head, the God-Man, she communicates the vigor of His life to all her members. And she does this through the ministrations of His Spirit, the Advocate of Love and Truth. It is in and by the Holy Spirit that Christians are changed from being timid, isolated men into becoming zealous apostles, with God-inspired passions for their fellowmen. We need but witness those frightened eleven locked in the upper room in Jerusalem before the coming of the roaring wind and the tongues of fire loosed them from their spiritual paralysis. The third Person of the Trinity, Absolute Love Personified, is the soul of the Catholic Church's life and mission of sanctity and mercy. Charity is the new fire that this Spirit has cast upon the earth. This charity has forged millions of martyrs, confessors and virgins who have heroically spent themselves for their fellow man. This charity continues to create millions of saints today on both sides of the iron and bamboo curtains. The Holy Spirit, Substantial Love Himself, creates the human society of divine love known as the communion of Saints. Communist humanism, on the contrary, has its own fire, the fire of militant hatred. With the sword of this fire it forges socialist society. Its proletarian torchbearers bring the world not truth and love, but propaganda, terror and war. Nothing, perhaps, conveys this spirit of fiery hatred more clearly than the opening words of the *Communist Manifesto:* "A spectre is haunting Europe—the spectre of Communism," write Marx and Engels. They conclude this famous document with a call to arms in a total war against society:

> The Communists disdain to conceal their views and aims. They openly declare that their ends can be attained only by the forcible overthrow of all existing social conditions. Let the ruling classes tremble at a Communist revolution. The proletarians have nothing to lose but their chains. They have a world to win.
> Working men of all countries, unite![47]

When we analyze the claims of the Catholic Church and communism on the meaning of history and their respective roles in it, we find, as we should now expect, diametrically opposed interpretations. Communist humanism claims it can scientifically prove that it alone gives history existence, direction and substantive meaning. History for communism is the self-manifestation of evolving matter in the process and development of socialist society. History is only the battlefield of economic forces in the affairs of men. Communism's historical law of evolutionary revolution focuses its main concern on the future. The present only matters if it changes everything so as to hasten the arrival of classless humanity. Dialectical materialism is the physical and thought power behind history's unfolding. Revolutionary violence is the catalyst speeding history to its chiliastic community. Unfortunately for the theory, there

---

47. Marx and Engels, *Manifesto of the Communist Party* (1848) translated by Samuel Moore, (Moscow: Foreign Languages Publishing House, n.d.).

is an irreducible contradiction in this dialectical process of history. If communist society is the final end in history, what further reason has the historical process for continuing in existence, as eternal, on-going and advancing when the final goal is attained? Does history cease when socialist society arrives? Is there no future then for man? Does the evolutionary, revolutionary nature of matter now change completely, becoming static and sterile? These contradictions in historical materialism have never been resolved.

The Catholic Church, for her part, has a consistent and ever advancing explanation of its life and role in the meaning of history. For her, sacred history is the whole of history; profane history is merely a subdivision of the universal history of cosmic salvation. The history of salvation embraces not only the history of mankind, but the whole of cosmic history. The creation of the world is act one in the history of salvation. It begins God's plan to perfect all creatures in His Incarnate Son. The central act of history is the Incarnation and mission of the Son of God to save man. The last act of history will be the second coming of Christ in power and glory to close the books on time, judge all men and create the new heavens and earth of eternity. The Church's concept of one, salvific, world history is based on Christ's revelation of the oneness of mankind, the uniqueness of the Incarnation and redemption and the sole destiny of creation, its glorification in Christ and God in eternity. All other events in history—some more directly, others more remotely— are related to the central act of the Incarnation.

In the beginning and up to the first coming of Christ in the fullness of time, God performed stupenduous works, *magnalia Dei,* so as to reveal to man the mightiness of His ways and wisdom. When Christ, the Summit of history, appeared, God performed in His Son miraculous works, *mirabilia Dei.* These are the last and supreme historical events. Christ is thus not the term of reference for a continuous line of events; He is the absolute summit and termination of history, in the sense that there can be nothing beyond Him. In Him the possibilities of human development are exhausted. And in founding His Church, Christ has identified it with Himself and His mission so that she too is the summit of history, His prolongation in time and into eternity. Finally, the last act of history can be considered as the Summit, Christ and His triumphant Church, being received into transcendent glory, a new, metacosmic creation, the deification of the communion of saints. It is all one drama. And the Catholic Church realizes in herself that mysterious paradox which Communism tried but failed to harmonize within itself. Although the time process continues in the life of the Church, and the last day or chronological end of the world is in the future, nevertheless, the ultimate, perfect reality and meaning of history is already present in the Person of the Incarnate Word and the society of His Church. There is not, because there cannot be, any greater human exaltation beyond Christ and His Church. In them we have a beginning fulfilled and yet, paradoxically, comprising all futurity.

The present is a period of "waiting for the sons of God to be made known." It is the "last times" during which is accomplished the gathering in and completion of the new creatures of whom Christ is the First-born. History has already fulfilled its full meaning and mission in Christ and His Church. It was God's loving design, centered in Christ and His Church, to give history this fulfillment by subsuming everything in them. The coming of the God-Man at the end of the world to judge mankind and the coming of the Messiah from the beginning to liberate man from sin and to inaugurate His new society, the Catholic Church, these two ends of history come together in the God-Man. Yet there is nothing deterministic about man's mission and destiny in these "last times." He is to work out his salvation "in fear and trembling." The Catholic historian is always face to face with the interplay of human will and the responsibility of man for his actions. Human beings decide and their decisions have tremendous influence in the formation of the flow of historical events. Christians are not meant to remain idle during this period of waiting. They have a challenging mission, dangerous and daring enough to exercise their powers of thought and love. St. Peter reminds Christians of this: "All so transitory; and what men you ought to be! How unworldly in your life, how reverent towards God, as you wait for and *hasten* the day of the Lord."[48]

So the Catholic Church and her members have a revolutionary work of their own to perform; under the guidance of the

48. 2 Peter 3 : 9.

Holy Spirit and urged on by His love, they are to catalyze the coming of the Lord on the last day. Theirs is a mission requiring courage, that readiness to win society over to Christ through self-sacrificing persuasion, whatever the hardships demanded. Theirs is a task that demands the exercise of a suffering zeal, that attitude of soul which habitually takes the side of man against falsehood and evil because it characteristically sides with the revelation of God in Christ. But, above all, theirs is a crusade of unshakable hope, the specific virtue of sacred history. For hope, founded on the revealed promises of God, looks patiently, faithfully, in the teeth of insurmountable odds towards the future, in a life of expectation endured in the time process, convinced that God will establish His kingdom in glory as the culmination of history. The object of hope is the final end of history, the full meaning of history—the salvation of the whole human race in the company of Jesus and his Church. And the hope of the Catholic Church is founded on an historical deed of her Founder, the universal Man who has risen from the dead by His own power and has gone ahead as God-Man into His eternal kingdom to prepare a place for His followers: "I ascend to my Father and your Father, to my God and your God."[49]

In this period of waiting for its future society of perfect man, Communism is by no means idle either. It works zealously at its own mission. And what is its task? The making of violent revolution to *hasten* the advent of socialist society. On what scientific or historical evidence is this utopia founded? On none. Marx's profession of the inevitable, golden, socialist future is the result of an irrational, blind act of faith. It is an *a priori* not an *a posteriori* doctrine, willed not proven, founded on no objective evidence nor on any incontrovertible authority. Indeed, current history has for some time now been proving that Marx and Engels were poor prophets, in error about what they predicted for man and society. For in the realm of economics, capitalism has reformed not gotten worse; though not perfect yet, it is not dying but flourishing. And in the realm of politics, socialism has been disintegrating and mankind is revolting against, not seeking, the security of its serfdom. How has communism reacted to these historical realities? In irrational rage and with unutterable violence. Unable to create, even in embryo form, its dream of a future society, communist humanism

49. John 20 : 17.

has set about sacrificing the perfection and happiness of its contemporary faithful to the future happiness of mankind. It inflicts unimaginable suffering, torturing and exterminating millions today for the sake of a messianic mirage in the dream of an impossible future. How can the unborn posterity of today's faithful become a perfect socialist society in the future through the torture and degradation of their ancestors? In the name of a future, hallucinatory humanity, supposed to be dwelling in an ever receding millenium of future happiness, communist humanism cheapens, insults and brutalizes current human life. It has been plowing under, during the last fifty years, real, living generations of imperfect men for the sake of highly abstract generations of possibly perfect men to be born someday from the uncertain womb of history. Eugene Lyons writes of this maniacal policy thus:

> By 1934, when I departed from Russia, nothing was left of the high mood of dedication, traces of which I had still found among the communists six years earlier. The very vocabulary of idealism had been outlawed. "Equality" was lampooned as bourgeois romanticism. Excessive concern for the needs and sensibilities of ordinary people was punished as "rotten liberalism." Terror was no longer explained away as a sad necessity. It was used starkly and glorified as "human engineering." Means had blotted out ends and have held this priority ever since.[50]

Quite the opposite of this savage society with its barbaric policies, the Catholic Church cares for, cures, sanctifies, liberates man today. Today she is already the perfect society. Today she divinizes man and his social institutions. To every man who joins her she gives the germ of divine life through her sacramental activity. Today her members are growing in this divine life which is destined to mature fulfillment in eternity. The Church sacrifices no generation to another. Each generation is precious to her for its own sake and because Christ redeemed it; each generation is loved for itself in God; each generation is taught, trained and guided in truth and sanctity. And each generation is given the sublime task of handing down to its children the divinely social life it received in love from its ancestors. There is nothing hallucinatory in the Catholic

---

50. *Workers' Paradise Lost,* p. 380.

Church and her sacramental life; she and her work are practical, founded on an historical Person; they are real with the plenary power of all dimensions of reality—the divine and the human. The history of the world for two thousand years and up to the present has been the era of the Church. The future belongs to her too, for she is the only human institution guaranteed immortality both in time and eternity.

As for communist humanism, it will never be the wave of future history. It has already been characterized as "a spent wave of the past." History will record its death and burial. And the Catholic Church will pray over its corpse. Death is its only future. At its fiftieth anniversary, it was hated by its own people and distrusted by the entire world. Its science, art, technology, politics, every phase of its inter-human relationships, have failed to gain credibility or legitimacy because all its activities subserve its power cliques and its false ideology. As its imperial colonialism expands, its people shrivel. Yet its swollen condition is already a sign that whatever vitality it originally had is now on the decline. Perceptive, longtime analysts of communism are indicating the symptoms of its disintegration. Doctrinal rigidity has produced *rigor mentis* in its theoreticians. Sclerosis of the mind has led to paralysis of policy. Excessively on the defensive, communist countries have ringed themselves with iron and bamboo curtains, massive walls, mined zones, electrified barbed-wire, Migged skies. All this to keep slaves from freedom and free men from investigating what is hidden behind those walls. Heresy and disillusionment are rampant among its students; national parties are fracturing and satellites are breaking out of the communist orbit, veering toward free, open courses. Civil war and anarchy have exploded in the Asian communist compound. Cynicism, creeping demoralization and stark fear grip its officialdom, which sits atop a volcano of a billion seething souls planning to erupt in raging vengeance when their hour has come, as come it must.

With its ideology a catastrophic failure, its leadership mediocre, its superstructure rotting and its masses defiant, how long can its naked military might hold this massive concentration camp together? For no man of civilized sensibilities would seriously consider communism's national and international states genuine societies. These "termite colonies" are even now sick unto death; their disease is terminal. It may take a long or short time, but the death of communism is inevitable. A day will come when the forces of decay and revolt within will coincide with the forces of assault and freedom from without; then communism will crumble, be wiped from reality, to be remembered only, like Nazism, Fascism and Japanese militarism, as a horrible nightmare that plagued the human race for over half a century. At present communism's death warrant is written in the soul of every man who loves God, his fellow man, freedom and his Church. The execution of communism will take place when God in his inscrutable wisdom reveals the proper time and brings together the proper forces. Moreover, because communism is so essentially and intensely anti-Christ, anti-Catholic, anti-Christian and anti-religious, the weapon that will be most efficacious in its execution is the fiery sword of Christ's truth and love as incarnated in His Church.

It should now be evident why the Catholic Church must formally and firmly resist communist atheism either unto its conversion or destruction. Every constitutive element of the Catholic Church is directly opposed by a constitutive element of communist humanism. If communism is true, the Church must be false; if communism is good, the Church must be evil; if communism is reality, the Church must be myth; if communism is history, the Church must be legend. And if Catholic dogmas are the truth, then the whole gamut of communist doctrines are falsifications. For communist humanism is a deliberate transposition of Christian revelations into secularized, pseudo-scientific doctrines. Indeed, Marx received from Hegel that philosopher's explicit transmutation of the body of Christian truths into a rationalistic system of natural truths. The one Catholic truth Marx and his followers failed to treat and transmute—the sacramental nature of the Church's being and activity—is the very one that Hegel failed to transpose, for as a Lutheran theologian, Hegel only knew a Protestant Christianity that had already lost the deep significance of the sacramental.

The Catholic Church resists communist humanism not only for her own survival, but for the survival of what is essentially human. She sees in the mental derangement and emotional frenzy of this militant, atheistic humanism the latest, most organized, most pernicious incarnation of antihuman, anti-God diabolism. And she has no alternative but to follow the warning of St. Peter, her first Pope, in matters of religious warfare: "Be sober, be watchful! For your adversary the devil, as a roaring lion, goes about seeking whom he may devour. Resist him, steadfast in the faith, knowing that the same suffering befalls your brethren all over the world."[51]

The Costs of Communist Barbarism

Our assessment of communist atheism must be far more than merely speculative. As we have already seen, communist humanism demands of its followers not merely faith but deeds in support of that faith. In this it is at one with the Catholic Church, which applies the criterion of its divine Master when determining its good members and, above all, its heroes of sanctity: "By their fruits you shall know them." Communist humanism, therefore, should certainly not take it amiss if we apply its own criterion to its performance in history for the past fifty years. What has communist humanism done *to* man, *for* man in the fifty years of its power? And we are speaking here not of abstract socialist man, the man of the future who does not exist, has never existed and can never exist. We want to know what communist humanism has done for real men, the men it saw, heard, touched in the cities and country places of the world. We want to know the stubborn facts of its historical conduct.

Let us first consider communist humanism's respect for human life. British journalist D. G. Stewart-Smith, in his study of this aspect of communism entitled *Defeat of Communism,* estimated that this militantly godless movement killed some eighty-three million persons from 1917 to 1964. Of these more than forty-five million were its own Russian citizens. Other sources, and there are hundreds of reliable ones, give varying figures. But no matter how the figures differ, they all record human slaughter in the millions and establish the irrefutable fact of communism's utter contempt for human life in its maniacal pursuit of its abstract goal. Eugene Lyons relates that at Yalta, when Winston Churchill expressed sympathy for the

51. 1 Peter 5 : 8–10.

enormous number of Russians killed in the war, Stalin passed this horrible holocaust off with a shrug of his shoulders, revealing that his collectivization of the farms program against a rebellious peasantry exacted far more lives than the war.[52] When one realizes that the Second World War cost Russia from fifteen to twenty million lives, one is left aghast at the numbers of its own citizens liquidated by communism through its purges, executions, deliberately imposed famines, liquidations of kulaks and the high mortality rates fostered by inhuman conditions in concentration camps.

And how does communist humanism treat the living? Through its techniques of degradation, it impoverishes men and grinds them down to indescribable perversions. It keeps man bound to a time-terrestrial leash like a chained animal. It places a premium on lying and treachery, shatters families by sudden arrests; it systematically persecutes all religious faiths and practices, bans sacred books, burns holy objects and herds Christians, Moslems and Jews into prison camps solely for religious reasons. It robs every man of his God, honor, a transcendental vision, a life of creative freedom. Terrorism is its normal interpersonal policy. Dr. Mihajlo Mihajlov is presently in prison because he revealed in his book, *Moscow Summer,* that "millions of Soviet citizens languish in death and forced labor camps." Moreover, he was the first to reveal publicly that the original death camps were not founded by the Nazis, but by the communists, in 1921 near Arklangelsk, where the Kolgomor camp was established with the sole end in view of physically obliterating its inmates. In the years of the great Stalin purges in Russia, 1936–1938, "over three million people disappeared from the earth's surface in the Soviet Union," according to the late Moshe Pijade. The slaughter of tens of millions of men, women and children shocks one's conceptual and imaginative powers, but when one reads of hatred sown among members of the same family, the execrable sadism of communism leaves the whole person numb with horror. Eugene Lyons records this unnatural practice of spiritual cannibalism:

> Other regimes may have induced young children to spy on their parents—it remained for the Soviets to erect a monument to Pavlik Morozov, a little monster who informed on

52. Eugene Lyons, *Workers' Paradise Lost*, p. 355.

his father and mother and got them executed. The Pavlik episode occured in the 1930's in a village in the Sverdlovsk area. Peasant neighbors were so infuriated by this action that they killed the boy, thus creating a martyr memorialized in metal in that village and held up as a model for all good little communists.[53]

What is communist humanism's attitude toward freedom of inquiry and expression? We have already seen that the profession of communist humanism imposes as a practical necessity the duty to destroy free societies and their free activities. Having walled in their own serfs against the flow of reports, researches and critical evaluations from free world print, radio, cinema and travel, the communist overlords exercise absolute control over schools, news media and intellectual and social associations of any kind. Their censorship is absolute; they feed their own people and the outside world only authorized truths, doctored facts, sovietized history. Even communist professors are not free to research and publish in their particular specialities immune from censorship. The teaching profession is always in mental servitude to party demands. Scholarly criteria are tailored to the needs of ideology and current policies. Textbooks from kindergarten on are slanted to conform with Marxist-Leninist doctrine and the prevailing policy thrust. Communist history is the most creative history extant, surpassing in imagination even many historical novels. André Gide, after a journey through Russia which cured him of early rosy illusions about communism, reported: "I doubt that in any country of the world, even Hitler's Germany, is thought less free, more bowed down, more terrorized."[54]

Concurrent with severe censorship at home is communism's intense indoctrination abroad. This intellectual infiltration takes place especially in the universities of the free world. Communist professors and speakers fill classrooms and lecture halls, systematically indoctrinating millions of eager minds to conform to communist doctrines. Abusing the blessings of academic freedom, these dedicated, trained professors deftly seduce young minds to pseudo-truth and inflame noble emotions to pseudo-ideals, thereby prostituting the learning pro-

53. *Ibid.,* p. 376.
54. Quoted by Eugene Lyons, *Workers' Paradise Lost,* p. 365.

cess. Warning universities of this systematic indoctrination and its treacherous techniques, Fr. Costanzo, S.J. offers a wise critique of this matter and suggests an enlightened policy on how to thwart it:

> The members of the Academy have duties toward the society of which it is itself a beneficiary. I am motivated by a deep conviction that academic freedom should not be entrusted to those who would work for its destruction by subverting the free society within which a free academy may exist and flourish and which they deny wherever they are in dominant control. No one may reasonably claim the right to work for the denial of these rights to others. We are not obliged to tolerate, in the Academy or out of it, those who would not tolerate us if they had the power; nor are we obliged to tolerate those who would subvert the civil order under the cloak of freedom of study and teaching. Academic freedom, like the Bill of Rights, is not a suicide pact.
> . . . A Communist teacher exploits the privileges of academic freedom because by training, purpose and dedication he intends not to teach but to twist and torture the truth. He is neither reliable nor trustworthy.[55]

Conclusion

Communist humanism does not liberate man; it delivers man into his own hands to do with himself what he will; this is slavery. For, once man rejects God, he has no place to go but back into himself and there lies the agony of isolation. Thus, the revolt against God is the prelude to all serfdom. For the essence of man's freedom is that he be able to transcend himself, the material things of earth and choose to live in companionship with God. Indeed, it was in order that man might enjoy freedom that God, Absolute Liberty Himself, made man in His own image and likeness. He made him a little less than the angels. But communist humanism, in delivering man into his own hands, really renders man captive to the material world below man. Communist humanism, by ripping man down from God, the source of all freedom, makes man less than man.

55. Rev. Joseph F. Costanzo, S.J., *The Academy and The City,* pamphlet printed by Cork University Press, Dublin, 1961, pp. 12, 13.

There is a law of creation which is unchangeable and is tragically enforced in the lives of men. It can be expressed thus: Cosmic captivity constricts a creature more rigidly the further it recedes from God in essence and activity. When the freest of creatures, the angels, fled from God in revolt, they became constricted in their own hatred, spirits hardened in chosen evil. They became also inmates of the prison of hell, subjected to the tyranny of the angel who led their revolt. Similarly, when free men reject God, they become walled-in by their own hatred, hardened in chosen evil. Moreover, they become slaves in the prison of the very cosmos which drew them away from God. Wherever it has dominated, communist humanism has erected walls that have isolated human spirits as well as human bodies. Behind its visible, iron curtain is also drawn around every human soul the infinitely more desolate curtain of spiritual isolation. Many have committed suicide through the madness induced by the torture of spiritual incarceration. Those who have survived to tell of their agonies, unanimously relate that the presence of God, whose Spirit breathes where He will and cannot be bound, sustained them through the communion of His loving companionship.

For without God, human freedom, dignity and the infinite value of the human spirit are severed from their principle of truth. And without God there is no longer any infinite Defender of these human values who can obligate man, under sanction of reward or punishment, to reverence the divine likeness in his fellowman. Man is free when he clings to God. In the words of the God-Man, "The truth shall make you free."[56] But to cling to God—*adhaerere Deo*—is to cling to Absolute Truth and to enjoy inner freedom. A Daniel in the lions' den or the three youths in the fiery furnace are free because God is with them. Communism, on the other hand, teaches man to cling to matter —*adhaerere materiae*—to cling to creatures in preference to God. But for man to subject himself to matter is the equivalent of his choosing to sink below himself, to become captive to the cosmos and its iron laws of determinism. Freedom is rooted in the spiritual, in the divine; servitude is rooted in the material, in the creaturely. Communism immerses man in matter, in the creaturely, in man himself. And there is no greater tyrant over

56. John 8 : 33.

man than man himself. For when man becomes his own God, as in communist humanism he inevitably does, this self-idolatry becomes so arrogantly irrational that it demands the life of every human being as its victim. It is in communist humanism that the metaphysically irrational extremes of Feuerbach and Hobbes meet and, paradoxically, complete each other. When Feuerbach's dictum, "Man is man's only God"—*Homo homini Deus*—is professed and practiced, then Hobbes's dictum, "Man is a wolf to his fellowman"—*Homo homini lupus*—eventually becomes the jungle law and practice of an organized Godless society.

Our conclusion is inevitable. There are psychic as well as physical cancers. Communist humanism is a psychic malignancy. It rots every cell of society; it produces predatory man; it organizes predatory parties and invades, contaminates, ulcerates all organs of society. Its metastatic zeal is messianic and, unless checked by divine remedies, will extinguish human life and speed to completion the social, spiritual disintegration it has initiated. As a secularized perversion of the genuine messianic community—the true Church and people of God—the power of communism will have to be destroyed essentially by the power of God. But man, who cannot live without God, will have to return to God and rededicate himself to the Will of God. For as Dostoevsky has said: "If God is nothing, everything is permitted; if God is nothing, everything is a matter of indifference."[57] Thus man will only liberate himself from the slavery of communist humanism by living in communion with God. For God, who created man without his consent, will not save him without his cooperation, not even from that ultimate spiritual evil, the cancer of communism.

57. Feodor Dostoyevsky, *The Devils* (*The Possessed*), transl. by David Magarshark (Harmondsworth, Middlesex: Penguin Books, 1953), p. 126.

CHAPTER V

Comte: Social Humanity as God

AGAINST A BACKGROUND OF BURGEONING DISORDER in the chaotic aftermath of the French Revolution, in an atmosphere of flagrantly avowed and triumphally marching atheism, Auguste Comte, the great Social Synthesist, thrived and created his vast *Cours de philosophie positive.* He is a typically French thinker whose ideas do not rise directly from Kantian or Hegelian roots, though his ideals have much in common with his German contemporaries. In the same year (1842) that Feuerbach published *The Essence Of Christianity,* Comte published his massive classic. Both authors presented man with a new idol. Commenting on both works, Emile Saisset noted: "Herr Feuerbach in Berlin, like Monsieur Comte in Paris, offers Christian Europe a new god to worship—the human race."

Disturbed and depressed as he observed the futile agony of France, of Europe struggling to recover from the cataclysm of the Revolution, the Red Terror, the fall of the Bonaparte Empire, Comte felt called to the mission to replace disorder with order, to bring about the total reconstruction of society. He gradually became convinced that the greatest hindrance to the ordered advancement of society from its material and cultural poverty was the unchecked fermentation of the revolutionary spirit. Revolution had already crushed the Ancien Régime, dissolved the power and coherency of the Church, rendered existing institutions morally and economically ineffective, disoriented the thoughts and beliefs of men and sent society wandering off in all directions, its actions ungoverned and misdirected. A new society had to be created over the ruins of the medieval hierarchy that was once the Church and State. A new faith had to replace the decadent belief of tired Christianity; new feelings, new loyalties, new moral purposes, a new order of thought and action had to recall scattered society from its drift in order to reconstruct it along lines that would assure its progress in the new, advancing complex age of industrialization.

But Comte realized that his social reconstruction demanded a reliable foundation in knowledge. The new society, the new humanity would have to rest on man himself, on his responsible assumption of power to govern himself according to positive principles. God, metaphysics, transcendent destinies, traditional beliefs, religious rituals and feelings had all failed man; they had led him to the precipice and cast him into the abyss of chaos. There could be no returning to smashed idols. Man's destiny, henceforth, was in his own hands not God's; his society was to be his own creation not the Church's; his religion was to be his worship of himself. Thus would man finally achieve mental, social and theological coherence and cohesion. In his final days Comte prided himself on having actually realized this encyclopaedic blueprint, this triple synthesis that provided man with a way of life capable of solving all his problems and fulfilling all his highest aspirations. But before scrutinizing the Comtian synthesis, a brief view of the man and his manners is in order so as to place his work and character in proper perspective.

Auguste Comte was born on January 19, 1798, in the year VI of the French Republic, son of ardent Catholic parents who were deeply distressed that the child was not permitted to be baptized. For all churches had been closed and baptism of children was forbidden, indeed punished by law, since 1793. At the age of nine he entered the lycée at Montpellier, where he was born and grew up. He was a brilliant student with a phenomenal memory, retaining and able to recite back flawlessly whole poems and pages read but once. A child prodigy outstanding in mathematics, he was at fifteen ready to attend the École Polytechnique, the highest institution of technical learning in France. But because of his youth he was required to work another year on higher mathematics at the lycée. Now his extra year at the lycée proved a blessing for he came under the tutelage of a remarkable professor, Daniel Encontre, theologist, philosopher-mathematician and dramatist who kindled in Comte an enthusiasm for exact sciences and broad culture.

Though a prodigy, Comte was also a problem child. Product of the revolution, he was in revolt against all authority, against all conformity. He drew special delight from destructive activities. At fourteen he claimed he was already an atheist. "I don't believe in God," he would repeat incessantly. And it appeared that in Comte's case this revolt against God was not mere boyish bravado. Even at this early age he was expelled from the École Polytechnique for being the ringleader of a group who arrogantly refused to observe school regulations. After a year spent in the rigid, royalist regime of his family, Comte traveled to Paris and in 1817 found a position there as Secretary to the famous Saint-Simon. Comte was then only nineteen years old.

Six years under the brilliant Saint-Simon matured the genius of Comte. He drank in many of the ideas and aspirations of Saint-Simon's astonishingly fertile mind. Saint-Simon was the continuer and developer of theories set out by the Voltairean Condorcet, the Italian philosopher Vico and the English savant Francis Bacon. Condorcet had already called for a science of society based on a study of history; in Vico could be found "the law of the three stages." In his major work, *Industry,* Saint-Simon developed his ideas of the industrial society of the future and called for replacing theological morality with positive industrial morality. At his death in 1825 Saint-Simon had just about completed what he hoped would be his greatest work, *New Christianity.* In this he called for the establishment of the future society that would be founded not only on industrial organization for technical progress, but also on belief in a Su-

preme Power and in the brotherhood of man. This conversion
of his master from promoter of materialistic man in a humanistic heaven to apostle of religious man in a Christian millenium was too much for Comte. As a fervent intellectual
atheist, he could no longer remain with Saint-Simon in the
position of secretary and collaborator. He broke with his master and struck out on his own. But the seal of his master was
forever branded onto his soul, for Comte left deeply cultured
with Saint-Simonian motifs. The seeds of Positivism planted by
Saint-Simon were to produce a plentiful harvest. At first resentful and indignant over his master's relapse into spiritual and
moral emotionalism, Comte refused to admit any influence on
his own work from that fallen intellectual power. In a moment
of graciousness, however, even the egotistical Comte relented
and confessed his debt to his master. In a letter to a friend,
quoted by Durkheim, he said: "I certainly owe a great deal
intellectually to Saint-Simon, that is to say, he contributed pow-
erfully to launching me in the philosophic direction that I have
clearly created for myself today and that I will follow without
hesitation all my life." And to the same friend he wrote in 1818:
"I have learned through this relationship of work and friendship with one of the men who sees furthest in philosophic politics. I have learned a mass of things I vainly would have sought
in books, and my mind has made more headway these six
months of our connection than it would in three years, had I
been alone."[1]

When master Saint-Simon died in 1825, the mantle of this
ingenious visionary of new ideas fell upon Comte, the disciple,
methodical thinker and builder of new systems. Comte was
only twenty-seven when he developed "the law of the three
states." With his work, *Fundamental Principles of the Positive
Philosophy,* he set out on a vast adventure which, in its three-
fold thrust and campaign into theology, philosophy and physics, aimed at the immediate, orderly reorganization of the
World and Humanity.

Perhaps the most profitable method for comprehending Comte's atheistic positivism is to compare it with Kant's critical
philosophy. Both Comte and Kant are convinced of the sterility

1. David Shillan, *The Order of Mankind as Seen by Auguste Comte* (Norfolk
Lodge, Richmond Hill, Surrey: New Atlantis Foundation), p. 4.

of speculative theology and metaphysics. Kant does, however, admit some slight meaning and usefulness to discussions about noumena, things-in-themselves which exist beyond the grasp of science. He does not reduce all rational activity merely to the procedures of empirical sciences. He admits that some mental activity transcends scientific endeavor. But, in the last analysis, reason, despite its metaphysical labors, never achieves valid knowledge of God, ethics or religion. For his part, Comte rejects metaphysics and theology as sources of natural or superior knowledge. Since anything they propose as true cannot be verified by scientific methods, they contribute fictions, not facts, to human learning. True, these fictional viewpoints are useful and even necessary as evolutionary and historical *moments* on the ladder of humanity's climb from its depth of superstition to its summit of positive wisdom. Kant's attitude toward metaphysical and theological disciplines is *critical,* ending in his rejection of them as sources of true knowledge. Comte's attitude toward science is uncritical but *positive.* Since, for Comte, scientific methods alone capture and reflect accurately the real world, science alone gives real knowledge. Thus, in the end, both Kant and Comte equally despair of the mind's ability to attain the transcendent. Kant, by his idealism, has sealed himself off from full reality in the prison of his own mind. Comte, by his positivism, has immersed himself totally in the prison of his senses, refusing even to admit the possibility of transcendent being.

Comte's positivism also bears a strong resemblance to Hegel's historicism. Both aspire to formulate a comprehensive view of reality through an all-inclusive, omni-competent system. Both systems are dynamic with the power of historical, evolutionary development. Comte's famous "law of the three stages" of human evolution, revealed in unfolding history in relationship to every science, has an Hegelian flavor of inevitability and indispensability. Both Comte and Hegel subtly use their respective systems as instruments for the demolition of philosophies of life which have preceded their own, especially for the destruction of the Christian metaphysical and theological viewpoint. The technique is to claim that the time for the Christian ideal is past. Christianity has served its propaedeutic role in the historical unfolding of humanity's ascent to a superior scientific, political, social and cultural synthesis. For Hegel that superior synthesis and reality will be cosmic Reason's fully achieved self-consciousness; for Comte that superior synthesis will be fully rational human society perfected by positive philosophy.

Moreover, the basic affinity of Comte's atheistic adventure to those of Marx and Nietzsche, despite their obvious differences, is perceptively reported by Henri de Lubac:

> To anyone observing the great spiritual currents of our age from a certain altitude, positivism will seem less the antagonist than the ally of the Marxist and Nietzschean currents. By other methods, in another spirit and in competition with them, it strives for the same essential object. Like them, it is one of the ways in which modern man seeks to escape from any kind of transcendency and to shake off the thing it regards as an unbearable yoke—namely, faith in God. "To discover a man with no trace of God in him" is how M. Henri Gouhier defines Auguste Comte's self-appointed task.[2]

The Venture of Human Progress

Comte founded his atheism on the discovery of a fundamental law to which the human intelligence is necessarily subjected. A study of the development of human intelligence throughout history, Comte claimed, revealed that the human mind, in every branch of its knowledge, necessarily ascended through three successive theoretical conditions: the Theological or fictitious, the Metaphysical or abstract, and the Scientific or positive. To be more specific, it is the dynamic nature of human intelligence to employ in its progress three methods of philosophizing whose dispositions are radically different and essentially opposed, namely, the theological, metaphysical and positive methods. The result is that man has produced mutually exclusive philosophies and systems in his attempt to interpret cosmic, human history with scientific, rational consistency. According to Comte, the theologically fictitious stage of human knowledge is a necessary point of departure, representing man-

2. *The Drama of Atheist Humanism,* p. 78.

kind's mental infancy. The metaphysically abstract stage is merely transitional, representing mankind's mental adolescence. But the scientifically positive stage is fixed and definitive. It represents mankind's fully mature achievement of a perfectly rational society. We shall now examine important aspects of Comte's system.

From Fetishism to Atheism

The first stage of man's intellectual development can be designated as the theological enterprise. According to Comte, "Each of us is aware, if he looks back upon his own history that he was a *theologian* in his childhood, a *metaphysician* in his youth, and a *physicist* in his manhood."[3] Man begins his thinking by conceiving phenomena of all kinds as products of the direct, continuous action of supernatural beings. In his mental hunger to grasp the nature of beings, of first and final causes, of all reality, man conceives entities largely in terms of analogies with his own being and activities. Consequently he ascribes to purely natural phenomena feelings, thoughts and volitions that are characteristic of his own responses to reality. In this primitive stage his thoughts tend to be animistic and anthropomorphic. Man sees everything under the categories of plan, purpose, order, will, thereby seeking the explanation of the existence and activity of everything in terms of an indwelling and guiding spirit. The first question bothering man as theological quester is "Who is the cause of this vast universe of diverse beings?" And the second follows immediately, "Why?" The question "How did it all come about?" is scarcely important until the first two queries are answered satisfactorily. Identification and justification are so much more important to the theological mind than explanation. Thus, according to Comte, from the theological standpoint the universe is conceived as a spiritual order of myths. Its animating purposes are in things as effective agencies, causing them to behave as they do. Thus each phenomenon is really personified and every process is an action guided by a supernatural cause. Within this "fictitious stage," there are three developments that comprise the whole

3. Auguste Comte, *Cours de Philosophie Positive,* Société Positiviste, 5 editions, (Paris: 1892–1894), Vol. I, p. 4.

history of religion—fetishism, polytheism and monotheism.

In Comte's ingenious theory, "man everywhere began with the crassest fetishism." In his fetishistic belief and worship man revered physical objects as though they were alive, had feelings, expressed purposes of their own and exercised magical powers for the rise or fall of his fortunes. But eventually his irrational devotion to these magical powers failed to satisfy man's intellectual hunger or solve his social problems. Moreover, the sorcerers who petitioned these supernatural beings on behalf of the faithful, far from becoming their guides to spiritual order, became agents of spiritual oppression by using their spiritual activities to gain power over the people and their affairs. Thus, in his effort to attain liberation from the slavery and darkness of fetishism, man proceeded to the belief and practice of polytheism. Polytheism is an ascent from the torpor of fetishism. Within the polytheistic milieu there takes place the gradual simplification of pluralistic animism. At this stage invisible, semivisible "gods" replace fetishes. These gods, who are quite similar to human persons, are held responsible for the whole history of phenomena in man's daily living.

But even the gods failed to be satisfactory guides to meaningful order for mankind. Blighted as they were with human passions and pettiness, they were quite frequently agents of cataclysmic tragedy for man. They had mankind going round and round forever in a radically vicious and monotonously hopeless circle. There was a desperate urge to break out of this prison of fate and to run forward with intellectual freedom. Thus man did escape to the monotheistic plateau in his theological enterprise. In the succession of his different phases of development, monotheism is intermediate between the theological and the metaphysical state. Monotheism consolidates all the gods into a unified godhead. Spiritual powers are concentrated into the hands of the One God who is conceived of as creating the whole universe, imparting to it its own powers, activities, purposes, yet, nevertheless, as governing his universe simultaneously by himself and through cooperation with his lesser agencies, seeing to it that his final goal is inevitably attained whether free creatures promote or oppose his plans. But monotheism contributes to man's development no new principle for advancement. Being nothing more than reduced, concentrated polytheism, it preserves the fantastic elements of backward theology. The One God is essentially the same stuff as the many gods; he functions to solve the same problem; the Providence is really fate, gradually and cleverly transformed.

The second state of man's advancement to mental maturity is known as the metaphysical transition. Why transition? Comte's explanation is again masterly. Although the theological phase of man's evolution was an indispensable first step forward, it was nevertheless, also purely temporary, preparatory for further development toward the stage of positive science. Yet theology and physics are so diametrically opposed that they need a mediator to construct a bridge between them. That bridge-builder is metaphysics.

> Theology and physical science are so utterly incompatible, their conceptions are so radically opposed that before renouncing the ones and using exclusively the others, man's intelligence had to have recourse to intermediary conceptions of an amphibious nature; the very intermediate character of these ideas was calculated to bring about the transition in a gradual way. All this indicates the natural destiny of metaphysical conceptions.[4]

Man's penchant for thinking animistically now begins to disappear. As he grows in reflective dexterity, a metamorphosis takes place in his mental and spiritual outlooks. He begins to produce abstract ideas from linking phenomenal facts in greater and greater complexity. Thus the primitive theologian gradually develops into the subtle metaphysician. Now the metaphysician rejects the view that nature is the divine creation of a providential God. Man's conceptions begin to move away from theology towards physics through the medium of "etherealized" universals. The supernatural influence of God, gods and spirits is replaced by mysterious essences, causes and substances. True, these bloodless concepts are related to both theology and physics, but they are leaving the realm of fiction for the realm of reality; they are on the threshold of science. Indeed, the characteristic thrust of the metaphysician, as opposed to the theologian, is not so much to vivify and personify

4. *Ibid.,* Vol. I, pp. 7–8.

wind or sea or lightning as to "reify" essences, causes, potencies. The metaphysician replaces invisible divinities with the invisible *logos.* Yet his so-called proofs remain products of immagination, not of science. Though at bottom remaining a "shade of bastard theology," devitalized, inconsistent, ambiguous, yet metaphysics fostered the coming of man's scientific maturity at least in the negative work of dissolving the concepts of the theological stage. Nevertheless, because of its ambiguity, because of its secret fascination for its lost God and its pining for the fleshpots of theology, metaphysics may be "the most dangerous obstacle to the final establishment of a true philosophy." The western world has been too long addicted to its boastful spirit of always proving everything. It will have to throw off this chronic malady of its transitional youth and pass directly into the health and peace of the positive state.

The third stage of man's mental evolution towards progress and unitive maturity is known as the state of the scientific synthesis. Just as the theologian had to disappear that the metaphysician could arrive, so also the metaphysician must die that the physicist might be born. In this stage of positive science, the scientist will gradually, but inevitably, take possession of all the territory successively lost by theologians and metaphysicians. In this phase of his adulthood, man no longer searches for transcendent or immanent causes. He simply desires to discover the empirically verifiable laws that govern and explain the phenomena of nature. Physical nature, of course, replaces a personal God or an abstract First Cause, as the source of order in the whole universe. The mind now investigates and concludes solely through the criterion of *experience.* The metaphysical mode of thought began to cede ascendency to the positive philosophy when the metaphysicians themselves divided into rival camps over the existential status of universal concepts. Realists opposed nominalists in this controversy. Once they had introduced skepticism over the reality of universals, the metaphysicians effectively undermined faith in the reality of any transcendent beings whatsoever.

But positive philosophy bypasses such metaphysical controversies as so much sterile logic-chopping, for it maintains that logical analysis alone is incapable of settling the question of existence. The positive scientist sees all events as parts of a constant order of phenomena. Each being and event is the invariable product of some antecedent condition or combination of conditions. The mind now applies itself to the study of the laws of phenomena and their variable relations of succession and coordination. The sole means to valid knowledge now becomes the findings of experience. This knowledge will be gathered and collated through observational reports, the accumulation of particular data and the formulation of general hypotheses and theories which realistically and reasonably connect these facts with other facts to form systematic, scientific disciplines of learning. Such natural, scientific knowledge of the world establishes propositions about the regular connections among phenomena. Such propositions can be proven only by testing. Thus all human knowledge is knowledge of the world as men experience it. But since the world and man are in evolution, all human knowledge is limited, never final, never absolute. Thus the major tendency of the positive mind is to substitute the relative for the absolute in all cases. The positive mind knows no essences of things nor even their modes of production. Everything that develops spontaneously is necessarily legitimate for a certain time; there are no eternal truths or principles of human conduct. All man can know is the relations between facts in the mode of succession or similitude. We know that relations existing under the same circumstances are constant. This constancy of interlinking resemblances and consequences among phenomena constitutes the laws of the universe and of society. The essential causes—originative, final, efficient—are unknown and inscrutable.

The tragedy of mankind's development up to Comte's time was that positive philosophy had not yet succeeded in effectively killing off the parasite of metaphysics. Though positivity had, through its secret action from the very beginning, destroyed the theological addictions of the human mind, yet it had failed to lay claim to all realms of phenomena; its universal rule had not yet been accomplished. There remained large areas in human affairs, especially in man's social activities, to which the positive philosophy had not yet applied its empirical method. And Comte knew precisely what was needed most and that he was the man of genius destined to bring about the maturation of evolving society by the discovery and application of what he called "social physics."

> Everything, then, can be reduced to a simple question of fact: Does positive philosophy, which in the last two centuries has gradually undergone so great a development, encompass today all realms of phenomena? It is evident that this is not the case; consequently, a great deal of scientific work remains to be done in order to give positive philosophy the character of universality that is necessary for its definitive constitution . . . There remains one science to complete the system of sciences of observation—*social physics.*[5]

Comte claimed that his "social physics" (he later coined the term "sociology") had introduced the last stage of development in the physical domain of man's progress. This positive science was to make a study of the moral phenomena existing in all human societies. With the appearance of Auguste Comte on the stage of history the hour of the positive age has finally struck. From the beginning of mankind's quest for maturity, the movements of theology and metaphysics propelled man, however haltingly and subconsciously, out of his primitive anarchy toward social fulfillment in science. Along this arduous, historical ascent anyone who had made a real contribution to science was a forerunner and foreknower of positive wisdom. In more modern times, however, men of great genius had accelerated the advent of the positive millenium. Comte regarded Bacon, Descartes and Galileo as prophets, indeed, founders—cofounders with himself, of course—of the excellent method of positivism. Since their time and henceforth, only the positive mind will develop valid knowledge because it alone is gifted with the power of logical coherence. Nor is there any fear that positive philosophy's character will undergo any substantive changes. It will develop merely by accretion, for it will advance by applying itself to all phases of social life, thereby creating and disciplining new social sciences. Once it has acquired the character of universality, positive philosophy will forever exclude and replace what was once the superiority of theology and metaphysics. Future generations will examine the two discarded

5. Comte, *op. cit.,* Vol. I, pp. 12–13.

methods as interesting relics of on-going history. Theology must wane and disappear as physics waxes and advances. Once in power and unopposed, positive philosophy will not so much deny and reject God as dismiss and forget Him. For the positive mind has already empirically observed that the theologico-metaphysical problem of God is "devoid of meaning," since it is one of those "undiscussable hypotheses" of such "profound inanity" that they "do not lend themselves to denial any more than to affirmation." Thus positive philosophy is unaware of the existence of a real, personal God. It is aware that such a myth can exist only in the imaginations of men. But having passed far beyond that infantile state of man, positive progress views the God-idea as the key idea in a cultural system that has long ago been swept into oblivion by the winds of evolutionary history.

From Atheism to Anti-theism

In his first letter to Comte, dated November 8, 1841, John Stuart Mill, British empiricist, remarked that, despite the openly anti-religious spirit of Comte's work, that work was having great influence among the different classes of savants in England. In his reply to Comte's first letter to him, dated December 18, 1841, Mill explained why he, unlike Comte, had to hide his own atheism, carefully keeping it out of his philosophical works:

> Doubtless you are not unaware of the fact that here in England the writer who would openly profess anti-religious, nay more, anti-Christian, opinions would compromise not only his social position, which I believe I could sacrifice for a sufficiently noble cause, but also and more seriously, his chances of being read. Already I am risking much by carefully putting aside, from the very outset of my work, any religious viewpoint, abstaining from declamatory praises of providential wisdom, usually employed by the philosophers of my country, even by the unbelievers. I rarely make allusions to this order of ideas, endeavoring, above all, not to arouse in the ordinary reader any religious antipathies. I believe I have written in such a manner that no thinker, Christian or unbeliever, can be mistaken about the genuine character of my opin-

ions. I rely somewhat, I admit it, on a worldly prudence which here in England prevents religious writers in general from proclaiming unnecessarily the irreligion of the scientific spirit of any value.[6]

Comte informed John Stuart Mill in a letter on July 14, 1845, that he also did not take kindly to being called an atheist. But the reasons for his displeasure at this appellation were not of a prudential nature. Survival in a certain social status or fear of being banned from a large readership were scarcely hazards for the bold atheist writer in nineteenth-century, laicized France. Comte objected that the name atheist "does not apply to people like us in any but the strictly etymological sense." True enough, we scholars of science do not believe in God, but we have no common cause with the metaphysicians who profess atheism. They dally with theism by constantly seeking the origin of the world, of man, of the absolute moral law, nostalgically seeking forever their lost God. They would return to the womb of theism. Thus the position of atheism is too puerile for minds of our positive, scientific stamp. Atheism should never harden into mere, sterile negativism. Like theism, it too should be only a temporary experience, a transitional stage toward progressive, systematic positivism. Nor did Comte reject the name of atheist because he wanted to remain an agnostic, as some scholars have claimed. For him it was never a question of being unable to say Yes or No to the existence of God. His writings leave no doubt about his decisions and thoughts about the validity of God and supernatural religion. Just as he despised mere negative atheism, so too he abhorred the paralysis of agnosticism.

Comte was not, therefore, an ordinary atheist. He planned to go beyond atheism through a positive program. His historical, positivistic dialectic was aimed at delivering the *coup de grâce* to a dying theologism. By marshaling a concatenation of empirical sciences against theology, Comte was assured that his mission to obliterate these myths would be eminently successful. So thorough is Comte's campaign to eliminate God as an illusion of man's arrested youth, so zealous and successful is

6. *Collected Works Of John Stuart Mill;* Vol. XIII, The *Earlier Letters Of John Stuart Mill,* Edited by Francis E. Mineka, (University of Toronto Press: Routledge & Kegan Paul, 1963), pp. 491–492.

that campaign, that Comte must be compared not to pale atheists but to those famous, antitheistic God-killers—Feuerbach, Marx, Nietzsche and Heidegger. When his great synthesis is completed, there will simply be no room for belief in God. Ancient dogmas will have lost all their meaning; they will consequently be forsaken as discredited, irrelevant myths, hopelessly out of touch with the modern, advanced situation of society. Thus, for Comte, mere atheism was too timid a stance against God. It remained vulnerable to theistic counter-attacks; it was a partial, an inadequate emancipation from the tyranny of God. Since atheism is always rooted in the metaphysical mode of thinking, it posed the threat of the return of an avenging God. For atheism is constantly reopening inquiries into theoretical problems. The trouble with the eighteenth-century atheists is that they argued their way merely to a denial of God; they established no positive program to keep God banished from human society. Comte himself would provide that positive program, the system of empirical and social sciences. Comte's system would provide the completely adequate emancipation from God that man's maturity demanded. He posed his problem and indicated his solution in these words:

> Although I have long denied any solidarity, whether dogmatic or historical, between true positivism and what is called atheism, I must, at this juncture, add a brief but pointed explanation in regard to this mistaken notion.
> Even in its intellectual aspect *atheism represents no more than an inadequate emancipation* since it tends to prolong the metaphysical state indefinitely by continually seeking new solutions of theoretical problems, instead of ruling out all accessible researches as inherently fruitless. The true positive spirit consists above all in perpetually substituting the study of the invariable laws of phenomena for the study of their causes properly so called, whether first or final, or, to put it briefly, it seeks to ascertain *how* rather than *why*. It is therefore incompatible with the vainglorious musings of a vague atheism about the formation of the universe, the origin of animals, etc. So long as we persist in solving the questions proper to our childhood, we are in a very bad position for rejecting the naive method which our imagination brings to bear on them and which is, indeed, the only one suited to their nature. Thus confirmed atheists can be regarded as the

most inconsistent of theologians, since they occupy themselves with the same questions but reject the only suitable
approach to them.[7]

Thus, even though atheism represents a natural, progressive
evolution in human thinking, Comte, prophet of the great Western revolution, refuses to remain in this rut of negativism. His
positive program for the reconstruction of society calls for the
liquidation of "reactionary beliefs and anarchic dogmas," a
preliminary necessity for human regeneration. In a spirit of
utter detestation, Comte let loose a stream of sarcastic ridicule
against "theological figments" and the reign of an effete God.
His plan was to bring about the dethronement of this decrepit
God who ruled despotically over "the long minority of mankind" through the instrumentality of organized religions, particularly Catholicism, all of which were presently rotten to the
core. The positivism of Comte was aimed at shocking atheists
forward into becoming anti-theists. The battle cry of their
regime of science would be: "Nothing is absolute, everything is
relative!" With God and his metaphysician-mourners driven
forever from the human predicament, a new spiritual power
would be free to unify mankind in universal maturity.

From Anti-theism to Religion Without God

On August 1, 1842, Comte sent to the printer the sixth and
final volume of his vast work, *Cours de Philosophie Positive.*
The date is significant for it represents a turning point in the
life and work of the author. That same day his wife Caroline
left him forever. For seventeen years their tempestuous marriage had been marred with countless dissensions, three separations and now the final break. In fairness to Caroline, she
really tried to make the marriage a success and was responsible
for whatever degree of happiness it managed to have. She even
agreed to stay on, attending Comte's needs under unbearable
conditions for their last two weeks, as he completed the sixth
volume. Recalling the final separation twelve years later
Comte wrote: "That day I felt terrible. I felt as if my health was
ready to break down and that I was to have the awful mental

7. Auguste Comte, *Système de politique positive,* (Paris: Société Positiviste,
1912), pp. 73 and 88.

episode of 1826, as a result of similar conditions of disturbing influences."

Brilliant seminal philosopher that he was, as a person Comte was impossible to live with. He was egotistical in the extreme, violently self-willed and insanely jealous. He could not get along with anyone, neither his colleagues, his publishers, his students nor his wife. He hated all opinions and authority other than his own. With his wife gone, he was alone, isolated socially and academically in a world from which he had also banished God. True, his just completed grand synthesis of positive philosophy was destined to influence greatly the progress and scientific thinking of the nineteenth century. But that was still in the future. He was bitterly alienated, incapable of returning thanks even in mere words to former loved ones. Yet his self-confidence and conceit were colossal. He exulted in having eliminated God as a vague, incoherent, even disastrous being. He prided himself on having accomplished his intense passion to destroy God.

Nevertheless, despite his extravagant, outrageous self-confidence, Comte was uneasy and unhappy. He was refused reappointment for a professorship at the Academy of Sciences in 1844. Idleness and isolation are scarcely the conditions for further creative work. Without a job, without followers or friends on the continent, without income, without money, Comte was forced to go begging to his friends in England through John Stuart Mill. Arrogantly he suggested that his English disciples should support him and thus grant him the financial freedom he needed to continue his creative work of social reorganization. Although Mill and his friends did send some funds, they advised Comte frankly not to expect fund-raising to be a regular affair on his behalf. To help himself financially he could take a boarder or write articles for English journals. Comte accepted the funds, but indignantly rejected the advice of his benefactors. He had other books to write. He was disturbed over the possibility that the religious and metaphysical vacuum which he had created might prove disastrous. Some new reality and religion must fill the place vacated by God and play the role formerly exercised by Christianity. As he had himself complained often enough, pure atheism was sterile because it left utterly frustrated the human needs satisfied by God and Christianity. There was the real danger that if this vacuum were not filled by positive doctrines and a positive religion, a new transcendent God and supernatural religion would seize the soul of humanity and its last state of imbecility would be worse than its primitive or godless state.

It was at this time that an event happened in Comte's life which was to transfigure him from being historian-philosopher into becoming "the High Priest of the Religion of Humanity," as John Stuart Mill expressed it. In April 1844, on a visit to a friend's hotel apartment in Paris, Comte met Madame Clotilde de Vaux. Immediately he became Clotilde-intoxicated, forming a passionate attachment to her. He admits that this attachment caused a "moral regeneration" in him. This "angelic influence," this "incomparable passion" aroused in him speculations far superior to those of his positive philosophy. His passion for Clotilde always remained in the courtyard of friendship, though Comte was eager to marry the beautiful lady. From Clotilde he gained the insight into the true source of human happiness: "One cannot always think, but one can always love." Under the influence of this radiant lady, who united in herself all that was morally and intellectually admirable, human sentiment and love began to displace intellect as the Lord of Comte's being. Under the spell of this passionate agony, Comte plunged into the work of his "second career," the revision of his philosophic system and its completion with his system of love. When Clotilde was cut off by death a year after their first meeting, Comte was at first inconsolable, but then vowed to immortalize her before all the world. From then on his speeches, lectures, books announced that Comte had become the apostle of a new redemption of humanity under the patronage of his Saint Clotilde, the perfect image of Humanity, even as Dante's Beatrice had been the perfect image of his Philosophy. Comte wanted all men to love the human race, all human beings, as he loved Clotilde. For Clotilde represented the human tenderness Comte had been denied and had denied himself all his life. Now, in her honor, he would transform the philosophy of positivism into the religion of positivism; i.e., into the religion of Humanity. His adoration of her memory effected major changes in Comte's personal character, sentiments, speculations. Now Comte, the cold positive scientist came forth

from the flames of his grand passion as Comte the compassionate lover and founder of the religion of humanity; the science
of humanity was replaced by the religion of humanity. As we
shall see in our examination of his system of religion, Clotilde's
influence did ennoble and soften somewhat Comte's character
and feelings, yet in the end, his passion for her seduced him
into a system of speculation and conduct that delivered him up
to lunacy.

Though he expanded his philosophy into a religion, Comte
did not bring back either the God of the Christians or their
theology. He did, however, draw his ideas of moral, hierarchi-
cal and sacramental discipline from the Catholic Church for
which he had great admiration, considering it the immediate
and necessary precursor of the Religion of Humanity. In fact,
he will attempt to make an alliance between Catholicism and
Positivism so as to graft its "social genius" onto the tree of
Positivism. The Religion of Humanity, therefore, is without a
God, or rather, Humanity is man's new God. Man's belief now
clings to Humanity, no longer to God, so that Comte has created
a religion without belief in God, a religion of the infidel. Instead
of squandering his efforts at worship on an illusory God, man
can now completely satisfy his religious appetite by directing
his thoughts, feelings and actions toward his own Humanity.
Soon, according to Comte's prophecy, Paris will replace Rome
as the religious capital of the world and Notre-Dame the
basilica of St. Peter as "the great temple" of mankind. In Notre-
Dame the statue of Humanity will have as its pedestal the altar
of God and the fallen God himself will be its footstool. Thenceforth each man's obligations and devotions will be paid to this
"Grand Être" which represents the real and ideal Humanity,
comprising the past, present and future of the Human Race
conceived as a continuous, progressing whole and holy Reality.
Worshiping a Collective Existence without knowable beginning or end will revive in men that awesome feeling for the
infinite which represents a metaphysical hunger in man and
which formerly was satisfied by the Absolute Illusion. Thus will
the God of Abraham, of Jesus, of St. Paul, of the Christians be
replaced by the God of Humanity. And everywhere "the servants of Humanity" will either convert or drive out the servants, or rather, "the slaves of God." On this point Comte was

adamant. He excluded from positions of leadership in his kingdom of Positivism "Catholics, Protestants and deists," i.e., "all the various slaves of God," for they are troublesome and backward forces. "While the Protestants and deists have always attacked religion in the name of God, we must discard God, once and for all, in the name of religion."[8]

Comte's religion is certainly not scientific; it is more a theory of vitalism, a sort of mystical revelation, a lyrical image of the "Grand Être." Its driving force is faith in, hope for and love toward the human race. Guided by history, reflection and compassion, Comte feels the intimacy of the connection of every age of humanity with every other. The great drama, the prolonged epic of man's earthly destiny unites all generations indissolubly into a single Great Being worthy of worship. To be sure, Comte's idea of what is worshipful Humanity is quite different from Feuerbach's idolized Humanity. Feuerbach divinized the abstract species of Humanity and made *Humanitas Universalis* worshipful. Comte's Great Humanity, on the other hand, is composed, in every age and condition, solely of those who have lived worthy and noble lives. Thus only individuals of character who throughout the ages have contributed by their lives and accomplishments to the social advancement of humanity are deserving of living man's veneration. Unworthy humans, criminals, even so-called great men like Nero, Robespierre, Bonaparte and others—all who destroy human harmony and hand down only disorder and hatred are excluded from incorporation into Adorable Humanity. Whereas whoever has assimilated and handed on the wisdom of the ages, whoever has cooperated in the drama of man's ascent to mature Humanity—such giants live on in us and to such spiritual titans do the living owe gratitude, reverence and worship. These are, in the words of Comte, "the dead who govern more and more those who are alive." In Humanity, therefore, not in God, "do we live and move and have our being." Just as Feuerbach advised men not to return from their own Humanity to the God of alienation, so Comte warned men not to leave the never ending congregation of great men united in Humanity for the God who formerly kept them as slaves. Men are to remain

8. Auguste Comte, *Lettres inédites à C. de Blignières,* Vol. 1, p. 107, quoted by de Lubac, *Drama Of Atheist Humanism,* p. 101.

forever united in the only true religion, the religion of Humanity.

The Cult of Humanity

In order to foster the Religion of Humanity as the only road to salvation opened to mankind, Comte had to expose Christianity as the religion that led man down the road to serfdom, depravity and destruction. Without delay he dismisses Christianity's doctrines as myths devoid of all truth. He goes on to concentrate his attacks against the spirit of Christianity, which he contrasts and separates from Catholicism. Christianity is hostile to the human race and the human condition. It begets idlers, unnaturally preoccupied with death, indifferent to earthly ideals, dreamers of happiness in the solitude of heaven. Consequently, its ethics is egotistical, exaggerating the importance of the personal or individual to the detriment of the social. Christianity is at bottom immoral because it is inherently antisocial. And it is antisocial in two glaring ways. First it is anarchic, making each man an absolute like God himself and encouraging him to subordinate the world to his own ego. Second, it is selfish, seeking isolated, personal sanctity and salvation without regard to the welfare of Humanity at large. Why even fetishism and polytheism were far more compassionately social, for they kept the individual harmoniously blended into the great social body working and motivated by altruistic ideals. But Christianity sees society merely as an accidental agglomeration of individuals, composed of transitory individuals obsessed exclusively with their private destiny. For Christians' cooperation in the salvation of others is merely a means for furthering their own salvific careers. Others are instruments to be used or discarded in so far as they aid the ego. But should one be surprised at this auto-erotic conduct of Christians? After all, "Christian egoism" is merely the image of "Absolute egoism" modeled on the Absolute, Isolated, Inaccessible God. St. Peter epitomized Christian isolationism in one of his hortatory maxims thus: "Let us look upon ourselves on earth as strangers or pilgrims." And St. Paul kept Christians in a nomadic spirit of disengagement with these words: "We have not here a lasting city, but we look for one which is to come."

Thus Christianity produces an army of individual pilgrims cautiously, circumspectly seeking solitary salvation. It atrophies man's social instincts, his noblest powers, through failure to exercise or satisfy them. Even when it urges men to love their fellow men as themselves, Christianity provides an eminently selfish motive for this love, thereby vitiating it too with the spirit of egoism. Love others as yourself not from compassion but for the sake of the love of God, of getting God on your side, of possessing God. Thus Christianity begets cold, calculating men, hermits wherever they are, in direct touch with Absolute Being, unavailable to their fellow men, to social interests and solidarities for the purposes of collective order. Is it any wonder, therefore, if Christians are arrogant, rebellious, at base, intellectual, social and religious anarchists? If history proves anything, it proves that Christianity is responsible for the chaotic revolution of our times, for the mystic enthusiasm that is pitting man against man, nation against nation and the world against Humanity.

Among the documents of Christianity criticized by Comte, the Gospels came in for special scorn. He rejected them for "the mental and moral void" which prevailed in them. Moreover, reminiscent of Nietzsche's wrath against Christ, Comte too displayed a shockingly jealous hatred for the person of Jesus. He banned Christ from the Calendar of Positivist Saints, considering Him as "essentially a charlatan," a religious adventurer, the false prophet and founder of a false religion.[9] Socrates and Plato were likewise denounced as monotheists who had a devastingly deleterious influence on mankind right up to the present. Secretly such monotheists were aspiring to personal deification under different guises, under the appellation of Son of God, Troubadour of Wisdom or Herald of the Ideal.

St. Paul, on the other hand, Comte praises profusely, for he prevented the contributions of Jesus to the Religion of Humanity from being purely destructive. St. Paul is the golden link between Catholicism and Positivism. He purged Christianity of its selfishness and guided it through Catholicism toward Positivism. He is on the Calendar of Positivist Saints, one of the three—Caesar and Charlemagne being the other two—whose

9. Auguste Comte, *Catéchisme Positiviste,* Réédition, (Paris: Garnier, 1909), pp. 11, 353, 358.

memory is given solemn worship annually. St. Paul is the greatest precursor of Auguste Comte. His special merit is due first
to his enunciation of the doctrine of the perennial war that
rages between nature and grace. This valuable doctrine out-
lined the entire moral problem. For, fictional though it was, this
doctrine was nothing more than a provisional compensation
for monotheism's radical incompatibility with the natural instincts of benevolence and sympathy that impel all creatures
to mutual union among themselves rather than to isolationary
adhesion to their Creator. "The imaginary conflict between nature and grace was thenceforth replaced by the real opposition
between the posterior mass of the brain, the seat of personal
instincts, and its anterior region, the distinct seat of the organs
for the sympathetic impulses and the intellectual faculties."[10]

Secondly and in a more marvelously direct way, Paul an-
ticipated in feeling the true vision of Humanity in that inspiring word-picture, "We are all members of one another."
Thirdly, his teaching that true freedom is found in complete
submission was to become a fundamental law of the Religion
of Humanity. Such are some of the outstanding social doctrines
whereby St. Paul corrected the anarchic egoism of Christianity
and replaced it with the good news of a socially ordered Catholicism. Positivism, endowed with superior lucidity and equity
because of its doctrine of constant relativity, was destined by
history to call forth Paul from the shadows of the past and
reveal him to the present as the true founder of Positive religious principles improperly called Christian. To be sure, Paul
was responsible for history's ignorance of his truly noble work.
The founding of Western monotheism required a "divine revealer" who would announce and establish "the separation of
the two powers," assigning Christian monotheism a temporal
role with spiritual power for the achievement of an eternal
destiny, while leaving to Caesar the management of this world.
But Paul, in his humility, preferred to be only an apostle, not a
divinized founder. He knew that the "divine revealer's" role of
necessity called for "a mixture of hypocrisy and spellbinding,"
a role far below his noble spirit. Hence, Paul gladly left the first
place of founder to one of the adventurers who, in imitation of
pagan forerunners, often attempt to inaugurate monotheism

10. *Ibid.,* p. 299.

while claiming simultaneously to have attained personal deification. Thus, with admirable abnegation, for the success of his
apostolic mission on behalf of monotheism, Paul consented to
accept with veneration a "bogus founder," a man-made God as
the idealized architect of Western monotheism. Commenting
on Comte's ingenious explanation of St. Paul's conduct and
relationship to Jesus, de Lubac writes: "Evidently Comte was
not altogether devoid of a novelist's imagination. St. Paul coming to worship Jesus sincerely, because the latter saved him
from the necessity (always hateful to an upright man) of let-
ting himself be worshipped, is a pretty idea to have hit upon.
The great apostle was within an ace of infecting his admirer
with his own enthusiasm . . . The latter, however, regained
possession of himself; it was sufficient for him to recognize 'the
true though involuntary, usefulness' of the part played by
Jesus, which was limited to dispensing Paul from the necessity
of self-deification, without, however, ceasing to fulfill the condition essential to Western monotheism."[11]

Through Paul, then, the monotheistic tradition of Christianity, which was initially narrowed and hardened in egoism,
thawed and socially expanded its character. Under the leaven
of Paul's social doctrines egotistical Christianity expanded to
the nobility of compassionate Catholicism. And the manner of
development was rather startling. For under the aspect of apparent continuity, Christianity, perhaps the worst form of religious egoism, evolved into its opposite, Catholicism, a good
form of religious sociality. Now, with the advent of Comte himself, Pontiff of Positivism, Catholicism would evolve still further into its opposite. Though socially superior to Christianity,
Catholicism was still infected with its egotistical, absolutist,
One God. Comte was determined to eliminate the God of Catholicism, immanentize its mission in temporal power and political wisdom, after having rejected Christ and the Gospels. Once
monotheistic Catholicism was transformed into its opposite,
atheistic Catholicism, its faith and doctrines would evaporate,
its morals would be thoroughly rinsed of any supernatural
stains and its institutions and authoritative structure would be
reestablished in the most social of all religious realities, the
Religion of Humanity. Thus would be accomplished the evolu-

11. Henri de Lubac, S.J., *The Drama Of Atheist Humanism*, p. 112.

tion of the worst religion into the best. *Corruptio pessimi optima,* from Christianity to Catholicism to Positivism. And the cure of souls would pass into the mission and jurisdiction of the positivist clergy. "The more I scrutinize this immense subject, the more I am confirmed in the feeling which I already had twenty years ago, at the time of my work on the spiritual power, that we systematic positivists are the true successors of the great medieval men, taking over the social work from where Catholicism has brought it."[12] Comte, in a word, planned to incorporate into his own religion everything that was true and useful in Catholicism, everything, that is, except its dogmas. The religion of Humanity was to make use of the organization, *regime,* worship, cathedrals, even clergy if possible, of the Catholicism of the Middle Ages. How did Comte plan to effect this marvelous transformation? Was a desecrated, desacralized, secularized Catholicism, now known as the Religion of Humanity possible? For Auguste Comte is was a thrilling, realizable, messianic mission.

We have already seen that the High Priest of Humanity was enthralled with the social genius and organization of the Catholicism of the Middle Ages. Its greatest human achievement, "the miracle of Papal hegemony," had been established in those days. The splendor of the Catholic feudal system had been the work of Charlemagne and Hildebrand. But it had its roots in the Catholic priesthood, product of Paul's genius, which had perseveringly built itself up over the ages of anarchy during the Christian persecutions and emerged so strong that it went on to construct the incomparable social masterpiece called Catholicism. Founded on the separation yet mutual cooperation between the two powers, the medieval unity represented "Catholic organization, Catholic constitution, Catholic systematisation" at its best. Society was unified and sanctified by the spiritual teaching power of the Church and ruled effectively in peace by the political power of the Christian kings. Evangelical anarchy was conquered by the theologically omni-competent papal oracle; political anarchy by the all-powerful royal throne.

Yet there already existed within this monotheistic monolith

---

12. Auguste Comte, *Lettres d'Auguste Comte à John Stuart Mill* (1841-1845) (Paris: 1877), p. 359.

doctrinal and liturgical currents which could breach the fortress of faith in One God and lead on to the eventual establishment of the Religion of Humanity. Comte proves to be a man of masterful imagination at discovering and linking up doctrines of Catholicism which are heralds of Humanity's religious apotheosis in Positivism. There is, for example, the doctrine of the Incarnation. In a more sublime degree than any previous polytheistic mystery, this mystery unites mankind with the Absolute God and thus already manifests "our growing tendency towards a real homogeneity between worshippers and worshipped." A formerly isolated trinity is now indwelling in Humanity. This communal homogeneity is further advanced through participation in the mystery in which each man takes the body of the Deity into his own body. Thus the God of Catholicism is slowly being assimilated into the God-Humanity, the God of Positivism. Then, too, the cult of the saints moves towards the displacement of the worship of the One God by the worship of the many great Humans, the worship of Humanity. What we have here is a form of polytheism evolving into the cult of Humanity. But, if the cult of the saints revived polytheism for the sake of Positivism, the worship of the Virgin—the highest poetic creation of Catholicism—introduced an even more radical break with monotheism. For "this sweet creation of the Virgin" reintroduced fetishism, thereby disposing souls in a wonderful manner for "positive worship." The Virgin-Mother becomes the truly human mediatrix of Humanity. She, not the Eucharist, is the bridge of transition from Catholicism to Positivism. The image of the Virgin-Mother is the prototype of the Goddess of Positivism, Humanity.

Thus far we have briefly treated the Comtian version of the evolution of religion from Christianity to Positivism. Now we must give some of the details of the Comtian cult of Humanity. "The necessary basis of the human order is the entire subordination of man to Humanity," according to Comte.[13] For man is and lives through Humanity. The Human Race, therefore, should be the focus of all his speculations, affections and worship. The human race is the new Supreme Being, composed of "its own worshippers, substituting herself for God." Positive worship begins with the worship of Humanity and proceeds to

13. Auguste Comte, *Synthèse Subjective,* p. 24.

develop into a Positivist Trinity by means of the principle of fetishism. "A trinity which admits of no change" guides "our conceptions and our adoration, both always relative, first to the Great Being, then to the Great Fetish and lastly to the Great Environment."[14]

The Great Fetish is the Earth, which is alive with a blind, profligately generous will, anxious to nourish all men copiously. The Great Environment is Space, that animated receptacle which kindly receives in a passively blind way all the phenomena of destiny. Man is obliged to adore all three living members of this trinity. The unity of the three and their services to men should dispose the positivist faithful to cultivate the sentiment of sympathy by developing in themselves gratitude for whoever serves the Great Being, Humanity. Though he called these poetic fables at first, Comte wanted his followers to take them as real beliefs eventually, because they would develop sympathetic emotions and aesthetic inspirations, thereby "perfecting our unity". Commenting on Comte's fantastic teachings and fetish-worship, Maritain writes: "The spectacle of the high priest of humanity warming up his sympathetic instincts, and those of his disciples, at the fire of his own laboriously combined fables, and offering his and their hearts to imaginary, deliberately invented beings, is a remarkable indication of the degradation to which the intellect could be exposed in the nineteenth century."[15]

Now there were private as well as public devotions in the Church of Comte. Private prayer was not a matter of addressing the Great Being or petitioning favors of it. It rather consisted in a mere outpouring of feeling. And it was practiced in two activities: a commemoration followed by effusion. In commemoration, the memory and imagination summoned up in all their vividness the image and life of the physically absent person. In the effusion that followed this realistic reproduction, each person could use his own formulas, positions of reverence in his prayerful observances which were to last two hours every day, divided into three parts: at rising, in the middle of the working hours and in bed at night. Such daily worship Comte paid to Clotilde de Vaux for thirteen and one half years after

14. *Ibid.,* p. 24.
15. Jacques Maritain, *Moral Philosophy* (London: Geoffrey Bles, 1964), p. 324.

her death. He felt that all men should love and worship the human race as he loved and worshipped his Clotilde, who was the glorified image of Humanity. The spectacle of the Pontiff of Positivism, on his knees before the armchair and bouquet of flowers—a relic of the happy, Wednesday visits of Clotilde— reviving with intense concentration her radiant figure and then rekindling his emotions to exalted stages of elation, is one of the most tragic examples in all history of a genius's loss of mental health, clearly traceable to his rejection of the God of reason and revelation.[16]

The public *cultus* of the Religion of Humanity was also well organized. It consisted of eighty-four festivals a year, with at least one a week devoted to the progressive glorification of Humanity. For Comte, who exhibited a delirium for directing human life under the reign of sentiment with the same cosmic regularity that guided stars and planets, there had to be instituted nine instead of seven sacraments. These sacraments were nine solemn consecrations, performed by the priests of Humanity, of the great transitional stages in life: birth, education, marriage, choice of a profession and so forth. Even death

16. "As soon as he rose, at half-past five, he prayed for an hour, a prayer made up of a commemoration and a great pouring forth of sentiments. The commemoration lasted for forty minutes. Comte, kneeling before the armchair-altar, would evoke Clotilde's image, recite some verses in her honor and relive in thought and in chronological order, the whole year of happiness he had lived with her . . . The pouring forth of sentiments would last twenty minutes. Comte, kneeling before Clotilde's flowers, would first of all evoke her image and would recite some Italian verses, then he would arise and come closer to the altar and, standing, he would address invocations to his beloved in which he mixed the language of the mystics with the expressions of his love. He would say to her: '*One*, union, continuity; *two*, ordering, combination; *three*, evolution, succession . . . man becomes more and more religious—submission is the foundation of authority.—Good-bye, my chaste eternal companion.—Good-bye, my beloved pupil and worthy colleague. Good-bye sister. Good-bye dear daughter. Good-bye chaste spouse! Good-bye holy mother! Virgin mother, daughter of your son, good-bye. Addio sorella. Addio cara figlia. Addio casta sposa, addio sancta madre! Virgine Madre, figlia del tuo figlio, addio.' Then he would kneel again and with open eyes would repeat some sentences from the beginning of the commemoration. Finally, on his knees before the altar-chair in its slip-cover, he would invoke Clotilde again, speak to her and would repeat three times: 'Amem te plus quam me, nec me nisi propter te!' At ten-thirty, the same ceremony would begin again and would last twenty minutes; this was the prayer for the middle of the day . . .
"Finally, in the evening, a new commemoration which he made sitting up in bed, a new pouring forth of sentiments once he had lain down, and always the same thanksgiving, the same verses, the same mystical sentence from the Imitation of Christ." George Dumas, *Psychologie des Deux Messies Positivistes, Saint-Simon et Auguste Comte* (Paris: Alcan, 1905), pp. 214–216.

was sanctified by a sacrament, called the sacrament of transformation, for it was considered as the passage from objective
to subjective existence—the living in the memory of our fellow
creatures. Personal immortality in eternity was denied by the
religion of Positivism. The good Positivists who have died are
sufficiently recompensed by being gathered up into the collective adoration of the Great Being. This is the only kind of immortality—existence in the posthumous adoration of mankind
at large—that is professed by the Religion of Humanity. Then,
seven years after death, the last sacrament may be administered. It is a form of canonization and consists in a public judgment by the priesthood of Humanity on the merits and memory
of the dead. Those judged and found worthy, as a result of their
outstanding lives, of further honors are then solemnly incorporated with the Great Being and their remains are publicly
transferred from their civil to their religious resting place—"to
the sacred grove which ought to encircle each temple of
Humanity."

It would be useless to enter at length into further details of
the Comtian cult of Humanity. Essentially an organizer, Comte
had a mania for minute regulations and prescriptions. Spontaneous living shriveled under his breath and freedom fled at
his touch. Sufficient is it to indicate that Comte had guardian
angels too—Clotilde, his chaste companion, Rosalie Boyer, his
venerable mother and Sophie Bliot, his servant—glorified by
him. All the faithful of Positivism were to be aided by similarly
chosen angels. Then there was the Positivist calendar of the
saints, which recorded those who had received the ninth sacrament, that of incorporation. Moreover, Comte fostered the worship of the Virgin-Mother, as the ideal limit upward, above
sexual instinct, of womanhood which perpetuates human life
in a holy social function. Marriages were held to be rigidly
indissoluble—except for the cause of conviction of crime—for
the family was held as the essential type of all society. Second
marriages were not permitted and married couples had to take
a vow of eternal widowhood. Here was an absolute monogamy
rendered irrational by an odd, Manichean twist. Indeed the
whole dogma and liturgy of the Religion of Humanity is full of
sayings and doings that leave one flabbergasted. Assessing
somewhat its extravagant ideas, de Lubac writes:

Objectively, this religious system is an illusionism; subjectively, is his religious life anything but an illusion put into practice? Clotilde was for her worshipper the symbol of Humanity; but was not Humanity, in so far as it provoked all these effusions, chiefly an irradiation of Clotilde? . . . Comte was one of those men who, as the saying goes, "grow devout as they grow grey." A vulgar expression, but is not the reality vulgar too? . . . Apart from all question of dogma, one cannot take seriously the musings of a man who never understood a word of the Gospel and who sank deeper, every day, into a monstrous egocentricity; the crude and lachrymose "consolations" to which Comte innocently abandoned himself in his sanctuary cannot be taken for genuine spirituality.[17]

The Ethics of Atheistic Altruism

In characterizing any system of ethics it is necessary to investigate the philosophical thought upon which it is based and out of which it evolved. For morality, as a class of values or code of conduct or quest of destiny, is really the prolongation of metaphysical convictions into practical life. Normally, the *logos,* or controlling principle of one's adherence to truth, becomes enfleshed in one's daily activities. Allowing for fallen man's periodic failures through wickedness or weakness, a man convinced he is made for absolute truth will usually try to fulfill his obligation to seek and speak the truth. In the case of Comte, as we have already seen, there exists no constant, inflexible, absolute cause—no who or why—of the universe of beings. Thus, there exists no absolute truth, no unchanging principles of being, no metaphysics. There exists only a phenomenal order of related beings which give up only relative truths. "Everything is relative, that's the only absolute principle," Comte had written while constructing his scientific system of positivism.[18] Thus, for Comte, metaphysics had passed into oblivion as a science. Today's truth may be false tomorrow. Truth as such is relative; it is mutable. There is no assertion which is absolutely true. Lévy-Bruhl, in his work on Comte, has written that positive philosophy "abandons the chimera of unchangeable truth. It does not consider today's truth as abso-

---

17. Henri de Lubac, S.J., *The Drama Of Atheist Humanism,* pp. 135–136.
18. Auguste Comte, *Système de politique positive,* Vol. IV, Appendix, p. ii.

lutely true, nor yesterday's truth as absolutely false. It ceases to be critical towards the whole of the past."[19]

Now a morality flowing from the total relativity of truth must itself be totally relative. It is not surprising, therefore, to discover that Comte holds that all moral values are relative. Already as a young man he had written: "It is no longer a matter of carrying on endless discussions to determine which is the best government; absolutely speaking, there is nothing good, there is nothing bad; everything is relative, that's the only thing absolute; so far as social institutions are concerned everything is especially relative to time."[20] Comte had here caught hold of a valid insight. The dimension of time does help to form values. As one of the molding circumstances of a human act, it contributes to the reasonableness or irrationality, the good or evil of acts which by themselves are indifferent morally. But though circumstances modify the morality of certain human acts, there remain many human acts which are good or evil in themselves and no time or circumstances will change them. Everything is not subject to time nor measured by it. The value of some human actions are valued as good or evil beyond the dimension of time. They are transcendentally good or evil. It is not true, therefore, to say that absolutely speaking there is nothing good, nothing bad; that everything is relative to our time. Comte's absolutizing of his own principle of relativity is a contradiction in terms that reveals the irrationality of his position. Writing about these Comtian inconsistencies, Maritain says:

> Moreover, as a matter of fact Comte could not and did not hold to his principle. For him it is an absolute truth that the positive state is the definitive state of humanity. He holds as an absolute truth the law of the three stages, whose necessity derives from *the nature of the human mind* and is demonstrated on that basis. He holds it as an absolute truth that the edifice of the positive sciences must be crowned by sociology. He holds as an absolute truth the necessity of completing the objective synthesis with the subjective synthesis, and the positivist reorganization of knowledge with the positivist reorganization of religion. He holds it as an absolute truth that political

19. Lévy-Bruhl, *La philosophie d'Auguste Comte* (Paris: Alcan), pp. 87–88.
20. Auguste Comte, in *Revue Occidentale,* May 1884, p. 331.

unity is chimerical unless it is based on intellectual unity, and that every reform of social institutions has as a prior condition the reform of philosophy, of religion and of education. There is not the least trace of relativity in his certitude that future generations will bless his name and his work. Always he is dogmatizing, retrenching, regenerating, excommunicating, reconciling, pontificating. As a matter of fact no one is more absolutist than this herald of relativity.[21]

With this in mind, let us examine briefly the Comtian ethics of altruistic atheism. The science of sociology had demonstrated to man that the social, human community—Humanity —is the Great Being which is advancing society, through the tragedies of history, to the unity of communal maturity. Now the whole mission of religion is to cooperate with this progressive advancement. The social good of the human race becomes, thus, the ultimate standard of good and evil. Moral discipline consists positively in developing as highly as possible the sympathetic instinct that will lead men to sacrifice themselves to the social good. Negatively, moral goodness consists in cultivating utter repugnance to egotistical instincts and actions. The golden rule of Comtian ethics is: *"Vivre pour autrui,"* To live for the other. To love our neighbor as ourself is evil because selfish. We should endeavor not to love ourselves at all! Thomas à Kempis enunciated the perfect moral law of the religion of Humanity. *"Amem te plus quam me, nec me nisi propter te!"* That I may love Thee more than myself, nor love myself save for Thee![22] All moral education and discipline have one purpose: to guarantee the conquest of egoism by altruism. How did Comte plan to accomplish this noble end?

Well, since no great society has ever maintained or developed itself as a moral power without a disciplinary force of some caliber, Comte established in his fellowship of Humanity a new priesthood. "The positive priesthood," the "spiritual priesthood of Humanity" was to direct the moral development of the faithful of Humanity. But on whose heads, among all the members of this Church, would the ordaining hands be laid? Why, on the

21. Jacques Maritain, *Moral Philosophy* (London: Geoffrey Bles, 1964), pp. 286–287.

22. Auguste Comte, *Catéchisme Positiviste,* Réédition, (Paris: Garnier, 1909), p. 35.

heads of the scientists, of course! The godless, positivist clergy was to be recruited from the "masters of synthesis who would direct students of synthesis in the positivist schools attached as a regular thing to the temples of Humanity." A long scientific training is demanded for those who will one day govern the Church of Humanity. But only such scientists as evince a scientific spirit of integration must be advanced to the priestly career. Comte rejects as intellectually narrow those scientists who specialize or who gather empty learning by mechanically accumulating facts. The real scientist worthy of the priesthood is the one who subordinates analysis to synthesis, progress to order, egoism to altruism. Moreover, the priest-scientists should be men of encyclopaedic minds, avoiding aridity by synthesizing in themselves the various branches of learning, along with poetry and philosophy. Using the principles and privileges of relativity, the scientist-priests should propound truths which answer the needs of the heart over those of the head. Having become master synthesists, they should strive also to become synergists in the service of sympathy.

The priests of Humanity are to be supported by endowments voted by the State but administered by themselves. They are to be excluded from riches, from political power but must rule their own households as masters. They may not inherit, nor receive *stipendia* from any other functions, neither from writings nor teachings. They are to live solely on their small salaries, maintaining the complete disinterestedness needed to counsel and guide the faithful wisely. To win over the masses, they must be poor like the masses. Up to the age of thirty-five, they are allowed to change their careers from theorist to practitioner and vice versa.

The dictates of the Religion of Humanity indicate the tasks that the priesthood of Humanity must perform. They are to establish doctrinal unity and ethical harmony. They decide what must be taught and thought. They must require of the faithful blind faith in their dogmatic and moral doctrines. Persuasion should first be used to win over the critical, but if that fails, stronger measures like social ostracism or economic boycott or eventually eviction from the Church may have to be applied. There is no free thought nor free conscience in the regime of positivism. Being in the definitive state of man's maturity, men have no longer any need for revolutionary theology. The old beliefs have been surpassed; all is new, final and fixed in the positive millenium. The principle of intellectual criticism is now the forbidden fruit that will introduce anarchy into the paradise of positivism. The new priesthood must, therefore, guard against the return of the scourge of metaphysics. Total emancipation and total subjugation are simultaneous realities in the society of Humanity, the former from the Catholic, the latter to the Positivist faith.

And what are the priests of Humanity to do in fostering the faith? "All the precepts of Catholicism regarding the submission of reason to faith are so many programs to be carried out." "We must not lessen them but go beyond them," says Comte.[23] Moreover, one need no longer fear the total submission of reason to faith for it is equivalent in Positivism to the total submission of the mind to the heart, of personal to social instincts, of man to Humanity. Already in his *Cours de philosophie positive* when he was systematizing man's objective world, Comte had revealed his mind concerning critical opposition to his doctrines. "The social order will always be incompatible with permanent freedom to reopen, at will, an indefinite discussion of the very foundations of society." Therefore, "systematic tolerance cannot exist and has never really existed except in connection with opinions regarded as indifferent or doubtful."[24]

In his *Système de politique positive* when he was organizing man's subjective world, Comte drew the rigorous conclusions of his former principle and applied them to the discipline of his religion. Contrasting scientists and believers in his new Church, Comte taught that the priest-scientists had demonstrated knowledge of the dogmas of the positive faith. Hence they needed faith less than the unlearned faithful. They were to be the spiritual fathers who could demonstrate the faith to wavering minds. But it would be unreasonable for the people to demand that everything be proven. The faithful must be willing to believe spontaneously and practice faithfully the truths of positivism even without demonstration and full understanding or any understanding at all. This disposition of total trust

23. Auguste Comte, *Lettres à Henri Dix Hutton,* 767, quoted by de Lubac, S.J., in *The Drama of Atheist Humanism,* p. 140.
24. Auguste Comte, *Cours de philosophie positive* as quoted by de Lubac, S.J., *Ibid.,* p. 142.

is absolutely fundamental for a mature social order. Believers must venerate their priesthood and submit with love to the discipline of blind faith, eschewing useless discussion which leads only to anarchic doubt and obfuscation. In true submissiveness of mind the believer must obey the authority of the priest.

And that authority is not meant by Comte to be an empty word. He puts teeth into authority. For when spurned and disobeyed, it must know how to enforce its commands. Action must complete its convictions. Comte advises that all the conduct of the believers be subjected "to examination by an inexorable priesthood." Heresy, as a perversion, must be mercilessly purged from the body of the Church. The priests are to unmask "false adherents" to the Comtian religion and thus root out that "revolutionary malady" which pits arrogant, individual infallibility against the valid teachings of the official hierarchy of the Church of Humanity. The priests too, even with their "scientific faith," must also practice the virtue of veneration as the clearest sign of their priestly vocation. Moreover, their spirit of veneration will be an unmistakable proof of their devoted loyalty to the Founder, First High Priest and Supreme Spokesman of Humanity, their Pontiff, Auguste Comte. Indeed, all, priests and people, owe to the Pontiff of Positivism, absolute obedience in thought, heart and deed, for he alone has the power to bind and loose the faithful.

The Despotism of Atheistic Humanity

Every idol measures its worshippers. Moloch, devouring slain and burning children, revealed the ghastly depravity and mad idolatry of its faithful. No greater calamity can afflict a people than its rejection of a worship that transcends, in wonder and reverence, to the all-holy God. For every idol is a total tyrant; it demands everything of its victim, self-immolation to the extremity of annihilation. And the idol of Humanity is no exception for there are no idols friendly to man. Moreover, the true God, dethroned, cannot for long leave behind a vacant throne. A dead God does not extinguish the line of deities. Nor can a rejected faith long remain without a replacement. The Comtian city, consequently, with its god-idol, Humanity, was destined to become a compound of cosmic confinement for all men who would be ruled by a "sociocracy" under the guidance of "sociolatry." Indeed, the idol of Humanity imposed upon its citizens a thoroughly harsh, arrogant, intellectual dictatorship. The priests of Humanity were obligated to think for their disciples. Every man was called upon to bow down blindly before the superior minds of his fellow men, the scientist-priests. And this submission, one of total obedience and veneration, was to commit the whole man, from his inner depths to his overt actions, to these oracles of Humanity. In this era of Humanity the principle of intellectual criticism was forever proscribed as the anarchic enemy of the instincts of the heart. Indeed, the faithful must acquire a suspicion and even hatred for scientific or purely intellectual enterprises. The mortal sin and political crime in the "sociocracy" of Auguste Comte was to practice the art of abstraction and ratiocination. And to control this heinous activity, Comte, Pontiff of the Religion of Humanity, had to set controls to the reading of his subjects. He selected one hundred volumes of science, philosophy, poetry, history and general knowledge. These were to satisfy every positivist mind. All other books, newspapers, periodicals might quite profitably be consigned to the flames. The faithful ought to imitate the example of their Pope. The great regenerator of Humanity had adopted a rule to which he very rarely made exception. He abstained systematically from newspapers, periodicals, scientific publications, from all reading whatever except a few favorite poets in ancient and modern European languages. This abstinence he practiced for the sake of mental health. By restricting themselves to those one hundred books the faithful would also enjoy the benefits of this *"hygiène cérébrale."*

Despite his doctrine that everything is relative, Comte displays a towering intolerance of anything that he does not approve. The great regenerator of Humanity, looking around at the animal and vegetative kingdoms, went on to suggest that all species of these beings not useful to man should be systematically annihilated. Of course, he who could not produce nor reproduce a single species, would determine which were useless and had to be eradicated. Amused at the arrogance of the regenerator of Humanity, John Stuart Mill observed: "Mankind have not yet been under the rule of one who assumes that he knows all there is to be known, and that when he has put himself at the head of humanity, the book of human knowledge may be closed . . . He does not imagine that he actually possesses all knowledge, but only that he is an infallible judge of what knowledge is worth possessing."[25] This naive intolerance of the infallible judge of the Church of Humanity is most instructive. It clearly proves that intolerance is not the particular privilege of those who believe in the Absolute God. At least these latter respect the natural and supernatural mysteries of life, thereby admitting man's infinite intellectual horizon and permitting the ennobling activity of reflection and speculation in wonderment about the transcendent. But Auguste Comte, on the other hand, has decreed the end of all mysteries forever and for everyone, thereby gluing the gaze of mankind in horror on the Moloch of Humanity. It is this idol of Humanity that extinguishes and devours the minds of its worshippers. So much for the intellectual dictatorship of atheistic Humanity.

It cannot be recalled enough that the positivist redeemer of mankind not only wanted to do man's thinking for him, but would also teach man how to love. Love for him has its source solely in the feeling of sympathy and the instincts of sociability. The feeling of love is, therefore, autonomous, welling up in man independent of and, indeed, often in opposition to his intellect. But what could a love whose source is thoroughly divorced from intelligence achieve? The answer is that love, severed from its head in reason, becomes a mad tyrant. Because love is solely oriented toward the other, toward society, it calls for man to exercise perfect hatred toward himself. Men should endeavor to starve all personal desires, denying themselves all subjective gratifications. This, at first, sounds like enlightened asceticism until we hear Comte exhorting his priesthood of Humanity to deaden personal passions and propensities by desuetude. After all, organs are strengthened by use and atrophied by disuse. Women and priests "will accomplish the entire abandonment of wine and other physical stimulants when alimentation has become sufficiently nutritious." This idea is odd enough, yet reasonable compared with what follows. What Maritain calls Comte's "headless love" soon demands the impossi-

25. John Stuart Mill, *Auguste Comte And Positivism,* (The University of Michigan Press: an Ann Arbor Paperback, 1961), pp. 180–181.

ble, total abstinence from the use of sex! "It is possible," he encourages his sociological priests, "to effect if not the atrophy, at any rate the inaction of that instinct now stimulated unduly by the brain." Comte has come a long way from his dissolute youth; he has developed into a love-intoxicated celibate in the twilight of his "second career" and would subject his followers of all ages to his own unnatural asceticism.

It should be reported too that the tyranny of Comte's decapitated love renders the practice of the virtue of justice impossible. In the Church of Humanity individuals have no rights whatsoever; they merely have duties and all their happiness will be attained in the fulfillment of their social duties. Well, then, if no one has any personal rights, no one has any claim on others to respect his person. Thus, social sympathy for others is totally arbitrary and not obligatory. It will be guaranteed merely by the holy influences of the positive religion, the priest-scientists and the regenerator of Humanity. Comtian love is decapitated because it is cut off from God, from reason and from the individual person. Such love is an amazingly contradictory activity. Though thoroughly atheistic, it attempts to adore tenderly the idol of Humanity while leaving no room in man to love his own being and destiny. But how can a love which hates self-being, be directed in love to other beings? The attempt is doomed to failure.

The tragedy of such "headless love" is that it never discovers others. Decapitated love has lost its reason and direction. It cannot tend toward others as persons with rights, but only toward them as objects for social sentiment and services. As Gabriel Marcel has indicated, unless the other is encountered as a "thou" and not as an "it," love becomes impossible. But in order to discover the other as a "thou," love must be founded on and guided by reason. Love must see, through the spiritual light of reason, the goodness of the "thou" before it can embrace the "thou" in its gift of self-donation. True love is the intelligent, free mutual self-donation and reception of the "I-Thou" embrace. There is no true love in the Religion of Humanity. For the idol of Humanity demands not intelligent, free, gift-giving of persons, but the exercise of sentimental hedonism toward itself. This is an abortive counterfeit of love.

Moreover, a love that does not complete and consummate

justice is a mere sentimental effusion which enslaves man in a degrading manner to the object of his effusion. And this is what happens to the citizens of the Comtian kingdom. "The idea of right," writes Comte, "has to disappear from the political, as the idea of cause from the philosophical domain. For both notions refer to wills above discussion . . . All human rights are as absurd as they are immoral. As divine right no longer exists, the notion must pass completely away, as relating solely to the preliminary state, and directly incompatible with the final state, which admits only duties, as a consequence of functions."[26]

Thus, Comte more thoroughly than most philosophers, radically expels the notion of natural law, denying that human individuals possess by nature any rights whatsoever. And his priests, though vowing never to seize temporal or political power in the kingdom of Humanity, effectively gain just such power through the weapon of despotic love. They govern souls and direct the political powers with motivations arising from the primacy of this "headless love," pointing the way to the purely temporal millenium of the Comtian kingdom with this cry of their High Priest of Humanity: "Love for principle, Order for basis, and Progress for end."[27] In such a manner does the great idol of Humanity strip the hearts of its worshippers of their rights to invoke justice and subject them mercilessly to the Sisyphean fate of performing loveless, meaningless duties.

The Lessons of Sociolatry

The religion of Humanity is thus seen to be a form of fetish worship. Comte wanted it that way because the fetishistic attitude toward nature is realized as a religion of feeling, not at all of intelligence. Comte was convinced that his fetishism would cultivate universal love. However, historical experience demonstrates that fetishism cultivates universal fear. The superstition of the fetishist makes him believe that his fetish is alive, can help him in war, cure him of diseases, grant him prosperity or afflict him with evils. The degrading effect of fetishism consists in forcing man to such irrational conduct, to such an an-

26. *Catéchisme Positiviste,* Réédition, pp. 298–300.
27. *Ibid.,* p. 59.

tagonism to the true knowledge of nature. Yet Comte insisted on a marriage of fetishism and Positivism! And their offspring was a sociocracy ruled by the dictatorship of an atheistic priesthood. Poor positivist sinners were made to feel the full weight of its "real coercive power." Sinners are subjected to the severe judgment of an inexorable priesthood. In the presence of members of their families, before relatives and friends summoned together for the occasion, they are scolded and warned about their critical views. Should this measure fail to convert the wayward, a public censure is pronounced against them in the temple of Humanity. If even this severe punishment proves inefficacious, the ultimate weapon is used against the hardened sinners. They are sent into social excommunication either for a time or forever. And this is done "in the name of the Great Being" before whom "the absolute unworthiness of the false servants is solemnly proclaimed." Such false brethren are thus rendered incapable of sharing in the duties and benefits of human society. Continually exposed to the "examination of an inflexible priesthood," the faithful must live an open, totally socialized existence. Religious and social privacy are banned and the Great Being becomes the Big Brother. Informers, functioning everywhere, are encouraged to report to the priesthood what may be amiss with their brethren. The Great Being's eyes and ears snoop into every phase of human endeavor, thereby suffocating every sigh for freedom. Thus, decapitated Comtian love, i.e., love without justice, becomes a tyrant and destroys the society it planned to ennoble. The idol of Humanity becomes man's most inhuman god. Its theological dogma and its liturgical functions can be said to have created a form of cannibalistic narcissism. For both are based on the cruel creed that the great social god, Humanity, progressively matures the more voraciously it feeds on its self-immolating members. Is this messianic, atheistic religion, which worships the great Social Whole, an unattainable myth? Not in the designs of Auguste Comte. Listen to the High Priest issuing militant orders to his godless priesthood:

> Seize hold of the world of society, for it belongs to you, not according to any law but because of a manifest duty, resting on your exclusive capacity to direct it properly, either

as speculative counsellors or as active commanders. Let
there be no dissembling the fact that today the servants of
Humanity are ousting the servants of God, root and
branch, from all control of public affairs, as incapable of
really concerning themselves with such affairs and understanding them properly . . . Those who cannot seriously
believe either in God or in mankind are morally unworthy,
so long as their sceptical sickness lasts. As for those who,
on the other hand, claim to combine God and Humanity,
their mental inferiority is at once evident, since they propose to reconcile two wholly incompatible regimes, and
thereby prove themselves unaware of the true conditions
of either . . .[28]

Such, then, is the atheism of the religion of Humanity. In
practice it creates the tyranny of a totally socialized society. In
its civic and religious functions the individual is wholly bound
over to the great Social Idol. And the Great Being, the Great
Fetish and the Great Environment cooperate to swallow him
up. Can it be said that the menace of the Comtian idol is still
with us today? *Père* de Lubac certainly thinks so:

To my mind it is, on the contrary, one of the most dangerous (menaces) that beset us . . . Many of the present
campaigns against individualism already derive their inspiration from the ideas of Comte and his disciples, too
often at the cost of the human person . . . The "accomodations" and "alliances" favored by Comte have already
borne fruit. They were followed by a period of spontaneous
assimilation, and the faith which used to be a living adherence to the mystery of Christ then came to be no more than
attachment to a social programme, itself twisted and div-
erted from its purpose. Without any apparent crisis, under
a surface which sometimes seemed the reverse of apostasy, that faith has slowly been drained of its substance.[29]

Although much has changed since Comte wrote his vast syn-
theses, the positivistic mentality is very much alive today ex-
erting enormous influence among scientists and moral
philosophers, not to say sociologists. Scientism, which holds
that to prove something one has to do what is done in natural

28. Auguste Comte, *Lettres Inédites à C. de Blignières,* pp. 35–36; also quoted
by de Lubac, S.J., *op. cit.,* p. 149.
29. Henri de Lubac, S.J., *The Drama Of Atheist Humanism,* pp. 157–158.

science, is quite vigorously alive in this age of science. Though there is no necessary, inherent transition from research in science to acceptance of atheism, so many scientists have followed that road that to be a scientist has come to mean being an atheist. Le Dantec, French scientist who died in 1917, is puzzled by the anomaly of the man of science who is also a man of faith. In his view, one man is an atheist by virtue of the same laws by which another is hunchbacked. A deterministic biological process determines whatever a man becomes.[30]

But besides living in the age of science and scientism, we are also living at the apex of the age of relativism. And M. Comte, with his principle of relativity, has contributed greatly to the arrival of this age. Under his guidance *amor humani generis* displaced *amor Dei*. With the divorce of the human from the divine love, human deformation, not reformation, resulted from the Comtian messianism. Truth was identified with the opinions that survived in the harsh, competitive market of ideas. It reflected what was wanted from reality, not what was there and offered by reality. Ethics, even among Christians of all denominations, was identified with what was being done in reality by the majority, not with what ought to be done by all rational men. The situation, and men were part of that situation, created the ethics relevant to the needs of the times. Do we not have in these two modern situations both a dogmatic variation on the Comtian principle of relativity as well as a liturgical refinement of his adoration of the Great Environment? Moreover, the goals of modern Christians have also become quite Comtian in orientation. Increasing interest and messianic zeal is focused on creating a better social world in which the individual tends to be totally absorbed by the collectivity. True, there is a hue and cry for expanded rights, individual and social, a cry that would be choked off by the supreme Pontiff of Humanity. But even here the motivation for these rights is quite Comtian, not Christian. It is Comtian in the sense that the Christians, indeed often the clergy, that flock to the banners of expanded rights, are more zealous for the creation of a humane, secular society than for the coming of the king-

30. F. Le Dantec, *L'Athéisme, (Paris: 1906), pp. 9 and following; also quoted by William A. Luijpen, O.S.A., Phenomenology And Atheism,* (Pittsburgh: Duquesne University Press, 1964), p. 55.

dom of Jesus Christ in the hearts of all men. Certainly, the same zeal could be just as easily inspired by the Holy Spirit, but the point is that the social apostles themselves disassociate themselves from the Gospel, preferring to be inspired by the spirit of the times, the spirit of sympathy and social instinct for Humanity.

It seems, then, that it is always the same myopic sickness that is afflicting the atheistic scientist, moralist and sociologist. The malady arises from a double illusion. First, the illusion that transcendence by man to metaphysics, a supernatural religion and a tri-personal Absolute God is a fantastic, superstitious, crude enslavement of the whole man and his society. Second, the illusion that man's choice to remain below, in the physical sciences, to discover there that God and the World are one is the only way of liberating and ennobling the human spirit. Only the reality of God and the leap of faith to Him can dispel this double illusion and restore sight to a blinded age. For if the example of Auguste Comte and his atheism of Humanity proves anything, it clearly demonstrates that those who refuse to rise above the adventures of time are condemned to suffer serfdom under idols of their own fashioning.

Part Two

Gods as Passions of the Heart

To kill God is to become god oneself; it is to realize already on this earth the eternal life of which the Gospel speaks.

The Myth Of Sisyphus
Albert Camus

To sum up, modern atheism is not a conclusion reached by objective reasoning, nor is it the result of an examination of reality which includes new aspects or probes deeper than earlier examinations and thereby discovers either some new truth or some error in the old reasoning. Atheism is to be sought not in the reason but in the will. Atheism springs from the revolt of the man who has written personal freedom large on his banner. Like Prometheus modern man desires to shake off the burden of God "and the dream of service to God" to awaken to conscious possession of himself. He refuses to obey anyone or bend a knee to anyone, including God, because he insists on being his own lord and lawgiver.

God on Trial
Georg Siegmund

Heinrich: Ah! Let Him damn me a hundred times, a thousand times, provided He exists. Goetz, . . . If God doesn't exist, there is no way of escaping men. My God, this man blasphemed, I believe in Thee, I believe. Our Father which art in heaven, I would rather be judged by an Infinite Being than judged by my equals.

The Devil And The Good Lord
Jean-Paul Sartre

CHAPTER VI

Camus: The God of Absurdity

WITH THE ADVENT OF EXISTENTIALISM IN THE TWEN-
tieth century, scarred with two world wars and a continuing
chain reaction of lesser wars and revolutions, the assault
against God has been wrested from the leadership of the systematizing adventurers. Like Nietzsche before him, but for
radically opposite reasons, Kierkegaard despised the constructors of logical, utopian, atheistic humanism. Both Nietzsche
and Kierkegaard admitted that the existence of God and His
theophany in Christ and Christianity was the sign of contradiction destined for the salvation or bankruptcy of the human
race. In his life and writings Kierkegaard vehemently rejected
the smug complacency and sham sanctity of the secularized
Christianity of his day. He fearlessly, even ruthlessly, returned
to the tragic truths of the Scriptures and he boldly embraced
the harsh sacrifices that are consequent for a life of witnessing
to Christ. Nietzsche, on the other hand, despaired at the sight
of the counterfeit Christianity of his day. He dramatically pro-

claimed its bankruptcy, the death of its God, the dishonesty of its morals, the cowardice of its people, the impending extinction of its structures in the rise and rule of ruthless Superman. Both of these prophets suffered the lonely lives that are the lot of moral reformers, for they trenchantly diagnosed the sickness of contemporary man and were angrily rejected by their unbelieving societies. Alive, they were considered madmen; dead and revisited through the events of the last sixty years, the acuteness and veracity of their analyses have established them as seers of major importance. Neither of these seers suffered or died for a system of clean, cool concepts. On the contrary, Nietzsche's voice in the wilderness of the Enlightenment called for the replacement of the dead God by the acme of man, vigorous, adventurous Superman who would hopefully liberate man from a decadent Christianity and lead him to perfect self-realization. Whereas Kierkegaard, the melancholy celibate, fought to liberate the individual person from submergence in his own dark tendencies to evil or from flight into the false security of collectivized systems so as to bring him, through the daring leap of faith, to full subjecthood in an alliance of love with the personal, transcendent God of Abraham and Christ. Moreover, both prophets were consumed at an early age by the zeal of their missions. At forty-five Nietzsche succumbed in a psychotic delirium, torn apart by his frenzy for Dionysos and his rage against Christ. Kierkegaard fell paralyzed in the streets of Copenhagen after publishing his greatest polemical blast, *The Attack On Christianity,* against the soft clergy of counterfeit Christianity. He died a few weeks later at the age of forty-two.

In the heyday of the Rationalist Era such systematizers as Kant, Hegel, Feuerbach, Marx and Comte located the center of the human personality, and indeed of all society and history, in human reason and in the science and systems of thought arising therefrom. This was already a violent break with the Christian vision of man which grounded the center of human personality in faith in the person and mission of Jesus Christ the God-Man whose life, death and resurrection oriented man towards eternal fulfillment in the bosom of the Divine Transcendence. St. Paul had already gone far beyond Aristotle's reason when he announced to the Athenians that faith in

Christ was the true center of man's personal dignity and destiny. Thus from the moment of her foundation Christianity has harnessed faith and reason into an harmonious, spiritual force in quest of transcendent salvation, in hope here, in fulfillment hereafter. This harmonious adventure of "faith seeking understanding" and "understanding seeking faith" established the thousand years of Medieval Unity as the Age of Faith and the Age of Reason. Christian Revelation, far from constricting intellectual vision or diminishing human love, opened up infinite horizons for both by revealing previously unknowable, even unimaginable, sublime verities that immediately became loadstones which unleashed in man intense, penetrating, insatiable intellectual and amatory activity.

Eventually, however, the internal harmony of Christianity was shattered. The religious revolt of Protestantism rent its doctrinal, liturgical and jurisdictional unity. The marriage between faith and reason ended in a divorce sued for by the Enlightenment. The collaboration between Church and State collapsed with the French Revolution and the rise of the laicized State. Thus Christian times slowly changed into secular times. As man's spiritual center of gravity shifted from faith to reason, his intellectual focus on transcendent reality became blurred and his intense delight with the good news of Revelation soured. With his vision now diminished to the limitations of pure reason's horizons and his love repressively riveted to time's transient realities, man embarked on the adventure of creating his own encapsulated world-order where he ruled as his own God. Thus, whereas formerly in the Age of Faith his love for truth and goodness—natural and divine—ruled supreme in his aspirations, now in his Age of Revolt his love for life—for the plenitude of cultural, progressive, terrestrial life —gained a thrilling ascendency in his soul. The ideal of liberated, progressive humanity was henceforth set up as his new, absolute standard for the evaluation of all reality. Under the scrutiny of this reasonable standard everything, faith in God and God Himself, were judged. With faith diminished or lost and love cooled or extinguished, the subject of God was weighed in this balance and found wanting. It was perfectly logical, therefore, for the systematizers to deny the possibility of faith in God, to announce the death of God and to erect systems that proved these truths.

When the savants of the Enlightenment dethroned and banished God from the temple of Christianity, they replaced Him in the Cathedral of Notre Dame by enthroning the Goddess of Reason in the person of a celebrated actress-beauty. The Lady of Reason displaced Our Lady of Faith! Their new speculations succeeded in shifting man's major concerns from interest in God to interest in man, thereby disrupting the nature and destiny of man and the organic society he had created and was directing Godwards in the Ages of Faith. The concern for man and his happiness in time naturally enough bore fruit in the elaboration of a new ethics, the ethics of self-seeking. To be sure, self-seeking was to be controlled personally by moderation and balanced socially with altruism. But the foundation for moral integrity had now been radically changed. No longer was man obliged to be morally good so as to attain his salvation by adherence to a God-willed natural order of things and, thereby, to God himself. The radical change now indicated that man's most urgent moral obligation was to satisfy his instinctive desire for happiness in such a way as to improve himself, his fellow men and the human condition.

Based upon this loss of faith in God and the new-found, absolute faith in the ultimate perfection of humanity—to be achieved solely through the marvelous projects of man himself —the new morality of the atheists of the eighteenth century was seen to be mundane, humanitarian and self-serving.

For centuries, then, the world of faith and the world of pure reason have been contesting for the souls of men. Faith has been calling men to adhere loyally to absolute truths and eternal moral values—God, His revelation and the Ten Commandments. The Renaissance and the Enlightenment, on the contrary, have been proposing their own set of absolutes as replacements for those of Christianity—man, his personal happiness and the common progress of humanity. In the cause of a holy life, Christianity has been encouraging men to worship God in Christ, to curb their passions and to love and serve their fellow men in God. In the cause of a happy life, the Enlightenment has been challenging men to worship man, to satisfy their private passions and to work for social progress in the name of Humanity. Is it any wonder, then, that the world of God and the world of the godless have become fatally alienated? Though co-existing in the same milieu, the men of faith in God and the men of faith in man are today experiencing the cumulative and still mounting harshness of centuries of contradiction and schism over God, Christ and the destiny of man. Each group is proclaiming in the desert of a "broken world" a contradictory doctrine and mission for man. The world of believers beckons men to imitate the ideal of the saint—the man of Christ, who grows in grace through a life of humility, self-denial and the sonship of God. The world of atheists, on the other hand, calls all men to imitate the ideal of the secularist—the man of culture, who grows in euphoria through a life of civility, self-indulgence and the cult of his own conscience.

Thus the salient, psychic fact of modern history is man's divorce from concrete communion with God, his flight from religion, his unrooted homelessness in a society that has been progressively secularized for the past five hundred years. Disoriented through the rupture of his ties with Church, sacred symbols, sacraments, religious rites and salvific dogmas, man has succeeded in despiritualizing nature and losing reverence for himself and his fellow man. Indeed, secular man has created an efficient technocratic world and a Humanistic Society that does not hesitate to use him as a machine, among many other marvelous machines of his own creation, for the ambivalent activities of producing a paradise of economic plenty or unleashing the whirlwind of world wars and the fury of atomic annihilation.

Does humanity still thrill today with that enthusiastic spirit of reason and power that moved the Renaissance and Enlightenment to liberate mankind from the God-infested structures of the Middle Ages? Does modern man still enjoy supreme confidence in the New Science that heralded his complete conquest and control of himself and the forces of nature? Has the secular ethic, as embodied in triumphant capitalism and humanitarian socialism, been able to guarantee mankind permanent economic prosperity? Has the compassionate, democratic, laicized State been successful in outlawing war and maintaining peace with honor? History is a stubborn, implacable witness to the hideous truth that rationally secularized, technocratic society, far from having prevented the encompassing darkness of the forces of hate, actually stripped mankind of its spiritual defenses and left it naked to the madness of its logical systems. Such ghastly humanisms as Nazism, Fascism and Communism, to mention but three modern, man-made social plagues, are at bottom logical systems and brutal enterprises of human reason which is vehemently divorced from divine natural reality and arrogantly assured of its supreme self-sufficiency.

When human *hubris* collapses it brings its whole world crashing down upon its head. There is no denying that in the beginning humanistic forms of *hubris* wonderfully advance man's scientific world. They create also prosperous, literate, well-informed societies. Yet, paradoxically, simultaneous with such public achievements, humanistic systems of *hubris* generate a regression in society toward the total externalization of life and the depersonalization of the individual. Rational man then becomes superficial man, incapable of contemplation because he is poured out on things. Moreover, he is left spiritually starving for the food of concrete relations and feeling with his fellow men. Wracked with anxiety over being treated as a number, a case, a mere abstract shadow of himself, rational man develops into alienated man. Thus he becomes a stranger to God, an enemy to nature, a tyrant or slave to the gigantic politico-economic apparatus that he either dominates or serves. The ultimate desolation is that rational man becomes alienated even from himself—disoriented, displaced, despairing—identified no longer as a person but with a function. Caught in a rational ordering of society that reduced his existence to a void signifying nothing, modern man expressed a radical revulsion for such omni-competent constructions in a movement called "the existentialist revolt." It is that movement of modern protest against rationalism which we must consider now, a movement that engendered several varieties of existentialist atheism.

Existentialism And Religious Belief

Soren Kierkegaard (1813–1855) was *par excellence* one of the greatest revolutionaries against that impersonal, abstract

1. David E. Roberts, *Existentialism and Religious Belief* (New York: Oxford University Press, Galaxy Books, 1959).

thinking which was scientifically constructing closed systems of mental truths. In opposition to these ivory-tower constructions, Kierkegaard shunned the ritual of systematization in his reflections as a blight that kills the meaning of truth for daily existence. Rather he reflected and wrote in answer to personal anxieties in which he and his fellow men were individually involved. Philosophy in his work became reflective biography. He grappled with the vital concerns of individuals from the inner standpoint of their subjecthood and salvation. In the arena of human conflict he refused to adopt the attitude of the spectator-judge who would hand down analyses and verdicts over moral struggles that were no personal concern of his. On the contrary, Kierkegaard considers problems as a participator, confrere and co-sufferer with all individuals in the crises of immediate experience. He tells us of himself that all his work revolves around his own tragic experiences. In this sense he is existentialist to the core and has rightly earned the distinction of being recognized by all as the founding philosopher of existentialism. For as a passionately personal thinker who was constantly reflecting on his own experiences, he spoke up most convincingly for the intuitive, instinctive, mysterious in the spiritual itinerary of individuals. His great concern was always the individual's personal encounter with Christ. The agonizing choice for every man is, "Will I say Yes or No to God?" Again his own life demonstrates his answer to this challenge. Brought up by a father who was deeply religious but afflicted by the torment of guilt over the heinous crimes of blasphemy and adultery, it was not surprising that as a youth Kierkegaard revolted against his family and for a time even abandoned Christianity for the easy, cynical, dissolute life of the average student. This driftless existence led him to the valley of despair and he even contemplated committing suicide. However, in 1836 he experienced a moral conversion which was completed two years later by a religious return to Christ and Christianity.

Thus Kierkegaard's existentialist thinking began with concern for Christian realities and proceeded to its commitment through the study of the existential personages in Sacred Scripture. In all his works he treats and analyzes the personal encounter of individuals with God, Christ and Christianity and

their mutual relationships of reconciliation or rejection consequent to freely made decisions. Being, thus, a personal thinker
interested in the unique subject who must respond in crisis and
anxiety to the call of God, Kierkegaard despised the standoffish-
ness of the abstract creators of systems. "It is intelligence," he
wrote in his *Journals,* "it is intelligence and nothing else that
had to be opposed." A great intelligence himself, who rever-
enced this creative power of man, Kierkegaard, nevertheless,
set out not to degrade intelligence but to expose and curb its
arrogant attempts to explode the "myth of God" and thereby
divinize rational humanity in His place. He saw his mission as
one of delivering man from the arid imperialism of the intellect. That was the negative side of his calling. On the positive
side, he aimed at restoring man to the inner depths of his personal life, however painful that process would be. Regarding
himself as a Christian Socrates, Kierkegaard deliberately became a gadfly to abstract, romantic, complacent Christianity,
prodding it away from its easy life and convenient conscience
toward the crisis of making a choice for the cross of Christ. To
live in the truth, under the eye of God, with a self-commitment
ventured in the dreadful leap of faith into the presence of God,
such witnessing constituted the test and triumph of choosing
one's real self, of achieving one's real existence.

Since the contemporary existentialist revolt began as a
frankly Christian movement, it follows that this important
mood of thinking cannot be equated, as is often erroneously
done, with Jean-Paul Sartre's brand of atheistic existentialism.
The fact is that Sartre himself admits that there are at least
"two types of existentialists: a first group who are Christians
and among whom I number Karl Jaspers and Gabriel Marcel;
and on the other hand the atheistic existentialists, among
whom I number Heidegger and myself."[2] Sartre himself is on
the average twenty years younger than the authors he mentioned and he had published nothing at all when Gabriel Marcel
had already developed the broad outlines of his Christian, existential philosophy. Troisfontaines, explaining the more positive view of the revolt, writes: "We shall be able to define
the existentialist movement as a philosophy of subjectivity, of
selfhood, whose fundamental doctrine proclaims man's free-

2. Jean-Paul Sartre, *Existentialism and Humanism* (London: Methuen &
Co., Ltd., 1966), p. 26.

dom in the accomplishment of his destiny, and whose principal method is consequently that of description or phenomenology."[3] What the Christian and atheistic existentialists have in common is that they all agree on the supreme importance of the individual subject. They affirm that on his individual use of freedom will depend the sort of man each person will become, for each person is in the hands of his own counsel and anguished at the responsibility for himself that is solely his. Where the two forms of existentialism differ radically is in the total opposition of the atheistic form to the Scriptural interpretation of man and his destiny given by Christian existentialism. Atheistic existentialists like Sartre and Merleau-Ponty pervert and secularize the religious themes explored by Christian existentialists. Before mentioning some of the major themes analyzed by all forms of existentialism, it is well to recall that all contemporary existentialists are phenomenologists, that is, they render explicit, by means of concrete description in depth, what is usually only implicit in the experiences of our daily lives. Most men usually live on the surface of their experiences. Phenomenologists, as skilled observers, analyzers, thinkers and writers, progressively and vividly lead men into the unsuspected richness of their daily experiences.

To contrast further the theistic from the atheistic emphases among the various representatives of these two principal camps, it may be helpful to enunciate some of the themes that have preoccupied these philosophers, for they reveal the burning issues in the radical struggle between Christianity and contemporary atheism. Here we shall merely enumerate the special themes of three Christian—Kierkegaard, Jaspers and Marcel—and three atheistic—Camus, Sartre and Merleau-Ponty—existentialist thinkers. Needless to say, since this work is an essay on the theological adventures of some contemporary atheists, we shall give below a fuller exposition only of the thought of the atheistic thinkers mentioned. In addition to the thought of these three thinkers, we shall investigate the existentialism of Heidegger who, though he objects to this classification, is usually identified and analyzed as an atheistic existentialist.

Among the Christian existentialists, then, the special themes

3. Roger Troisfontaines, S.J., "What is Existentialism?" *Thought,* Fordham University Quarterly, Vol. XXXII, No. 127, Winter, 1957–1958, p. 516.

of Kierkegaard's work may be extremely summarized and simplified in two formulas. First, the only decisive marks of an authentically Christian existence are despair and dread. Second, that which alone is capable of raising a human life from the despair of the aesthetic through the reform of the moral to the fulfillment of the authentically Christian existence is the acceptance through faith of the absurdity of God's revelation. St. Paul accepted it when he testified that Christ crucified was a stumbling block to the Jews and foolishness to the Greeks. The spirit of this truth is caught in Tertullian's cry of faith: *"Credo quia absurdum!"* ("I believe because it is foolish!")

Jaspers developed his existential thinking around the following human experiences. The free choice of ideals and a destiny mold the human I of each individual. But these ideals and hopes are doomed to shipwreck in the world of tragic events. Nevertheless, each disaster ought to be deciphered as one of those "limiting situations" that foreshadows my death which is the ultimate seal of my finitude and contingency. Instead of succumbing to despair within this tragic milieu, each individual should accept his lot with a philosophical and religious faith that reveals such events as accurate signs indicating the only road to the Transcendence of God, who always remains when all else fails.

Marcel, a personal thinker *par excellence,* reflects on such of his experiences as can be shared by anyone—fidelity, hope, love —and arrives at the following concrete conclusions: A person's authentic human existence is determined by the use he makes of his freedom. The dreadful decision no one can escape is whether to say Yes or No to God, the Supreme Personal Existence and Absolute Thou in whom every creature finds its meaning. But all personal existences, whether divine or human, are mysteries in the sense that they transcend or escape every intellectual attempt to solve them as problems and are inexhaustibly open only to affective contemplation and communion. The fulfillment and plenitude of personal existence is achieved, therefore, only in the eager decision to live with God.

The atheistic existentialist thinkers, despite their differences, are in agreement on some very important issues. They agree with Nietzsche that "God is dead," certainly for themselves. And they mean the God of Judaeo-Christian revelation.

For them all revelation has been proven by science, reason and experience to be a fairy tale. They agree also that the Christian moral code is as dead as its Christian God. Thus they proclaim in a triumphant manner the logical conclusion of Dostoevsky's character. "If God is nothing, everything is permitted." But even more, theirs is also the gloomy finding that, with God defunct, everything is a matter of absurdity, futility and annihilation. Each expresses these conclusions in his own way and from his own experiences.

Camus, gifted novelist and dramatist, holds that the world is bereft of any reasonable significance. Man's experience of the universal absurdity of existence arises from the confrontation of his own appeal for clarity and charity to a world that responds with irrational, cruel silence. The inhumanity, indifference, cruelty of nature and man's own tragic temporality, always mercilessly terminated by death, make the belief in a good God nothing more than a wishful thinking, an escape into superstition. The real world is in itself Godless, valueless. To give life meaning, man must revolt against the absurd, reject the escapism of suicide and faith, and become, as it were, an atheist saint by an active life of self-commitment to the audacious exercise of freedom and pride in their fullest degree. Personal and social greatness is achieved only by self-commitment to the revolt against the absurd and one's dire destiny.

Sartre is not so much a man for whom "God is dead," as one for whom "God is impossible." For he argues that the very idea of God is self-contradictory. His fundamental premise is the affirmation of pure phenomenon as the sole existent. There exists no other real existence than the phenomenon of existence itself. Once the relationship of the phenomena of consciousness and the world is clarified, philosophy has fulfilled its function. An Absolute Being called God, that would include and transcend both consciousness and the world, simply cannot exist. For phenomena, as they manifest themselves, reveal no ultimate foundation or transcendent origin for their existences; they simply are there in an absurd and superfluous manner. It follows that man alone gives meaning to things and creates all values—aesthetic, moral, political, economic, social and personal—in every phase of his existence. He does this by the courageous exercise of his individual and unlimited freedom. His greatness lies in his decision to live freely for a cause of his own choosing, in his ejection of the temptation to bad faith which consists in a flight from the responsible exercise of his freedom into the security of uncommitted conformity.

Merleau-Ponty discovers the wonderment and authenticity of human existence in the freedom and contingency of man the subject. Truth, values and their eternal development arise from the dialogue between man and the world. There is no God because if there were an Absolute, Necessary Being, He would necessarily exhaust the indefinability of man, destroy man's free subjecthood and, as Truth Himself, render futile man's thrilling quest for truth. Man, himself "a weakness" at the heart of the thing-like beings of nature, is nevertheless the center where all cosmological events find their meaning and become history. Though living in the dizziness of contingency, man must not retreat from himself or refuse to choose this very contingency within the world. Flights to religion, especially to Catholic Christianity, or to humanisms like contemporary communism are retreats from contingency into occultism. They are acts of treason by man against being man and abandonments of his search for truth and values.

This brief presentation of some existentialist positions indicates the opposite directions taken by various philosophers of our times. Their main differences are arrived at by the same concrete process. Each writer analyzes his own experiences, which are often radically different from, even contradictory to, those of the others. Their varied, indeed unique, visions express the disagreements which send them off on distinct, irreconcilable, humanistic missions. It will be wise to recall this truth as we explore now four contemporary varieties of existentialist, atheistic humanism.

Albert Camus (1913–1960) Atheism of Absurdity

Albert Camus was born in Mondovi, Algeria, November 7, 1913, of Breton and Spanish parentage. He was raised in North Africa by his Spanish mother under dire circumstances, for his father was killed when Camus was only a year old. Education was expensive and hence difficult for Camus to pursue. He had to hold many jobs, therefore—one of them was playing goalie for the Algiers football team—and, by winning scholarships as well, was able to achieve the master's degree in philosophy at the University of Algiers. Shortly thereafter he arrived in Metropolitan France to work as a journalist. He was active in the Resistance Movement during the German occupation of France, where he edited the clandestine paper *Combat.* He very early gave signs of genius as a writer, when his skillful newspaper exposé of the abominable ghetto conditions among certain groups of Algerian natives provoked rabid reactions but, nevertheless, moved the French government to remedy the social scandal. Before the war he had written a play, *Caligula* (1939), and during the war, but prior to his self-commitment to the Resistance, two books which made him instantly famous: his first major philosophical essay, *The Myth of Sisyphus,* and his first novel, *The Stranger,* both in 1942. In 1951 *The Rebel,* his second major philosophical work, appeared and at once his break with Sartre began. In 1957 Camus was awarded the Nobel Prize for literature, the youngest man (at forty-three) to receive the award since Rudyard Kipling was chosen in 1907 at forty-two. In the final year of his life Camus compiled twenty-three essays, lectures and interviews which he felt represented his maturer thought and which he wanted preserved in English. This collection, constituting his third major philosophical work, was published posthumously in 1961 under the title *Resistance; Rebellion; Death.* A novel, *The First Man,* was in process when Camus came to his untimely end at the height of his genius in an automobile accident on January 4, 1960.[4] The tragedy is emphasized by the thought he had written as recently as 1958, in the preface to a new edition of *L'Envers et l'endroit:* "I continue to be convinced that my work hasn't even been begun."

Camus, like Kierkegaard, is the very antithesis of a philosopher system-builder. His philosophy is grounded in his own psychological concerns arising from his experiences and his reflections on the meaning of these for the whole of mankind. Thus all his works—plays, novels, theses, short stories, essays and interviews—are far more self-confession than artistic fiction, though they are, fortunately for the reader, these as

4. David E. Denton, *The Philosophy of Albert Camus* (Boston: Prime Publishers, 1967).

well. Early in his career when he was writing his plays
Caligula and *Cross Purpose (Le Malentendu),* Camus was
deeply shaken by the experience of what he called "the absurd." In *Cross Purpose* he puts into the mouth of the mother,
who with her daughter kills a boarder staying at their inn for
his money, only to find to their horror after the deed that the
mother committed filicide and the daughter fratricide, these
words: "But then this world we live in doesn't make sense, and
I have a right to judge it, since I've tested all it has to offer, from
creation to destruction."[5] In this drama Martha, the daughter,
is the atheist in bitter rebellion against her harsh lot of poverty,
hard, menial work, spinsterhood at a young age in a country
where the sun never shines but where rain, fog and dampness
shrivel the soul. And now she and her mother are rich, free to
live in the islands of sunshine and happiness about which they
dreamed so long and ardently! But the unspeakable truth has
destroyed in them now the capacity for happiness and freedom.
The mother moves on to suicide. Martha rants against heaven:
"I hate this narrow world in which we are reduced to gazing up
to God!"[6] But ranting against a non-listener is sheer futility. She
must vent her spleen where she can find some satisfaction, on
a human listener. Poor Maria, wife of the murdered Jan,
becomes that shocked listener when she calls for her husband
and receives the news of the tragedy that has struck his
playacting, homecoming surprise. In a calloused report of the
crime that deliberately rises to a crescendo of cruel hatred,
Martha, herself now determined on suicide, attempts to destroy
the faith of Maria.

> We did to your husband last night what we had done to
> other travellers before; we killed him and took his money
> . . . If you *must* know, there was a misunderstanding. And
> if you have any experience at all of the world, that won't
> surprise you. (Jan was not recognized on his return home
> after a twenty year absence.) . . . Your tears revolt me
> . . . But fix this in your mind; neither for him nor for us,
> neither in life nor in death, is there any peace or home-
> land. For you'll agree one can hardly call it a home, that
> place of clotted darkness underground, to which we go

5. Albert Camus, *Cross Purpose (Le Malentendu),* translated by Stuart Gilbert (Harmondsworth, England: Penguin Books, Ltd., 1965), p. 145.
  6. *Ibid.,* p. 148.

from here, to feed blind animals . . . We're cheated, I tell you. Cheated! What do they serve, those blind impulses that surge up in us, the yearnings that rack our souls? Why cry out for the sea, or for love? What futility! Your husband knows now what the answer is: that charnel house where in the end we shall lie huddled together, side by side . . . try to realize that no grief of yours can ever equal the injustice done to man.

And now—before I go, let me give a word of advice. I owe it to you, since I killed your husband. Pray your God to harden you to stone. It's the happiness He has assigned Himself, and the one true happiness. Do as He does, be deaf to all appeals, and turn your heart to stone while there still is time. But if you feel you lack the courage to enter into this blind, hard peace—then come and join us in our common house. Good-bye, my sister. As you see, it's all quite simple. You have a choice between the mindless happiness of stones and the slimy bed in which we are awaiting you.[7]

The Myth of Sisyphus abounds in evidences of the absurd. Its thesis is that the feeling of the absurd arises from the daily confrontations between man and his world. The consciousness of the overpowering hostility and indifference of nature, of the fickle temporality of human life, of its inevitable cancellation by death, of the deadening monotony of a technocratic routine, of the unattainable otherness of people or even of our very selves, of the arbitrary and protracted sufferings of innocent children, all these evidences of despotic capriciousness and many, many more prove beyond a shadow of doubt that the world is irrational and that man, wandering around as a stranger in this wilderness of inhumanity is on a path that leads to nothing, to death. In the face of such an endlessly accumulating litany of afflictions, human reason, by instinct questing for purpose, justice and happiness, stands stunned, utterly frustrated and confounded. Desperate in his hunger for clarity and charity from the world and his fellow men, man becomes angered by their indifference to his aspirations and takes refuge in hedonism or instinctualism or stoicism. How else escape from the heartless silence that confronts his exasperated "Why?"

Other existentialist thinkers, each in his own way, have tried

7. *Ibid.,* pp. 151–156.

to escape this unbearably absurd exasperation. Camus examines three spiritual sorties and rejects them as illusions not solutions. Kierkegaard embraced the absurd by leaping beyond reason, beyond the "indescribable universe where contradiction, antinomy, anguish or impotence reigns," to the affirmation of God in faith. Jaspers's leap to the Transcendent springs from his faith in the acceptance of tragic experience as the only path to meaning. Chestov too leaps in faith beyond reason, from the absurd in reality to an absurd God. What intellectual suicides! All three of these thinkers "deify what crushes them." In reality, they do not transcend but transform the absurd. The absurd is God! "His greatness is his incoherence. His proof is his inhumanity."[8] Against these attempts to escape reason Camus protests that in reality there is nothing beyond reason. The absurd world is *de facto* godless; within it there exist no absolute values.

Moreover, there is no other world for man to inhabit. And Camus would have men with "the courage to be" directing this world's formation. Yet, he is profoundly aware that the utterly absurd poses its own total solution, the abandonment of life's tension in the act of suicide. Camus unequivocally rejects suicide as the solution to the feeling of absurdity. Suicide is surrender to absurdity; that alone, not any moral considerations, renders it objectionable. Killing oneself amounts to confessing that life is unbearable, suffering useless, commitment not worth the trouble. In reality, recognizing the absurdity of life is not the end but only the beginning of its spiritual adventure. The way to conquer the absurd is to give it meaning. The way to give it meaning is to refuse to submit oneself to it. The way to stand free of the absurd, and thereby give it meaning, is to rebel against it. True, the absurd ceases in suicide but so does man and the greatness of his drama. What is this but an irrecoverable loss of freedom, an absolute negation of reason?

Sisyphus is the most inspiring hero, who demonstrates how to make the absurd live. He embraced the absurd tragically yet triumphantly. Condemned by the irate gods to push a huge rock eternally to the summit of a steep slope, only to watch it eternally rush down to the plain again, Sisyphus conquers the ab-

8. Albert Camus, *The Myth of Sisyphus*, translated by Justin O'Brien (New York: Vintage Books, 1955), pp. 25–26.

surd by consciously revolting against it. He despises the solution of suicide or the submission of faith; he becomes stronger than the rock, superior to his fate through the defiant scorn he hurls at the gods. His greatness is achieved in his revolt, in the unequaled human pride that spurns divine consolations or hopes. His enlightened reason and absolute will pulverize the gods and reduce their world to ridicule. As for man's world, Camus has Caligula testify against it:

> Really this world of ours, the scheme of things as they call it, is quite intolerable. That's why I want the moon, or happiness, or eternal life—something, in fact, that may sound crazy, but which isn't this world.[9]
> ... This world has no importance; once a man realizes that, he wins his freedom ... There's nothing in this world made to my stature. And yet I know ... that all I need is for the impossible to be. The impossible![10]

Now what manner of life may a man of the absurd live in the face of the impossible? Clearly, in a meaningless universe moral obligations are non-existent and all is permitted. But, Camus tells us, "All is permitted does not signify that nothing is forbidden."[11] Absurdity and impossibility simply render all consequences of human activity morally indifferent. Thus, crime is forbidden not because it is immoral but because it is childish and stupid. The experience of duty is as morally indifferent and legitimate as any other experience. All human actions, being free and morally indifferent, have no qualitative but merely quantitative differences. Thus, man can live with "divine irresponsibility," there being no God to answer to. Of course, one is free to live virtuously through caprice.

In his novel *The Stranger* Camus created the hero of quantitative morality. Meursault is, in the words of Sartre, "one of those terrible innocents who shock society by not accepting the rules of its game."[12] In all his experiences Meursault acts like an innocent, amoral, human animal. Whether he is at work, swimming in the nude, at his mother's funeral, attending a

9. Albert Camus, *Caligula,* translated by Stuart Gilbert (Harmondsworth, England: Penguin Books, Ltd., 1965), p. 34.
10. *Ibid.,* p. 34 and p. 97.
11. Albert Camus, *The Myth of Sisyphus,* p. 50.
12. Jean-Paul Sartre, *Literary and Philosophical Essays* (New York: Collier Books, 1962), p. 30.

comedy in the theater, in the arms of his mistress, killing an Arab or experiencing boredom while confessing an atheism of unconcern to the judge, each experience is as morally valueless as the other for Meursault. What Camus is demonstrating in Meursault is his own conviction that it is impossible to justify moral values through reasoning. The absurd man or the Christian saint? It is a matter of quantity versus quality; the saint chooses human actions of quality. He accepts responsibility, the realities of sin, guilt, remorse, punishment as well as their opposites—virtue, peace, reward. On the other hand, though the absurd binds and demands responsibility, it admits of no sin, no guilt, no remorse. There is only amoral experience; people can learn from past experience so as to live more fully in the future. Thus, the Don Juan who fulfills himself to capacity in the realization of his experiences even though he knows these experiences have no ultimate meaning; the soldier who fights for a cause even though he knows it is doomed to failure in the desert of history; the artist who creates to capacity even though he foresees himself and his work doomed to extinction, these are all examples of heroic men of the absurd who live in the lucid awareness of absurdity, who make life worth living by turning its lost causes, after the example of Sisyphus, into conquests of revolt and personal sacrifice in the very teeth of a nihilistic future. Thus Camus would save man from the pessimism of suicide through a three-fold ethical spirit. First, scorn for the gods which will preserve the man of the absurd from philosophical suicide. Second, pride of revolt which will preserve the man of the absurd from physical suicide. Third, the passion for happiness which will lead the man of the absurd to become the master of his own fate, the conqueror of gods and tyrants. All three—scorn, the resolve to revolt, the passion for optimism—enable the man of the absurd to go beyond the nihilism of suicide to the summit of self-commitment to human greatness.

Knowledge in the Face of Absurdity

Camus admits the possibility of limited knowledge, but he denies the possibility of any knowledge of anything beyond the human condition. Man knows only what he can touch, what offers resistance. Beyond the human condition nothing exists.

Hence knowledge of an Absolute that transcends the human condition is meaningless. Camus represents man's progressive advance in his process of knowing by the three phases of sensationism, perception and construction.

Sensationism represents all knowledge as the fruit of sensory experiences. This is tentative, relative knowledge, subject to the manipulations of consciousness and leading to few generalizations and even fewer conclusions. But from this base of sense experience do the phases of perception and construction proceed. Now the sensationist character *par excellence* is represented by Meursault in Camus's novel *The Stranger*. The reader, as he follows the story which is narrated in the first person by Meursault himself, sees the colors of the ocean, sky, sand; feels the hot sun of Algeria invade his body; thrills to a swim in the blue, smooth ocean that cools his whole being. Meursault, amazingly observant of objects, people, nature which he captures in vivid detail, narrates all in bright, short sentences. The very crime committed by Meursault is a crime of sensation. It flows from no motive of envy, hatred, greed nor revenge. Meursault fires a gun five times into an Arab because the cumulative, crescendoing sensations of consuming heat caused by the blazing sun, scorching sands and withering winds compelled some reaction of relief, if he were not to go stark mad. Nothing so abstract as love or hate pulled the trigger.

When he treats of the phase of perception in man's knowledge, Camus makes the following observations. Abstractions, as such, are always non-verifiable, hence they are non-objects, non-knowledge. Man's knowledge is contained within the absurd limits of things capable of being perceived. Now perception simply records things passively. Meursault again is the acme of the humanly animated movie film. He records everything; each flash upon the imagination of the reader is a short, descriptive event that simply unfolds. But Meursault explains, synthesizes nothing. Sartre says of Camus's view on perception that "the universe of the absurd man is the analytic world of the neo-realist."[13]

Obviously, Camus knows that man is an incurable explainer of his experiences. And when his explanatory efforts attain the expertise of the philosopher so that he creates categories, laws, systems of ordered being, his end product is not true knowledge,

13. *Ibid.,* p. 40.

but simply artificial construction raised on the foundations of sense knowledge and perception. Though denying they are true knowledge, Camus has no objections against mental constructions as such. What he despises is the substitution of these ghosts of reality for concrete reality and, far more, their individual constructors themselves. For history records that constructors of abstract reality who attempted to impose their mental creations as substitutes for the vital world of reality have developed into the most murderous tyrants of humanity. Take for example know-it-all Marxism which explains history dogmatically from beginning to end, insists it knows the outcome of the future now and justifies its slaughter of today's man for the sake of tomorrow's classless creature. Its Garden of Eden remains in time but is placed at the end.[14] In that position it can seduce more men to Marxism. According to Camus the Christians are as condemnable as the Marxists for they too claim to know for certain the ends of history which they, unlike the Marxists, place beyond time in an eternal paradise or hell. God and eternity make time meaningful, bearable for them; they subordinate and transmute the absurd to the Absolute. More recently a liberal humanism, such as the abstraction of Man-himself, has been afflicting human beings. It has substituted the human for the divine absolute, the one no more verifiable than the other. Liberal Humanism is but Christianity in the last stages of its development; it is the religion of Humanity. Just as Christianity divorced men from themselves for an abstract God, so liberal humanism divorces individuals from themselves for an abstract humanity. All of these faith systems are based on the arrogant presumption of a certain knowledge of what is beyond the human condition and what the future must inevitably be. They have perpetrated mass murders, cruel displacements of millions from their homes and even now continue a progressive pulverization of the human individual, always, to be sure, in the name of an abstract justice, truth, freedom and salvation. The price for the realization of their bloodless phantoms is the shedding of the real blood of unnumbered millions of individuals.

The frustrating fact is that man lives in an unreasonable world with a power for knowledge which is absurdly restricted to sense findings. He will be forever, therefore, a stranger to

14. David E. Denton, *op. cit.,* p. 38.

himself and the world, for he will never be able to comprehend the total range of either. Camus has man involved, then, in an absurd world, with absurd limits to his knowledge, on a mission doomed to long-range failure—despite its short-range accomplishments—to get beyond the nihilism of absurdity through the practice of a morality of rebellion against the absurd. Perhaps a further look should be taken at his ethics of rebellion.

In his second major philosophical work, *The Rebel,* Camus shows that he was tired of the nihilism and negativism of his earlier work. He seeks a way out of his nihilism through a more positive affirmation of man's ideals and possibilities. Rebellion is the answer to nihilism. In his ethic of rebellion Camus synthesized three cultural currents of the Christian West: the passionate commitment of the Hebrew to moral rectitude in a world to be saved; the noble attempt of the Greek to establish reason, balance and beauty as rulers in a world to be loved; the humane efforts of the Existentialist to liberate the unique individual from the tyranny of abstraction and restore him to his sublime, frequently irrational, subjecthood in a world to be transformed through the solidarity of all men.

It will be noticed that Camus rejected the religious elements of all three cultural currents. God, temporal messianism, salvation and damnation are ruled out as childish plunges into irrationality. Secular counterparts, too, that strive to replace religious utopias with humanistic utopias are also ruled out as deifications of history that dehumanize man. Over two hundred pages of the work are dedicated to rejecting the metaphysical rebellion of artists and writers and the historical rebellion of the politicians. They deny the world, degrade man and resort to murder to change both.

What then is the nature of Camus's rebellion and how is it to be contained so as to prevent it from escalating endlessly until it has obliterated human society? Camus's ethic of rebellion demands a rebellion against extremes; it stresses the Greek notion of moderation, a reaction toward the middle. Reasonable limits are set to rebellion, so history, science, logic and morality demonstrate, by the common human nature of man which naturally shuns extremes and gravitates toward the golden mean. Camus appeals here to the Mediterranean tradition for humane moderation as against the "Nordic Dreams" of intemperance. In his critique of this explanation, Cruickshank writes: "This idea of rebellion is obviously both non-Christian and non-Marxist. It emphasizes nature rather than history, moderation rather than extremism, human concern rather than abstract ideology, the dialogue rather than the directive . . . It is no doubt obvious that the guide in Camus, as distinct from the spokesman, is vague about details and sometimes has recourse to a lyrical, personal language that uses such terms as *pensée solaire* and *espirit méditerranéen.*"[15]

Camus and the Atheism of Resentment

Camus seems to be a thorough atheist. But he did not develop any technical, *a priori,* intellectual framework to sustain his atheism. On the other hand, however, he was obsessed with concern for the religious aspects of man's life. All his works treat quite seriously such topics as God, the meaning of life, sin, guilt, innocence, suffering, death and how to face the future. He wrote hostile criticisms about organized religion, especially against Christianity. What then were the causes and aspects of Camus' atheism?

Perhaps Meursault, in *The Stranger,* epitomizes the content and spirit of Camus's atheism. Meursault, the atheist, living an apparently monotonous life bereft of any project or hope, experiences, nevertheless, happiness. He is condemned to death by the judge and the people, not because he murdered an Arab, which he openly admits, but because he is a total stranger to any hierarchy of absolute moral values, a stranger, therefore, also to the legalistic society in which he lives. Yet in defiance of this verdict, Meursault attains a sort of peace in the very end. On the verge of being beheaded, he has discovered "for the first time the tender indifference of the world." He gives himself up fully to that indifference. As he realizes that this experience of indifference has such a remarkable, fraternal affinity for his free spirit, Meursault can exclaim: "I feel that I have been happy and that I am so even at this instant." Meursault has discovered happiness in and through the absurd indifference of the world and of his fellowmen. He has fallen in love with the absurd. Thus, when the chaplain visits him to plead the cause of God and the salvation of his soul, Meursault defiantly cries

15. John Cruickshank, Introduction to *Albert Camus, Caligula and Cross Purpose,* (Hammondsworth: Penguin Books, Ltd., 1965), pp. 18–19.

out: "All your certitudes are not as precious as a single hair of a woman." What Meursault loves is concrete, sensuous reality —the sun, ocean, sky, light, heat; living bodies, his own, those of his fellow men, but above all, the body of woman and he loves all this despite its indifferent harshness to man. As for God and kindred abstractions, he despises "ideas" over which men murder men.

Camus is Nietzschean in his rebellion against the sterile abstractions of the professors. Indeed, he proudly admits his spiritual descent from this philosopher who mocked faith in God as a mental malady. Though tinged with rationalism to the degree that he refused to seek truth beyond what appealed to his reason, Camus's unbelief is really nourished from another source, the experience of absurdity in daily life. Rationalism disposed him from atheism; resentment against the absurd moved him to embrace total unbelief.

One day when he was a boy of sixteen, Camus went for a walk with his friend Max Pol Fouchet. It was a beautiful day. In a short time, their attention was drawn by a crowd that gathered on the road ahead. On arrival at the crowd, they saw in their midst the body of a small Arab boy just crushed to death by a bus. The poor mother was sobbing out her despair; the father stood shocked in silence. Helpless, Camus and his friend started to move on. Then turning abruptly, Camus pointed first to the crowd and then to the blue sky: "You see," he said, "heaven is silent."[16]

This experience was crucial for Camus. His vivacious, delicate sensitivity was shocked by the sensuous experience of death which moved brutally, absurdly at the heart of life. He never got over this experience; the tragic event colored his entire view of the world; it left him dazed, wounded forever. He transformed this wound into his cure. One is reminded of Ivan Karamazov who rejected a world where a single child would be made to weep. Such a small life snuffed out by a stupid accident. One is also reminded of the child of Othon, the judge in Camus's story, *The Plague.* The child suffers horribly in the presence of Dr. Rieux and Fr. Paneloux before succumbing to the absurd bubonic plague. Dr. Rieux, unable to comprehend an

16. Charles Moeller, "Aspects de l'athéisme dans la littérature contemporaine," in *L'Athéisme Daus La Vie Et La Culture Contemporaine* (Paris: Desclée & Cie, 1968), Tome I, Vol. 2., p. 127.

abstract God who wills the death of children, complains to the priest: "That little child, you know this very well, was innocent." How then could it have been punished for its sins, as the priest had preached? Fr. Paneloux protests that "this sort of thing is revolting because it surpasses our understanding. But perhaps we should love what we cannot understand?"[17] Dr. Rieux remains adamant in his rebellion against a conception of love that decrees the agony of children.

Camus's atheism, according to Moeller, is a Gordion knot twisted together by the strands of ignorance and resentment. Camus never really belonged to any religion. His grandmother, of course, insisted on his making his First Communion for the purpose of preventing difficulties later on in life. He was instructed for a few days in a superficial way by one of the neighboring vicars. "I do not begin with the princple that the truth of Christianity is illusory," Camus said in 1949. "I just never joined Christianity, that's all." Moreover, he never found an answer in Christianity for the harsh poverty in which he was raised. To make matters worse, religion was hopelessly mixed up with politics and Camus detested this alliance. He especially hated the triumph of the Church in the Spanish Civil War where Nazi and Fascist forces were aiding the Franco side. The political regime established by Franco was to be a block between Camus and any effort to comprehend religion. But the shock of the Hungarian revolution and slaughter made him revolt against Communism and understand better what Spain had to purge itself of. Yet his experiences as a journalist led him to the conviction that religion was one form of myth about the Absolute in whose name men oppressed their fellowmen. It was this suspicion of duplicity and hypocrisy that led Camus to say in a conference to Christians in 1949:

> In reality what is the world looking forward to? This world, 80 percent of which lives outside of grace, is face to face with the problem of evil. My generation has lived in the revolution. They have uncovered unutterable hypocrisy in morality. They have witnessed the murderer justified, torture accepted as mere disability. The floors of the Gestapo premises on Rue Pompe would reverberate with the cries of the tormented, but the brave porter who

17. Albert Camus, *The Plague,* translated by Stuart Gilbert (Harmondsworth, England: Penguin Books Ltd., 1967), p. 178.

cleaned the rooms declared: "I'm not concerned with what my tenants are doing . . ." It is time to shatter this conspiracy of silence.[18]

Nevertheless, Camus paradoxically rejected the idea of sin. Or if there is sin in life, it cannot be despair of this life so much as hope in another life. Hope is perhaps the greatest evil for humanity. For such hope reduces man to the sterile attitude of resignation. But to live courageously means never to be resigned to reality as it is. Even so, despite this rejection of sin and guilt, Camus, in his story *The Fall,* demonstrates that the atheist does suffer from an inner compulsion to confess his guilt, especially when this guilt arises from dereliction in one's social responsibilities. The novel is a monologue of a formerly respected Parisian lawyer, now an atheist habitué of the Amsterdam waterfront, who confesses his life to stranger after stranger while drinking liberal quantities of gin at one of the shady harbor alehouses. What disintegrated his former state of self-satisfied harmony with himself and high-society life in Paris was his failure to come to the rescue of a young woman who one night in his presence jumped into the Seine from the Pont Royal and drowned. He had listened to the drowning woman's cries going downstream until they died away, frozen in fear, without moving a muscle to help her. His atheism was social not intellectual, springing from the social, learned circles in Paris where God was out of fashion. But the famous criminal lawyer, reflecting with his friends at the bar, analyzes this spirit of atheism with deep insight.

> The word "God" has lost its meaning; it's not worth the risk of shocking anyone by using it.
> Take our moral philosophers, for instance, with their moral seriousness, loving their neighbors and all the rest —nothing distinguishes them from Christians except they don't preach in churches. What, in your opinion, keeps them from becoming converted? Human respect, perhaps, respect for men; yes, human respect. They don't want to start a scandal, so they keep their feelings to themselves. I knew an atheist novelist, for example, who used to say his prayers every night. That didn't alter anything. How he gave it to God in his books? What a dressing down, as one might say. A militant freethinker to whom I spoke of this

18. *Vie Intellectuelle,* April 1949, pp. 337–338.

raised his hands—with no evil intention, I assure you—to heaven: "You're telling me nothing new," that apostle of free thought sighed, "they're all like that." According to him, 80 percent of our writers, if only they could avoid putting their names to it, would write and hail the name of God. But they do not sign their names, because they love themselves, and they hail nothing at all because they loathe themselves, according to him. Since they cannot keep themselves from judging, nevertheless, they make up for it by moralizing. In short, their satanism is virtuous. An odd epoch indeed![19]

Here then is the atheism of Albert Camus. It is an atheism that is dynamically concerned about the individual and his society. And this social concern for the individual is a mark of our generation. The Spanish Civil War, the World War, the Resistance, the Hungarian Revolution, all these violent events have been the fruits of an already spiritually "broken world," to use the phrase of Gabriel Marcel. This world was for Camus a place of unredeemable distrust in regard to whatever was not immediately and sensuously known by experience. The tragedies of the times aroused in Camus the spirit of never abandoning man in his present condition of suffering. Repairing to God for help was a premature, an immature, futile activity. There is no time to waste in aiding men for "too many chariots have already bogged down on the road and need human help to send them freely on their way." Forget the rendezvous of prayer and repentance with God. According to Camus, man has already grown beyond such childishness. Indeed, man has already grown beyond dependence on the God of science as well.

> Contemporary incredulity no longer rests on science as at the end of the last century. Both science and faith are denied today. And this is no longer merely the skepticism of reason against miracles. It is a passionate unbelief.[20]

Siegmund calls the atheism of Camus an "inherited form of atheism." He explains that Camus, and most modern atheists for that matter, are the intellectual offspring of whole generations of philosophers and literary savants who, from Hegel's time on, cultivated the cultural prejudice of no longer reflect-

19. Albert Camus, *The Fall,* translated by Justin O'Brien (New York: Alfred A. Kropf; London; Hamish Hamilton, 1956), p. 99.
20. *Vie Intellectuelle,* April 1949, p. 349.

ing themselves, nor allowing others to reflect, through the censure of ridicule, on the scientifically formed proofs and the existential insights recorded by thinkers and mystics in favor of the existence of God. He quotes Fuerstenberg's lament against this close-minded, arbitrary intolerance of theological discussion as being "a sorry example of a tabu which is itself dogmatic, unskeptical and unscientific." Like many of his predecessors, Marx in particular, Camus simply accepted atheism as a fact no longer needing proof nor any further intellectual probing. Hence he never posed this ultimate question. He accepted the premise that existence had no meaning. This premise had to be true because of the desperate feeling of the absurd that ravaged his own soul and was so widespread in the war-torn world around him. Blanchet's insight on this matter is quite perceptive. Camus insists on taking absurdity as a starting point because he is an atheist "by birth" and "from his sense of solidarity" with his disillusioned, disbelieving world.[21] Camus identified himself with the masses. And for him "the working masses, worn out with suffering and death, are masses without God. Our place is henceforth at their side, far from teachers old or new."[22] Thus a society that had for centuries walled in its inhabitants against a Transcendent God, a birth and training within that theologically beseiged society and a sense of solidarity with the suffering masses trapped inside its walls "obliged" Camus to remain loyal to the cause of atheism. He explicitly states this in his writings: "The movement of pure rebellion is climaxed in the shattering cry of Karamazov, 'If all cannot be saved, what's the good of saving one!'" Camus and arch-rebel Dimitri Karamazov are agreed on this atheism of revolt.

Toward the end of his life Camus's atheism seemed to become nuanced with a nostalgia for God. He protested that his was not a disbelief of a banal sort. It is true that his distrust of the Churches still possessed him before his violent end. Yet between 1947 and 1951 there seemed to be a "lurch" in his career towards Catholicism, for he had met some dedicated Catholic fighters in his work in the Resistance who did not share his belief that the human condition was fatally absurd.

21. Georg Siegmund, *God on Trial* translated by Elinor Castendyk Briefs (New York: Desclée Company, 1968), pp. 415–416.
22. Albert Camus, *The Rebel*, (New York: Alfred Knopf), p. 303.

But he was frightened away by the Church's retrenchments on the priest-workers' movements and by her warnings in *Humani Generis* against dangerous doctrines. Camus saw in these restrictions of the Church fresh signs of the absurdity of the world which he had hoped to escape in Catholicism. Despite his refusal to accept any restrictions against intellectual and social activities that were beneficial to toiling man, Camus maintained an intense interest in religious matters to the end. On two occasions in 1957 he expressed his interest publicly. In an interview given to *Le Monde* in August of that year, Camus said:

> I do not believe in God; that is true. But I am not an atheist for all that. I would even agree with Benjamin Constant that irreligion has something vulgar about it and . . . yes, something trite.[23]

In another interview given to *Daghens Nyheter* in December of the same year on the occasion of his receiving the Nobel Prize for literature, Camus expressed with deep feeling these sentiments:

> I am aware of the sacred, of the mystery in man. And I do not see why I should not confess the emotion I experience before Christ and his teaching. I fear, unfortunately, that in certain quarters, especially in Europe, the avowal of an ignorance or limit to man's knowledge would only appear as a weakness. If these admissions are weaknesses, then I accept them with strength. I have only respect and veneration for the person of Christ and for his history. I do not believe in his resurrection.[24]

In this last statement one senses the influence of Marcel on a Camus progressing toward a deeper understanding of the human person. The two dramatist-philosophers differed strongly over Catholic Franco's cause against Communism in Spain. But this writer knows from speaking to Marcel that the two became good friends, visited each other to discuss their common concern for a free, humane society and that, as a result of this mutual cordiality, Camus's antagonism to faith as

23. *Le Monde,* Paris, August 1957.
24. *Daghens Nyheter,* Stockholm, December 1957.

a possible help to the understanding of this absurdly brutal world seems to have mellowed. Camus's evolution as an atheist seems clear enough. The challenge, revolt, choice of the absurd, the agitated romanticism of the early years have all disappeared. True, Camus's inability to express belief in God remains, for he remains constricted by rationalism. Moreover, he never gets beyond the facile, Gidean negations about the Christ of the Gospels. Nevertheless, there is a real advance. Camus, the atheist, venerates Christ and in doing so hungers for God. Perhaps no expression in his works more graphically describes the eternal tug of war in his soul between: defiance of the absurd and concern to help others; love for the individual and distrust of the collective; the rejection of God and the need for transcendence than the words of Jonas the artist in *Exile and the Kingdom.* Unsuccessful in solving the dilemma in his professional life between the isolation needed to create and the involvement needed to live, Jonas, after working months in isolation on his masterpiece, collapses over a canvas found to be completely blank save for one word in small letters at its center. And the viewer of the canvas cannot tell whether the word is "solitary" or "solidary." In his own life, then, Camus seems to have opted for a "religion" described in his first work, *L'envers et l'endroit,* in these words: "Once again the worst evil is to cause suffering." An analysis of this atheistic humanism shows that this religion is a humanism without a Church, a rationalism without dogmas, a naturalism without cruelties, a moralism without sanctions, an individualism without God.

CHAPTER VII

Sartre:
The Changing of His Gods

JEAN-PAUL SARTRE WAS BORN IN PARIS IN 1905. HE studied at the École Normale Supérieure in that city, and later, in Germany, he attended Husserl's lectures and studied under Heidegger. He later taught philosophy at Le Havre and Loan, after which he returned to Paris and taught at the Lycée Condorcet. During the war, on his return to occupied France from internment in a German prison camp, he played an active role in the Resistance. One of his plays, *The Flies,* fooled the Nazi censors who passed it, not realizing that under the guise of Grecian mythology, Sartre presented as a hero Orestes who revolted against the tyrant Gods and killed their human Gauleiters in order to liberate the people. After the war he left the teaching profession and since 1946 has spent his time writing and editing the magazine *Les Temps Modernes.* His first novel, *Nausea,* established him quickly as a giant in the literary world. It probed concrete human situations which vividly exemplified doctrines and analyses of reality previously propounded in his philosophical works. Novelist, dramatist, essayist and philosopher, Sartre in all his works boldly admits he is a man for whom "God is dead" and man alone is master of his own destiny. Just about every literary work of Sartre's is didactic in essence. His dramas are thesis-dramas, that is, they demonstrate, popularize, indeed propagandize, his philosophical doctrines. His famous play, *The Devil and the Good Lord,* pretends to establish the non-existence of God and the uselessness of reward for the saint or punishment for the sinner. His novels are also thesis-novels. They depict human beings as sickened by the fundamental, metaphysical experience of nausea, that realization of the primeval, intrinsic absurdity of all reality. They represent consciousness not as a progressive conquest of material beings, but as a "sickness of being" which creates nothingness at the very heart of the fullness of being. Sartre's literary works demonstrate how freedom is a curse in man's consciousness, how man is condemned to be free. The novels, plays, short stories—even the first installment of his autobiography, *The Words*—depict human beings as trapped in a spiritually decaying civilization complicated by social injustice, war and psychological compulsions, yet inescapably called upon to face up to their responsibility to exercise their liberty for its own sake, in any manner and for any causes they themselves deem worthwhile. For there are no meanings to reality, according to Sartre, save those that man himself desires to place there and "there is no difference between getting drunk by myself and leading a nation." In the novel, *The Reprieve,* which is the second of a tetralogy entitled *Roads to Freedom,* Matthieu Delarue receives a letter from Daniel Sereno in which this pederast narrates his conversion to Catholicism. It reads in part:

> . . . I am seen, therefore I am. I need no longer bear the responsibility of my turbid and disintegrating self; he who sees me causes me to be . . . And I say to God: Here am I. Here am I, as you see me, as I am. What can I do now? You know me, and I do not know myself. What can I do except support myself? And Thou, whose look eternally creates me—do Thou support me. Matthieu, what joy! What torment! At last I am transmuted into myself. Hated, despised, sustained, a presence supports me to continue thus

forever. I am infinite and infinitely guilty. But I *am*, Matthieu, I am. Before God and before men, I am. *Ecce homo.*[1]

Rationalist philosopher and free-thinking atheist that he is, Matthieu is disgusted by this conversion and throws the crumpled letter out the window of the speeding train with the exclamation: *"Quelles Vieilleries!* [What rubbish!]" We have in this reaction a true illustration of Sartre's attitude to God, faith and religion. Yet he was not always so hostile to religious realities. A look into his childhood as depicted by himself in *The Words* will reveal the early influences in his genesis to godlessness.

Because his father died when he was two years old, Sartre, an only child, puny and delicate of health, was brought up together with his child-mother at his grandfather's home where, by his own admission, he was thoroughly spoiled and developed into a "bogus child."

> Until the age of ten, I was alone between one old man and two women ... I was an impostor ... I could feel my actions changing into gestures . . . I had been convinced that we were born to playact to each other . . . Lacking more precise information, no one, beginning with myself, knew what the hell I had come on earth to do ... But I remained an abstraction ... I *was not* stable or permanent; I *was not* the perpetuator-to-be of my father's work; I *was not* necessary to the production of steel; in short, I had no soul . . . I felt superfluous so I had to disappear. In other words, I was condemned, and the sentence could be carried out at any time.[2]

Sartre goes on to admit his hunger for God as the solution to his aimless existence. Brought up in the Catholic religion, he looked for a remedy from emptiness in the Almighty, who made him with a meaning and a mission. Existence for God's greater glory was an ideal that could have lifted him to fruitful being. But the God he was introduced to at home, while fashionable, was unacceptable. He craved for a Creator and was given a Big Businessman. He was disgusted with what his family had to offer. He analyzed its failure to give him the true God. His

1. Jean-Paul Sartre, *The Reprieve,* translated by Eric Sutton (London: A Penguin Book, 1966), pp. 345–346.
2. Jean-Paul Sartre, *The Words,* translated by Irene Clephane (London: A Penguin Book, 1967), pp. 54–61.

family had been blighted by the gradual dechristianization which was planted in the Voltaire-seeded *haute bourgeoisie.* The weed of disbelief took a century to spread through every level of society. In many a European family circle, faith was but a religious name for the breath of liberty unleashed by the French Revolution; baptism was a symbol of one's independence. To be on the baptismal rolls was to be considered normal, a citizen. When one grew up, one could do what he pleased about his faith. Anyway, in those days when Europe was still nominally Catholic, it was considered harder to acquire the faith than to lose it. On conditions in his own family which were like the above, Sartre expatiated in the following manner:

> Charles Schweitzer (my grandfather) . . . never missed an opportunity of poking fun at Catholicism . . . I was in danger of being a victim of saintliness. My grandfather disgusted me with it for good: I saw it through his eyes, and this cruel folly sickened me with its mawkish ecstasies and terrified me with its sadistic contempt for the body . . . I was both Catholic and Protestant and I united the spirit of criticism with that of submission . . . I was led to unbelief not through conflicting dogma but through my grandparents' indifference.[3]

Although he testifies that he still believed and said his night prayers before retiring, Sartre admits that his grandfather's anti-clericalism and anti-popery succeeded in turning his emotions against the faith and he gradually thought less and less often about the good God." He then relates his final break with God in an incident which drew from him anger and blasphemy.

> For several years longer, I kept up public relations with the Almighty; in private, I stopped associating with Him. Once only I had the feeling that He existed. I had been playing with matches and had burnt a mat; I was busy covering up my crime when suddenly God saw me. I felt His gaze inside my head and on my hands; I turned round and round in the bathroom, horribly visible, a living target. I was saved by indignation: I grew angry at such a crude lack of tact, and blasphemed, muttering like my grandfa-

3. *Ibid.,* pp. 63–64.

ther: *"Sacré nom de Dieu de nom de Dieu de nom de Dieu."* He never looked at me again.[4]

It would be misleading to conclude that Sartre simply assumed atheism from then on without a look back. Unlike Camus, Sartre was not accepting unexamined the atheism inherited from his family and cultural milieu. This tradition of atheism was still too much perfumed with the fragrance of God. Sartre wanted to cleanse it completely of any religious odors. Thus, far from dismissing the problem of God as an absurd discussion about a nonentity, Sartre posed the ultimate questions again and attempted to solve them to the satisfaction of his own mind and temperament. He did this in two philosophical works, his major work, *Being and Nothingness,* and another important work, *Existentialism and Humanism.* That he felt he had solved these problems to his own satisfaction is recorded in *The Words:*

> I have just told the story of a missed vocation; I needed God; He was given to me, and I received him without understanding what I was looking for. Unable to take root in my heart, he vegetated in me for a while and then died. Today, when he is mentioned, I say with the amusement and lack of regret of some ageing beau who meets an old flame: "Fifty years ago, without that misunderstanding, without that mistake, without the accident which separated us, there might have been something between us."[5]

Frequently, while reading passages like this in *The Words*—and in all his works for that matter—one is forced to the conclusion arrived at by Marcel "that there is in Sartre a certain taste and propensity for scandal." Yet Sartre is serious and impressive in his philosophical efforts to establish atheism scientifically, whatever his psychological and cultural prepossessions may be.

The Metaphysical Absence of God

In *Being and Nothingness* Sartre, like Heidegger in his own work before him, rediscovers and deepens his sense of the

4. *Ibid.,* p. 65.
5. *Ibid.,* p. 65.

finiteness and contingency of all existence. He starts his reflections with "subjectivity," with the idea of consciousness. We experience that consciousness is always consciousness of something. And that something is always a finite object quite other than the conscious subject, although the subject is aware of itself too in the act of its consciousness. Now our consciousness of a thing does not bring that thing into existence, but discovers it there in reality. Unlike Descartes, we do not have to prove the existence of the eternal world in our consciousness. The world is there already given.

Now neither beyond, nor under, nor above finite existences does anything else exist. Nothing is really in existence save the phenomenon of existence itself. Thus such transcendent realities as God, infinity and universal natures are mere chimeras. Now the being of objects, the being of the world is called by Sartre *l'en-soi,* that is, "being-in-itself." This is the being of experience, of phenomenon which the conscious subject experiences, examines and knows. This transphenomenal being is full of its own being; it is opaque; it is self-identical being without any potency or abilities to change. Yet it is neither created nor necessary being. It is simply there, gratuitous, *de trop,* that is, superfluous. Now the other fundamental mode of being is the being of the conscious subject. Sartre calls this mode of being *le pour-soi,* that is, being-for-itself. Man is that conscious being. Now conscious man is bound to reality and in some inexplicable way has come forth from reality. Man too is necessarily finite, uncreated, contingent, gratuitous, *de trop* or superfluous. Conscious being, unlike unconscious being, is not self-identical being; it has potencies, is able to change, indeed is in constant flux. For when a man is conscious of something, he is conscious of it by way of being a distance from, a negation of, the object known. And here we discover the nature of consciousness, of thinking, of choosing. Now what separates conscious man from his object known is nothing. For consciousness comes into being through the secretion of nothingness, through the denial of reality, through the refusal to decide. Thus, there is a rift, a fissure, a cleavage in "human reality" which cannot be described because it is nothing. Thus, nothingness lies at the heart of consciousness. Man is the being through which nothingness comes into the world. Sartre does not say that consciousness achieves separation from its object, that is, that being-for-itself is totally separated from being-in-itself. For conscious man is constantly reconstituting himself as separation from in regard to every particular object experienced. As we have seen, consciousness is always contingent, always dependent on the being of phenomenon, though always seeking in vain to become united with it.

Now man, as conscious being, not only separates himself from objects external to himself, but he also separates himself from himself by constituting his past as unchangeable, phenomenal history. Man's being is temporal, historical. Indeed time is created by his consciousness. Thus the world of history comes into being by the act through which conscious man separates himself from phenomenal being by projecting himself into the future. How does conscious man separate himself from his past? By his exercise of liberty, according to Sartre. Man is always far more than his past because he is constantly projecting himself from it moment by moment into the future by freely denying what he is so as to become what he is not yet, something other than his being. His body, opinions, feelings, desires and projects are constantly changing. Man is an existence seeking his essence, what he is to become through the exercise of his freedom. The true me is presently unknown, in as much as I am free to continue constituting myself through the exercise of my liberty, until death supervenes and extinguishes all my possibilities. Death alone reduces conscious being to *en-soi,* to being-in-itself—immutable, self-identified, forever unconscious. The dead man is reduced to being equated with his whole past and to remaining forever nothing but an object for the living.

Man's freedom can thus be described as man separating himself from his past "by secreting his own nothing." Man's essence is what he freely makes or made of himself up to the moment of death. Thus man is forced by his freedom to flee himself in order to catch himself. Yet he never consciously escapes nor catches up with himself. He is really fleeing into nothingness, nowhere, haunted by his perpetual instability and contingency. He would gladly put an end to this eternal exodus and the anguished nausea of always losing and never finding himself. He would love eventually to become equal to himself, to capture the solidity and permanency of his body—*l'en-soi,* being-in-itself—which as transphenomenal being is non-temporal, fully itself and absolute. Man actually strives to fill the nothingness of his freedom with the plentitude of peace that comes from the plentitude of being. The whole fundamental project of each man's existence, in his flight into the future, is to achieve this self-identity of being-in-itself without, however, ever losing the consciousness of being-for-itself. It is the drive for the unification of *pour-soi* with *en-soi,* toward consciousness' self-grounding as conscious being-in-itself, so as to overcome the basic metaphysical experience—nausea and the affliction of contingency. But his ideal is doomed to failure. It is an impossible project. For consciousness is presence to oneself through distance from oneself, whereas being-in-itself is necessarily absence or that fissure or rift so essential to consciousness.

Now the unification of *pour-soi-en-soi* in one subject, if raised to infinity, would constitute the person of God, the Infinite, Free, Absolute Plentitude of Being—the infinitely conscious self-identity. But consciousness and self-identity are mutually exclusive. Thus God not only does not *de facto* exist. God really cannot exist. The idea of God is a contradiction. There can be no God. And hence man's striving after God is doomed to utter failure. For God is the same thing as the absence, the metaphysical absence and impossibility of all being. Here, then, is Sartre's final judgment, after some seven hundred pages of metaphysical virtuosity in *Being And Nothingness.* God is merely the imaginary cure for the incurable cleavage that exists at the center of human beings. He is an illusion for man nauseated unto death. Man's longing for God is irrational, unpardonable for if God could, *per impossibile,* exist, his presence would demand the death of man's free consciousness. For God and other consciousness, God and other freedom could not exist without the Absolute destroying the contingent. Man commits suicide when he creates God. One of the final passages in *Being And Nothingness* sums up Sartre's doctrine on the metaphysical absurdity of all reality and the human project with polemical vigor and bristling contempt. "The passion of man is the exact opposite of that of Christ, for man loses himself as man, in order that God may be born. But the idea of God is contradictory, and we lose ourselves in vain; man is a useless passion."[6]

The Consequent Absence of Mandatory Morals

Sartre deliberately drew the logical conclusions from his atheism, no matter how shocking they were. Indeed, the more scandalous the conclusions the more shameless he is in forcing men to face them. He takes a measure of pride in his brutal honesty. In a passage reminiscent of St. Paul's, "I have fought the good fight; I have finished the course; I have kept the faith. For the rest, there is laid up for me a crown," Sartre writes: "Atheism is a cruel, long-term business. I believe I have gone through it to the end. I see clearly; I am free from illusions; I know my real tasks and I must surely deserve a civic prize."[7] Again at the end of his famous lecture, *Existentialism and Humanism,* delivered at the Club Maintenant and repeated privately to afford his opponents an opportunity to state their objections, Sartre concluded: "Existentialism is nothing else but an attempt to draw the full conclusions from a consistently atheistic position."[8]

Now the most important conclusion which Sartre drew from his atheism was this: Since there cannot be any God, there cannot be logically any universally mandatory moral law; there cannot be any absolute fixed values. Dostoevsky was right when he wrote, "If God did not exist, everything would be permitted." And that is existentialism's starting position. Man alone creates his own values; he is incurably free. Man *is* freedom. There are no values nor commands from above, nor from within himself—as from a permanent nature—that can legitimize his conduct. Man is alone, with the full responsibility to create himself through the exercise of his freedom. Thrown into an absurd world, he must choose his own values for he cannot help acting in this world. Even should he opt for suicide, he does not escape choice nor action. Certainly his acts are performed with motives, but he chooses which motives he

6. Jean-Paul Sartre, *Being and Nothingness,* transl. by Hazel E. Barnes (London: Methuen & Co., Ltd., 1966), p. 615.

7. *The Words,* p. 157.

8. Jean-Paul Sartre, *Existentialism And Humanism,* translated by Philip Mairet (London: Methuen & Co., Ltd., 1966) p. 56.

will make efficacious. And the choice of values and motives depends on the project to which man chooses to commit himself. Thus, as a free, self-transcending subject, man inevitably projects an initial, freely chosen ideal in the light of which he constitutes his values. Man is the sole source of values, his freedom being their foundation. Man alone is responsible for everything he chooses or refuses, for whatever he does or refuses to do.

Man's liberty is, therefore, unlimited; it is absolute. But then also he bears an absolute responsibility. Freedom is always a summons to action for needs to be fulfilled, for goals to be achieved, for a personal history to be consummated. Though the conditioning factors of life and its surroundings supply the raw material of my motives and ends, yet I must choose to assume and change my historical situation. Free actions prevent me from ever coinciding with myself or any form of being, no matter how radically I transform myself or my environment. There is no peace for man in life for freedom prevents him from becoming a thing. The freedom which is my liberty remains total and infinite, even though death haunts me at the heart of each of my projects. Death is the reverse side of my projects. Yet death is not an obstacle to these projects; it is merely their destiny elsewhere; death is beyond my subjectivity; it is there the moment I'm gone.

Moreover, man's liberty is quite arbitrary. One man's chosen meanings, actions and goals for himself and this world are as good as another's, even if the two are contradictory. It is impossible to demonstrate their "rightness" or "goodness" by showing how each conforms to norms, structures or authorities beyond freedom itself. Then too, man's freedom is ambiguous, precarious, since at any moment it may turn away and undercut everything formerly valued and achieved. For man is never sometimes free and sometimes predetermined; he is either wholly always free or never free at all. Now because of the awful power and responsibility entailed in the exercise of his freedom, man experiences dread in making his choices. For in choosing, he is creating his essence; he is perceiving the "nothing" that separates that essence from that choice. His perception of the "nothing" is the source of his experience of dread. Man, thus, becomes conscious of his liberty in dread, in the anxiety that he may destroy himself, his future, his goals by the decisions and actions he undertakes.

Now it is from this dreadful experience of his nothingness that there arises in man the temptation to flee the exercise of liberty, to shun the responsibility of giving the world, his life and his actions meaning and direction. The responsibility of making himself and his world lies heavy on each man's shoulders. Yet the man who renounces his absolute freedom by referring his choices to God, or fatalistically to his predetermined essence, his physico-psychological compulsions, his insurmountable environment, his Church, party or society whom he delegates to do his deciding for him, such a man is in "bad faith." He is not a liar, for liars deceive others by representing falsehoods as truths. Yet he deceives himself by attempting to mask the truth from himself. And this is "bad faith," inauthentic existence. Such men are "cowards" and "scum."[9] Of course, the possibility of "bad faith" is always present; it is inherent to the structure of consciousness and liberty. Only men in "bad faith," according to Sartre, live inauthentic, immoral lives.

It follows from man's burden of absolute freedom and responsibility that he never has a right to complain. He should find nothing foreign in life. For what he feels, experiences, decrees or whatever happens to him are his own. Is he mobilized for war? If he goes, it is his war; he has declared it, for he could avoid going to fight by suicide or desertion. There are no accidents in life. Every event is an opportunity for self-commitment. The individual's exercise of freedom gives each event value and direction. Therefore, without remorse, regret or excuse, man, all alone, ought to carry the tragedies of the world and not expect anyone to lighten his burden, for no one can. Sartre admits that all of men's projects are absurd and doomed to failure in time and obliteration by death. If this is so, why should man not rather succumb to despair and suicide? Why commit oneself to a project which is "a tale told by an idiot signifying nothing?" Because suicide, despair, flight are "bad faith," inauthentic, immoral existence. Freedom and its exercise are Sartre's absolute, each man's absolute. Man should exercise his freedom for its own sake, curse though it is, and in any manner whatsoever. Sartre would have man live and die in

9. *Ibid.*, p. 52.

a manner which is the reverse of T. S. Eliot's poetic lines: "This is the way the world ends, this is the way the worlds ends, this is the way the world ends, not with a bang but with a whimper." Sartre would have man remain committed to his project in life until it all ends "not with a whimper but with a bang." And the bang is the explosion of liberty. Each man should go on living vigorously, with defiant exercise of liberty, with the possibility of sinning and damning himself in the exaltation of selfsufficiency. This is man's meaning and glory, the exercise of his liberty for its own sake. And it makes no difference how he is exercising it so long as he is consciously exercising it. For all human activities are equivalent, all, in principle, doomed to failure. "And this amounts to the same thing whether one gets drunk alone or is a leader of nations."[10]

Neither are there any calls from heaven for men to assume special missions. Sartre demonstrates this teaching from the life of a Jesuit he met while in a German prison camp. The priest's father died while the boy was very young. The family sank into poverty. The boy became a charity student at boarding school with its inevitable social stigma. Because of his dependent position, he was denied certain academic honors he had earned. Later he was rejected by the girl he loved. And as if that were not enough, his military training was a dismal failure. Then the meaning of his whole sorry existence suddenly dawned upon him. God was calling him to work for His cause in His vineyard. How else explain the concatenation of catastrophes? He followed God's direction and became a Jesuit priest. Was all this God's doing, really? "No," says Sartre. That man alone assigned those signs of tribulation their divine meaning. He could just as easily have read into those signs God's call for him to become a carpenter. How explain that he did not discover this meaning in his tragic existence? The answer, says Sartre, is that the young man had no desire to become a carpenter. Therefore, he alone was fully responsible for becoming the person he became, because he chose to make the Jesuit priesthood his project in life, and to interpret all events as being meaningful for that goal alone.[11]

Ultimately, therefore, each individual creates his own being,

10. Jean-Paul Sartre, *Being And Nothingness*, p. 627.
11. Jean-Paul Sartre, *Existentialism And Humanism*, p. 38.

values, history, world-meaning and moral law. As a free subject, isolated and alone, each individual, in his isolation and
loneliness, constitutes his world and cuts his own tablets of
moral law. But what happens when individuals confront each
other with conflicting worlds and morals? The answer to this
question leads us to Sartre's social philosophy.

The Social Impossibility of Interpersonal Love

We have thus far seen in Sartre's philosophy that nausea is
the primal metaphysical experience of man's consciousness of
the absurdity of the world. Simultaneously, dread is the fundamental moral reaction over the "nothing" secreted and perceived by man in the exercise of his absolute freedom. We have
also discussed the sheer futility and impotency of man's practical striving toward self-unification in conscious self-identity;
in a word, the impossibility of his becoming God himself. Now
we will investigate the estrangement which Sartre tells us is
the basic, inherent characteristic of man's relationship to his
fellow man.

When Sartre removed the divine Other, he still had to contend with the plurality of intelligent subjects. Hegel found the
existence of so many other intelligences scandalous. He arranged things so that his One Spirit would descend into history
and eventually remove this scandal by absorbing all other intelligences into his totally self-conscious Spirit. For Sartre too, the
presence of anyone else is an intolerable situation. "The first
duty of the creature," he had taught, "is to deny its creator."
That dismissed the Absolute Other. But there was not much he
could do about the indignity of being surrounded by a world of
other free individuals. He could not free himself from their
circumscribing looks and intrusions into his life. His infant's
resentment at the presence of others, therefore, should be kept
in mind as one studies his analysis of the interpersonal relationship.

According to Sartre, the interpersonal relation is one of isolation; its social atmosphere is one of conflict. "While I attempt
to free myself from the hold of the other, the other is trying to
free himself from mine; while I seek to enslave the other, the
other seeks to enslave me. . .Conflict is the original meaning of

being-for-others."[12] And the first hostile act in the conflict is inflicted by the "look." The other as look dispossesses me, steals my freedom, reduces me to an object to be used for his interests. The other breaks into my egocentric consciousness, reveals to me my nakedness, limitations, contingency. Indeed, the other regarding me as I cannot regard myself, holds a secret against me. The other haunts me continually with the suspicion of the existence of the Absolute Other. Why? Because the essential interpersonal conflict over unification in love is the same sort of illusion as the conflict of contradictory beings—en-soi-pour-soi—in God. It follows that love is as impossible as God. There can be no love, therefore there is no love between human beings. How does Sartre explain this impossibility?

I can never "get inside" the other's subjectivity. We are intrusions into each other's lives, without ever being able to control each other's freedom or subjecthood. And love is the project seeking this control. Thus, the interpersonal relationship remains essentially one of isolation while paradoxically functioning as attack and counterattack to reduce each other into objects through the complete domination of the other's liberty. Unity with the other is, therefore, unrealizable both in theory and fact. Its realization would necessarily entail, as in Hegel's dialectically evolving Spirit, the annihilation through absorption of the other.

Now love is the primitive relation to the other. It is man's project for possessing not merely the body, but the liberty, the whole person of the other. Love wants to reduce the other "to being a freedom subject to my freedom."[13] Love, as a unification or fusion of two freedoms, is destined to eternal frustration. In all his novels and plays, Sartre's characters try to engulf the freedom of the other. But though separation is surpassed, isolation is never surmounted even in the most intimate of relations. Lovers strive to become absolutes, the ultimate meaning of life to each other. Instead they remain outsiders, strangers to each other. "My original fall is the existence of the other," Sartre writes.[14] For, in terrible reality, to love is to choose to be either dominant or dominated, or each in turn. At

12. Jean-Paul Sartre, *Being And Nothingness*, p. 364.
13. Jean-Paul Sartre, *Being And Nothingness*, p. 366.
14. *Ibid.*, p. 263.

its maddest extremes, love may drive one to transform himself for the pleasure of the other into a thing; love then becomes masochism. Or at the opposite extreme of madness, love may attempt to pulverize the other for its own pleasure and power; love then becomes sadism. But these perversions are merely the bipolar sexual extremes of the love-project which is inherently contradictory. Love is the futile, endless attempt to merge two bodies, two liberties, two selves. This sado-masochistic love-project pervades the whole work of Sartre as an ineradicable stain. Every other subject for him is a "drain" through which my universe leaks away. Others steal my world, my person, my liberty. And the persons in his drama *Huis Clos (No Exit)* discover to their despairing frustration that *"L'enfer, c'est les Autres;* "Hell is other people." Adam's original sin or fall was not the eating of the apple; it was the arrival of Eve. For sin, as the failure and fall of man's being, is the presence of others. Now far from reconciling me to myself, the intrusion of others shocks me into a realization of the cleavage within my own conscience. In Sartre we are back again to Hegel's and Nietzsche's Master and Slave relationship and morality. The lover seeks the mastery of his beloved whom he must enslave; he demands "the beloved's freedom first and foremost."[15] From the enterprise of seduction, which begins with the look, through language, indifference, desire, to the perversions of hate, masochism and sadism, Sartre has few peers as an analyst of the techniques used by man to dehumanize his fellow man. Thus love in Sartre displays a triple power of destructibility. First, it deceives man into striving to become the Absolute Other, to attain a unification hopelessly out of reach. Thus it begets in man perpetual dissatisfaction. Second, through love the other reduces me to an object, thereby afflicting me with perpetual insecurity. Third, the presence of many others besides my beloved threatens our mutual, absolute relationship thereby arousing in us perpetual shame.[16]

In the drama *The Devil And The Good Lord,* Heinrich, the Bishop of Worms who betrays the city to its besiegers, expresses Sartre's convictions on the impossibility of inter-personal love in this absurd world.

15. Jean-Paul Sartre, *Being And Nothingness,* p. 370.
16. *Ibid.,* p. 377.

. . . God had made it impossible for man to do good on earth . . . Completely impossible! Love is impossible! Justice is impossible! Why don't you try and love your neighbor? You can tell me afterward what success you had . . . If only one man should hate another, it would be sufficient for hatred to spread from one to another and overwhelm mankind . . . The world itself is iniquity; if you accept the world, you are really iniquitous. If you try and change it, then you become an executioner. The stench of the world rises to the stars.[17]

The Rage Against God

Whatever life and strength it has, all atheism, negative or positive, has its power from its awareness of God. It is a parasite that feeds on God. Comte and Marx substituted Humanity —the scientific priesthood and the proletarian masses—as the God of positivism and socialism who would explain, justify and fulfill the course of world history for the temporal happiness of society. Sartre, on the other hand, divinizes the individual. Each individual, in his absolute denial and rejection of God, establishes himself as the ultimate creator of meaning, missions and morals in a world of endless discord and contradiction. The only authentic enterprise capable of achieving human greatness is the life totally committed to the revolt against God, religion of any kind, but especially against Christianity. It is hardly surprising, then, that throughout his literary works Sartre challenges man to act alone, boldly, without any other justification for his deeds than to defy and destroy God. In *The Flies*, Orestes has just killed his mother in an act of rebellion against the whole moral order of God. He flings this defiance into the face of the offended God: "You will have no power over me except the power which I myself acknowledge. You created me but you did not have to create me free. You are God and I am free. We are both equally alone."[18]

In the drama, *The Devil And The Good Lord*, Sartre sets out to prove that God does not exist and that, even if he did, he

17. Jean-Paul Sartre, *The Devil And The Good Lord, and Two Other Plays*, transl. by Kitty Black (New York: Vintage Books, 1962), pp. 62–63.
18. Jean-Paul Sartre, *No Exit and Three Other Plays*, transl. by Stuart Gilbert, (New York: Vintage Books, 1963), p. 122.

would be a cruel, useless tyrant. His hero is a German cavalry officer of the sixteenth century, named Goetz. Goetz performs evil for the sake of evil, but above all because evil provokes God. He rejects doing good because "what is good has already been done . . . by God the Father. As for me, I invent."[19] He kills his brother and rejoices over the deed because by it he made "God's heart bleed." "God is the only adversary worthy of me. I shall crucify God tonight," he boasts, as he plans to massacre twenty-thousand inhabitants of the city of Worms. The reasoning behind this prospective massacre is quite perverse. "God's suffering is infinite and that makes the one who makes Him suffer likewise infinite." When the prophet Nasti attempts to persuade him to abandon his nefarious plan, Goetz objects vigorously:

> But what do I care for mankind? God hears me; it is God I am deafening and that is enough for me, for He is the only enemy worthy of my talents . . . It is God I shall crucify this night, through you, and through twenty thousand men, because His suffering is infinite and renders infinite those whom He causes to suffer. This city will go up in flames. God knows that. At this moment He is afraid; I can feel it, I can feel His eyes on my hand, His breath on my hair, His angels shed tears. He is saying to Himself: "Perhaps Goetz will not dare . . ." exactly as if He were a man. Weep, angels; I shall dare. In a few moments I will march in His fear and His anger. The city shall blaze; the soul of the Lord is a hall of mirrors, the fire will be reflected in a thousand mirrors. Then I shall know that I am an unalloyed monster.[20]

When it is desperately pointed out to Goetz that to do good is far more difficult than to do evil and infinitely more godlike, He is fascinated with this reasoning, abandons his plan against the city and agrees, on a bet, to live for a year and a day as a hermit-saint. Goetz enters upon a strange Sartrean life of penance. He fasts and vows perfect chastity. Yet, despite this vow, this remarkable monk continues to keep his mistress. But, of course, the arrangement becomes perfectly reasonable when it is realized that his mistress's presence is essential to his peni-

19. Jean-Paul Sartre, *The Devil And The Good Lord and Two Other Plays*, p. 46.
20. *Ibid.*, p. 55.

tential life, since Goetz also emplys her to whip him in a traditionally masochistic ritual. The conversion is never more than
a spiritual perversion, despite Sartre's efforts to convince us of
its authenticity. The peasants themselves can smell its hypocrisy. In the end, a year and a day later, when the city of Love
he worked to establish is destroyed by war, Goetz, in bitter
disillusionment, turns on the silent God who abandons even
those who serve Him.

> I alone. I supplicated, I demanded a sign, I sent messages
> to Heaven. No reply. Heaven ignored my very name. Each
> minute I wondered what I could BE in the eyes of God.
> Now I know the answer: nothing. God does not see me, God
> does not hear me, God does not know me. You see this
> emptiness above our heads? That is God. You see this gap
> in the door? It is God. You see that hole in the ground? That
> is God again. Silence is God. Absence is God. God is the
> loneliness of man. There was no one but myself; I alone
> decided on Evil; I alone invented Good.. I, man. If God
> exists, man is nothing; if man exists . . . Heinrich, I am
> going to tell you a colossal joke: God does not exist . . . He
> does not exist . . . Joy, tears of joy. Alleluia! I have liberated
> us. No more Heaven, no more Hell; nothing but earth . . .
> Farewell to monsters, farewell to saints. Only men exist.[21]

Back to the life of crime goes Goetz with a vengeance. He
brings his comedy of good to an end with a murder. In a struggle
to the death with the possessed priest, Heinrich, Goetz stabs his
opponent mortally. His new cause is to be a man among men,
to fight for mankind's betterment. He assumes command of the
peasant armies and plans a war against their exploiters. But to
do this successfully, he tells the prophet Nasti, that he must
begin again at the beginning. When Nasti asks what that beginning is, Goetz explains:

> Crime. Men of the present day are born criminals, I must
> demand my share of their crimes if I want to have my
> share of their love and virtue. I wanted pure love: ridicu-
> lous nonsense. To love anyone is to hate the same enemy;
> therefore, I will adopt your hates. I wanted to do Good:
> foolishness. On this earth at present Good and Evil are
> inseparable. I agree to be bad in order to become good . . .

21. *Ibid.,* pp. 141–142

I killed God because He divided me from mankind, and
now I see that His death has isolated me even more surely.
I shall not allow this huge carcass to poison my human
friendships . . .[22]

Sartre is fond of attacking Christianity. His animus against
the Christian God seems to be a classic case of the souring of
a disappointed lover. As his estrangement from the Christian
God became more and more embittered, Sartre, after the manner of a modern Voltaire, caricatured the image, dogmas and
history of the Christian religion. He loved to use its theological
language for the joy he experienced at always perverting it. He
held it against God that man was trapped in an absurd rat-race
of existence in a cruel world. He deeply resented the frustration and gloom of being superfluous. "I had been told over and
over again that I was a gift from heaven, much longed for,
indispensable . . . I no longer believed this, but I still felt that
you were born superfluous."[23]

Unfortunately, the relatives and friends of his family milieu
were incapable of introducing Sartre to the majesty of the true
God of revelation, the divine mission of Christ and the sublime
destiny of each man through his call to membership in His
Church. Sartre himself has spoken of a public dechristianization which deplores the style and manner of the faith. He describes in piquant terms the family performance at Sunday
services. "On Sundays the ladies sometimes went to Mass, to
hear some good music or a well-known organist: neither of
them was a practising Catholic, but the faith of others helped
them to ecstatic enjoyment of the music. They believed in God
just long enough to enjoy a toccata."[24]

Moreover, Sartre can never quite rid himself of the obsession
that God is looking at him. He fights against this vague menace
all his life, in his own experiences and those of his main literary characters who are really his alter egos. Just as the look of
God had frightened and angered him when he had set fire to a
mat, so too, on a memorable occasion when he was going to
school, he again encountered God and again had to dismiss
Him.

22. *Ibid.*, pp. 145, 147.
23. Jean-Paul Sartre, *The Words*, pp. 104–105.
24. *Ibid.*, p. 19.

> One morning, in 1917, at La Rochelle, I was waiting for some companions who were supposed to accompany me to the *lycée;* they were late. Soon I could think of nothing more to distract myself, and I decided to think about the Almighty. He at once tumbled down into the blue sky and vanished without explanation: He does not exist, I said to myself, in polite astonishment, and I thought the matter was settled. In one sense it was, because I have never since had the least temptation to revive Him.[25]

Sartre has not given the temptation to revive God the slightest opportunity to present itself. The reason is that he has been so busy mocking and deriding the mythical God of the Christians. He has traveled a long road of estrangement from God between the age of thirteen, the end of his life-period covered by *The Words,* and his present exalted arrogance toward the deity. As a boy, his parting with God vibrates with tremulous regret and nostalgia. "I needed God . . . He was given to me . . . Unable to take root in my heart, he vegetated in me for a while and then died . . . there might have been something between us." Forty years later, regret and nostalgia have degenerated into scornful derision. In perhaps the most blasphemous scene he has created throughout his many dramas and novels, Sartre, incarnated in Goetz, wallows madly in a Luciferian assault against the crucified Christ. Goetz's mistress, Catherine, in a dying, delirious condition and pleading for a priest to hear her confession, is brought to the church in the presence of Goetz and laid at the feet of the life-sized crucifix. The priests flee the church, refusing her any last sacraments. The faithful remain to mock and consign her soul to hell. In a rage, Goetz clears the church and, alone with the dying sinner, addresses the crucified Christ, begging a sign of Catherine's salvation:

> Lord, these sins are mine. Thou knowest it. Render to me what rightfully belongs to me. Thou has no right to condemn this woman since I alone am guilty. Give me a sign! My arms are ready; my face and breast are prepared. Blast my cheeks; let her sins become pus oozing from my eyes and ears; let them burn like acid into my back, my thighs and my genitals. Strike me with leprosy, cholera, the

---

25. *Ibid.,* pp. 155–156.

plague, but redeem her! Didst Thou die for mankind, yes or no? Look down on us: mankind is suffering. Thou must begin to die again! Give! Give me Thy wounds! Give me the wound in Thy right side, the two holes in Thy hands. If God could suffer for their sins, why cannot a man? Art Thou jealous of me? Give me Thy stigmata! Give me Thy wounds! Give me Thy wounds! Art Thou deaf? Good heavens, how stupid I am! God helps those who help themselves! *(He draws a dagger from his belt, stabs the palm of his left hand, then the palm of his right hand and then finally his side. Then he throws the dagger behind the altar and leaning forward, marks the breast of the Christ with blood.)* Come back, all of you! The Christ has bled. See, in His infinite mercy, He has allowed me to bear His stigmata. The blood of Christ, my brothers, the blood of Christ is flowing from my hands. Fear no more, my love. I touch your forehead, your eyes and lips with the blood of our Lord Jesus Christ . . . Die in peace . . . The blood of Christ, Catherine.

Catherine dies in the presence of her new saviour with these words: "Your blood, Goetz, your blood. You have shed it for me."[26]

Irrational Assumptions of Sartrean Atheism

It is now time to evaluate the symmetrical appearance of the Sartrean synthesis of reality. His first exceedingly gratuitous assumption is a metaphysical assertion. Rejecting previous forms of dualism, Sartre apodictically presents, in the first chapters of his *Being And Nothingness,* his own radical dualism. It states that all being is divided into *l'en-soï,* being as it is in itself, and *le pour-soi,* human consciousness. There is no being beyond these. Now the world of objects, that is, non-human reality, is so strong, so dense as to be completely meaningless. By contrast, human reality is so weak, so contingent, that it is confounded with nothingness. Radically, then, all being is absurd, superfluous. No proof is attempted to establish the truth of this dualism. These are, in reality, a matter of choice; no proof is needed for what one chooses to postulate. Here is Sartre's basic act of faith. The following six hundred

26. Jean-Paul Sartre, *The Devil And The Good Lord and Two Other Plays,* pp. 101–102.

pages of his book elaborate and defend this metaphysical dogma.

Whereas other thinkers explained consciousness in terms of a spiritual dimension and higher fruition of the superior being, man, Sartre holds the opposite. Other philosophers have demonstrated that the world's many characteristics of unity, beauty, intelligibility, order and diversity, already present ontologically, become humanly actualized in the awakened and appreciative mind. But for Sartre, the conscious mind is a hole, a tear, a secreter of "nothing" in the otherwise solid wall of being. This perverse, unproven axiom sets up the specious proof for the non-existence of God. For it establishes, by pronouncement alone, the absence of order, meaning, direction in the world. Discord, contradiction, nothingness, chaos reign at the heart of each thing and within the ensemble of all things. The two types of being metaphysically oppose each other; they render God, not only non-existent, but impossible. For God, in order to exist, would have to be the self-identification of Infinite Consciousness with the world of objects. But on Sartre's initial assumption, consciousness and the world of objects are mutually exclusive. Moreover, since there is no consciousness apart from the world—for consciousness is always consciousness of something—God not only does not exist, but *creation ex nihilo* is also impossible. For creation would presuppose God already existing as a conscious subject before there were objects to be conscious of. Now this situation would deny the very nature of consciousness. Of course, Sartre assumes here that God is conscious of beings other than Himself in a way that is identical to man's consciousness. But if we admit that God's consciousness is supposed to be like man's in a univocal sense, then certainly we cannot conceive God's creating the world. Thus, by an initially optional division of all being, by an imposition of inherently contradictory definitions on these modes of being, by the arbitrary announcement that God could only be the unity of these contradictions, were they raised to the infinite and personalized degree, Sartre has conveniently pre-arranged that God not only does not exist, but cannot exist. For God would have to be the identification of the ideal with the real, something consciousness reveals to be utterly impossible. The Sartrean atheism, therefore, is founded on the metaphysical misinformation that all being is inherently: contradictory, meaningless, absurd and superfluous.

Of course, the Christian thinker sees the basic error in Sartre's ontology. Consciousness is not a lack, a minus of being; it is rather a fuller achievement, a plus of being. If man's consciousness appears for no reason at all, if it has no relationship to an absolute consciousness, then all thinking is impossible. For thinking is a pursuit that presupposes a pursued. And truth is the reality so avidly pursued. Now if the thinking process "secretes nothing" as its inevitable product, instead of grasping fuller truth, then truth is non-existent and Sartre's own philosophizing is undermined. Moreover, the Christian mind sees no contradiction in the unification of infinite, dynamic self-consciousness and immutable, infinitely perfect being. For the Christian this is exactly what God is, in so far as the human mind can grasp Him darkly. God is utter, total Self-consciousness, sheer Dynamism while simultaneously being pure, immutable, permanent Being. For the Christian does not know how these paradoxical characteristics cohere in the Absolute Being; he cannot explain their presence in a positive manner. Yet he knows that there is no contradiction, that these characteristics are not mutually exclusive. And he knows this truth in a negative way, from the very analysis of the concepts involved. Sartre, in placing a contradiction between these aspects of being, is concluding beyond the evidence that is available. Moreover, what the Christian mind knows through the deductions of native reason in a negative manner, it also knows more amply and positively through the revelation of faith. The one God is infinitely self-conscious because He is three Divine Persons. This God knows Himself perfectly in the Person of the Absolute, Substantial Word. He loves Himself in the Person of the Substantial Spirit. The Christian at least has the intrinsic, metaphysical consistency of the concepts garnered from philosophical reflection and the external, revelationary testimony received from the God-Man to assert and defend his adherence to God. Sartre has neither the one nor the other of these sources of truth to corroborate his atheistic ontology. As a matter of fact, Sartre never claims that his ontology can *demonstrate* the truth of his atheism. It is with him more a matter of choice. In the final analysis, God does not and cannot exist for Sartre because Sartre wants it and prearranged it that way.

We pass now to the moral assumption for the non-existence of God. It states that: God is irreconcilable with human freedom. For, if God as Absolute Liberty existed, then man would be caught in the inescapable strait jacket of determinism. If God the creator determines what it means to be human, then freedom has vanished into man's total dependence upon God. But to be free means to be a subject, which is what man is. And far from being produced as an essence according to a pre-conceived plan of God, the "Superior Artisan," man rather falls into existence through the exercise of his power of choosing. Thus, being totally independent of a non-existent God, man is absolutely free to create his own values, whatever he will become in himself and whatever the world will mean to him. Sartre falls into the metaphysical trap of presupposing that the definition of essence excludes freedom. Moreover, he merely assumes that the definition of existence demands that it always precede essence. Once again, as in the case of being, the origin of liberty is utterly absurd; it has no metaphysical or reasonable foundation.

On the contrary, the Christian sees that capacities come with every new being, every new nature. Freedom is present as a potentiality even before the child begins to exercise it. Where does it come from? Sartre holds that freedom, like all being, is superfluous, absurd; it comes from nowhere. He calls freedom a "sickness" of human existence. The Christian, on the other hand, sees liberty as an essential qualification of the human individual, a gift given freely by God with the gift of human nature itself. True, liberty is an ambiguous power capable of destroying its possessor according to his responsible or irresponsible exercise of it. Once again Sartre makes God and man free in an univocal sense; once again he fails to understand the paradoxical nature of the freedom in God and the freedom in man. If God's absolute freedom were identical to man's freedom, then, of course, we could not conceive how man could be free. He would be a mere automaton or puppet directed wholly by the divine decisions. But, of course, this is not the case; man is conscious of directing himself by his own decisions. God is absolutely free, yet He does not suffocate the freedom of man. How are the two freedoms possible, if man is totally dependent on God as a creature? We are again in the presence of a mystery, a truth above and beyond, but not against, reason. But Sartre superficially concludes that this relationship must produce determinism. Sartre rejects all mysteries, except the mystery of the absurdity of all reality. For the Christian, freedom is a mysterious gift from the Absolute Freedom, God. For Sartre, freedom is a mysterious curse from the absolute Absurdity of the World of Reality.

Yet Sartre is right and does man a great service when he analyzes the relationship between anxiety and freedom. Each person alone must decide whether he will seek the divine or the demonic. Despite the awful responsibility involved, man must not allow the feeling of dread to paralyze him. He must choose or suffer the degradation of "bad faith" and immoral existence. Sartre is unhappy about having to face life and its decisions alone. It is most distressing to him that God's support is unavailable. For man, isolated and unsupported, is condemned to invent himself every moment. In this nostalgic analysis Sartre unwittingly witnesses to the truth that God is real, that He stirs the soul of man by arousing his metaphysical hunger, conscience and liberty for the Absolute Other. Man cannot remain unmoved when he contemplates the abyss between God and himself, between reason and revelation, between the message from God and the message from himself. Sartre again serves man well by insisting that his misgivings over these sacred decisions cannot be surmounted merely by dispassionate proofs, norms and principles. Witnessing to truth and moral causes must also be made through decisive action. Truth and meaning are not only attained in thinking but also in action.

But Sartre's conclusion is all wrong. Man does not have "to go it alone" in an absurd world with the desperate exercise of his unlimited freedom. God and religion are not merely human projections, as all intellectual atheists from Hegel to the present teach. The reality of God is quite compatible with each man's reason and freedom, since Absolute Intelligence and Liberty is essentially diffusive of itself and is the very source of man's endowment with these spiritual powers. Thus in reality the presence of God is not a projection, but a call to communion. And religion is the dialectic of that communion, a dialectic of truth and love, of sacrifice and self-donation. True, this communion does not of itself remove anxiety from the human condition, for during the temporal testing period of the dialectic there is always the possibility of man's fall into infidelity. Thus, Sartre's error consists in making man's freedom the whole meaning and story of life. The unrestricted exercise of each man's freedom cannot begin to give an adequate account of the world, human beings, truth, morality and man's destiny. To say that it can is to identify all values—true or false, wicked or noble—with the capricious choices of all men. From that erroneous principle there can only emerge a project for social suicide. We now wish to evaluate that project.

What can be said of Sartre's social assumption that intersubjective love is impossible? First, this teaching is built upon the fundamental doctrines of atheism and the absolute freedom of man. In that sense it is both an assumption and a conclusion. It is an assumption in so far as it is not at all demonstrated to be a universal truth. It is a conclusion in so far as it is a logical result of Sartre's break with the Absolute Other and his seizure of unlimited liberty for each man. The Christian thinker rejects Sartre's narrow explanation of the role of the other in interpersonal relations. It is not true that the only role of the other is to achieve the destruction of my subjectivity. Nor is that my goal in relationship to the subjectivity of my fellow men. The other is not always a hostile, conniving, seducing starer, plotting how he can dominate me. The purpose of intersubjective relations is not to dominate or be dominated. It is simply not true that no other intersubjective relationship is possible than sado-masochistic interaction. It is a travesty on love to reduce it to being merely one form of domination along with seduction, hate, desire and cruelty. Christian thinkers reject this sick analysis of man's social relationships.

Commenting on the Sartrean explanation of the nature and ends of intersubjective relationships. Marcel, philosopher of communion and Sartre's most trenchant living critic, writes:

> It is clear that the whole of this dialectic, with its undeniable power, rests upon the complete denial of *we* as subject, that is to say upon the denial of communion. For Sartre this word has no meaning at any possible level, not to speak of its religious or mystical sense. This is because in his universe, participation itself is impossible: this, philo-

sophically, is the essential point. There is room only for appropriation.[27]

Indeed, Sartre's rejection of grace and graciousness is so complete that he even degrades the human activity of gift-giving into a form of seduction for the purpose of dominating others bodily and spiritually. His distortion of the essential nature of the love of generosity is but a further hateful impudence against the sublime reality of genuine mutual human love. "To give is to appropriate by means of destroying and to use this act of destruction as a means of enslaving others."[28] It is clear that the root of Sartre's metaphysical pride is that he refuses to admit his creaturehood. He refuses to be gracious enough to accept any gift. For him to receive anything in joy would make love possible. But already he has proven that love is impossible. For him to receive a gift is incompatible with being free. Indeed a truly free being denies that it has ever received anything. A free being is incapable of expressing gratitude, incapable of giving because incapable of receiving. Thus, the joy of gratitude, the ecstasy of mutual self-donation, the communion of beatific companionship are perverted by Sartre into satanic sorties in social relations for the purpose of dominating and depersonalizing others.

How, then, are men to be brought together for social action, if love, friendship and mutual trust are impossible? As if delighting in the fascination of exaggeration, Sartre calls for *terror* as the only positive force that can oblige men to become social. Terror creates the collective consciousness needed for communal action. Terror is the condition and cause of solidarity, even of brotherliness, for it alone guarantees that "my neighbor will remain my brother." "Sartre," writes Molnar, "needs the drama of extremes—fraternity growing out of terror which he omniously calls 'mortal solicitude'—in order to breed global collectivism. In fact, it is precisely terror with its climate of fear which discourages brotherliness and breeds violence."[29]

Christians see in the initial relationship of man with God, a

27. Gabriel Marcel, *The Philosophy of Existence* (New York: Citadel Press, 1968), p. 76.
28. Jean-Paul Sartre, *Being And Nothingness;* p. 594.
29. Thomas Molnar, *Sartre: Ideologue of our Time* (New York: Funk & Wagnalls, 1968), p. 109.

communication of gifts and a communion of destinies in mutual love. The Transcendent Lover bestows being, dignity, mission, destiny on man as the other whom He has loved and called into His presence. The Transcendent Lover gives Himself freely without any hint of trying to dominate the freedom of man, but rather honoring him with an invitation to collaborate with His Benefactor in the venture toward human sanctity and happiness. Neither is the No of conflict the only answer men give to the call of their fellow men. Indeed, millions of martyrs, confessors, virgins, saints from all walks of life have answered Yes to the invocation of God to live with Him. And in answering Yes to God, they have also said Yes to their fellow men. Nor is the essence of man's relationships incarnated in the look of hate. For Sartre, every look is a look of hate, every embrace a "kiss of death." Granted that the kiss of Judas is always a possibility, the fact is that it is not the only possibility; it is not the only and predetermined eventuality in man's social life. If it were, where would be that vaunted, unlimited freedom Sartre claims for man?

There is also the look of love, genuine, disinterested, concerned with the happiness of the other. This look expresses a will to communion, to service, not to domination. The look of God creates human persons: "I have loved thee with an everlasting love, therefore, have I drawn thee, taking pity on thee". The Gospels record that the look of Christ raises up, restores, saves man. The look of Christ melted Peter into repentance; the look of Christ transformed Magdalene from sinner into saint; the look of Christ raised in an instant with Himself into paradise a blaspheming thief on the verge of hell. The person of every child is created by the loving looks of its parents and relatives. The truth is that man thrives as a person under the light of the approval of others. In the end, the look of love conquers the look of hate. It is never Christ who flees the gaze of Satan; it is Satan who flees the look of Christ and begs for asylum in swine. But the look of love creates subjectivity in both lover and beloved because in its expansive climate of mutual self-donation the lovers achieve the plenitude of their beings as persons. In every inter-subjective relation, in every society the last word on its social vigor is not concerned with the mind but with whether one loves. Sartre does not love; he does not even love himself, for according to the abstractions of his mind, love is an impossible ideal. Society is a jungle of scheming tyrants seeking to dominate one another. Such a social philosophy can only beget a society of murderers or a society of suicides, depending on whether men decide to seize power or despair over attaining the grace of communion.

In the spirit of ethical adventuresomeness, Sartre attacks what he calls "the spirit of seriousness" and equates it with "bad faith." When men appeal to a universal moral law in the hope of dodging hard decisions, they are acting false roles. When men immerse themselves in God, prayer, religious services or transcendent activities of any kind, they are fleeing the tasks of freedom for this life. Thus Freudians with their libidos, communists with their classless society, Christians with their heaven, anyone who deceives himself about the present duty by concentrating his faith on the future, all these are hiding behind "the spirit of seriousness" but living in "bad faith." What then is good faith in Sartre's social philosophy?

Good faith is practiced by the man who works to liberate himself from his own egotism and to collaborate for the freedom of others. Thus, when Sartre, in the day of the underground Resistance, schemed and worked for the freedom of France and French prisoners, he was living in "good faith," for he was living for others. This was certainly a morally good activity. No Christian would quarrel with this selfcommitment. But the question arises: How is such commitment to the good of others possible under the Sartrean social theories? For under this theory of universal social conflict in interpersonal relations, such commitment to the welfare of others is well-nigh impossible. According to Sartre, men do not know what is good for other men since they have no nature, no values, no liberty, no destiny in common. Moreover, each man's exercise of liberty is always aimed at enslaving others. Sartre's theory denies the possibility of common sociality among men, yet in practice he now demands self-commitment to others. Moreover, his phenomenological descriptions of interpersonal activities stress egotism and conflict, frustration rather than social fruition. It is this inconsistency between doctrine and deed that has led the Marxists to dismiss Sartre's thinking as "the last, convulsive effort of the alienated individual in a dying bourgeois world."

For all its vaunted phenomenological method, Sartre's philosophy is in its main themes a product of pure subjectivism, a creation of a mind divorced from concrete reality. Sartre, is, in a word, the worst kind of rationalist, the kind that expresses contempt and irreverence for concrete reality and favors a towering love for the disembodied mind. He himself testifies in *The Words* how he became that way:

> A Platonist by condition, I moved from knowledge to its objects; I found ideas more real than things, because they were the first to give themselves to me and because they gave themselves like things. I met the universe in books: assimilated, classified, labelled and studied, but still impressive; and I confused the chaos of my experience through books with the hazardous course of real events. Hence my idealism which it took me thirty years to undo.[30]

The truth is that Sartre is still confusing "the chaos of my experience through books with the . . . course of real events." The truth is that even today he has failed to undo his idealism or rationalism. Who, but a man hopelessly divorced from the hostile to the sacred, concrete mystery of parenthood, could have written this unrealistic nonsense against human love: "The rule is that there are no good fathers; it is not the men who are at fault but the parental bond which is rotten. There is nothing better than to produce children but what a sin to *have* some!"[31]

It is tragic to watch Sartre move from idol to idol in a vain effort to replace his banished God. The sign of the sacred has shifted from Catholicism to belles-lettres, to fame as a writer, to revolution on behalf of social causes under the banner of socialism and Marxism. Today Sartre admits his complete disillusionment over his chosen idols: ". . . I know quite well that no one is waiting for me. I have renounced my vocation but I have not unfrocked myself. I still write. What else can I do?"[32]

Sartre has rendered mankind some useful services. He has analyzed sin with deep penetration. It is the bitter estrangement from God and from our fellow man. It is the great divine-human schism. He has exploded the secularized myths that

30. Jean-Paul Sartre, *The Words*, p. 34.
31. *Ibid.*, p. 14.
32. *Ibid.*, p. 157.

guarantee man happiness in and through temporal achievements. No present, no future earthly condition of man will ever
make life worth living. He has stressed once again, in a stark
manner, man's personal responsibility for making his own being and world. He has focused the mind and heart of man on
his great power of freedom with all its dangerous possibilities.
He has ruthlessly unmasked the poses men take to escape hard
decisions. He has re-created the confrontation between freedom and grace. He has forced the collectivized atheism of Positivism and Marxism to come out from behind their protective
wall of science and politics in order to prove to the individual
that absurd existence is worth living. He has put their panaceas
to a severe test.

But in the last analysis Sartre's philosophy leads logically
and directly to despair and suicide. His doctrine of salvation
leads man to the abyss of social atomism. His first and final
word on life, liberty and love is that they just happen and are
always absurd, contradictory and doomed to frustration. His
world of atheism is a kingdom of nothingness plunged into
intellectual darkness, convulsed with spiritual hate and peo-
pled by inhabitants who curse God and destroy each other in
their vain attempt to seize His vacant throne.

CHAPTER VIII

Heidegger:
"Waiting for the New God"

PERHAPS THE MOST PROFOUND CONTEMPORARY source of inspiration for the "death of God" school of philosopher-theologians is the systematic phenomenologist-philosopher, Martin Heidegger. Heidegger was born in 1889 in Messkirch, a region in the Black Forest of Swabia. A man who has remained close to the soil while developing into a solitary thinker, Heidegger has never left this austerely beautiful land high up in the mountains. He was brought up a Catholic and for a short time was a novice in the Society of Jesus with the aim of studying to be a priest. Before developing his own thought, he learned Scholastic thought well, passed through the training of the Neo-Kantians and subsequently experienced the direct influence of the great Husserl, the founder of phenomenology. In fact, it was in close contact with Husserl, to whom he later dedicated his master work, *Being And Time,* that he worked out his own method of philosophical analysis and exposition. In 1927, while Professor of Philosophy at the University of Marburg, he published his greatest work, *Being and Time*. His first published work had been his thesis for lectureship, *Duns Scotus's Doctrine of Categories and Concepts*.

Heidegger openly took his philosophic stand and orientation in the European tradition of philosophy, but he boldly ambitioned becoming its modern Aristotle, his main aim being to construct an ontology whose new basis would finally answer the long-neglected question: "What is the meaning of 'Being'?" He was convinced that neither Aristotle himself nor the long line of great Western thinkers since him had addressed themselves properly to this problem. In the course of pursuing the solution to this central problem, Heidegger coins his own technical terminology. It is extremely unfamiliar and extraordinarily hard to cope with even for the professional philosopher. For in taking up the meaning of being afresh, Heidegger admits he will have to destroy traditional ontology. Thus he makes use of the peculiar, run-on word structure of the German language, often resorting to elaborate puns to express the content of his reflections. An eminent classicist, master of Greek and Latin, he digs back into the root meanings of words to develop startling neologisms that substitute new meanings for old, familiar ones. If this philosopher is so ambiguous and well-nigh impossible to decipher, it may be asked, "Why bother to tax the minds of readers with a discussion of his thought at all"?

The reason is, as we have indicated above, that Heidegger has had and is still having an all-pervading influence upon the existentialists. Though Heidegger has dissociated himself from Sartre and emphasized their differences, he and Sartre are still in agreement on some important points. Both these philosophers set out to establish a universally valid philosophy whose main concentration is the existence and not the essence of things. Theirs is an existential, phenomenological ontology. Its purpose is to answer the question: "What is existence; in what does the being of existence consist?" Both analyzed the "Cogito" of Descartes and renounced it because his abstractions fail to reach the being of existence. Both replaced Aristotle's and Kant's abstract categories of being with their own phenomenological, existential categories to describe the phenomenon of existing things. According to Sartre and Heidegger, this description alone has the value of proof because it unveils the evidence of the phenomenon of concrete existences under all their aspects. Moreover, Heidegger and Sartre agree that man's fundamental personality is established by his free choice of his destiny, a choice that has no other justification than itself and is the first, absolute principle in the human being, that which explains his whole life. Then too, Sartre's conception of Nothingness reflects Heidegger's direct influence on him. Moreover, if one examines contemporary Protestant, existential theologians, one finds that Heidegger's influence on them is vast. The thought of such theologians as Brunner, Bultmann, Tillich, Van Buren, Robinson and many others is steeped in Heideggerian thought-forms.

In 1020 Heidegger succeeded Husserl at Freiburg to the Chair of Philosophy where he continued to teach until the end of the Second World War. He supported the Nazi regime when it came to power in 1933 and, in the same year, was elected Rector of Freiburg University.[1] Though he later became disillusioned and resigned his post as Rector in 1934, he never publicly rejected Nazism. As a result of this entanglement, he was for some time forbidden to teach in Germany when the Allies began their occupation. Today, however, he continues to write as a recluse and his influence in the world of thought is probably greater than it was before the accession of Hitler to power. In an interesting speculative exercise as to how such a profound philosopher, whose thought stresses the independence of the individual, could ever have been lured to favor Nazism, Roberts advances four conjectural considerations.

> First, his sense of closeness to the soil, especially his native Swabian land. Second, the influence of Nietzsche, which prompted him to feel that Western civilization had become spiritually bankrupt and that a radical transvaluation of values was needed. Third, mystical tendency which had nowhere to go except to associate itself with his

1. In November 1933 Heidegger, just established Rector of the University of Freiburg by the will of the Nazi Party which had been voted into power, issued a proclamation to the students of the university. It said in part: "Not theorems and 'ideas' be the rule of your being. The Führer himself and alone is the present and future German reality and its law. Learn ever deeper to know: that from now on each and every thing demands decision, and every action responsibility. Heil Hitler!" See Dr. Hans Jonas, "Heidegger and Theology," *Review of Metaphysics*, XVIII, December 1964, pp. 207–233.

feelings about the homeland. Fourth, a stress upon reso-
luteness and courage which could easily be channeled in
the direction of political decision and martial virtues. But
these remain mere conjectures, and the qualities to which
they call attention have continued to characterize his
thinking since the Nazi debacle as well as before it.[2]

The Problem of Being and Human Existence

According to Heidegger, to inquire into the meaning of Being
is not a grammatical questing at all. It is rather a seeking of the
Being of beings. But what particular being is best suited for
study in the construction of a new ontology? The approach to
ontology via cosmology, the path taken by the classical philosophers, has failed to consider the meaning of Being. Heidegger's
new approach to Being is the being of man. He begins his search
for the meaning of Being by searching the being of the ques-
tioner himself. For man who raises the problem, as "being
there"—*Dasein* is Heidegger's word for him—has a special relation to Being. Man's very investigation of Being is a mode of
being. But Heidegger has no intention of studying man for the
sake of giving a cultural or sociological or psychological account of him. For him, man is the most important instance of
being because man has the capacity to wonder and thus to
philosophize in a contemplative manner. Thus, man should be
able to discover the relationship between his own particular
being and the structure of Being in itself.

But what precisely is Being in itself for Heidegger? Is it the
absolute, ultimate Being, the utterly Transcendent Being in the
sense of God? No, for according to Heidegger, God, if He existed, would be a being among other beings. And Heidegger is
not interested in beings or a being; his whole concern is with
Being in itself; he is seeking the Being of beings. Thus, a study
of man, who raises the problem of Being, is primary and essential to the meaning of the Being of beings. For man alone
among all beings is open to Being and its existential structure.

Man being there *(Dasein)* is existence *(Existenz)*. He cannot
be defined as a static essence, as a rational animal, because

2. David E. Roberts, *Existentialism and Religious Belief* (New York: A
Galaxy Book, Oxford University Press, 1959), p. 149.

man is always potential being, a potentiality of being. Continually in advance of himself, man projects himself into the future, thus transcending himself. Ontologically man is a being-in-the-world; this is his fundamental constitution, his innermost essence. "World" is that whereto man transcends so as to be what he is and to become what he is to be. Actually, man is "thrown" into the world and left there to his own devices and responsibility. There, in his "thrown" condition, man finds himself dynamically related to other things and persons. As a result of this relationship, he exists, necessarily preoccupied and concerned with "the other," but not with this or that particular other. Thus, active concern and preoccupation with other beings-encountered-in-the-world is a constitutive characteristic of man's existence. For man exists as being-in-the-world in advance of himself, concerned and preoccupied with the other. As he moves forward to realize his possibilities, man is concerned with the encounter with other beings and men. It is through his concern and preoccupation that man constitutes the world as a meaningful system of objects. His concern establishes objects in intelligible relations to one another and to himself.

In his contrast between the world of men and the world of things, Heidegger sees the world of objects as the world of tools and utensils. Objects are instruments at hand; they exist for the use of men. The sea *is* for the fisherman what he drags in order to get fish—food. It is, of course, quite another thing for the merchant marine, the naval strategist or the sailing enthusiast. Each takes his meaning of the sea from the inner concern that constitutes his being. Thus, man is a being-in-the-world concerned with things as instruments which will help him in his drive forward to realize his chosen projects. Now man's practical point of view of things is, of course, not his only viewpoint. There is a great variety of perspectives and viewpoints. For one example, scientists study the sea objectively, not as an instrument, but simply to discover its physical composition. Both viewpoints, practical and scientific, are useful but neither is exclusively privileged. Preoccupation with things takes a variety of forms which give birth to different yet complementary, meaningful systems. Man's concern, of course, is not responsible for the stark "thereness" of things but for the meaningful patterns and systems which form his individual world. Each man discovers himself as an individual subject only as a being "thrown" there within the world and as a subject in relation with other subjects.

Social being-with, social intersubjectivity adds another dimension to the constitutive being of man, complementing his preoccupation with things as tools. Heidegger expresses this dimension of man's being thus. The human person is in the world as a member of "the anonymous one," *(das Man)*. This fundamental social interdependence reveals man as being immersed in a maze of conventional mass human reactions and as participating in established ways of feeling and thinking. Being-in-the-world means being-with for man. Each individual lives largely in terms of "what he does" or "what he does not do." Man's private viewpoint arises only on the basis of a common world constituted by the concern which is a fundamental characteristic of man seen as a member of "the anonymous one." "My" world presupposes the world of "the anonymous one." Man is, thus, not an isolated ego, but oriented toward the realization of his possibilities. For he is a being necessarily interrelated with the world of things and the world of persons.

Now because of his immergence in the world of things and persons, man will never be able to escape completely from the impersonal form of existence which roots him in membership with "the anonymous one." Yet man must make the effort to rise out of "the anonymous one" if he is to attain his true selfhood. Two paths are open to each individual. First, man can freely settle down in a life immersed in "the anonymous one" so that he is absorbed in crowd-consciousness, thereby choosing security and assurance at the cost of personal responsibility and resolute self-direction. Once man does this, he sinks into what Heidegger calls "unauthentic existence." Or second, man may, within limits of course, assume personal responsibility for his destiny, freely choose his possibilities and, above all, accept his destiny to death. This way of life would constitute "authentic existence" for man. Thus, "thrown" into the world, finite, abandoned to his own resources, and destined to death, man is called upon to achieve the realization of his possibilities and thereby to interpret the world in the accomplishment of his chosen projects.

It is true, alas, that the ultimate possibility, one which annihilates all other possibilities in the end, is death. Man is a being who transcends himself dynamically toward the future, the being who is "thrown" into the world and destined to death. This tragic future presents man with a major decision, the dilemma of how to live. Shall he interpret himself as just one thing among others in the world and thereby subordinate himself to things? Or shall he pursue his possibilities in such a way that they become the achievements for which he exists? If he chooses the former way of life, he decides for unauthentic existence and thinking. If he chooses the latter way of life, he enters the life of authentic understanding and existence. But even if the decision is for the nobler, harder way of life, man's testing does not stop there. For the decision must be renewed continually until death, since it is always possible to fall away from higher resolves.

Perhaps the most important result of his obscure consciousness of contingency, finiteness, dereliction and destiny to death is man's fundamental experience of "dread." Heidegger distinguishes between "dread" and "fear." Fear is directed toward some definite being whereas dread is not. Dread is a fleeing, panic reaction to a threatening state of affairs, to "something" which renders the very atmosphere of life harsh. Now because he is free, man may attempt to flee the responsibility of his possibilities so as to remain safe and secure at the level of "the anonymous one," thereby deluding himself that in this way he will escape the experience of dread. He may plunge into the realm of the commonplace, thinking, talking, doing trivia, squandering his intellectual powers in curiosities, novelties, gossip, in any superficial, uncritical undertaking that may distract him from the restlessness of dread. In a word, he may choose to enslave himself in externalized anonymity. For Heidegger, this choice to flee his true selfhood, this decision to become a bogus person is the fall that constitutes man's Original Sin. Nevertheless, man's flight from his authentic self never escapes the gravitational pull of dread; dread accompanies man everywhere. That "something"—he can never specify it as a definite thing—that is threatening him is as ever present and inescapable as the air he breathes. While in this state of flight and self-estrangement, man sees death as something that happens not to himself but to "the anonymous one." He thus refuses to face and embrace dread, to live an authentic existence. Dread, therefore, destroys him as a true self.

But if he overcomes the temptation to fall away from his true self to the groundless irrelevance of everyday anonymity, man's very experience of dread will be a force that drives him to the achievement of his possibilities. He will, then, attain the plenitude of his true selfhood through an authentic existence *sub specie mortis.* Instead of running away in dread to the slavery of a bogus self, he will be running forward, despite dread, to the freedom of his authentic self.

Pursuing his phenomenological scrutiny of human existence, Heidegger then introduces what he considers the most fundamental characteristic of the human structure. "What is the Being of *Dasein?"* he asks. "It is defined as Care," he answers. And Care *(Sorge)* is composed of three moments that reflect man's total situation. First, man, discovering himself in existence before he knows the meaning of existence, is concerned with what he is to be. *Existenz* means being-in-front-of-oneself or self-projection. Thus as man is *Existenz,* it must be asserted that futurity characterizes him. Man's running forward toward his potentiality is the ground of his futurity. Care, then, is the first element in his existence arising from his concern with what he is to be. Secondly, man discovers he is in the world as "thrown." His concern over this "thrown" condition of his existence is the second constitutive element of Care. This phase of Care grounds man in the past. Thirdly, man's being-with others in the world, his entangling relationships arouse particular preoccupations that constitute the third element of his care. This moment of Care grounds man in the present. Care, then, is tri-temporal, but its primary element is futurity. Man is thus structured in temporality in his inmost being. His being is, therefore, projection from nothingness toward nothingness. Once he has freely accepted his "throwness" into the world and his relations there toward others, once he has willingly decided to run forward toward his unique potentiality known as death, which involves his existing no longer, man then authentically constitutes his past and present by reaching out responsibly toward his future. It is when man accepts the potentiality of his death that he experiences the whole meaning of isolation, for death severs all relations to others. Man has no possibility of escaping the dread connected with his running toward his death. Each man's death is irreplaceable, though each man can be replaced. Where death is the experience, no one can take my place. Each man has to do his own dying. Running away from death through immature attempts to avoid dread only estranges man from his innermost self and betrays the truth that he is essentially preoccupied with death. The authentic attitude toward death enables man to accept his potentialities and their limitations. *Sub specie mortis* man is enabled to see all other possibilities in their brutal finitude and, entering into death as an inevitable personal experience, he will also be able, through his ensuing experience of isolation, to accept the extreme potentiality of his existence as that of a full and final renunciation. Indeed, the very indefiniteness of the moment of his death will then become for man, not an occasion for an endless postponement of considering it, but the occasion for his continual confrontation with the Nothingness of death. Dread of death attunes man to Nothingness.

When he treats of the human conscience in its relation to authentic and unauthentic existence, Heidegger reveals his novel doctrine on both conscience and guilt. Conscience, on the unauthentic level of existence, merely listens to others in order to join in accepting what is commonly said and done. But the call of conscience on the authentic level of existence arises from the true self. Speaking in silence, the authentic call of conscience rejects the lure of the crowd and the commonplace; it drives the true self toward its solitary accomplishment of its potentialities. Authentic conscience arises solely from the self, not from God, nor from social mores, nor from social pressures or any source outside the self. The voice of conscience is that mysterious source within man which, strangely enough, drives the true self away from normal, daily human existence because it finds this insipid, inadequate and destructive of man's independence.

Now it is the cry of conscience that awakens guilt in man. Guilt is fundamentally related to a deficiency, the absence of a mode of being which the individual might have become. Thus all guilty feelings, arising from individual faults and evil deeds, presuppose man's basic condition of being guilty. Authentic existence does not flee the experience of guilt; rather it accepts the guilt of failure to realize one's potentialities; it makes use of this guilt as the starting line for human existence, the foundation upon which the individual will project himself toward his possibilities. Thus, man will choose his true self only by embracing his own guilt. For, he will thereby heed the cry of conscience which is the herald of authentic existence. Heidegger describes this willingness to accept dread, death, conscience and guilt as an openness of being, a resolve to become one's true self even though forced to remain in the world tied somewhat to "the anonymous one." It is the spirit of this openness and bold resolve that founds authentic man in genuine human fellowship. Such resolve creates mutual understanding among solitary, authentic individuals who transcend their dismal surroundings by mastering them. Such resolve transforms mere transitory activities into permanent deeds of inner development. Heidegger rejects every attempt to locate the ultimate source of conscience, guilt and resolve in an immortal self who transcends the world and time. There is no self which is beyond man in the midst of his world, beyond man's time, dread, Care, death. There is no Being who gives man his personal identity. Personal identity has to be achieved by each individual in the fires of resolution, isolation, independence, in the condition of "throwness," dread and destiny to death.

Heidegger proceeds to unravel the role of man in history. He has already established that man can never exist outside temporality. He revealed man as caught up in three "ecstasies" (*ekstasis:* literally, "standing out") of future, present and past. Now man discovers the meaning of his own existence by studying the history of mankind. Unlike brute animals and objects which act and are acted upon by a process that is unintelligible to them, man creates history as well as being formed by it. He is *the* historical being because he alone reflects and makes decisions. Volcanoes, canyons and mountains do not have a "history" in the strict sense; they certainly undergo the processes of change, but have no say in these changes. The same is true of the animal world. It is man's decisions that determine the possibilities of authentic existence. Through these decisions man can cull from the record of his fellowman. Man's reflections and choices enable him to use the past of history as the launching pad to the future, instead of preserving the past in an accumulating mass of petrified lumber. Man chooses to perpetuate the valuable achievements of his heritage. On the level of authentic existence this means that man is intelligently selective of what he will conserve and perpetuate; he does not blindly nor automatically conserve for the sake of conserving. Man chooses to keep alive his kinship with the genius and culture of the past ages. Consequently, the acceptance and perpetuation of tradition as a living presence is, at the same time, the projection of the genius of this tradition toward the achievement of man's present and future potentialities. Thus the core of history is found in individual existence. On the other hand, the unauthentic approach to history reverses this process. Merely noting down what has happened, it fails to analyze or take a firm stand on events and accomplishments of the past. Moreover, it sees the individual as an insignificant moment on the unintelligible world process. The objective approach to history is sterile because it never attains reality; it merely catalogues it. Decisions alone lead man to understand world history and his role within it. The reflection, choice and authority of the free individual in judging history are recognized by other free individuals only when that individual authority preserves and projects human achievements worth repeating. Historical facts in themselves are dead and meaningless; they come alive with pertinence to the present and future only when they are related to man's personal decisions today because they were vital to man's decisions in the past. Subjectivism in this process of creating true history through personal decisions will be avoided by fidelity to facts and an immergence in a sound ontology.[3]

The Essence of Truth

In his discussion on the essence of truth, Heidegger continues his "phenomenological destruction" of traditional ontology. He does this by fitting his meaning of truth into an expanded con-

3. Martin Heidegger, *Being and Time,* transl. by John Macquarrie and Edward Robinson (Oxford: Basil Blackwell, 1967). This is the *magnum opus* of the author, containing his reinvestigation of the meaning of Being in a terminology so new and difficult that we can only hope we have done minimal justice to his thought in this section on his ontology.

text of his distinction between authentic and unauthentic existence. He rejects the traditional definition of truth as the conformity of the mind with the object. He objects that this theory of truth is founded on Christian theology. As long as the human intellectual and concrete things were viewed as created by God, it was natural to conclude that just as creation was in conformity with God's ideas of it, so, in an analogous manner, man's ideas could be brought into conformity with the world of creation, thus attaining human truth. God, as the intelligent, unique source of an harmonious creative plan was the foundation for the possibility of any human knowledge. So too, if truth consists in conformity between thought and thing, then error would necessarily consist in the nonconformity between judgments and the objects to which they refer. Now Heidegger is against supernatural explanations of truth, for he holds that theology is not needed to explain the essence of truth. That reason is able to conform to the world should be obvious, for the human mind develops in interaction with the world of other minds and things.

How does the mind, then, conform to the object? Thought differs so radically from the object that conformity between them seems impossible. The object is concrete, material, spatial; thought of the object is abstract, immaterial and nonspatial. What takes place when thought represents things to human consciousness without altering the things represented as they are there in the world? Heidegger says that somehow the object "comes across the open" into man's conscious mind. Now this openness and accessibility of the object cannot be the product of the mind, neither man's nor God's, for consciousness receives objects that are already accessible; it does not make them accessible. Heidegger's ontology, therefore, rejects the process of finding truth in propositions created by the mind. For him, truth cannot arise in the mind unless it is awakened by the object. But this awakening is not an automatic process. Indeed, to submit willingly to adherence to a truth made available by the object calls for an act of freedom. Thus the difference between true and false thinking is grounded in freedom. Not that the truth content of a statement depends as such on the act of volition. The freedom indicated here is not the plaything of caprice; rather it is the liberty which is constitutive of the structure of Being. This fundamental liberty reveals itself as saying Yes to what-is as it is. Such freedom willingly participates in the openness of things. Thus truth does not come about by conformity between two utterly disparate beings—thought and thing. Rather truth is created through the free participation of man in the luminous "coming across the open" of things. Objects are the realities that open and reveal themselves; minds are the consciousnesses that must expose themselves for their reception. A mind exposes itself through participation in the revelations of objects. Freedom and truth, then, coincide where the participation of mind in the revealed nature of what-is occurs. *"The essence of truth is freedom,"* says Heidegger, emphasizing this statement with his own italics.[4] And, he continues, "Resistance to the proposition that the essence of truth is freedom is rooted in prejudices, the most obstinate of which contends that freedom is a property of man and that the nature of freedom neither needs nor allows of further questioning."[5] In reality it is not man who possesses freedom as a property, but rather freedom that possesses man. It does so in such an all-pervading manner that it endows him with the relationship to what-is-in-totality, a relationship that is a distinctive characteristic of man in history.

When he goes on to treat truth from the aspects of authentic and unauthentic understanding, Heidegger points to natural science as a clear example of unauthentic understanding. Natural science, through its process of technical domination, falls into untruth by dissimulating and concealing the truth of Being. For untruth is always a form of dissimulation. Therefore, science as a source of real truth has to be debunked. Of course, scientists gather many facts, announce formulas, develop techniques and predict results. All this is done not in the name of truth but of power and control. Scientists are not interested in the total being of any individual thing, in the what-is or the meaning of Being. Thus they are never open nor attuned

4. Martin Heidegger, *Existence and Being,* Containing: a) An Account of *Being and Time* by Dr. Werner Brock; b) *Remembrance of the Poet* translated by Douglas Scott; c) *Holderlin and the Essence of Poetry* translated by Douglas Scott; d) *On the Essence of Truth* translated by R. F. C. Hull and Alan Crick; e) *What Is Metaphysics?* translated by R. F. C. Hull and Alan Crick, (London: Vision Press Ltd., 1968), p. 330.
5. *Ibid.,* p. 332.

to whatever is revealed by beings. That is why scientists fail to experience wonderment or the magic and mystery of the universe and of existence. The scientist finds it a monotonous fact that the sun rises and sets every day, for he is concerned only with the mastery of things. Hostile to the revelatory character of Being, scientists reject metaphysics in favor of technics and manipulation. On the other hand, whenever what-is as a whole manifests itself and man becomes attuned to it through participation, then this event of truth goes far beyond the petty calculations of science. This event soars towards the incomprehensible, incalculable dimensions of Being. For it is mystery that underlies participation in essential truth; it is mystery that pervades the whole of human existence. Estranged from the truth from the outset of his quest for knowledge, man often mistakes his preoccupation with gathering facts about objects as the essence of truth. This is the scientist's great mistake. Practical knowledge is not part of the revelation of truth. Moreover, to ignore the mystery of Being does not abolish it; neither is it annihilated when it is neglected. The dilemma always remains for man. He must choose between a world of projects, plans, dominations and a world of truth and mystery. He must choose authentic or unauthentic knowledge. To prefer mechanics to metaphysics is to prefer estrangement from human potentialities and reduction to the status of objects themselves. To prefer the mystery of Being to the manipulation of things is to accept the adventure of freedom to move forward toward one's highest possibilities and fullest, genuine self. Man is not the measure of all things; he must return from mechanics to metaphysics, from living in error to living in truth, if he is to save himself from the tyranny of technologization and mass society. Once again Heidegger brings us back to the courageous resolve that is needed to make the decisions which will liberate man from the masses mired in mechanics to join the solitaries seeking mystery.

But the decision to live in genuine metaphysics will demand another encounter with dread, Heidegger warns man. The essential miseries of human existence stem from the fact that Being also contains the negation of what-is. Being-there *(Dasein)* affirms simultaneously the essence of truth and the extreme non-revelation of truth. Thus Being and Nothingness hang together. This is true, according to Heidegger, "because

Being itself is finite in essence and is only revealed in the Transcendence of *Dasein* as projected into Nothing."[6] But it is dread which reveals Nothingness. Thus the man who resolves to pursue the mystery of Being is also prepared to suffer the dread of Nothingness. For man's freedom, which is grounded in Being, is simultaneously founded in Nothingness. When man, therefore, participates in the mystery of truth it means that human liberty also accepts the presence of Nothingness within the ambit of its freedom. For freedom consists in transcending Nothingness. For Heidegger, Nothingness seems to be something positive. It can perhaps be explained through the distinction between the brute thereness of being *(das Seiende)* and the conscious existence of the human being *(das Sein)*. Between these two classes of beings there is Being-as-such which is, as it were, their relation of union. This type of in-between Being is the meaning which man gives to brute being as he reflects upon and uses it. Before man gives it meaning, the world of beings is positive being, to be sure, but it is still undetermined and chaotic. Without meaning it is not yet Being in the strict sense of the word. One can, therefore, call the as yet meaningless world Nothingness. Man is born into this Nothingness and he will return, via death, to this Nothingness. During his life span, however, his courageous resolves of freedom enable him to transcend this Nothingness. Through the exercise of his freedom he commits himself to accept the challenge of Nothingness; he imposes meaning upon this Nothingness and thereby raises it to the status of Being. Man attains mature achievements in truth and liberty when he organizes his existence in a meaningful manner between the two Nothingnesses bordering his birth and death. Only thus can he live an authentic existence. From this phenomenological doctrine arises Heidegger's famous formula: *Ex nihilo omne ens qua ens fit.* "Every being in so far as it is being is made out of nothing."[7]

Christian philosophy, of course, is in complete disagreement with Heidegger's formula. The Scholastic philosophy holds that *ex nihilo nihil fit,* but this is in the context that defines Nothing as the absolute absence of all being. But, since God always exists, the Christian formulates his principle in a more realistic way. *Ex nihilo fit—ens creatum.* He is forced by the evi-

6. *Ibid.,* p. 377.
7. *Ibid.,* p. 377.

dence of creation to conclude in this reasonable way. But since God is Being in such an absolutely transcending and superior way and degree from the being of creatures, the Christian divides being into *Summum Ens*—God—and *ens creatum*—creatures. God is then seen as drawing creatures out of Nothingness, but by the omnipotent power and fullness of His Own Being. How this is done is the mystery of Being, because to be able to grasp the how of creation would be equivalent to comprehending exhaustively the essence of God, an impossible achievement for a limited intelligence.

What then is Heidegger's conclusion about philosophy as the source of truth? He teaches that philosophy is autonomous as a human activity. Philosophy cannot acknowledge any outside authority, nor expect nor receive any support from natural science or theology. The art of philosophizing alone, which is the art of living in commitment to Being through the courageous resolve of liberty, can discover and maintain the laws of truth. To be sure, philosophy is not an enterprise of pure reason apprehending eternal essences, as the Greeks and Scholastics taught. Rather, philosophy is the historical act of the total man. Only in piercing to the structure of man as he lives in history does man succeed in comprehending what it means to say that Being includes knowing, that man is to be understood in the last analysis as a freedom founded in Being and Nothingness.

An Atheism of Ambiguity

On the basis of the first volume of his *Time and Being (Sein und Zeit)*—the other two volumes of Heidegger's philosophy have not yet appeared though eagerly awaited for the past thirty years—Heidegger's thought has often been branded by professional philosophers and theologians as an existentialist form of modern atheism. In my opinion, there are very good reasons for this conclusion, even though Heidegger himself in his *Letter On Humanism* has vigorously protested against the atheistic interpretation of his philosophy.[8] It is true that he

8. Martin Heidegger, Letter On Humanism, from *Philosophy In The Twentieth Century*, ed. W. Barrett, H. D. Aiken, (New York: Random House, 1962), p. 294. "Through the ontological interpretation of *Dasein* as Being-in-the-World, there is neither a positive nor a negative resolution of a possible Being-towards-God."

never explicitly denies the existence of God in forthright language. But his whole phenomenological method of philosophizing and his descriptions of the human predicament inevitably suggest that reality is nothing more than the existence of godless man in a godless universe.

A phenomenological method of philosophizing which forbids the thinker from reflecting beyond the immediate, concrete evidence at hand in his analysis of contingent existence must lead to a self-enclosed philosophic atheism. This type of philosophy appears to be, if one may formulate an expression, a phenomenological positivism. The very analysis Heidegger makes of the inner, metaphysical structure of Being brings him to the conclusion that Being is essentially and necessarily finite and temporal. Naturally enough, if this conclusion is true, then an infinitely Necessary Being who transcends time and change, is simply ruled out, of no concern because it is non-existent. One suspects that Heidegger sees this inevitable conclusion of his thought and it is for this reason that he has simply dropped the question of God, proclaiming in rather Delphic terms that he neither affirms nor denies God. He quickly affirms, however, that his refusal to raise the question of God as an important and agonizing problem for man must not be put down to indifferentism. It is simply that on the level of existential analysis where man is "thrown," conscious and destined to death, the existence of God cannot be raised as a problem. Why not? Heidegger's explanation deserves adequate consideration because it contains a profound commentary on the contemporary chaos that exists in the wasteland of mass society. Though agreeing with him for the most part in his perceptive description of the spiritual disintegration of our age, we cannot imitate either his stoical stand of silence about God or his flight into the mysticism of poetry as the only valid mood and response against the triumph of technocratic society. For reasons to be exposed later on, we consider both the mood of silence and the flight into poetry sterile and misguided answers to the challenge of moral and metaphysical chaos.

Heidegger, in a deeply spiritual sense, is a philosophic heir of Nietzsche. In a series of conferences given during the Third Reich, Heidegger expounded on Nietzsche's saying: "God is Dead." He pointed out that this proclamation was the bell-symbol that tolled the tragic end of Western man as a Christian. The expression "God is dead" has undermined the whole vision of an intelligible world that transcends the sensible world. It has weakened not only Christian belief but the whole tradition of Western metaphysics. Not satisfied with expounding this saying of Nietzsche's, Heidegger went on to reinterpret it. He explained that when Nietzsche announced that "God is dead," the proclamation remained an anti-proclamation, that is, it continued to be addicted to what it opposed. It continued to arouse a world-wide upheaval of nostalgic emotions that deplored the absence and hungered for the return of the dead God. Heidegger suggested that Nietzsche's thrust against God ought to be pushed to its limits. After all, even Nietzsche considered the "Death of God" to be only a transitional event. Thus the movement against God should so develop that no trace of the emotional trail left behind should be allowed to remain to indicate the direction or place in which God had quietly and unobtrusively sunk into oblivion.[9] Once the old God, with his old norms of transcendent truth, goodness and beauty had vanished, then the authority of the old God would be replaced by the authority of liberated man, the new man, the man of reason and committed conscience. Nietzsche's atheism was a step in the right direction; it was a nihilism leading to a greater self-consciousness in man through which the essence of modern man would come to fulfillment. Then, creative activity, no longer the monopoly of a defunct God, would become the characteristic activity of man. And just as Nietzsche called for the "transvaluation of all values," so too modern man's new ethic would no longer have fixed norms. The final step, of course, would be achieved in man's maturation when he ascended to the position of being the executor of his absolute will to power. Heidegger seemed to be teaching that God had to be annihilated and every trace or memory of his Being erased from the consciousness of man if man were to become authentic man.

For Heidegger, however, the modern age is still slightly sickened with nostalgia for God. To be sure, it is an age of metaphysical and theological rot. A whole spiritual movement that impoverishes the spirit of man while it coddles his body and titillates his superficial interests is in the ascendency at pre-

9. Georg Siegmund, *God On Trial*, pp. 433–434.

sent in politics, education, religion and the world of work. Technocracy has produced depersonalized individuals, stampeding human herds, faceless nations, vast military blocks, all swallowed up in the devitalized life of unauthentic existence. The madman in Nietzsche's *Joyful Wisdom* had predicted this dreadful happening, man's confrontation face to face with Nothingness. "What are these churches now," he cried out, "if they are not the tombs and monuments of God?" Concerning modern man's attitude toward God and religion, Heidegger records that, despite his nostalgia for God, man's traditional beliefs have evanesced into thin air. Man has become so obsessed with things—inventing, accumulating, consuming them—that all gods, even the Christian God, have been driven from his consciousness. Man has lost touch with the experience of the "holy." His everyday world is no longer sacred; rather it has been vulgarized, secularized, desacralized. Thus despairing of salvation for this fallen world from either the classic or Christian God, Heidegger turns toward the poet as the new savior. And the poet who has inspired his vision and inflamed his soul is his beloved J. C. F. Hölderlin who lived from 1770 to 1843 in Germany.

Following the lead of Hölderlin, Heidegger placed the poet, as the new priest and prophet, between the gods and the people. "He is the one who has been cast out—out into that *Between,* between gods and men. But only and for the first time in this Between is it decided who is man and where he is settling his existence."[10] Moreover, Heidegger fully accepts Hölderlin's obscure, prophetic witness for modern man. Its content and program, in a world which has driven out the divine, is as follows: "It is that Hölderlin . . . first determines a new time. This is the time of the gods that have fled *and* the god that is coming. It is the time *of need,* because it lies under a double lack and a double Not: the No-more of the gods that fled and the Not-yet of the god that is coming."[11] Heidegger tells us that his philosophic attitude is one of expectant waiting for "the new god." We live in a new spiritual situation, in the time of "God's fall." Heidegger, who broke with the Catholic Church and rejected

10. Martin Heidegger, *Existence And Being*, Essay "Hölderlin and the Essence of Poetry," p. 312.
11. *Ibid.*, p. 313.

Christ because he could not, even as a youth, convince himself
of the existence of God according to St. Thomas's proofs, now
determines to live in the everpresent consciousness of "God's
self-withholding." The philosopher must join the poet in waiting on mountains farthest apart for the coming of the "new
god" from the bosom of the word of Being-itself. For both Hölderlin and Heidegger this messianic expectancy is a secularized
form of the Judaeic yearning for the first coming and the Christian eagerness for the final coming of God. There is nothing
transcendent in a supernatural sense about their non-Christian
piety. Moreover, during this period of waiting, it would be
ridiculous to talk meaningfully about God and things divine.
For we live in an age of transition whose chief chaotic characteristic is silence about God. Discussion about God today can
only produce distortion, falsehood, even blasphemy. All one can
do is silently, within himself, "call for the new God," without
succeeding in making him appear, as no one has succeeded
hitherto.[12] The hour has not yet come for the dialogue with the
new divine being, if it will ever come in our lifetime. And
Heidegger quotes his beloved poet, "the shepherd and guardian
of Being," to demonstrate this truth:

> Oft must we keep silent;
> We lack holy names.
> The heart may beat and break,
> Yet speech remains unsaid.
>
> But alas! our generation walks
>   in the night,
> Dwells in hell, without the divine.[13]

Secularized Theology as Atheism

Despite Heidegger's protestations that he is neither an atheist nor a theist, the perceptive student of his thought comes
away from his works impressed with having encountered a
new type of modern thinker—the secularized theologian. We
notice that Heidegger says nothing explicitly about religious

12. *Ibid.*, p. 192.
13. *Ibid.*, p. 261.

faith, eternity, immortality, the religious dimension of Being and of man which is superior to natural conscience and metaphysics. Heidegger places the highest achievement of man in the attainment of authenticity which results from obedience to the call of his conscience, a call from himself and hence an obedience to himself. In *Being and Time* Heidegger reduced the meaning of human life to its temporal possibilities. Death alone was the absolute which structured into wholeness the individual's existence. In the first phase of his thinking, therefore, Heidegger emphasized the man-in-the-world relationship with other beings. There was, of course, no mention of a God-man relationship. Then Heidegger abandoned his ontological relationship because it remained too humanistic and did not succeed in transcending metaphysics as he had hoped. Thus in the second stage of his interpretative analysis of Being he attempted to define man and the world on the basis of a definition of Being itself. This procedure was the reverse of his first phenomenological exploration. In the first exploration he attempted to define Being through his analysis and clarification of man's understanding of Being. In his second study he placed all the emphasis of his thinking on Being rather than on man. This time he sought the meaning of Being not in everyday world revelations of man's experiences but in the writings of the great philosophers and poets. Once again in the second stage of his thinking the relationship between man and God or between beings and God was not even raised for consideration. Eventually Heidegger also had to abandon this second method of his thinking as an acceptable criterion of the meaning of Being. It contained untruth mixed with truth. In the third phase of his thinking about the meaning of Being Heidegger selected a few great figures for guidance who, in his words, "possessed a more essential vision of being." Thus having rejected man's everyday experience and the traditional philosophers as sources of light on the nature of Being, Heidegger finally became his own judge and authority on who is a source of light on the nature of Being. Without any objective criteria, he alone determined who were the inspired authors, prophets and mystics of Being. He inserted their works as canonical in the Bible of Being. It is in this third stage of his intellectual endeavors that Heidegger becomes prophet and mystic of Being himself.

Versényi has written an incisive analysis of this mystical procedure:

> In his attempt to make visible what is Wholly Other, and to make enter into an entirely different dimension, Heidegger engages in a kind of negative theology and mysticism: he gives forth sibylline utterances whose only concrete content is the rejection of all human experience and insight. This is not a sudden development, for already in his second hermeneutic period Heidegger's descent into the poverty of thought was accompanied by a gradual elimination of concrete significance and existential import from his thought. But this process is now completed: Insisting on the ineffability of his ultimate Ground, the incomprehensibility of the Play of Being, and the total otherness of his Region of disclosure, Heidegger has succeeded in overcoming humanistic metaphysics. But he did so at the price of relinquishing all philosophically articulate and articulable meaning.[14]

Once again among the mystics, prophets and poets who have cast brilliant light on the meaning of Being in the course of history, one looks in vain for a religious teacher or leader. The revelations of Christ about the mystery of the Being of Beings —the Divine Trinity—are nowhere mentioned. Heidegger the philosopher proves to be an arbitrary selector of authors. Moreover, he is quite dogmatic about the fact that his choices, uncorroborated by others, are the best and should be accepted unquestioningly by all. It is quite clear that Heidegger has cut himself adrift from his Christian moorings. He teaches mankind in his mystical language that men must presently endure in silence "the lean years," awaiting the "poet" who keeps in touch with the vanished gods. The "poet" will come eventually and open the gates to the city of the "holy." For the Christian faith which he has relinquished, Heidegger has substituted a secular faith in his select philosophers and poets. They are the prophetic heralds, along with Heidegger himself, of the coming Poet-God who will save mankind. This faith is mystical; it professes no definite doctrines; it adheres to no clearly identifiable God or gods; its highpriests—the shepherds and guardians of

14. Laszlo Versényi, *Heidegger; Being; And Truth;* (New Haven and London: Yale University Press, A Yale Paperbound, 1965), p. 163.

Being—are the mystic poets, the prophet-philosophers, the secularized theologians. Because secular philosophy had failed to reveal to man the meaning of Being, or to guide him successfully through finitude, dread, guilt and fear of death to authentic existence, Heidegger abandoned it for his mystical method of procedure. Now his secularized theology is announced as the only road to authentic existence, the gateway to the "gods" and their empire of "holy ones." In effect, Heidegger has become the herald of a "New God," the Isaiah of the Third and Final Testament, announcing the advent of an unknown-unknowable God, the very purpose of whose mission to man is inscrutable. And yet, despite this dark inscrutability, man is exhorted to prepare a welcome for this "new God" in dumb silence. Moreover, man's relationship to this "new God" is left so vague, so impersonal, so directionless that man is nonplused as to what to expect and what to do in an authentic way during "this time of need."

We have already indicated Heidegger's fascination for Nietzsche's thrilling, anti-rational addiction to mighty but extreme ideals. A religious loyalty to the earth, a lust for life as the highest of values, a zeal for planning and achieving terrifying experiences, the thirst for living dangerously, heroically, atop mountains, apart from the crass crowd and yet the fierce temptation to descend, shake the foundations of the trivial lives of the masses and plunge them into the abyss of tragedy. Faith in feeling, force, fate, indeed in Nothingness, all these ideals of passion led Heidegger to choose deliberately, even violently, an ontological order of ironclad immanentism in preference to God and God's providence of love in behalf of mankind. Landsberg characterizes the Hiedeggerian philosophy of fatalism as a "paradoxical mystery of extreme cruelty."[15] Indeed, in scrutinizing Heidegger's "New God" who is coming, one fears to discover that he is none other than Nietzsche's approaching God of Superman.

15. Dr. Goetz Briefs, professor with Heidegger at the University of Freiburg in the 1920's, related this incident to me in Rome where I consulted him on this study. Dr. Heidegger was chagrined at the carefree lives of people who, like fish swimming contentedly in the shallows, escaped danger by maintaining life lines with the shore of security—God, religion, the Church, traditional institutions. His mission was to cut those life lines, to liberate men for the dangers of the depths, for the authentic experience of the darkness of tragedy. Truly a Nietzschean mission!

Dr. Hans Jonas, himself an outstanding pupil of Heidegger, astonished at the sight of theologians attempting to justify their faith through the philosophy of his master, warns them of the utter disillusionment that awaits them as a result of this sterile activity. The Heideggerian highway of thought is the road back to pagan fatalism, to a deified cosmos:

> ... There is much secularized Christianity in Hiedegger's thought ... the vocabulary of guilt and conscience and call and voice and hearing and response and mission and shepherd and revelation and thanksgiving ... If we first ask how Heidegger came to adopt the Judaeo-Christian vocabulary ... *he* (Heidegger) might ... say that the Christian speech, and the disclosure of being laid down in it, are via our tradition an integral part of fate to which our thinking must respond, and therefore the language is genuine as *his* (Heidegger's) thinking response to the task as *conditioned* by history ... The theologian should resist the attempt to treat his message as a matter of historic fate ... as part of a comprehensive becoming ... as one element among others in a tradition and as itself something divisible, assimilable in part and left in part, ready for the pickings of the unbeliever ... But as regards the theologian—or should I rather say the believer—it seems to me that the Christian, and therefore the Christian theologian, must reject any such idea of fate and history as extending to the status of his own mandate. For one thing the Christian is said to be saved from the power of fate ... Second, that which saved him was, by the understanding of faith as distinct from the understanding of the world, not an event of the world and thus not an event of fate, nor destined ever to become fate or part of fate itself, but an event invalidating all dicta of fate and overruling the words which fate speaks to man, including the words of self-unveiling being. Nor is it, thirdly, itself a mere unveiling: the crucifixion ... was not in the first place an event of language. Must I say this to Christian theologians? It seems so ... The theologian cannot, if he keeps faith with himself, accept *any* system of historical fate or reason or eschatology as a frame to integrate his trust into —be it Hegel's or Comte's or Marx's or Spengler's or Heidegger's—for the simple reason that it is about "this world", ... and its truth at best the truth of this world ... The being whose fate Heidegger ponders is the quintessence of this world, it is *saeculum.* Against this, theology should guard the radical transcendence of its God, whose voice comes not out of being but breaks into the kingdom

of being from without. My theological friends—don't you
see what you are dealing with? Don't you sense, if not see,
the profoundly pagan character of Heidegger's thought?
Rightly pagan, insofar as it is philosophy, though not every
philosophy must be so devoid of objective norms; but more
pagan than others from your point of view, not in spite but
because of its, also, speaking of call and self-revealing and
even of the shepherd.[16]

The truth of the matter is that secularized theology cannot
make life worth living. Nor should the use of Christian categories applied in non-theological senses fool the forlorn reader.
When the center of all Being and, above all, of man's being is
rejected, the flight into mystical neologisms will not save the
situation. Sooner or later the truth will out. Without God—Absolute Intelligence, Liberty and Goodness—at the center of Being,
all beings fly off into directionless, meaningless chaos. St. Paul,
true mystic theologian, accurately enunciated the Christian
news of salvation. This news is the wisdom of God as revealed
in the Son of God made man. It is a wisdom radically opposed
to the wisdom of the philosophers and poets who refuse dialogue with God or the Son of God, the only God who can and has
wrought the salvation of man. "For, it is written, 'I will destroy
the wisdom of the wise, and the prudence of the prudent, I will
reject.' Where is the 'wise man'? Where is the scribe? Where is
the disputant of this world? Has not God turned to foolishness
the 'wisdom' of this world?"[17] Thus, the good news of salvation
is not dependent upon the philosophers or poets of this world.

Heidegger exhorted men to face death honestly as a way to
authentic, existential salvation in this world, since there is no
other spiritual, transcendent world. But the courage to be, live
and die for Nothingness is irrational and breaks down into
despair and suicide. How can Heidegger counsel man to live
purely and simply for death in the name of his meaning of
authenticity? St. Paul, on the other hand, demonstrates that the
world is incapable of delivering man from the despair of death.
We cannot save ourselves, nor can philosophers or poets save
us. Moreover, we do not live solely in or for ourselves. "You are
not your own. You are Christ's and Christ is God's." We are

16. Hans Jonas, "Heidegger and Theology", *Review of Metaphysics,* XVIII,
December 1964, pp. 207–233, pp. 214, 215, 217, 218, 219.
17. I Corinthians 1 : 19–21.

delivered from despair and death solely in Jesus Christ, the Son of God who has already come, already achieved our salvation and left us abundant powerful means to bring this salvation to the maturity of high, authentic sanctity. And we await the same known God who is to return. Moreover, we await him, not in silence, but in psalms, singing and good works. No poet or philosopher, however sublime, will ever replace the Son of God as the Saviour of all men. For, "He is the image of the invisible God, the firstborn of every creature. For in him were created all things in the heavens and on the earth, things visible and things invisible. . .All things have been created through him and unto him, and he is before all creatures, and in him all things hold together."[18] "Why is there any Being at all—why not far rather Nothing?" Heidegger had asked at the end of his inaugural lecture, "What is Metaphysics?" when he was appointed to the Chair of Philosophy in Freiburg as successor to his own mentor Edmund Husserl. Unfortunately, Heidegger at that time was in the position of another famous historical figure who had asked the question: "What is truth?" Like Pilate he had turned away from Christ and did not bother to find the answer in the Son of God.

As a matter of fact, when we analyze the epistemology of Heidegger, we find that he replaces eternal, transcendent truth with truth as a social-historical, on-going reality. Truth thus suffers the fate of all immanent realities; truth is essentially relative. Heidegger contends that the assertion that the sun revolves around the earth was not untrue before Copernicus discovered that the earth revolves around the sun. Truth is thus cut back exclusively to the subjective act of human knowledge and depends only on what the universe reveals about itself under present circumstances. What is presently believed as true is truth. There is no transcendent, immutable Personification of Truth Itself who can infallibly measure the truths expressed in history. Popular appeal and willpower make truth. No wonder Nazism could be easily espoused as a fateful historical truth. It enjoyed vast power, historical success and massive popularity. Truth in Heidegger is thus trendy, fickle, even contradictory. A philosophy is true when its hour of success has arrived; it ceases to be true when the hour of its contradictory

18. Colossians 1 : 15–17.

system of thought has struck in the process of history. Thus, already in his epistemology Heidegger had denied God who is Absolute Truth, the Source and Standard of all cosmic, historical truth. And yet inconsistently though unavoidably, Heidegger pays tribute to the reality of transcendent truth and absolute moral goodness by claiming throughout his works that his theory of truth is the only true theory and his standards of moral goodness are the only standards of authentically human conduct. And in making these claims Heidegger understands truth and moral goodness in the classic, immutable, even Christian meaning of those terms.

As for man's destiny to death, once again Heidegger's doctrine is a summons to suicide, intellectual, moral and social. This form of nihilism is no solution to the mystery of Being. St. Paul, the theologian of the resurrection had long ago answered Heidegger, the theologian of annihilation. "Behold, I tell you a mystery: we shall all indeed rise. . .For this corruptible body must put on incorruption, and this mortal body must put on immortality. But when this mortal body puts on immortality, then shall come to pass the word that is written: 'Death is swallowed up in victory!' O Death, where is thy victory? O Death, where is thy sting? . . . But thanks be to God who has given us the victory through our Lord Jesus Christ . . . And the last enemy to be destroyed will be death, for God has put all things under his feet,"[19] Instead of walking in futility of mind, clouded in darkness, estranged from God and courageously committed to death, the Christian accepts death with faith in the risen Christ, hope for his homecoming to God and gratitude for Christ's common victory over death. Only such a divine destiny to death can render life in time an adventure of self-transcendence, for it is an adventure into the life of God.

Another glaring disservice of Heidegger's night of nihilism is that it proposes to man, isolated from God, an ethic which, like that of Nietzsche, is beyond good and evil. The private, subjective conscience is made the sole source of morality. By courageous decisions of freedom it is to make authentic existence its goal in life, overcoming dread, mass mediocrity and death. But such mere teaching and exhortation to moral rectitude is uninspiring and indeed sterile, if the obligation to that moral good-

19. I Corinthians 15 : 53–55.

ness is imposed solely by the private conscience which enjoys a liberty restricted solely by itself, which is to say, an unrestricted liberty. We are reminded again of Ivan Karamazov's logical rule of morality: "If God did not exist, everything would be permitted." Thus Heidegger's ethic is reduced to being totally subjective, irresponsible, unrealistic and hence, inefficacious for producing moral goodness. For a merely subjective protest against the morality of the masses, when vastly outvoted by the masses, has no higher recourse or appeal to a Supreme Source of moral goodness and hence falls upon deaf ears. It is quite understandable, then, that in the face of the vast decadence of civilization effected by the tyranny of technocracy, Heidegger, in the last analysis, can only confront the void with the paralyzed stare of dread and the silence of despair. He seems to have forgotten his earlier exhortations that the man of historical authenticity must keep vital experiences of the past which can improve the present and prepare a better future. The fact that for two thousand years mankind has kept alive the life and deeds of Christ for the ineffable betterment of the whole human race is passed over in total silence in his philosophy, despite the fact that Christ has come to be looked upon as the center and full meaning of all history. The fact that twelve simple witnesses, in a world of Roman depravity far worse than ours, instead of keeping silence, raised their voices incessantly with the good news of divine salvation, seems never to have dissuaded Heidegger from his advocacy of quietism in the face of nihilism. The fact that their "voice and words which had gone forth into all the earth and unto the ends of the world" had converted a world of slaves into a world of saints is not even adverted to by Heidegger.

The lives of Christ, the apostles and of all men of true faith alone give the full, true meaning of Being, finitude, throwness, dread, care, crime, guilt, authentic existence and death. They speak not only in words and deeds but also in blood and death. And the meaning is love, Divine Love, incarnated in the Son of God and communicated through His Spirit to all men. Why is there being rather than nothing? Because He is love, because He is good, I exist, everything exists, everyone exists. "Greater love than this no man hath, that he lay down his life for his friends." It is a tragic pity that Heidegger, who knew Christ from his youth, did not in his phenomenological search for the meaning of Being, apply his great powers of analysis and exposition to the study of the existential commitment of Christ to to God and his fellow men. Had he done so, he might have spared himself the experience of the sickness of being which arises from the meaninglessness of life.

In a world of confusion which he had hoped to improve, it is especially catastrophic that his philosophy of nihilism merely succeeds in cutting man's breathing lines to the source of his life in God and leaving him to suffocate in the vacuum of atheism. For to deprive man of the atmosphere of God is to destroy him via spiritual asphyxiation.

CHAPTER IX

Merleau-Ponty: Man, The God of Meaning and Liberty

MAURICE MERLEAU-PONTY WAS BORN AT ROCHEFORT-sur-mer (Charente-Maritime) on March 14, 1908. He was Catholic in origin, well-informed about his faith and a solid Christian as a youth. In 1926 he was admitted to the École Normale Superieure. After receiving his doctorate from the Sorbonne in 1945, he taught first at the University of Lyons and then at the Sorbonne through the years 1949 to 1952. He was then nominated to the Chair of Philosophy at the Collège de France. His acceptance lecture on that occasion was eventually published under the title *In Praise of Philosophy (Eloge de la philosophie)*. In this work he revealed his thoughts on the nature and tasks of philosophy, the place of God in philosophy, and the personal as well as social functions of thinking and choosing that man must assume if he is to give meaning to his own existence, to the world and to history. Merleau-Ponty died at Paris in an untimely and violent fashion at the height of his powers on May 3, 1961.

Although he had long ceased being a philosophical theist,

Merleau-Ponty requested and received a religious burial service, indicating thereby that before his death he had certainly reopened the question of the possibility of religious belief and man's divine destiny. Since he situated himself within the authentically designated existential, phenomenological current of philosophy, it is not surprising that Merleau-Ponty's thought shows strong affinities to the thinking of J.-P. Sartre, M. Heidegger and G. Marcel. But the principal influence upon Merleau-Ponty's thinking by far was E. Husserl, especially the Husserl of the later period. Hegel was also a significant though less dominant force upon his work. Through his phenomenological method of analysis and reflection, Merleau-Ponty hoped to transcend the ever-present dichotomies in philosophy, subject-object, idealism-realism, contingent-absolute. He developed and transformed Husserl's phenomenology into a more concrete, realistic philosophy. His major work consisted in: first, detailed analyses of the sciences of man; second, a study of modern, classical rationalist philosophers; and third, an elucidation of the fundamental structures of human existence based upon man's immediate experience of the world, others and himself. His later works concentrated on aesthetics, political philosophy and the philosophy of history. In this chapter we will restrict ourselves for the most part to his study of man in his immediate cosmic, personal and social existential relationships.

Philosophy Without God

According to Merleau-Ponty, to be an authentic man means to live fully in relation not to God, but to the world and others. To be an authentic philosopher means to reflect on what is concrete and existential—man, the world, their relationships—not on theological absolutes—God and the history of the hereafter. True philosophy suppresses theology in favor of anthropology or sociology. One recalls here the philosophic themes of Feuerbach and Comte, to say nothing of the phenomenology of Sartre. When these themes are sung, Merleau-Ponty is a member of their chorus. Be that as it may, Merleau-Ponty notes that today no one attempts to prove God's existence with the classical arguments of the Scholastic giants, St. Anselm, St. Thomas or Descartes. God's existence is either assumed as proven or those who deny it are branded as atheists. Moreover, in assessing and answering the new philosophies, the theist can usually find a breached wall through which the banished God can be or has already been surreptiously re-introduced. But if one should fail to find the crack in the wall of such God-denying philosophies, then one disqualifies that system of thought with the epithet—hopelessly atheistic![1]

The trouble is, complains Merleau-Ponty, that too many critics of philosophic thought assume that every philosophy must inevitably arrive at the existence of the Necessary Being, if such a philosophy is to stand intrinsically intelligent and coherent, while simultaneously being illuminative of all that is. Often enough, then, a philosophy is defined negatively—for example, as being atheistic. But a negative definition does not present in a positive manner what philosophy really is. Merleau-Ponty laments the fact that even the serene reflections of de Lubac and Maritain presuppose that true philosophy must affirm God, not dismiss and then replace him with a pseudo-god. For no pseudo-god can support the omnipotent role of the ultimate Being who holds all things together in harmony physically and intelligently. Maritain and de Lubac have demonstrated that atheism destroys one God in order to enthrone another and that anti-theism lives parasitically on the true God by "an inverted act of faith."[2]

Certainly anti-theism exists, agrees Merleau-Ponty. One need only recall the classic system of Nietzsche's thought. But, insists Merleau-Ponty, atheism and anti-theism are not philosophies. They are inverted theologies; and theology is not philosophy. Savants ought to cease trying to give the final, definitive, omni-competent, omnipotent explanation of all beings by appealing to the existence of a Necessary Being. It is this obsessive assumption that divides philosophers and theologians into estranged camps of alienated, grieved wranglers. Is there no other alternative to this sharp-horned dilemma between theism and anthropothesim, between theology and "the apocalypse of Wonderland"?[3] Merleau-Ponty thinks there is. That is why he rejects both the affirmations of Christianity—the God-become-man-humanism—and those of "the mystique of Super-

---

1. Maurice Merleau-Ponty, *Éloge de la philosophie* (Paris: Éditions Gallimard, Paperback, 1960), p. 50.
2. *Ibid.*, p. 51.
3. *Ibid.*, p. 51.

man—the man-become-God, Promethean humanism. Philosophy simply does not exist nor flourish in such an imaginary realm of non-being. The true philosopher does not predict that in the end all human contradictions shall be resolved, nor that man, as a totally perfect being, will be the final fruit of the cosmic process of history. Like everyone else he does not know nor care to predict the future.

The true philosopher's message is quite different from such dogmatic predictions. He admits that the world has begun and is in the process of development. How? Or why? He does not know. He denies that man can predict his future by what has happened in his past; he denies that the idea of a destiny is inherent to things; he claims that this teaching about a destiny is not an idea, but a sort of metaphysical dizziness, a philosophic black-out. The true philosopher holds that man's relationships with nature are not fixed once and for all, for no man can predict what freedom can accomplish nor imagine what human morals or relationships would develop in a civilization that would no longer be haunted with competition and destitution. Thus, the true philosopher does not place his hope in any destiny, not even in a favorable one. On the contrary, he puts his hope in that which in man negates any destiny. The true philosopher hopes in his contingency and this negation is his point of departure for philosophizing. Should such a philosopher be called a humanist? No, says Merleau-Ponty, not if one considers man as a universal principle that can explain everything and substitute himself for everything. For nothing is explained through man, since man is not a force, but a feebleness at the heart of reality. Man is not even one cosmological factor among many others; he is a junction where cosmological factors are forever changing the meaning of himself and the meaning of history.[4]

But man is also attracted to the contemplation of all other natures as well as to the love of himself. His life and love reach out to too many things, to be exact, to everything. Thus, he cannot easily make himself the sole object of his own delight so as to lay himself open to the charge of engaging in "human chauvinism."[5] This very same ocean of being that eludes every religion of humanity, also knocks the props out from under all

4. *Ibid.*, pp. 52–53.
5. *Ibid.*, p. 53.

theology. It is true that theology undeniably establishes the contingency of all being. But it does this only by deriving that contingency from the existence of the Necessary Being. Thus, by resolving all problems, dilemmas, struggles harmoniously in the Necessary Being, theology, in effect, rids man of all contingency; it destroys philosophic wonderment. On the contrary, philosophy awakens man to his own and the world's existence; it poses the problems connected with both these existences; it drives man on, in an endless search, toward the solution of these problems. But, unlike theology, it never cures man of his curious searching, for it never finally solves the problem of existence. De Lubac discusses an atheism that seeks to suppress the very problem that gives birth to God in the consciousness of man. In reality, however, the philosopher knows this problem so well that he attacks it at its very root, thereby placing it beyond solutions that would suffocate it. Ideas, like that of the Necessary Being or of "eternal matter," or of "total man" appear quite dull and prosaic to the philosopher in comparison with that upheaval of phenomena and continual birth of beings taking place at every stage of a developing world. For it is this storm of burgeoning being that the philosopher is absorbed in describing. Placed in this dynamic perspective, religion is seen as only one of the expressions of the central phenomenon of existence, a non-authentic, non-philosophical experience. Atheism, therefore, cannot be a valid accusation against a system of thought because, in reality, atheism is philosophy seen through the eyes of a theologian. The theologian claims that atheism displaces and destroys the sacred. But philosophy does none of these things, because it is not concerned with God nor the sacred. But with what is philosophy concerned and what does it do? A careful look into Merleau-Ponty's writings should give us his answer to this important question.

Philosophy Condemns Man to Meaning

While Sartre takes his point of departure from Heidegger, Merleau-Ponty owes his existentialism in a special manner to Husserl and his late concept of the "world of life" (Lebenswelt). Merleau-Ponty philosophizes by using the analytic principles of phenomenology. He is a master in their use, pushing them to their subtlest ramifications. According to Merleau-Ponty, philosophy spends itself in phenomenological analysis, description, reflection and synthesis. Despite its careful excavations of lived experience, this philosophy gladly recognizes the essential incompleteness of its work and also its own provisoriness. There is so much depth and width to being that the most complete phenomenological scrutinies can never exhaust its reality. We can clearly distinguish Sartre's descriptive analyses from those of Merleau-Ponty by noting that objectively and thematically each author concentrates on a different aspect of man's existential mission in life. For Sartre, man is "condemned to *liberty;*" for Merleau-Ponty, man is "condemned to *meaning.*" As an intellectualist of serene temperament, Merleau-Ponty calmly denies God. He has a passion to understand reality. Sartre, on the other hand, as a moralist of vigorous temperament, violently denies God, often in a frenzied style. He has a passion for action. Yet both agree in rejecting theology for anthropology, metaphysics for phenomenology.[6] When we find out the exact sense of Merleau-Ponty's statement that man is "condemned to meaning," we will understand his philosophy and his atheism.

According to Merleau-Ponty, a philosopher is a person who seeks being with a hunger to see whatever reality is there to be seen and to report the truth about it all. The trouble with thinkers today is that they are no longer seekers; they are partisan commentators; they return to traditional systems of thought merely to defend them. Their convictions are founded less on the values or truths discovered by their own seeking than on the vices and errors they seem to discover in the thinkers they reject. In reality, however, man is an incarnate "I think." The marvelous event about him is the emergence of his subjectivity. Meaning, truth, value arise in the world only in and through the awakening subjectivity of the human person. Now man's seeking extends over the whole field of concrete reality. Moreover, man is set down into his own existence, into the world solely through his body. It is because his body enjoys concrete existence that it is indissoluble within and from the concrete existence of the world. Philosophy, therefore, will

6. Jean Lacroix, *The Meaning of Modern Atheism,* transl. by Garret Barden, S.J., (New York: The Macmillan Company, 1965), p. 45.

have to be understood as a search into the structural analysis of man's conduct in the world.[7] The particular characteristic of Merleau-Ponty's thought lies in the fact that he begins this search in the experience and contact with the world that takes place prior to any thought about the world. Thus he contacts and examines the world before any reflection about the world begins and he then contrasts this original, pre-reflective experience of the world with man's later, ordinary, elaborated reflections. Thus, for him, philosophic reflection has the task of awakening the original, pre-reflective experience of the world. It is precisely in reflection upon this non-reflective, pre-predicative presence of the world to man that philosophy must spend itself. All its affirmations will have to be derived from such a presence and from reflections that seek to clarify that presence. Now, the original and immediate unity with the world is experienced only in perception, which becomes, therefore, the exclusive object of phenomenological analysis. In more exact terms, the phenomenon, which is the object of philosophic reflection, has two moments: First, the mystery of the world as its foundation; second, the mystery of reason which rests on that foundation. Because of these two mysteries, man is simultaneously oriented outwardly and inwardly. He is, at the same time, both an Ego in a body and a thinking subject, present to, yet simultaneously absent from, the world. It is this tension in man—interior-exterior, present-absent polarity— that consitutes man's *ambiguity*. This ambiguity does not entirely express the imperfection of existence or of consciousness, but it does constitute the real, unique essence of man's existence. Moreover, this bipolarity is found to be functioning in a dialectical manner. But, whereas in Hegel there exists a destructive, tripartite dialectic, Merleau-Ponty presents us only with a bipartite dialectic, a reciprocal dialectic in which there is realized the alternate predominance of one of the two opposites.[8]

When the philosopher investigates the fundamental phenomenon of existence and its double dynamic direction, he

7. Johannes Lotz, "Ateismo e Esistenzialismo," article appearing in *L' Ateismo e Contemporaneo*, Vol. 2, one section of which treats of "L'Ateismo in Maurice Merleau-Ponty," (Torino, Italy: Società Editrice Intérnazionale), pp. 321–329.

8. *Ibid.*, pp. 321–329.

discovers that the core of this phenomenon is "incarnate meaning." Philosophy is, for this reason then, freely committed to comprehend the meaning of the world and of history. It seeks this meaning by retracing its steps to the most primitive experiences in which this meaning began to be formed. But in this quest for meaning, philosophy encounters irrational obstacles, contradictions, sheer nonsense which, however, the philosopher is in a position to reduce to a dialectic unity with meaning. Merleau-Ponty's investigations concentrate in a special manner on the meaning of the world. He discovers that all things form a true *con-text,* a weaving together (the Christian would say a witnessing together) for *one* world. When, therefore, the philosopher turns his mind toward discovering the meaning in man-as-a-subject, he discovers the meaning of *intersubjectivity* that prevails in reality and through which each person orients himself as an open being toward a dynamic encounter with the other through the acknowledgement of the other as a person. This clearly reveals that man has the responsibility to achieve the community.

Is there any explanation for the emergence of man's marvelous intersubjectivity? Merleau-Ponty considers the question itself and any answer to it pure nonsense. Explanations and answers destroy the wonder of contingent freedom. Sciences specialize in giving explanations. They try to reduce beings and their happenings to their antecedents, to their causes. Now in the domain of physical nature, where determinism is the universal law, explanation of forces, processes, actions and reactions is certainly in order. But man, the subject, is clearly beyond determinism; he cannot be explained. Any meaning we might advance as his explanation already *presupposes* him as a subject. The subject, therefore, who is acting in the first place as presupposing all explanation, is himself inexplicable. Man as subject is not determined by processes, forces, actions and reactions. Not completely anyway. For man is contingent; he is free.[9] Now the philosopher insists on maintaining the contingent freedom of man in the world. For it is through contingent freedom that man escapes the prison of necessitating processes. Moreover, human contingency makes human life possi-

9. Maurice Merleau-Ponty, *Phénoménologie de la Perception,* (Paris: Éditions Gallimard, 1945), p. 413.

ble; human contingency is the necessary milieu in which the life of truth, value and history flourish. Thus, for Merleau-Ponty, history is not a determined process. For free, contingent man creates history, not the way he creates machines, following faithfully the laws of physical forces and processes. Man makes history through his free, contingent decisions. And through his free, contingent decisions man makes himself. These decisions create meaning for himself, his fellow man and his world. Man, as a free, contingent being, therefore, is the source of all meaning. He is "condemned to create meaning." That is why man is never "guaranteed." He cannot hope in a fixed fate, but only in his own ambiguous creation of himself and his historical world. Those, therefore, who put blind faith in the inevitable growth of progress with the passage of mankind from present to future are hopelessly deluding themselves. Stultification and even regression are well within man's possibilities today, even as they were realized in past dark ages. We must never forget that man is not a *force* but a *faiblesse* in the heart of physical nature. He is not even a cosmological factor, but the cosmological center where all factors in the world meet, take and change their meaning while becoming on-going history.

Meaning arises, then, within the dialogue between man and the world. And this meaning is characterized by man as his truth and values. The world, isolated from the thinking subject, has no meaning. Man, isolated from the world and his fellow man, has no meaning. There is meaning only in a world-for-man, made human by the history created by human subjects. Within the subject-world communication and intersubjectivity, truth and values incontrovertibly exist; there really *is* the true and false, the good and evil. But, says Merleau-Ponty, the verb *is* here only has meaning if the knowing subject does not postulate an absolute "in itself," an absolute "for itself."[10] Whoever insists on first searching for and finding the absolute "for-itself-in-itself," thereby renders the human life of truth and values impossible. For, "metaphysical and moral consciousness dies on contact with the absolute because consciousness is itself—beyond the insipid world of habitually benumbed

10. Maurice Merleau-Ponty, *Sens et Non-sens* (Paris: Les Éditions Nagel, 1966), p. 167.

consciousnesses—the living link of the I with the I and of the I with the Other."[11] Man's involvement, through his body in the world and his involvement with others through intersubjectivity testifies unmistakably to the exercise of his liberty. It is true that his liberty is limited; each individual always lives hampered by situations that from time to time oppose and control him through social bonds. Man's liberty is, therefore, free to function only in a limited field of action. But to be restricted by conditions does not obliterate liberty, because man is capable of escaping his situation. He can, despite his social restrictions, make decisions to act this way or that. Man's destiny is thus to be sought in his zeal to fulfill himself toward the achievement of community. The ethical imperative drives him toward that goal.

In his treatment of liberty, we find that Merleau-Ponty is truly a philosopher of existentialism. He stresses that man's radical finiteness and contingency are bound up with his limited liberty. Contingency is defined as that causality which at a certain moment made man the subject emerge and which again at a certain moment will make him disappear. Merleau-Ponty finds in contingency no indication of any reality that transcends the world or man. Thus, contingent man is always and totally oriented toward the earth alone. Man's existence does not move beyond the solidarity achieved in intra-cosmic and intra-human relationship. For beyond the unique and irreversible appearances of existence there exists nothing. For that reason, man is fundamentally a metaphysical being; his metaphysical consciousness has, as its unique quest, daily experience. It follows that religion is merely a substitute for so-called positive humanism. Coherent philosophy is unconcerned with religion, a useless activity chasing a non-existent phantom. Coherent philosophy devotes itself to exploring the depths of the structure of human behavior. In a word, coherent philosophy plunges into the depths of man's social conduct. It unmasks as illusory every reality represented as existing beyond man and the world. Coherent philosophy is not ashamed to admit that the finitude of existence cannot be structured on any absolute or solid foundation; it truthfully admits that man's finitude is completely bereft of any security.

11. *Ibid.*, p. 167.

Indeed, coherent philosophy points out that both history and politics also lead man to this same truth. All existence, and especially man's, is totally relative and ambiguous; recourse to absoluteness is a vain recourse to nothingness.

The Case Against God

The impossibility of accounting for a God-dependent man as a contingent and free subject calls necessarily for the denial of the absolute. Indeed, it demands that the very idea of God be radically erased from the consciousness of man. God's existence would obliterate man's consciousness and render man's activities absurdly impossible. In the presence of a God of infinite truth, beauty and goodness, man is reduced to the level of an unemployed slave. His search for truth becomes unrealizable; his desire to create his own beauty is frustrated; his ideals for attaining moral goodness through his own efforts are rendered empty dreams. Indeed, in the presence of an omnipotent and omniscient God, man's liberty is destroyed.[12] On the other hand, no sooner is the absolute norm, founded on God, abandoned, than human powers rightfully claim their cosmic field for the vigorous development of their own projects. No sooner is God dismissed, than man is liberated, eager to pledge himself to the achievement of a perfection which the world has never yet known or suspected. Previously, with God fixing His gaze upon him, man felt himself overwhelmed to the very roots of his being. Under the scrutiny of God, he felt himself completely stripped of his powers, especially of his liberty. The profound and mysterious center of his being was an open book to that infinite Look. Under it, he could never enjoy privacy; his most ardent desires, his past, present, even future were totally focused and tabulated by the eye of God. Indeed, the stare of God so oppressed man that he experienced the shrinkage of his being to the state of a mere visible object, something to be handled, examined and used.[13] Thus, religion, in a special manner, came to be regarded, under the glance of God, as a modification of intra-human relationships. Religion taught man that since his intra-human life in time would never develop to satis-

12. Maurice Merleau-Ponty, *Sens et Non-sens*, (Paris: Les Éditions Nagel, 1966, edition of 1948), p. 356.
13. Maurice Merleau-Ponty, *Sens et Non-sens*, (Paris: Les Éditions Nagel, edition of 1948), p. 362.

factory maturity, he should dream of the next life where he would realize a deep, beatifying bond of social happiness with his fellow men. The presence of God, therefore, put man in an impossible position. No matter what circumstances man lived under, God demanded that he lead two contradictory lives simultaneously. He called man to strive for two orders of values at once—the human values of this life and the divine values of the next. The fulfillment of these contradictory calls is simply impossible and thus man becomes a complete failure, neither a human nor a divine achievement.

All the same and despite the foregoing explanations against God, Merleau-Ponty has always objected to having his thought branded as atheistic. He admits that, in a way, philosophy is unable to purge itself of the thought of God. "I think that it is naturally inherent for man to think of God. This does not, however, mean that God exists."[14] Because the existence of God destroys the wonderment inherent in true philosophy, Merleau-Ponty will have nothing to do with God in philosophy. Yet he refuses to call himself an atheist, though he admits that he does so only when he is provoked.[15] Moreover, the fact that men in general are preoccupied with God cannot be silenced by calling it simply an illusion. Men think and talk about God uninterruptedly and with implacable insistence. The novelty of God-thinking, or thinking-God, never fades; it is always influencing human thought in precise and all-pervading ways. Its very influence is revealed in Merleau-Ponty's thought itself. God, in the form of the Transcendent, haunts Merleau-Ponty when he tries to make the transition from the mystery of the world to the mystery of thought. He wonders how thought is possible. And immediately he is in the presence of the problem of transcendence. He has to consider carefully the conditions that make thought possible. On making this consideration, Merleau-Ponty declares that ordinary experience is a necessary, but not an all-explanative, condition for thought. This is his first step. But almost immediately another problem crops up. Why does being hurl itself into the adventure of thinking? How is thinking rendered possible from out of the most inti-

14. Merleau-Ponty, in a discourse given before The French Society of Philosophy, September 23, 1946.
15. Maurice Merleau-Ponty, "Deuxième entretien privé," in *La Connaissance de l'homme au XXe siècle,* Rencontres internationales de Genève, 1951, p. 250.

mate foundations of being? To the extent that Merleau-Ponty concluded that ambiguity was the unique answer to the problem of thought, he did not get beyond a provisory solution to this mystery. Merleau-Ponty was not able to complete his investigation in depth on the mystery of thought, nor to make secure his provisory solution by establishing its validity on solid, metaphysical foundations. Death overtook him while he was studiously preparing a major work on this question. The first part of this work and a large section of the working notes prepared for future development were published posthumuously under the title, *Le Visible et l'Invisible.*

The Case Against Christianity

In addition to rejecting God, Merleau-Ponty also rejected Christianity. He accused Catholic theology of doing away with man's contingency and freedom by deriving both from God, the Necessary Being. By offering man this retreat from contingency, Christianity betrayed man. For it prevented him from courageously taking up his mission to give meaning to himself and history. Through the temptation of its absolute God, Christianity stifled wonderment in man. For the man who has all the answers to the adventure of human life ahead of time is bound to be bored with existence. Christianity acts like the spoiler of a mystery novel who reveals the ending to the prospective reader, thereby prematurely sating his hunger for the quest and goal of mystery, and removing the very motive for entering upon the adventure. Merleau-Ponty finds the expression "Christian existentialism" a contradiction in terms. Such a philosophic stance is impossible in his eyes. True, there are outstanding philosophers, like Kierkegaard and Marcel, who are considered by their peers to be Christian existentialists. But thinkers who put these two words together in a meaningful way do not seem to see the illogicality of their position. The Pope, Pius XII, was a far more consistent thinker when he condemned existentialism as being contrary to Christianity.

Merleau-Ponty tends to agree with Maritain when the latter explains that the essence of Christianity demands the rejection of graven images. As Maritain sees it, the saint is an "integral atheist" vis à vis a God who would only guarantee the natural order of things, sanction all good and evil, justify slavery, the tears of infants and the agony of the innocent, all under the rationalization that these hardships are, in reality, sacred necessities for the fulfillment of the divine plan. Moreover, the saint is an "integral atheist" before a God who would sacrifice man to the cosmos so as to have it proclaimed everywhere and to all that He is the absurd "Emperor of the World." Maritain contends, of course, that the Christian God could never approve, much less perform, such cruelties. For the Christian God is the God who redeems the world and answers the prayers of men. For his part, however, Merleau-Ponty contends that the Christian God is unfortunately projected by the Catholic Church, in word, deed and demand, as being just what the title "Emperor of the World" implies. According to Merleau-Ponty, the Catholic hierarchy uses terminology about the Christian God that represents Him as the Despot of the World. He admits, to be sure, that there are among Catholic theologians, especially among the avant-garde French and European group, more mollifying, humane expressions that depict the nature and conduct of a more humane Christian God. But the official expressions emanating from the top, from Rome, still insist that God is the Maker of the World and the manipulator of men's destinies. And, insists Merleau-Ponty, the contingency and freedom of man as subject are simply incompatible with the existence of Absolute Thought, Absolute Will, Absolute Power—all identified in the Absolute Emperor of the World.[16] Christianity, therefore, destroys the human adventure to achieve meaning on earth; it opposes a heaven of infinite power to an earth of infinite prospects; it divorces a mythical history, already consummated in God, from real history, heroically evolving and branded with meaning through the ambiguous, contingent, committed activities of man. The Christian has reduced philosophic wonderment to an empty formula. He is prematurely celebrating a victory already assured in history. For his enemy, Satan and his kingdom of darkness, is already vanquished. Indeed, the Emperor-God of the Christian is also his Conqueror-God. It is a lesson gleaned from history that eventually occultist thought shows its mark.[17]

16. Maurice Merleau-Ponty, *Éloge de la philosophie*, pp. 55–56.
17. Maurice Merleau-Ponty, "L'homme et l'adversité," in *La Connaissance de l'homme au XXe siècle*, Rencontres internationales de Genève, 1951, p. 74.

The Radical Ambiguity of Christianity

As he examined the essence of Christianity, Merleau-Ponty found it wanting not only because of its metaphysical ambiguity but also because of its historical non-dependability. In certain periods of history he found that Christianity worked with man in his search for progress and meaning. In other periods Christianity opposed man's quest for values and truth. Why this historical equivocity? Is Christianity an authentic partner of man in his quest for social maturity or not? Many learned Christians of the high caliber of Père Daniélou argue that in principle and substance Christianity is the best ally man has in his earthly struggles for self-advancement. Its history of civilizing, sanctifying service to man for two thousand years presents unimpeachable evidence of this truth. Certainly, such learned Christians are the first to admit that history also reveals that many Christians have betrayed man in his quest for truth and values. But these traitors were not failures because of Christian truth and morals but in spite of them. These historical failures betrayed man in so far as they freely fell away from the ideals of Christianity. The teachings and example of Christ, the Founder of Christianity, cannot be held responsible for these failures, any more than the treason of Judas can be attributed to the goodness of his Divine Master. There are unfortunate incidents in the past of Christianity; there are unfortunate incidents in the present of Christianity and the future of Christianity will be afflicted with its failures as well. Christians ever remain free to face or flee the ideals of Christianity. Neither God nor His Church will force Christians to be faithful to themselves. Christians, from Popes to peasants, are peccable. It is because of human depravity that scandals arise, not because of divine generosity. Indeed, perhaps the hardest test of a Christian's faith is the scandal he receives from his fellow Christians. But Merleau-Ponty is not convinced by this distinction between the substantial goodness of Christianity and the accidental evil of depraved Christians. Often, he complains, the Christian "will plead guilty for the past and innocence in regard to the future."[18] Merleau-Ponty's objection against Christianity goes deeper than the historically good or bad deeds

18. Maurice Merleau-Ponty, *Sens et Non-sens* (Paris: edition of 1948), p. 353.

of Christians. He admits there have been saints and devils among Christians. But he insists that Christianity, in the last analysis, is incapable of siding with man because its ambiguity is an essential sickness, a sick constitutional condition deeper by far than any outward deeds. And he bases his complete distrust of Christianity on his discovery of a doctrinal distinction intrinsic to Christianity, the distinction between its "internal God" and its "external God."

Catholicism is hopelessly and fundamentally ambiguous because Catholics are called upon to believe in an internal and external God. Catholics practice a "religion of the Father" and a "religion of the Son." Somehow the two are compatible to Catholics; in reality, they are not, in the eyes of Merleau-Ponty. "The kingdom of God is within you," Catholics are taught. And so they find God in their inner souls, for God is more intimate to man than man is to himself.[19] Thus God's testimony to Himself in the interior souls is alone valuable. With God dwelling within man, no external force may be used to coerce man to faith. Now faith in a God who dwells within man is a faith characterized by the dimensions of eternity and invincibility.[20] Thus experiencing himself eternally stablized in an unshakable faith placed in his indwelling God, the Christian dismisses the temporal as of no significance. Even when the Christian violates his own conscience, he falls morally, yet he believes he creates nothing, for evil is an absence of being, of good. Sin, in this conspectus, becomes unreal. But, and here is that startling ambiguity again, the good also has no real significance for the Christian. For the good which abides in man's interior spirit, ultimately abides in reality in God who is more intimate to man than man is to himself. And, moreover, since God is infinite goodness, man can neither produce nor offer God any goodness of his own human volition. It follows, says Merleau-Ponty, that there is no good that man can perform.[21]

Man, analyzed under the aspect of his faith in an eternal God, sinks into the abyss of meaninglessness. His earthly destiny is of no great importance. Naturally then, a sort of fatalistic resignation paralyzes his will; he accepts whatever comes his way,

19. Maurice Merleau-Ponty, *La Connaissance de l'homme au XXe siècle*, Rencontres internationales de Genève, 1951, p 356.
20. *Ibid.*, p. 356.
21. *Ibid.*, p. 356.

tragedy or happiness. "Thy will be done" is his motto in life. And so the Christian isolates himself with God within his soul. "We have not here a lasting city, but look for one which is to come." The Christian is thus always stargazing into eternity. But in this very situation we again come face to face with that Christian equivocity. For the Christian's lot hereafter is also dissolved into nothingness. Is not his God always adorable? "Let us repose in him," expresses a program of idleness for all eternity. Thus faith in his indwelling God strips man of love for his own life. Prostrate, paralyzed and denuded before his guest-God, human history loses its meaning, coherence and reality for the inert adorer. In the presence of his abiding God the Christian sinks into the coma of quietism.[22] In the apt phrase of Hegel, the Christian is asleep in "the reign of the Father."[23]

But when God enters history as the Incarnate Son, the Christian's religion, or rather man's religion, takes on an orientation of truly perplexing obscurity. With the Incarnate appearance of the Son of God in history, the Christian's faith shifted from the internal to the external God. Now he was called to the practice of the "religion of the Son." For his God has moved from the interior of man's soul to the exterior of man's history. Whereas before, God was a hidden God, dwelling in inaccessible light and in the depths of souls, now God's life is dated with a specific time; His travels are localized in definite cities and towns; His deeds and words are recorded in explicit, historical books and even His very death and final destiny are recorded on exact sites that have become historical, holy places of pilgrimage. Because God entered the world in this manner, the Christian finally came to see the world as a precious place that has to be humanized and sanctified. History, too, has taken on great importance in his eyes as the milieu in which God taught truth, created values and achieved the salvation of the whole cosmos.

Moreover, God's advent in the flesh seems to have indicated that God the Father was not self-sufficient. He took up flesh, the world and history in His Son as if it were necessary for Him to complete His own perfection in this way. Were the assumption of man and the world necessary for the fulfillment of the Father? Was Hegel, after all, right in maintaining that God, in

22. *Ibid.*, p. 356.
23. *Ibid.*, p. 356 ff.

order to attain His full self-conscious identity, had to incarnate Himself in the dialectical and evolving processes of man, the world and history? Whatever the answer may be to this question, Christians, following the Son's example, no longer withdraw from the world in order to live for God. Now, in imitation of the Son of God, they are externally involved in the ambiguous development of the world, of good and of evil. Now Christians, like their master Christ, represent within themselves the contradictions of good and evil, truth and falsity, light and darkness. This means, in the estimation of Merleau-Ponty, that Christians are also "non-Christians." They are at once light and darkness, savory and insipid salt. Once again that ambiguity; for when Christians defect from God, their religion, their Church, they still remain Christians. Somehow they fall and do not fall, run away and remain, receive sacraments of life and remain spiritually dead, profess a faith of joy and live lives of unhappiness.[24]

Merleau-Ponty traces this oscillatory, maddening Christian duplicity to the schism within the Catholic faith between the "religion of the Father" on the one hand, and the "religion of the Son" on the other. "The paradox of Christianity, especially of Catholicism, consists in this—that the Catholic never clings either to the internal or the external God, but always takes a position that lies *in between* those two possibilities."[25] In other words, between the religion of the Father and Son the Christian is a middle-of-the-roader; he wants to practice both religions, but can dedicate himself to neither entirely.

Merleau-Ponty finds this Catholic duplicity and ambiguity illustrated in innumerable historical incidents. For example, the Catholic will give his life for his faith, but only because he is convinced he keeps his life in this manner. The Catholic surrenders to the darkness of faith, but only because he is convinced he is surrendering to the infinite light that is God. The Catholic founds his beliefs on faith, yet he is told by his Church, teaching infallibly, that one cannot be a Catholic who disbelieves that a rational proof of the existence of God is possible. The Catholic believes in God's immanent presence within himself and the whole universe, yet he simultaneously maintains

24. *Ibid.*, pp. 357–360.
25. *Ibid.*, p. 360.

God's utter transcendence beyond himself and the whole universe. History is sacred and important for the Catholic, yet it is secular and trivial also, for it is passing away. Everything is possible for a Catholic in God, yet everything is already determined by Infinite Wisdom. When it comes to daily practices and policies, the Catholic is progressist and integrist, revolutionary and conservative, orthodox and heretic. The Church is sometimes with God against Caesar, at other times with Caesar against God; she has sided alternately with the rich against the poor and with the poor against the rich. In a word, claims Merleau-Ponty, Christianity, expecially Catholicism, is hopelessly and utterly unreliable because essentially equivocal. Therefore, man who is dedicated to forging his own meaning, truth and progressive history, through his own creative and free resources, simply cannot count on the Catholic Church becoming his steadfast ally in this great human enterprise. Whenever her essentially ambiguous religious instincts, doctrines, liturgies and policies happen to coincide with his great enterprise, man can make use of Catholicism. But he must be on his guard, for in the last analysis Christianity will betray the authenticity of man's life, thought, ideals and history. Events over the ages have proven that Christianity leaves men nonplused even when it is not abandoning them.

A Critical Appreciation

Here we will search out and reflect upon the source, the form and the major arguments that sustain the atheism of Merleau-Ponty. The tap root of his atheism draws its nourishment from the rich, primitive soil of perception. The necessary return of the philosopher to this pre-predicative, pre-reflective field of human activity calls for his understanding of perception as that originally structured human behavior which includes every aspect of man's pristine experience, stressing especially the birth and growth of his consciousness. A more concrete consideration of existential man is scarcely imaginable. This type of philosophy concentrates on the incarnate I, the individual subject called forth into the world and endowed with a body that vigorously propels him into dynamic contact with the world and the community of things and men. Its phenomeno-

logical descriptions aim at unveiling the original, complex phenomenon of conscious experience in the hope of drawing authentic conclusions about what lies under that experience at
the core of man's being.

Now it is Merleau-Ponty's contention that for a philosopher
to reflect at all in this area of the dawn of wonderment, he must
reject God. Why? Because, he continues, once the philosopher
accepts God as the key to the myestery of being, then both the
mystery and wonderment over the mystery vanish. Moreover,
the philosopher burdened with belief in God is also incapable
of experiencing the thrilling, agonizing contingency of his own
being and the dangerous ambiguity of his quest for historical
meaning as he creates an authentic human community. A God
who answers questions before they are asked and determines
solutions to problems before they arise, kills the awe of wonderment, the thrill of contingency, the challenge of ambiguity. In
a word, belief in God violates the authenticity of human life,
belief in God renders authentic philosophy impossible. In attempting to evaluate these arguments, we will examine in a
phenomenological way the experiences of wonderment and
contingency so as to see if God's presence in the philosophic
quest of man for meaning, truth, value and historical community really renders the whole human enterprise sterile and impossible.

What is wonder or wonderment? Bacon has written that
"wonder is the seed of knowledge." A normal child, then, just
recently arrived in the world, with everything to learn, ought
to be an excellent human exemplification of the dawn and development of wonder. And so, on observation, we find he is.
Wide-eyed in pre-reflective, spontaneous awe at the magnitude,
magnificence and munificence of the world of beings, the child-
discoverer thrusts himself violently forward, all sensory systems open, toward whatever moves, shines, is colored, vibrates
or comes within his reach or prowling range. Wonder in the
child's overwhelming perceptions is seen as the exclamatory
opening and expanding exultation of the child's attainment of
new and more beings. Marcel, with intuitive genius, sees, below
the depths of these breath-taking discoveries, a metaphysical
dimension to man, an ontological *besoin d'être* which, from the
core of man's being, drives man into the ocean of being. Thus

wonderment testifies to the truth that man is essentially a being-with, that *esse est co-esse,* "to be is to-be-with." The activity
of wonder is, then, the subject's attempts at satisfying his metaphysical hunger for greater participation in greater being.
Wonder is man's first thrust into transcendence; it is man's
eternal effort to quench his thirst for greater and better grades
of being. Looked at subjectively, then, wonderment is clearly
seen to be man's metaphysical and physical advance in greater
participation of the being of other beings. To recall our child for
a moment, we notice that he is first lost in wonderment at the
presence of his parents. He is first drawn into, then upward in
being through the parental "cords of Adam," through the bodies, food, things, love and service of beings nearest and dearest
to him. Man's ascent in being always begins through realities
that are nearest to him. For these first awaken his wonder,
whet his metaphysical appetite, attract his whole being toward
the plenitude of being. Looked at objectively, wonderment is
seen to be related to other beings to be attained. There is more
being and "I must participate in that greater being" is the un-
verbalized truth underlying the child's quest in wonderment. In
reality, then, wonder is man's response of *Yes* to the alluring
call of other beings' *Come,* a call that vibrates with a thrill in
the awakening consciousness of man. Wonder is the spiritual,
gravitational plunge of lesser being toward fuller being, of
fuller being toward the plenitude of being. When a philosopher
of the genius of a Socrates or Plato or the neo-Socratic Marcel
asks himself what explains this metaphysical hunger that exists dynamically at the core of all being, he concludes that there
is implicit testimony in this universal phenomenon to the existence of the Plenitude of Being. He concludes that upon reflection on this concrete, universal experience of wonderment,
man must conclude to the existence of God, as the Plentitude
of Being. Contrary then to Merleau-Ponty's thesis, God does not
destroy true philosophy by stifling wonder. The truth is that
God is the hidden foundation for all wonder, the invisible but
ever-present loadstone that attracts back to Himself the creation He called forth out of nothingness and sent on its mission
of self-maturation.

The weight of history testifies to the fact that it is in a Godless
civilization that wonderment vanishes and that men despair of

ever achieving truth, value or creative communities. It is in Godless societies that men become bored, though surfeited with the comforts of their marvelous machines, and slide toward the seduction of social suicide. In reality, then, the initial pre-reflective, pre-predicative perceptions of man, as a brilliant dawn of wonder, already implicitly testify to the rising Sun of the Deity in the consciousness of awakening man, that Deity who is drawing man to Himself through the very activity of man's wonderment. St. Augustine experienced this wonder in his long, tortured quest for meaning and value. His observation about it has become one of the most inspiring insights of universal appeal: "Thou hast made us for Thyself, O Lord, and our hearts are restless until they rest in Thee." Wonder is now seen as the awed, agonized restlessness, the insatiable hunger of conscious man's drive for the possession of God. Chesterton pithily expressed the same truth when he wrote: "The world will never starve for want of wonders but only for want of wonder." Contrary to Merleau-Ponty, God guarantees man's authentic life of philosophy for He is the goad and goal of man's wonder.

What is contingency? A clear understanding of this notion is important, since traditional metaphysics argues from the contingency of creatures to the existence of God as the Necessary Being, whereas Merleau-Ponty argues from the same basis to the denial of God as the Necessary Being.[26] As might be expected the word has different meanings for each current of thought. In the traditional metaphysical sense, that being is contingent which has not the ground or reason of its being within itself. This means that no aspects of a contingent being, neither its existence nor activities, can find their full meaning within the being itself. Thus all creatures are contingent beings because they depend for their beings and activities ultimately on causes, reasons, agents outside themselves. Indeed, in the last analysis, all creatures are contingent because they depend totally upon the absolutely self-explanatory, self-contained, self-sufficient Being known as God.

Man's very activity of wonderment, which we have just

26. William A. Luijpen, O.S.A., *Phenomenology And Atheism* (Pittsburgh: Duquesne University Press, 1964), p. 308. Contains a fine chapter on Merleau-Ponty, but the book is marred by the exaggeration of blaming atheism on Christianity.

briefly analyzed, illustrates his basic contingency. In revealing his hunger for more being, it demonstrates the inadequacy of his own being, his dependence upon other beings for his self-fulfillment, ultimately his need for God as the sole solution to his contingency. The trouble with Merleau-Ponty's understanding of the notion of contingency is that it is an expression of an anthropological, not of the metaphysical, sense of the word. For Merleau-Ponty the contingency of man means that man "is not necessitated by processes and forces." In traditional metaphysics that definition would define the freedom, not the contingency of man. Of course, for traditional philosophy even man's freedom is contingent, for he is not the ground or full explanation of his limited freedom. That ground and explanation lies outside of man in Absolute Freedom who is God. But God, far from imprisoning man within necessitating processes and forces—Merleau-Ponty's contention—actually endows man with a participation in the liberty that comes down from Himself, the source of all freedom. It is God who creates man free and thereby challenges him to use his freedom to discover meaning, truth, values and community. The fact that God knows the whole system of creation and all its intermediate and final answers does not in the least diminish the free contingency of man. Even if man begins with God as the final answer and solution to all, he is left to work out the solutions to the problems of his world and societies through the use of his intelligence and freedom. And he must do this in fear and trembling, for ultimate failure and tragedy are well within his possibilities. The fact that man knows and accepts God in his knowledge as his last end and goal does not dispense him from the responsibility of earning that goal, nor from the danger of failing in the quest for God. Man is free and morally obligated to perform the good deeds and abstain from the bad deeds that will assure him success in his moral struggles. He is free to do evil and reject God, his fellow men, himself—as many men have done in history. Because he is free and intelligent, man suffers contingency in the very sense Merleau-Ponty wishes to preserve it through denying God.

Thus we see that the contingency of limited freedom in man has no other rational or metaphysical foundation than the necessary existence of the absolutely Free God. Moreover, the fact of God's existence does not reduce man to an idle automation, for God is not going to do man's work for him. If anything, then, the existence of God known and accepted only heightens the anguish of ambiguity. For once man realizes that God is the Supreme Goal he must attain yet can irrevocably lose, only then does he fully experience the crisis of his contingency. Kierkegaard has related graphically how the presence of God heightens the degree of dread in all man's decisions. The presence of God flings man this challenge: Will you choose for or against God? After all, God is transcendent and invisible. To choose these intangibles seems to man to be throwing himself into an unknown abyss; man recoils in dread from the chasm of transcendence. Either way his choice involves the survival or annihilation of his being. If Kierkegaard's phenomenological analysis does nothing else, it demonstrates in a powerful manner the truth that God does not, during this life, obliterate contingency; he sharpens and heightens man's consciousness of it by requiring of him decisions that determine his eternal failure or success. In a very true sense, man's destiny is in his own hands; that is how God arranged matters when He made man free. Christianity gives countless testimonies to this truth. When the Son of God appeared as a child and was received in the arms of Simeon, this holy man prophesied one drastic outcome of God's arrival in the flesh, an outcome that dramatically illustrates the ambiguous contingency of man: "Behold, this child is destined for the fall and for the rise of many in Israel and for a sign that shall be contradicted."[27] Far from leaving man with nothing to do because God is present and accepted, Christianity reveals God as demanding more of Christians to whom He has given more; Christ, by His coming and the example of His service to the world, to His fellow men and to God, challenges Christians to emulate His generosity.

We here summarize our response to the first part of Merleau-Ponty's objection to the existence of God; namely that God would destroy true philosophy through his destruction of man's experience of wonderment, ambiguity and contingency. First, we stress that the datum of original perception is an experience which is not merely sensory, but one which contains metaphysically constitutive elements that indicate man's thrust to-

27. Luke 2 : 34.

ward and grasp of the heart of Being itself, however implicitly. The internal-external phenomenon of human consciousness cannot be explained simply by human ambiguity, but must be seen, in its deepest foundations, as the metaphysical drive of man for union with the Plenitude of Being—God. Thus, the unity of conscious being, through other beings, with divine Being is solved not by appealing to the ambiguity of the pure univocity of being, but by having recourse to the ambiguity of the univocity of the plurality of beings. God is Being in the absolutely perfect degree; man and creatures are beings by participation in being; they are beings by the grace of other beings, by the grace of the Absolute. Hence they are limited, contingent, ambiguous beings, that is, *beings by analogy.* We, therefore, replace Merleau-Ponty's philosophy of contradictory ambiguity which he places between the internal and external, the one and the other, man and God, with the philosophy of the analogy of being. This philosophy of the analogy of being alone coherently accounts for the ambiguity of created beings and, paradoxical as that may seem, for the unity of all beings among themselves and with God. Above all, this metaphysical foundation of the analogy of being explains why philosophy, contrary to Merleau-Ponty's demand, can never succeed in freeing itself from the thought of God, but is, on the contrary, always forced to come to terms with Him. At the same time, the analogy of being also explains how philosophy's inability to free itself from the thought of God is already its first step toward proclaiming His existence.

Secondly, we maintain that the superhuman dimension of man's being should not be completely reduced to his intrahuman dimension. For the metaphysical is not the only aspect of man's being. Indeed man's metaphysical consciousness transcends the experience of the merely perceptible. Man's metaphysical consciousness reveals that there exist drives in man's nature which will not permit him to be held earth-bound, tied solely to intracosmic or intrahuman relationships. These superior drives reveal man's need for religion and explain his rejection of positive humanism as a substitute for religion. Thirdly, phenomenology does not coincide with philosophy. Phenomenological description of the exterior of beings needs to be completed and surpassed by a return to the internal, transcendental aspects of beings. Phenomenology does not supply a basis for metaphysics; it is too subjective; each philosopher claims truth from his own viewpoint. Metaphysics alone can save phenomenology from falling into subjectivism. For metaphysics alone affords the objective, transcendental foundation, criteria and norms which can complete and stabilize the valid findings of phenomenology. Fourthly, the "incarnate meaning" which Merleau-Ponty seeks in the unity of the world and in the human community, will, in our estimation, be solidly founded and developed only and ultimately under the light and love of the Transcendent Being, God. The Psalmist warns mankind that "unless the Lord builds the house, they labor in vain who build it." Moreover, history has testified, time and time again, that self-sufficient man, after constructing impressive and vast empires, only had them come crashing down to divide and destroy men in the confusion of tongues and fratricidal wars. Finally, we contend that an exclusively phenomenological description of contingency represents it as if it were a radical finiteness, or a casuality so absolutely simple that there is offered to man not the slightest hint of how to overcome it. In reality, we know, under the light of the transcendence of being, that all contingent existences are ultimately grounded in Being and, in the last analysis, in the Absolute Being who can and will cure all contingency."[28]

God and Christian Quietism

We now propose to answer Merleau-Ponty's social arguments against the existence of God. In an analogous formulation of the same argument in Sartre, Merleau-Ponty claims that once people are convinced they possess God, then, the human enterprise to create a more civilized world and meaningful history becomes an absurd, impossible project. For in God everything has already attained its perfection and man cannot improve on that. From a Christian viewpoint, our first observation would point out that the Apostles and first Christians would have been startled indeed to learn that the coming of the Holy Spirit was meant to confirm them in the idleness of waiting for the second coming of Christ. So stirred were they by the Holy Spirit that

28. Johannes Lotz, *op. cit.,* pp. 321–329.

they realized that, now that Christ had come, everything remained to be done; there was a world to be divinized. And with
incredible energy they spread the truth of God's entrance into
history all over the world. For the Christian even today, everything depends on man's cooperation with God. For each generation everything begins again; man has always the inspiring,
endless mission to humanize and sanctify society. Moreover,
from a philosophical point of view we can add that God, in His
infiniteness, does not possess within Himself what is human in
its finiteness, the human considered precisely as the finite human. Man's self-realization through his own human activity is
never, as such, contained in God. God and the human person are
separate beings; man has to work for his perfection, not expect
it gratis from God. Man's works, therefore, are far from absurd
or useless. Indeed, God depends on man's loving activity for the
return of primitive creation back to Himself as a sanctified gift
from the community of man. God expects this gift because He
has already taken up the human family into His divine family
through the grace of His divine Son. Thus there need be no
contradiction between man's orientation toward the world and
his orientation toward his Transcendent God. In fact there is no
contradiction between the "religion of the Father" and the
"religion of the Son." They are one and the same religion.
"Philip, he who sees me sees the Father," said Christ to His
apostle seeking a glimpse of the Father. The mission of the
Father and of the Son is identical. "God so loved the world that
he delivered up his Son for its salvation."

The truth is that man does not live "always *between* one and
the other; he lives always *in* one and the other";[29] he lives in
both, for both in God. As a matter of reality, Christians do take
this world seriously because "now is the time of salvation," of
their testing, of their decisions for or against their God and
their eternal salvation. The Christian lives in two tensions; he
develops and realizes himself in his tension to create holy history and in his tension to bear away the kingdom of God with
violence; that is, with zealous love. The Christian, in his daily
strivings, can never be satisfied either with the degree of his

29. A. De Waelhens, *Une philosophie de l'ambiguité, l'existentialisme de
Maurice Merleau-Ponty* (Louvain: 1951), p. 381.

success or with the efforts expended to attain it. Through success or failure he presses forward, not looking behind but ahead
to the ideal presented him by Christ. Christianity and quietism
are, therefore, seen to be mutually negating. Indeed, the Catholic Church is the only organized religion, to my knowledge, that
has solemnly condemned religious quietism. And her condemnation of quietism in religion could be reasonably expected to
extend to its use as a posture in every valid area of human
endeavor.

Merleau-Ponty also contends that the "look of God" violates
the liberty of man and reduces the human person to the status
of a mere thing. But Christ, the Son of God, testifies that God
is the Father of every man, the Father who bestows upon each
man whatever gifts he has of nature and grace. And among
man's God-given gifts is the gift of liberty. It is God who *de
facto* created a universe in space and time as an almost limitless field for the exercise of man's liberty. God is so sensitively
considerate of man's liberty that He allows man almost infinite
spiritual space within which to make his decisions. Man is so
completely free in determining his own destiny that history
bears witness to the infinite range of his choices. At times, man
has risen to the supreme heights, through his free cooperation
with God, of ecstatic union with God; he has chosen to become
a saint. At other times, alas, by his decision to rebel, he has sunk
to the abysmal depths of monstruous criminality, even choosing the ultimate, satanic crime of attempting to dethrone God.
"God is love," says St. John the Evangelist. And we know from
the example of Christ that the regard, the look of God, the look
of divine love attracts, raises up, forgives, heals and expands
the liberty of the human person.

In another argument against God, Merleau-Ponty goes
beyond a position taken by Sartre, if that can be imagined. It
states that religion reduces man to the posture of being an idle
dreamer. He dreams about the next life. It is in that life that
man expects to enjoy perfect, intrahuman harmony, an ideal
wholly unrealizable in this life. The result of this fixation on
otherworldly community happiness is that the religious man is
antisocial. Christians are estranged from the community of
mankind; they cannot be fully counted on to dedicate them-

selves to projects that foster intercommunion and intercommunity advancement. What about this charge of social exclusivism which leads to social divisiveness? First, it must be stated—and the truth of this statement must be evident by this time—that Merleau-Ponty either is not acquainted with true Christianity or he continually characterizes it to suit his own satisfaction and purposes. The last thing Christianity is, is exclusive. Wherever man is, from hottentot to eskimo, her missionaries have found him. And even the charge that Christianity seeks man exclusively for purposes of the next world will not bear historical scrutiny. For nuns, brothers, priests, Christian laywomen and laymen have been doctors, nurses, teachers, farmers as well as apostles of the gospel to the downtrodden of the world. As for Merleau-Ponty's definition of religion, we must point out that he has failed to grasp the essence of religion. For the essential significance of religion is this: religion is man's *community with God.* This is true even of false religions in which men form communities and rituals in order to honor their gods. But in the history of the Christian religion the highest, most reasonable, most noble and sacred community of man with God is realized. For in Christianity two communities are united in sacred love. The divine community of the Trinity has assumed the human community. Christ, God and Man, is the link of eternal love between them; the Church is the prolongation of Christ in time and the intrahuman bond that unites men with each other and with God in a service of love.

St. Paul, writing to the Ephesians and comparing their social lot before their conversion to Christ and insertion into His Church to their present infinitely improved social state, illustrates what a pallid reality natural community is without the transcendent ascent into the Divine Community of Love. He writes:

> And coming, he announced the good tidings of peace to you who were afar off and of peace to those who were near; because through him we both have access in one Spirit to the Father. Therefore, you are now no longer strangers and foreigners, but you are citizens with the saints and members of God's household; you are built upon the foundations of the apostles and prophets with Christ himself as the chief cornerstone. In him the whole structure is

closely fitted together and grows into a temple holy in the Lord; in him you are being built together into a dwelling place for God in the Spirit.[30]

It is to this sublime, intrahuman, divine community that Christianity invites all men.

In another objection, Merleau-Ponty pointed out to Christians that they were attempting to live two contradictory lives at the same time and under two standards of morality. We agree that there would be an undeniable contradiction in the conduct of Christians if these two lives and moral standards were completely contrary or in absolute opposition. As a matter of fact, however, no such contradiction exists because both lives and standards either intersect or the higher includes and completes the lower. As man develops in the context of his earthly existence, his life presents him with moral values that are essentially and indelibly rough, valid approximations of the sublime values found in the life of Transcendence. Natural moral goodness is completed and transfigured by religious sanctity; natural moral evil is an irrational debasement and can develop into religious dereliction. The life and values of Transcendence constitute the intimate core of moral nobility without which the natural life could not maintain even its normal, moral quality. There is no contradiction between natural and supernatural life or morals; they both ascend toward the perfection of God. Between the life of the wicked and that of the just there is the opposition of moral war, but that hostility is not due to God; it is due to the wicked who, in warring against God, destroy themselves.

Conclusion

Before we conclude this chapter we want to consider briefly the ethical dimension of Merleau-Ponty's thought. For him, as for traditional philosophers, liberty is inherent in every moral act. Man's liberty is, of course, limited by his limited opening to being and, hence, by his created nature or essence. Nevertheless, men possess true liberty, even if it is also restricted and conditioned by historical circumstances. Merleau-Ponty

---

30. Ephesians 2 : 17–22.

stresses that true morality consists in man's authentic search
for genuine harmony within himself and with others within
the community. Morality eschews, therefore, any utopian ac-
cord founded on unreal and sterile ideologies which only halt
man's search for valid harmony by presupposing that the whole
problem is already solved. The Christian Absolute, God, and the
communist Absolute, History, are cases of unreal ideologies
and phantom harmonies. For Merleau-Ponty, the moral imperative is linked up again to human liberty, not to God or History
or anything outside man himself. Moreover, man's liberty
should take as its commitment the good of the community.
Man's decision to abandon God is a positive moral commitment
to assume his daily responsibilities with all his heart. This commitment seeks no external guarantee for the attainment of
human truth and values. Rather, it stresses that man is determined to forge his own destiny freely. Merleau-Ponty's thought
on human morality comes down to being a positive, a-religious
humanism. Now we recognize in this morality, without the
slightest doubt, a very high goal of moral goodness. The interior
self-realization of man which subordinates his personal career
to the good of the community is truly admirable. However, the
individual's subordination to so social a goal is fraught with
danger precisely because Merleau Ponty has severed the person's transcendent bond with God. Godless, socially oriented
man, once exclusively immersed within the community, is
easily reduced to becoming the object of abuse. Our era is continuing to witness the frightful evidence of totalitarian systems pulverizing man with techniques of degradation for the
social good of the community.

Thus, we must say that it is not true that "the metaphysical
and moral conscience dies when it comes into contact with the
Absolute." Rather, the opposite is true; the moral conscience
dies when it breaks contact with the Absolute. The truth is that
man is powerless for truth, goodness or the liberty of justice
and ordered love when he abandons God. He then becomes
powerful in crime, as history implacably testifies. On the other
hand, religious humanism, or rather Christian humanity, allows man to escape the despair of social tyranny by inspiring
him to transcend toward the Principle of Liberty. Christianity
exalts man in his most intimate interior, holding him higher

than the community, more precious than the temporal and placing his destiny beyond the passing community of history in the eternally established community of God himself. Only by taking membership in the transcendent community of God can man escape individualistic self-confinement in autoerotic humanism. In the last analysis, it is man's religious relationship with the community of God which confers on the love and services he renders to the community of men their most sane and sacred significance. Man is not condemned to make his own relative meaning and ambiguous morals; rather he is called by God to achieve absolute meaning and to create, within the drama of meaning, a community growing in truth, advancing in moral excellence and forging its ultimate transfiguration in God.

CHAPTER X

Bonhoeffer: The God of the Saeculum

WITHIN THE LAST TWO DECADES THE CRUST OF MAN'S theological landscape has trembled and split wide open as a result of the volcanic forces that have exploded beneath it. For the Christian savant who has carefully followed the formation and development of the various layers of modern thought, this shaking of religious foundations was not unexpected. Indeed, it was long overdue. Underground pressures had been building against the city of theology for at least three centuries. In the previous chapters of this work we have briefly studied how the fault of philosophical and cultural atheism was formed. The city of theology was perched precariously over the development of this rockless fault. Eventually, when the pressures below could no longer be contained, the quake struck, a large section of the Christian city broke with a roar from the strata of orthodoxy and shifted suddenly downward into a "death-of-God" depression. This abrupt dislocation in the rock of dogma sent shock waves traveling with restless violence to the ends of the world of religion. Seismographic recordings in scholarly journals reported the magnitude of spiritual desolation caused by this crack in the Christian Citadel. A tidal wave of books, articles, reviews, seminars and international conferences inundated campuses and cities of the West, all of them obsessed with the new gospel about the death of God. For the benefit of the masses, popular weekly journals and radio-television documentaries sensationalized the news that Christian faith in the God of Revelation was crumbling everywhere.

What has been the result of this quake of faith? The list of casualties is appalling but we indicate here only the most dire disasters. Among theologians, credal continuity and coherence has been radically ruptured. In a sterile and self-contradictory venture the Godless theologians have substituted the suicidal science of a theology without God for the authentic discipline of theology about God. As irrationally might astronomers pursue an astronomy without stars or physicists a physics without atoms or biologists a biology without cells. Then too among the moralists chaos has supplanted consensus on what constitutes Christian morality. Moreover, the Secular City is now rising over the ruins of the Christian City. This new city promises its citizens an earthly paradise and a civilization that is founded on its new creed expressed in the following words: "There is no God! In man 'come of age' we trust!" Needless to say, this Godless City is doomed to even greater destruction than that which struck faithless cities before it. For the Godless City is built on the sands of a double fault—that of philosophical atheism and, now, of theological nihilism. When the underground, volcanic fires of disbelief, desperation and despair build to the point of violent friction that can no longer be suppressed, then the shining City of Godless, secular culture will explode and be consumed by fire like Sodom and Gomorrah and, like them, will disappear into the bowels of the earth as a City of Eternal Night.

But perhaps if Christians understood the past and present causes that are hastening Godless society toward self-annihilation, they might once again so bestir themselves as to change the face of the earth through a renewal of Pentecostal faith and zeal that God would be moved to spare and bless his cities. For, unlike cosmic earthquakes, which are determined by necessary physical laws and cannot be avoided, social upheavals do not occur in such a fatalistic manner; man chooses these freely with open eyes, often in defiance of God's offers to save man from himself. Man need only return to God in faith and repentence to be rescued from social suicide. With the hope of sparking just such a return, we will now briefly survey the remote and proximate causes for the rise of radical theology.

Old Seed For Radical Theology

Despite some decisive differences among the radical theologians—we will consider these later in other chapters—their death-of-God Credo sprang from a common ancestry. The plant of modern atheism took root in the seed bed of the Enlightenment. In those times the currents of thought were so wild and the floods of passion so violent that the rich soil of metaphysics and faith was swept into cultural oblivion. The body of God has not yet been recovered from that flood, which is called in the history books, "the Age of Enlightenment" or "the Age of the Metaphysical Revolt." Earlier, at the time of the Protestant Reformation, Luther had radically altered the concept of the nature of the Christian God. In his eyes God was the supreme Being of absolute sovereignty who decided the fate of men in a purely arbitrary manner, saving those He liked, damning those He disliked, always, of course, for reasons founded on His infinite holiness and goodness. Calvin hardened this cruel brand of predestination into a ruthless dogma of faith. Naturally, men shrank from this God who devoured their intellectual, volitional and personal existences. In the name of human freedom and dignity, the men of the Enlightenment turned against this despot-God who, as the exemplar of human rulers, was invoked to justify the unbridled political omnipotence of tyrannical princes and kings. If man hoped to regain his freedom and dignity, he had to bring down his political overlords. But, if he was to succeed in this revolution, man had first to overthrow the Lord of his overlords Himself. It was the Christian God who supposedly guaranteed the authority and despotism of Christian kings. Thus the metaphysical revolution had to precede the political upheaval and it had to be, by the nature of things, an assault against God and religion.

Rousseau created the euphoric atmosphere that fostered man's complete confidence in his own natural goodness and faith in the power of his reason. Robespierre, his devoted disciple, promulgated his master's doctrines and, in a famous speech of the 18th Floreal (May 7, 1794), from the tribunal of the Revolutionary Convention, decreed formally that the religion of civil humanity delineated in *Emile* was henceforth the state religion. According to Engels this establishment of a civil religion was the herald that announced that "the long hibernation of the Christian Middle Ages was over" and a new awakening, a new spring had arrived. In the exhilarating atmosphere of this new spring, all philosophical problems were going to be reassessed. D'Holbach in his writings at this time insisted that "the God who was on trial was the God of the Christians."[1] And He was being tried for His ill use of omnipotent power as well as for His abuse of man's trust in his Providence. D'Holbach thundered against God as the tyrant who had to be done away with. Much ahead of Marx he cited religion as a drug, writing that "religion is the art of inspiring mankind with enthusiasm. It is designed by those who govern to divert men's minds from the evils with which they are overwhelmed."[2] Voltaire himself had no use for God, heaping ridicule upon Him and the Catholic Church. But he urged the use of God and religion as a means of preventing the "vile mob" from awakening to injustice, for fear that the masses would violently disposses the affluent landowners. God and religious faith were to keep the mobs from thinking, for once they begin to think, everything is lost. The illusion of God would preserve the established order and prevent anarchy. Marx shrewdly remarked "that Voltaire taught atheism in his text and faith in his footnotes, and that the people believed the text, not the footnotes."[3] Though in the end he returned and died in the Catholic faith, Voltaire left behind a nation of agnostics whose faith he had sapped by the ridicule and mockery that filled his brilliant books. Voltaire altered the tyrant-God of Luther and Calvin into the deistic God of the Enlightenment. This was a God who abandoned the world to

1. P. Hazard, *European Thought In The Eighteenth Century* (New Haven: Yale University Press, 1954), p. 46.
2. P. T. d'Holbach, *Christianity Unveiled*, translated by Robertson and Gowan (New York: Columbian Press, 1795), p. 229.
3. G. Siegmund, *God On Trial* (New York: Desclée Co, 1967), Quoted on p. 149.

the devil, caring not at all for the miserable plight of humanity. Men rose against a God who had betrayed this world, demanding His annihilation. When the political Revolution, the Reign of Blood and the Napoleonic Wars added their vast carnage to this flood of free-thinking, the faith of France, eldest daughter of the Church, was almost obliterated.

Soon many German scholars, ardent admirers of such French men of letters as Diderot, d'Alembert, d'Holbach, Helvétius and Voltaire, joined the chorus of enlightened mockers. Hegel, Fichte, Feuerbach, Marx slashed with the pack at the Christian God and Church. They sought the revolutionary change of the existing order. But first the pillars of the Christian building had to be leveled. That meant that God and the Christian religion had to be destroyed. Feuerbach was acclaimed by the Neo-Hegelians of the left for having skillfully liquidated the Christian God. It was truly a feat of dialectical dexterity and consisted in the reversing of a Christian principle: God was the image of man, not man the image of God. Theology was anthropology not vice versa. Since this was the truth, it was time man dismissed God and lived up to his own image. Marx, the atheist of action, set to work reducing the Christian world to a desert swept clean of Christian institutions. His classless utopia could be built only on the ruins of the City of God.

With the arrival of Kant, a reaction set in against the illusion that Reason was supreme and omnicompetent. Originally a rationalist and man of the Enlightenment, Kant was shocked from his dogmatic slumber by the criticisms of the English empiricist, David Hume. Hume's empiricism made a skeptic of Kant, at least with respect to those "transcendental illusions" that Kant analyzed and found metaphysically wanting—the existence of God, the immortality of the soul and the liberty of man. Kant demonstrated that the idea of God was impossible for man. God's existence was incapable of metaphysical proof, even though God had to be cherished as a moral imperative of the human heart. At this point positivism replaced rationalism as the fashionable manner of thought in the twentieth century. For it was agreed by all that Kant had completely destroyed any objective knowledge of God. Thereupon the Enlightenment's superb collection of proofs for the existence of God—an exercise never intended to foster faith but to flatter the enlightened

—was thrown into the discard. Granted that all suprasensible realities were actually unknowable, scientism reduced man's knowledge to the mere experience of phenomena. Soon it became a truism that a God who was unknowable was actually nonexistent.

Following in the footsteps of the philosopher Kant came the theologian Hegel. He planned to create a philosophy that would end forever the eternal antagonism between reason and faith. He started with a terrible resentment against Christianity because it tortured him with a sense of sin and paralyzed the powers of his soul. The doctrine of punishment in hell for the evil-doer pushed Hegel's resentment against the Christian God to pathogenic proportions. This led him to reject all faith in a personal God. Nietzsche later is to hold this against God, that God keeps man forever frightened and sick so that man will always be dependent on divine medications. Both men accused the Christian God of being the cause of man's sick, alienated conscience. Both rejected the God of Christianity as the eternal enemy of man. In an effort to gain man absolute freedom, Hegel reduced the tri-personal Godhead to pure, boundless reason, to an immanent, impersonal Idea of the infinite, seeking self-achievement in nature and history. God and immortality were to be sought, not beyond or outside of man but within man, for man is fatalistically destined to the achievement of the religion of absolute freedom. In his thought Hegel succeeds in downgrading God to a mere dialectical "process." Clashing, twisting and unwinding in history, Hegel's God of Process succeeds in obliterating in Himself all metaphysical oppositions by incorporating the principle of contradiction.

Hegel reduced absolute transcendence to absolute immanence, eternity to time. Under his intellectual ministrations the finite became the infinite in the World Spirit whose development was locked in history. In effect, the infinite disappeared, for the only reality in history or existence is the closed circle of Abstract Thought fashioning itself as its own World-in-itself. Starting from the position of attaining man's absolute freedom, Hegel ended by telling man that his glory consisted in allowing himself to be kneaded into this collective, historical, necessary process of self-achieving Thought. The Christian longing for a transcendent happiness with God beyond time was now described by Hegel as sentimental dreaming, a despicable flight from the challenges of time, a cowardly fear of the good earth. It is from this very doctrine that Nietzsche's hatred of the Christian God will arise. Bitterly will he cry out a warning to man, a warning that is still echoing and reechoing in our day. "Brothers, remain true to the earth! Beward of the siren-God of Christianity who would seduce you from your earthly greatness!" This God is the cause of the interior disorder in man's unhappy self-consciousness. Already in Hegel we find allusions that God must die if man is to be cured. These allusions to the death of God in Hegel's works become announcements of God's actual demise in the works of Nietzsche. For both men, when man succeeds in finally identifying himself with God, the old God will die. Indeed the whole death-of-God movement takes its rise in this titanic adventure—the philosophic assault of man on heaven in order to recover for himself the treasures he squandered on God. Summing up Hegel's decision to revolt against the personal God of Christianity, Siegmund clearly follows that road of revolt to the dead-end of deicide.

> As we have seen, Hegel's intellectual revolution began with the fundamental religious decision he made against a personal God. The principle of dialectics made possible the suspension of Christian faith (instead of the radical denial of God which logically follows) by positing the philosophy of a World Spirit coming into its own in the world process; God is not simply cancelled, he is "only" radically reinterpreted. No longer is there a God who transcends time and space, all becoming and all sin; no absolute, divine opposite for man awakened to himself as a person. God is identical with the world. Never complete, he is forever in the process of becoming. Only at the completion of the world process will absolute thought *(das absolute Denken)* have come entirely into its own. The dialectic between finite and infinite is annulled. Noetically and ontically God and man are posited as one; human thought becomes the stage for infinite thought; only in man does the absolute attain self-consciousness. God and man are one and the same since God "is" God only to the extent that he attains consciousness of himself in man.
>
> A further consequence of this oneness of God and man is that the world's becoming is identified with the self-

becoming of the absolute spirit. Thus the infinite Creator becomes finite, while the creature is divinized. Titan-fashion, says Erich Przywara, Hegel with his identity of opposites usurps the very ground of God by laying hands on the inner rhythm of divine life.[4]

New Seed For Radical Theology

Now the idea of God, which was rendered *impossible* by the Kantian dichotomy between the cognoscible phenomena and the unknowable noumena, became for a new brand of modern positivism a *useless* idea. A form of linguistic positivism claims that all philosophical problems are problems of language. It denies all meaning to any proposition that does not arise from experience or cannot be verified by scientific proof. Now God, *ex hypothesi,* cannot be concretely experienced nor become an object of scientific investigation. Hence he is to be considered as nonexistent, as of no account in the world of human realities. More recently, the neo-positivism called structuralism, presently the fashionable rage in the intellectual circles of Europe, has taken to explaining the diversified manifestations of human reality from the viewpoint that all interhuman relations are held together merely by their constituent, crisscrossing, discontinuous elements. There is no need to seek a transcendent reality behind these human relationships which gives them meaning, unity, a temporal and eternal goal. Indeed, structuralism insists that the whole movement of history is discontinuous. It follows, therefore, that God as the key to the meaning and goal of human history, is rejected as a relic of a cultural system that has been lost in the past and forgotten by modern man.

Others have asked, "In our scientific age does the idea of God make any difference in the direction of human betterment?" And many have answered that it makes none at all, pointing out that the believer and the unbeliever have to make the same concrete decisions every day and no appreciable difference in the caliber of their performances shows up. Appeals to heaven do not improve economic, political, academic or civic achievements. Indeed, throughout history religious ideas, people and institutions have backed the most diversified products on politi-

4. G. Siegmund, *God On Trial,* Quoted on pp. 225–226.

cal and moral markets. In the name of God, armies have fought for radically opposed interests. Today the findings of such sciences as sociology, history and other human studies confirm the general feeling among men that the idea of God is simply *sterile*.

There are those too, and their number is growing, who object to the idea of God because they are convinced it is positively *harmful;* it is a roadblock to progress. Such people accuse it of conserving the unjust established order, indeed of justifying this order's existence, institutions and policies by appeals to transcendent reasons. Thus the static idea of God negates freedom and prevents creative human enterprise. As conservative, it encapsulates man in sacred, untouchable, intolerable structures. Once again it is the idea of God that is the cause of man's alienation against society, for it has repeatedly frustrated man's efforts to reform his communities. In a desperate effort, therefore, to throw off the yoke of God and the corrupt *status quo,* men have taken to the streets and campuses in violence. The idea of God, therefore, is the goad, the *agent provocateur* of total revolution. Paradoxically it has become this while working to bring men peace in another world. By directing man's gaze upward toward another kingdom, the idea of God has invited man to abandon himself to the designs of the Absolute Being and to leave unattended the sublime adventure of humanizing the only marvelous world at his creative disposal.

All of these accusations against God have been systematically developed and given the fashionable ring of genuineness over the past several centuries. We have seen how Feuerbach, Nietzsche, Marx, Comte and the existentialists have molded our age of atheism with their thinking tools and passionate ideals. It is now time to investigate how today's radical theologians have altered the tools and refashioned the atheism they inherited from such great savants. We will find that, thanks to the corrosive work of these philosopher-titans, the idea of God had become an embarrassing liability to a section of academic theologians. In an effort to dissolve their embarrassment at the presence of a retarded God in their homes, modern radical theologians decided to put God away decently. This caused a furor in the Christian family. We must now analyze and assess their case against God, studying the explanations they are presenting the worldwide Christian Community that is angered at what it sees as "the treason of the theologians."

Precursors of the Radical Theologians

It is within the historical matrix of the philosophico-cultural atheism already displayed that the "death of God" theologians were formed and given to the world. Today they have become famous through their works. Yet the transition of atheism from the citadel of thought to the citadel of faith did not take place all of a sudden. The way had to be prepared for this transition by the prophets of secularism, themselves able theologians. Though not "death of God" theologians themselves, these outstanding Protestant theologians nevertheless laid down the road their more radical successors would follow. Dedicated sincerely to God in their personal lives and works, they yet ironically became messengers of the "death of God" theologians; they unwittingly sowed the doctrinal seed from which would be harvested a school of professional undertakers who would decently manage the burial of God and religion.

A word must be said about the theological context in which these precursor theologians lived and worked. Without a look into the cultural atmosphere of their times, one would scarcely do justice to the thought of such seminal thinkers as Bonhoeffer, Tillich, Bultmann, Robinson and Cox. Mascall reminds us that, with the exception of Robinson and Cox, these men are products of German Protestanism. Now, as Alasdair Macintyre has astutely observed, modern Protestant theology is the child of euphoria and catastrophe. It developed in the womb of liberal idealism and was raised in the starkness of worldwide social upheavals. The liberal theologians at the turn of the century saw in man's phenomenal scientific and cultural progress the sign of God's approval of modern society. Suddenly, however, they were rudely shocked out of their secular faith in man's goodness and lost hope in his inevitably progressing utopia when they witnessed the indescribable carnage and destruction of two World Wars. Tillich and Bultmann were army chaplains, immersed in the agonizing experience of violent killing. Bonhoeffer was imprisoned and hung by the Nazis. Pietistic Protestant moralizing, against which Kierkegaard so violently revolted, was finally discredited in the face of such cataclysmic catastrophes. Christians steeped in tragedy hungered for faith and fortitude capable of sustaining their wretched lives in God. The wars had revealed the falsity and shallowness of a Christianity of consolations. Biblical Christianity, a Christianity of crisis and commitment, was rediscovered and once again preached to contemporary man.

At the head of the line of return from liberal reductionism to the absolutely transcendent God of Revelation stood Karl Barth. He relates a day of great disillusionment in his life thus: "One day in early August 1914 stands out in my personal memory as a black day. Ninety-three German intellectuals impressed public opinion by their proclamation in support of the war policy of Wilhelm II and his counsellors. Among the intellectuals I discovered to my horror almost all my theological teachers whom I had greatly venerated. In despair over what this indicated about the signs of the time I suddenly realized that I could no longer follow either their ethics and dogmatics or their understanding of the Bible and of history. For me at least, 19th century theology no longer held any future."[5] Later, in 1939, Barth was again shocked to see philosophers and theologians flock to the defense of Nazism.

Karl Barth in his famous *Commentary On Romans* radically rejected any efforts to translate God's revelation to man in philosophical or human terms. Paul had represented God as infinitely transcendent, totally other and totally beyond man. Revelation is an infinitely gracious condenscension of God to man, a pure gift of love incarnated in the Word of God, Jesus Christ. It must be received totally on God's terms. It helps to be pleased rationally with God's revelation, but pleased or not, man is consulted neither about its content nor its manner of promulgation. God challenges man to accept his revelation in complete faith, knowing full well that man may rationalize his rejection of this revelation. Nevertheless, rational argument about the faith is an exercise in arrogance. And man must take the respective consequences for his acceptance or rejection of that revelation. Moreover, evil is a mys-

5. Quoted by David E. Jenkins in his *Guide to the Debate About God*, the Westminster Press (Philadelphia: 1966) p. 74.

tery; in this life man cannot avoid or solve it. However, in Jesus Christ, the Word of God, he can be redeemed and saved from its tyranny.

Barth's neo-orthodoxy, as it came to be called, did not entirely escape liberalism's infection. It conceded that the Bible as the work of human authors could be fallible and yet, despite this flaw in the truth, it demanded man's adherence to its essential truthfulness and authoritativeness. This psychological dilemma of adhering wholeheartedly by faith to historical or factual error proved too much for reasonable men, as well it should. Harold O. J. Brown, Congregational minister, writes about this difficulty thus: "In effect, the neo-orthodox demanded a new kind of 'leap of faith' into the irrational. One was asked to believe in 'the great truths of revelation' in spite of all evidence . . . This irrational belief in traditional dogmas without a credible foundation in trustworthy revelation proved difficult for the neo-orthodox professors to communicate to their students."[6] The result was that neo-orthodoxy lost the academic field to the existentialist, demythologizing, rationalistic theology of Rudolf Bultmann and his disciples, who today have come to dominate Protestant theology in Germany and the United States in the persons of the already mentioned precursor theologians.

All of them—including Robinson, Cox and some Catholic American theologians—represent, each with his own distinctive indifferences, a strong reaction to the utterly transcendent supernaturalism and revelationism of the school of Barth, Brunner and Heim. Can the secularist emphasis introduced by these men into theology be explained as a much-needed, healthy swing back from that extreme supernaturalism which left man unconcerned about humanizing his cosmos and community? Whatever may be the answer to this query, it is indisputable that among these theologians God and grace are sought and found more often—indeed almost solely—in the realm of nature, man and history than in the realm of the supernatural, which seems to have been abandoned as a myth. Bonhoeffer leaves no doubt of the new emphasis in theology in his famous letters from prison:

6. H. O. J. Brown, "The Struggle for the German Church," in *National Review*, April 8, 1969, pp. 334–337.

Man has learned to cope with all questions of importance without recourse to God as a working hypothesis. In questions concerning science, art and even ethics, this has become an understood thing which one scarcely dares to tilt at any more. But for the last hundred years or so it has been increasingly true of religious questions also: it is becoming evident that everything gets along without "God," and just as well as before.[7]

Now, as we shall see more in detail in the following chapters; all "the death of God" theologians claim that Dietrich Bonhoeffer is the inspiration for their theology of readjustment and accomodation to modern man. The work that shook them from their theological lethargy is Bonhoeffer's *Letters And Papers From Prison.* According to David E. Jenkins, "Bonhoeffer is a martyr of the Christian Faith in the old and original sense of that term, viz. one who witnessed to the reality of his faith in conditions of great stress, culminating in suffering and death."[8] What was Bonhoeffer's mission in life? His ambition was to bring a world, estranged from God religiously and culturally, back to a fruitful reconsideration of the reality of the Divine and the significance of a Christian life of commitment. He strove to reactivate in the Christian way of life a specific social and biblical quality that could reconcile isolated, hostile Western culture to the divine and human ideals of its Founder. As a reformer, he became at once the iconoclast of the false conception of God abroad among Christians and the catalyst for a new theological openness to the modern world and the culture that shaped it.

According to Bonhoeffer, God, as the rescuer who drops out of the blue to handle man's insoluble problems or redeem his failures, is an idol. God as a universal anodyne is a caricature of the true God of the Bible. The God of the Bible is the God who is present in the world in weakness and suffering. Moreover, a misconception on the nature of the Christian Community must also be cleared up. The urgency for this clarification arose from the fact that the crisis between the world and the Christian

7. Dietrich Bonhoeffer, *Letters And Papers From Prison,* ed. by Eberhard Bethge, trans. by Reginald H. Fuller (New York: The Macmillan Company, 1953), p. 195.
8. David E. Jenkins, *Guide To The Debate About God* (Philadelphia: The Westminister Press, 1966), p. 99.

Community had produced a crisis within the Church itself. Not only was the nature of the Church in doubt but also what manner of life and policies she should follow in order to reclaim the world for Christ. Bonhoeffer approached the solution of this problem of the Christian Community through the terms of Ferdinand Tönnies, using his categories of *Gemeinschaft* and *Gesellschaft*—Community and Society—in an attempt to relate sociology and theology in a meaningful way to the Christian Church. He attempted to show how the Christian Community differed from other societies. In doing so, he rejected the answers of secular sociologists and religious apologists. He insisted that the specific difference between secular societies and Christian communities did not derive from the profession of faith in a transcendent God nor from the performance of religious rites in the latter to the exclusion of these in the former. For Bonhoeffer, Christian life is not dependent on any ecclesiastical structures or totally transcendent Power. On the contrary, Christian life consists in a life lived totally for the other in powerlessness and suffering. Thus the difference between Christians and atheists is not that Christians belong to a new religion but that Christians, in their concern for others, should seek their transcendent God "not in tasks beyond their scope and power but in the nearest Thou at hand, in man." God is to be found in every human form, in imitation of the Crucified who existed for others. In the modern world religion is no longer a necessary condition for justification. Perhaps only a "religionless Christianity" is relevant in our times for it alone will bring men to join Jesus in his sufferings for others. The challenge of the day is that Christians participate in the sufferings of God even if these come at the hands of a godless world. This calls for Christian immersion in the affairs and life of the godless world, not to gloss over its godlessness with a veneer of religion in an attempt to transfigure it.[9]

Man today takes the world seriously; he has grown out of a certain kind of infantilism; he depends no longer on religious fairy tales for an explanation of the workings of the universe; he no longer stands by, expecting miracles to rout his evils and problems. Rather he sets to work with the skills of science and technology to create a world of real hope and progress today

9. Dietrich Bonhoeffer, *Letters And Papers From Prison*, p. 224.

and in the immediate tomorrow. Modern man, in a word, "has come of age." Is Bonhoeffer telling modern mature man that he no longer needs God or religion or spiritual services, that he is now sufficient unto himself? The Christian reader, irritated at the imprecise, challenging and shocking language sometimes used by Bonhoeffer might be tempted to write him off as a man who, under the duress of his prison hardships, abandoned his faith in God and his allegiance to Christianity. But this would be a premature judgment. Bonhoeffer was writing, as a suffering prophet in prison, thoughts that moved him suddenly, that he had no time to work on reflectively and to balance carefully with the Scriptures. In one of his letters he expresses his own dissatisfaction with a prospective book on theology which he is outlining. "I am often shocked at the things I am saying, especially in the first part; which is mainly critical . . . But the whole subject has never been properly thrashed out, so it sounds very undigested."[10] Despite the fragmentary aspects of this theology, he does give incontrovertible proof of his deep faith up to the end. Powerless as Christ in his own Gethsemane of a Nazi prison camp, like Him also about to be violently edged out of this world, Bonhoeffer, in a letter dated August 1944, nine months before the Nazi hangman took his life, expressed his fidelity to God and Christianity in these eloquent words:

> All that we rightly expect from God and pray for is to be found in Jesus Christ. The God of Jesus Christ has nothing to do with all that we, in our human way, think he can and ought to do. We must persevere in quiet meditation on the life, sayings, deeds, sufferings and death of Jesus in order to learn what God promises and what he fulfills. One thing is certain: we must always live close to the presence of God, for that is newness of life; and then nothing is impossible for all things are possible with God; no earthly power can touch us without his will, and danger can only drive us closer to him. We can claim nothing for ourselves, and yet we may pray for everything. Our joy is hidden in suffering, our life in death. But all through we are sustained in a wondrous fellowship. To all this God in Jesus has given his Yea and his Amen, and that is the firm ground on which we stand. In these turbulent times we are always forgetting what it is that makes life really worth while.

10. *Ibid.*, p. 245.

We think that life has a meaning for us so long as such and such a person still lives. But the truth is that if this earth was good enough for the Man Jesus Christ, if a man like him really lived in it, then, and only then, has life a meaning for us. If Jesus had not lived, then our life, in spite of all the other people we know and honour and love, would be without meaning.[11]

Unfortunately, today many secularizing theologians are demanding Christianity's total conformity to the world in the name and writings of Bonhoeffer. Acquainted with Bonhoeffer's ideas through Robinson's *Honest To God,* he and they have made use only of this heroic German's *Letters And Papers From Prison* in a process that dilutes Christianity down to Bultmann's and Tillich's disincarnated, humanistic idealism. Thus, they have seriously misrepresented the abiding faith of a great Christian witness. René Marlé in his perceptive study, *Bonhoeffer: The Man And His Work,* tells us that "in Dietrich Bonhoeffer's theological thinking, prematurely cut short, the Church always held pride of place. It is indeed, then, in the concrete and historical community of believers that union with Christ and with God takes place (for Bonhoeffer) . . . In this connection he condemned the resentment which it is all too easy for the faithful to feel toward their Church and the 'dogmatic frivolousness' that so often precedes it."[12] The deep Christian convictions of Bonhoeffer were concretely and movingly recorded in his two books *The Cost Of Discipleship* and *Life Together.* But the secularists, anxious to read a position of atheism into Bonhoeffer's tentative theological speculations while in prison, hardly ever refer to these works. Yet Bonhoeffer never fell away from the allegiance to Christ, His revealed truth and His Church. Thus, the attempt to make of him the prophetic precursor of modern, ultra-liberal theological atheism is a grievous falsification. He was an impassioned defender of Christian doctrine and its irreducible demands. In a memoir, Lutheran Bishop Gerhard Jacobi wrote forcefully of Bonhoeffer's rock-like faith: "Dietrich Bonhoeffer never for a moment doubted in the trinitarian God. He would have fought

11. *Ibid.*, pp. 243, 244.
12. René Marlé, *Bonhoeffer: The Man And His Work,* trans. by Rosemary Sheed (New York: Newman Press, 1968), pp. 41, 44.

to the death our modern flirting with unbelief."[13]

But the question is justly asked: How have the secularizing theologians been able to succeed in using Bonhoeffer as an instrument with which to distort Christianity and erect upon this distortion a secular Church of easy, earthly salvation? First of all we must admit that this unwarranted truncation of Bonhoeffer's Christian faith is partially due to some of his infelicitous expressions and audacious theological distinctions. Taken out of context, they seemed to indicate that he was either "naturalizing" or even abandoning the truths of Christianity. As expressed, some of his ideas cannot be accepted by a true Christian. His distinction between the Christian faith and Christian religion would seem to make the Church which he loved so well useless and expendable. A religionless Christianity is the death of Christianity. His expression "man come of age" did not really mean, for him, man independent of God, but man able to do many more marvelous things because of his great discoveries in rapidly advancing science. Admittedly, he seems to reduce man's relation to God to man's life in "existence for others," a life similar to the self-donated life of Jesus. Moreover, he seems to deny the infinity of transcendence, admitting only transcendence toward the neighbor where God dwells. This doctrine seems to lock man's destiny in a time-space-matter immanence. Yet despite these imprecise, tentative theological speculations written in personal letters meant only for the eyes of an intimate friend, himself a staunch Christian and thus not prone to take scandal at such reflections, the last view we have of Bonhoeffer, five minutes before his execution, shows him in prayer before the Father and Jesus Christ who filled his whole life. The prison doctor records the scene: "Through the half-open door I saw Pastor Bonhoeffer kneeling in fervent prayer to the Lord his God. The devotion and evident conviction of being heard that I saw in the prayer of this intensely captivating man moved me to the depths."[14]

In her study in depth, *Life And Death Of Dietrich Bonhoeffer,* Miss Mary Bosanquet records how Bonhoeffer's ideas pushed to their pejorative and never-intended consequences,

---

13. *Ibid.*, cited on p. 61.
14. Arnold Lunn and Garth Lean, *Christian Counter-Attack,* (London: Blandford Press, 1969), p. 84.

were abused to erect a counterfeit Christianity. She writes: "Some of the phrases from Bonhoeffer's *Letters* have been appropriated and carried away like stones from a half-built church to be used as the foundations of theological superstructures for which he would have disclaimed any responsibility."[15] Moreover, the secularizers never understood Bonhoeffer's distinction between "ultimate" and "penultimate" truths. The "ultimate" things were in God's hands. Since he and his friend Bethge were in solid agreement on these Christian fundamentals, there was no need to discuss them in their letters. But the "penultimate realities" expressed ways of making Christian truths meaningful to the modern generation. How could the Christian Church identify with the modern world in order to save it and yet not lose her own identity as the Body of Christ? The secularizers interpreted Bonhoeffer as calling for the de-Christianization of Christianity as the only means of saving the modern scientific world. Yet in reality Bonhoeffer taught that Christianity must maintain its identity as the Body of Christ. And he even indicated the "secret discipline" she must continually exercize in order to remain faithful to her Founder and His message. That "secret discipline" called for Christians to devote themselves as a community to prayer, meditation, common worship and the reception of the sacraments. Religionless Christianity meant not capitulation but openness to the world, not isolation from but availability to others in a service that extended to them the true message of Christ and His charity. Indeed, Bonhoeffer rejected explicitly and in writing the demythologized gospel of Bultmann and the secularizers who were using new methods in biblical scholarship to filter out of Christianity any historical evidence of God's marvelous entrance into human history and the human family for the purpose of saving and divinizing man. He wrote:

> We have so far spoken of the present Christ; but this present-historical *(geschichtlich)* Christ is the same person as the historical *(historisch)* Jesus of Nazareth. Were this not so, we would have to say with Paul that our faith is vain and an illusion. The Church would be deprived of its substance. There can be no isolation of the so-called his-

15. Mary Bosanquet, *The Life And Death Of Dietrich Bonhoeffer*, (London: Hodder & Stoughton, 1968), Quoted by Lunn and Lean, *op. cit.*, p. 85.

torical *(historisch)* Jesus from the Christ who is present now ... The historicity *(Geschichtlichkeit)* of Jesus Christ comes under the twofold aspect of history *(Historie)* and faith. Both aspects are closely associated.[16]

We have had to treat Bonhoeffer in a study of modern atheism not because he himself ever flirted with the thought of denying God, but because some of his sayings have been constructed by the secularizers into a bridge that leads inevitably to the loss of all faith and the "disestablishment of all churches." In a world whose "figure" is changing rapidly, even violently, toward unbelief, underground churches and drop-out Christians, we had to set the record straight about this attractive, modern theologican and martyr and, by removing an effective weapon from the hands of false brethren, stem the stampede of the faithful out of the fold.

16. Dietrich Bonhoeffer, *Christology,* (London: 1966), pp. 71–76. Quoted by René Marlé in *Bonhoeffer: The Man And His Work,* p. 70.

Part Three

Gods as Myths of the Modern Mentality

The Resurrection is not itself a fact of history. Such an impossible marvel could only spring from mythology. The Resurrection cannot be historical because the return of a dead man to life here on earth merely revives a myth and its contradictions. The Resurrection for us is something clearly unbelievable.

Kerygma And Myth
Rudolf Bultmann

The overwhelming experience of the disciples is the great historical event which we call the Resurrection . . . Precisely what happened to the body we shall never know . . . Some will find it possible and natural to accept a literal vanishing or transformation of the elements which composed the flesh of Jesus. Others will think that what the disciples subsequently saw was a vision of Jesus alive: others again that it was what the psychic investigators would call his "astral" body. But all this is quite secondary . . . No, the proof of the matter lay for them within.

And it was clinched for them in what we call the Appearances. Exactly
how physical or how psychological these were, I don't think it matters.

Sunday Mirror (London)
December 22, 1963 p. 29.
John A. T. Robinson

I readily believe those witnesses who get their throats cut.

Pensées
Blaise Pascal

CHAPTER XI

Bultmann:
The Demythologized God

WITH HIS SMALL BUT IMPORTANT WORK *The New Testament and Mythology,* published in 1941,[1] Rudolf Bultmann established himself as an extraordinary but controversial leader of the revolution in Protestant theology. This work has aroused strong condemnations from many sides, especially from orthodox and neo-orthodox theologians, for it challenges and rejects traditional Protestant and Catholic doctrines. Moreover, it has plunged many young spirits into the darkness of doubt, detaching them tragically from traditional Christianity and delivering them instead to a purely philosophical existentialism that calls itself "the new and modern theology" or "the existentialist interpretation of the New Testament."

Basically Bultmann's theology takes its orientation from two deeply subjective preoccupations. First, there is Bultmann's

1. Rudolf Bultmann, *The New Testament And Mythology.* This essay can be found, along with a text of the violent debates it had given rise to, in the two volumes entitled *Kerygma And Myth.* There Dr. A. M. Farrer gives a penetrating critique of Bultmann's theory of demythologization.

concern for making the message of the Gospel meaningful and relevant to modern, scientific society. Secondly, and perhaps consequently, there is Bultmann's historical scepticism about the reality of the New Testament events. In his effort to gain for the Gospel a relevancy acceptable to scientific man, Bultmann developed a theology which called for the confrontation between the Christian message and myth. He undertook a selective, though rather thorough, demythologization of the New Testament message. Indeed, he went further and himself established just what the Christian message must mean for scientific man.

Bultmann's thesis is that modern scientific man simply cannot accept any longer the mythological stories strewn throughout the New Testament. After all, according to Bultmann, the New Testament writers were not writing history. Their times and their mentalities were saturated with prescientific, imaginary cosmologies and mythological legends. Moreover, there is nothing original in the New Testament myths. A quick review of their contents reveals this fact. There is that three-tiered universe of heaven, earth and hell. Earth is influenced by the powers of both heaven and hell; never is earth the master of its own destiny. Before the redemption, Satan and his minions controlled it; they temporarily seized it from the control of heaven and its legions of angels. Before the redemption, these evil spirits dominated man through their power of sin and death. When the redemption was accomplished in the life, death and resurrection of Christ, the God-Man, the grip of the underworld was broken. Now man is liberated from sin, death and Satan. Now he is capable of achieving salvation by choosing to live with God through his acceptance of Christ. The Cross and the Resurrection precipitated a cosmic catastrophe for the powers of hell and evil men; they simultaneously precipitated a cosmic celebration for the powers of heaven and saintly men. Soon the second coming of Christ will herald the final defeat of the powers of the nether world. At that time there will take place the resurrection of the dead and Christ's final judgment of all men and angels. In the meantime, believers united by faith in these saving events are incorporated in Christ through Baptism and the Eucharist which, along with the other five sacraments, work like physical causes to save and sanctify.

Now according to Bultmann such New Testament mythology merely reproduces the Jewish apocalyptic mythology of salvation in combination with the Hellenic gnostic myth of redemption. Both these pre-Christian myths proposed the dualistic doctrine of a world of men struggling for salvation from domination by a satanic underworld through a divine liberation from a world beyond. The Jewish myth hoped for a heaven on earth after the coming and conquests of the Messiah, while the gnostic myth predicted the descent from a luminous world of the Son of God clothed as a man who would by doctrine and deed liberate man and lead him to a celestial fatherland.

Modern scientific thought, according to Bultmann, has exploded all three mythologies. If Christianity is to avoid perishing like its Jewish and gnostic precursor-messianisms, it will have to demythologize its message and accomodate it to the needs of the scientific mind. Somehow it must keep the idea of revelation and of a non-mythological presence of God in history. For the mythology conceals rather than reveals the true message of the Gospel. Such fantasies as sin, Satan, a war between upper and lower worlds for the conquest of this world have been exploded by the development of the human sciences. Only a schizophrenic can believe these fictions today. Man has become his own master in the physical world through the incredible advancement of his reason, sciences and technology. His universe is closed upon itself, determined by its physical laws and no supernatural powers can irrupt into time to produce effects independent of these laws or of man's autonomous freedom. Man alone is responsible for his own and his world's social and scientific advancement. It is inconceivable, therefore, that modern man accept the fable that spirits and sacraments produce physical effects in history. As for a God who destroys his own innocent Son in order to save man through a vicarious redemption, such a story is too barbaric and repulsive to be accepted as reasonable. Indeed the whole effort to tie the Christian message to myths and images is vain and sterile. That is why many modern men have abandoned Christianity.

Nevertheless, Bultmann is not in favor of so complete a demythologization that no myths at all remain in the Christian message. Only those archaic, traditional representations which needlessly provoke revulsion in the scientific mind are to be dropped from the preaching of the Gospel. Indeed, Bultmann holds it against the Protestant liberal school of theology that it betrayed the Gospel message by totally demythologizing it. Liberal theology failed to maintain the radical incompatibility between God and man; it begot an insufferable overconfidence of man in himself; it removed the healthy shock and scandal effect of the message of the Cross, putting to sleep in man's consciousness his sense of insecurity, his need for redemption and his hunger for encounter with God. Liberal theology hid the scandal of the Cross and presented only the crown of human self-sufficiency. That is why its total demythologization, from Harnack on, was such a total failure.

Thus Bultmann's demythologization is only partial and highly selective. He would preserve the mythical image of corporal nourishment whereby the Body of Christ advances in spiritual growth. Though displeased with the image of a baptismal rebirth from spiritual death, he approves the mythical idea of salvation from acceptance of the preaching of the Word of God. The criterion of selection comes down to this: Authentic demythologization eliminates anthropomorphic images of transcendence offensive to the scientific mind; it rejects all images of direct divine intervention into human history because they reduce God to a reality of this world and man to a mere automation. The truth of the matter is that God is totally hidden, entirely out of science, history and the universe, while man is totally immersed in this world, obligated to achieve his authentic existence through the enlightened, responsible exercise of his liberty. Thus, authentic myths reveal the Gospel's message to be an existentialist challenge for man to understand himself fully and thereby to attain mature, authentic human existence. Against such an interpretation of myths in the Gospel the modern mentality will not in principle raise any objections.

Existentialist Interpretation of the New Testament

What does Bultmann understand by an existentialist interpretation of the New Testament? He frankly admits that his explanation of this expression is inspired by the philosophy of Martin Heidegger. We may recall that Heidegger's philosophy, as expounded in *Being And Time,* is essentially a transcendental analysis of *Dasein,* that is, of man thrown into existence in this world, yet facing up to his radical anxiety and destination to death by decisions that give himself and his world some transcendent meaning. Reflective introspection on the existential state of human existence reveals that men live in two opposing styles. Some men live an *authentic* human existence. They accept the dereliction of being thrown into existence from nothing and their destiny through death toward nothing. They realize that human existence is trapped in temporality from its superfluous birth to its annihilating death. Despite this radical absurdity and finitude, such men courageously give meaning to their lives and world, projecting themselves constantly forward into a future made meaningful through their serious, reflective, responsible exercise of liberty. On the other hand, those who live *inauthentic* existences flee the anxiety and insecurity of human existence; they take refuge in the common delusions of the masses; their beliefs, rules, ends, cares, ambitions are harmonized with those of the amorphous crowd in which they gladly lose themselves. They choose to be part of the *one, many, they*—preferring the peace of anonymity to the fight for subjecthood. Whereas those who live authentic lives choose to become subjects, I's, that is, coherent conscious persons making their own plans and decisions. Authentic persons, because of their commitments, are called by Heidegger *Dasein;* inauthentic men, because they have chosen to live like inanimate objects, are called by Heidegger *Vorhandensein.*

Utilizing such Heideggerian concepts and terms, Bultmann goes on to reveal the meaning of the Gospel relevant to modern man. This message is never theoretic nor speculative; it is personalist and existentialist. Therefore, most elements in the Gospel which seem to be objective representations or historical or doctrinal matters must be discarded. Only those elements that stress man's authentic existence and its existential conditions are to be retained. Thus, the kerygma of the Gospel proclaims that the true significance of Jesus is that He summons man to make the decision to face up to his dire destiny to death. In Jesus man receives a mature understanding of his precarious existence. The Cross and the Resurrection as salvation

events are recovered not as history but as personal commitments. The decision to encounter God in these events is really
the decision to achieve authentic existence. Faith alone,
achieved in man's affirmative encounter with God, leads man
to the acceptance of Heidegger's particular understanding of
human existence. Indeed the preacher of the Word of God
should stress this particular understanding as the true meaning of the Gospel, even using Heidegger's terms rather than
traditional teaching to expound the roles of God, Jesus and men
in the adventure of salvation. Heidegger's emphasis on man's
fall and tragic existence renders his philosophy most apt as an
existentialist hermeneutics, an excellent corrective of irrational mythology.

For example, let us apply this hermeneutics to the idea of sin.
Traditional theology tells us that sin is an *aversio a Deo* and it
invites us to sorrow for sin and a confession of it unto the grace
of reconciliation. But modern man is displeased with this idea
of aversion, confession, conversion, reconciliation in relation
to an offended God. He is no longer interested in such irrelevant
mythology because it does not cure his existential anxiety and
dereliction. Such abstract terminology leaves man cold and indifferent. But the preacher who shows man that sin is an irresponsible flight and a fall from authentic existence into the
banality of common anonymity will move man deeply by challenging him to get back to God by first getting back to his own
authentic human existence. He will show too that the existential character of pardon and reconciliation are human decisions and responsibilities. The fall will be seen not as an
impersonal inherited fault but as a cowardly flight. Thus the
sinner will be troubled and his refusal to accept the existential
meaning of the Gospel message to become his true self will
confront him with his personal perfidy. Thus too the scandal
and shock of the Christian message will be restored as the
mythological aspects are removed. Preaching the Word of God
in such an existential manner, Bultmann argues, goads man
toward faith in such a manner that it forces him into a deeper
understanding of himself and his human condition. For belief
and unbelief are not blind and arbitrary actions working automatically like magical charms, but they are a Yes or No made
with knowledge and freedom. Neither belief nor unbelief

should be founded on exterior signs—miracles, divine interventions, historical events, ceremonies and sacraments—but on interior encounter, motivation and decision. Faith is, therefore, founded on an apologetic of immanence, not on a fideism characteristic of so much traditional theology. Man is saved by faith, by his response to God who challenges him to an interior encounter with himself through man's acceptance of the Cross and the Resurrection not as historical events but as signs of God's calling. Moreover, the faith does not endow the believer with any superior state of being nor with a redemption conceived in terms of a cosmic process. For the decision for faith is not achieved once for all; it must be eternally renewed under each concrete challenge to infidelity. Then too the Spirit spoken of in the New Testament is not another mysterious Being; this would be irrelevant mythology again. The Spirit signifies merely the individual's achievement of the decision not to live selfishly any longer but to live for others, to love and serve his fellow man. Thus, the meaning of the New Testament accords substantially with the Heideggerian analysis of authentic human existence. Both messages are the fruit of a natural analysis and inspiration. Faith consists now in the decision for a natural commitment to authentic existence. Bultmann's pupil, W. Kamlah, drew the inevitable conclusions from his master's existentialist and naturalistic interpretation of the Christian message. Kamlah concluded that the life of faith is independent of any divine events that took place in Palestine in the first century; it is independent of the existence of any supernatural or divine being. Faith is the fruit of a particular philosophy, not of a divine revelation irrupting into human history. The demythologized Christian message turns out to be merely a nominally theistic existentialism evolving under the new hermeneutics into an atheistic philosophy, into an atheistic humanism. Faith is reduced to philosophy, one particular philosophy—Heidegger's—and the passage of man from the pagan to the Christian state is rendered utterly meaningless. For all that man has to do to attain the faith is to decide to live an authentic human existence, a feat needing no new religion, revelation nor divine intervention. For all men are capable by natural powers of becoming Heideggerian saints, *Dasein.* In the last analysis, in the hermeneutics of Bultmann, Christ and

Christianity have become the new mythology—irrelevant, because totally secularized, to the pre-scientific and the scientific mentality.

The Role of Christ in the Event of Salvation

Bultmann rejects traditional theology's explanation of the deed of salvation. Orthodox theology has consistently taught that Christians put their faith in events that actually happened in history. These events can be objectively dated and historically proven to have taken place outside the inner consciousness of men and even against their very opposition. But for Bultmann this belief in an objectively determinable history of salvation is irrelevant, scandalous mythology. According to him, once the event of salvation in Christ is demythologized, that event then has no objectively recognizable reality. Bultmann admits that in one sense the divine event of salvation has objective reality. He maintains that God has really accomplished in Christ something which has happened outside of man. But he denies that this salvation event is *recognizable* by man as an objective, historical event. On the contrary, this event eludes every human method of historical investigation. Reason cannot grasp or explain it. For the event of salvation is grasped only in the interior act of faith, within the decision each man makes to accept God.

But the question is asked, "How does the life of Jesus fit into the event of salvation, as the New Testament insists it does?" The New Testament represents Jesus as existing before the dawn of history as the Logos, the Son of God. Moreover, it identifies Jesus as that same eternal Son, incarnate in the man, Jesus of Nazareth, who saves mankind by His death on the Cross. It represents Jesus as a thaumaturge performing superhuman prodigies, even raising others and Himself from the state of death. Bultmann rejects all this. He explains that the New Testament is clothing the life of Jesus with mythology in these events. The reason for this embellishment of the life of Jesus is that His disciples wanted to stress the truth that God had decreed to save men through the life and deeds of the man Jesus of Nazareth. Hence the mythology of divine pre-existence and divine thaumaturgy as natural endowments of Jesus is not to be taken as historical fact but to be viewed solely as notification that God saves men in Jesus. When pressed to explain precisely how man is saved by the Crucifixion and Resurrection of the man Jesus, Bultmann responds by introducing a perceptive distinction in his interpretation of the salvation event, the distinction between *historisch* and *geschichtlich,* each word pertaining to a different historical aspect of an event.[2]

An event is historical *(historisch)* when it is a fact fixed in time, established by experience and verified by objectively historical methods. An event is historical *(geschichtlich)* when it is temporal reality, but one which cannot be fixed in time nor caught in experimental certification. Creation and the work of salvation are historical in the second sense, in the sense of *geschichtlich.* Yet the world and men, which make up the content of these divine events, themselves create History *(Geschichte)* and are simultaneously called historical *(geschichtlich)* in so far as they are viewed in their relationship to divine action and especially to the divine action of salvation. Now when Bultmann applies this distinction to the Cross, he produces the following explanation of the role of Jesus in the event of man's salvation. The Cross is an historical *(historisch)* event in the sense that the Crucifixion of Jesus is a fact fixed in past history, capable of indubitable, objective verification. But the Christian message has endowed this event of history with cosmic dimensions. It expresses these dimensions through mythological representations. What does the New Testament hope to attain by such mythology? It is its method for making man grasp the significance, the non-static, non-verifiable, historical *(geschichtlich)* capacity of the Cross. According to the New Testament, the Cross in the divine designs is endowed with the value of an historical *(geschichtlich)* event; that is, an event pregnant with meaning for the entire human race in its relationship to God. And that meaning and value consist in this, that in the Cross God has decreed and effected the liberation of man from the powers of the world. In the Cross God judges man

2. René Marlé explains that the single word for "history" can be rendered in German as either *Geschichte* or *Historie.* The distinction expresses "history as reality" and "history as science," terms used by Maurice Blondel. Bultmann uses this distinction to nudge God out of New Testament history back into invisible history.

and reveals to him his condition as a sinner along with his impotence to rise from sin to authentic existence by his own powers. In the Cross God enlightens man to the truth that if he admits his own impotence, he will be regenerated by the gratuitous mercy of God. In what precise sense, then, does God accomplish His decree to liberate man by the Cross? Bultmann responds thus: Certainly not in the sense that Christ has merited man's salvation by His death on the Cross. That interpretation proposes the myth of vicarious redemption, a theory obnoxious to the modern mind. The true message of the Cross is as follows: God's decree to save man, considered in its divine origins, is an act posited beyond time. The Cross accomplishes this decree by giving it expression and fulfillment in time. In the concrete Cross of Christ God manifests the condemnation that weighs on all men. In that bloodied Cross God notifies man of his condition of personal sinfulness, condemnation and crucifixion. In a word, then, the concrete Cross of Christ is not the accomplishment but the notification of salvation. This notification is prolonged throughout history for all men in the teaching of the apostles and the preaching of the ministers of the Church. The Christian kerygma re-presents the Cross event of the past in such a manner that the conditions for an encounter with God are ever present for contemporary man. Thus the eternal act of God's decree for salvation becomes in Christian preaching an enduring, temporal, a truly historical *(geschichtlich)* act, accompanying man throughout all ages, ceaselessly challenging him *hic et nunc* to ratify his encounter of faith with God.

Finally, man either accepts this decree of salvation as proclaimed in Christian preaching or rejects it. If he accepts salvation, he accepts it in faith alone. Bultmann, good Protestant that he is, cannot emphasize this fact enough. The event of salvation has taken place outside of man, true enough. But outside of man the event does not possess any transcendent dimensions. It does so only when it is clothed with otherworldly fantasies, too ridiculous to be accepted by modern man. Because of this lack of transcendence, the competent historian sees in the Cross of Christ a mere incident of past history, at best a miscarriage of justice in which an innocent man is put to death by his enemies; he does not see any enduring value to this event. Thus, the historical *(geschichtlich)* scope of the Crucifixion entirely escapes him, for there is no grasp nor understanding of the act of God save in actual faith. This is so true, the acceptance of the event of salvation is reserved so exclusively to faith that one can say that salvation is accomplished in the decision for faith itself. For faith is the operation of the Spirit, the gift of God, the act of God, the act of salvation *par excellence.* Thus Bultmann insists that the meaning of the Cross, when the event is demythologized, is as follows: "God judges me; God crucifies me. In revealing to me my impotence to liberate myself through my own efforts God invites me to accept the Cross and thus find authentic existence." On the other hand, the traditional doctrine which Bultmann rejects is as follows: "Christ has expiated for me and in my place; the Son of God has merited salvation for me through his death. By putting my faith in the Son of God I attain salvation and authentic existence as a man."

Thus, for Bultmann, the historical *(historisch)* event of the Cross has also an eschatologically historical *(geschichtlich)* significance; it is an event both for time and for beyond time. On the occasion of hearing the Christian message of the Cross, the potential believer is interiorly challenged by God to accept the divine decree for his salvation. In saying Yes to this challenge the believer attains simultaneously both faith and salvation. Yet he must continually repeat his Yes against every temptation to abandon God until his day of dying. Thus, man is saved by an interior act of faith, not by the myth of a past death of Christ on the Cross which is a vicarious act of salvation in itself. The Cross is used by God merely to notify man of His decree to save man. It is a signpost to the interior way of salvation, the encounter with God ratified by faith.

When he comes to consider the Resurrection as the event of salvation, Bultmann once again parts company with the New Testament narratives. Clearly the New Testament bases man's salvation as much on the Resurrection as on the Cross. But Bultmann's explanation is slightly different here than it is in his explanation of the Cross. He admitted the historical *(historisch)* reality of the Cross as an objective event that happened in the past under Pontius Pilate. But he denies the "empirical fact" of the Resurrection; the Resurrection is not historical in the sense of *historisch*. Scientific man cannot accept it; it is pure myth to proclaim that a cadaver has been reanimated. For this would call for an irruption of the divine, of the supernatural, into the human and natural, an eventuality already seen to be impossible. Thus for Bultmann Christ did not rise from the dead, did not live a glorified life on earth, did not show His glorified body to His Apostles, nor eat with them, nor send them on their missions to convert the world. None of these narrations were empirically observed by men. What then is Bultmann's meaning for the Resurrection in Christian preaching?

In order to understand his teaching on this event we must contrast it with his teaching on the meaning of the Cross. Now we recall that the Cross of Christ signified in time the decree God had made *ab aeterno* to save man. It notified man both of his condemnation and salvation, of his challenge to rise from inauthentic to authentic existence. Yet the Cross did not in any way signify man's triumph over death. Now the role of the Resurrection myth is to do precisely that, to notify man of his victory over death by his acceptance of salvation through faith. It was God who moved the disciples to proclaim the Resurrection myth. God utilized their mentalities, already preconditioned and attached to the mythologies of their Graeco-Judaic culture, to formulate the myth of the Resurrection. The action of God produced in their spirits an image of a corporeal resurrection in order to give them and the world an understanding of the triumphant value of the Cross. The Resurrection is thus a totally interior event, taking place solely in the souls of the disciples and their believing followers. The Resurrection is not an objective, corporeal, observable event. To profess faith in the Resurrection, therefore, is merely to accept in faith, not an historical *(historisch)* objective event of past history, but simply the triumphant scope of the Cross. The Cross is the factual drama that happened in history; the Resurrection is merely the realization within the souls of Christ's disciples that the Cross is also a victory over death. Yet both Cross and Resurrection are merely expressions of the event of salvation which is accomplished in the souls of men as they say Yes throughout history to God in the encounter of the faith. On the occasion of the preaching of the Cross and Resurrection men are challenged interiorly to accept by faith *hic et nunc* the decree of salvation made *ab aeterno* by God but accomplished eschatologically in time through man's interior adherence to God.

Evaluation of the Bultmannian Hermeneutics

Bultmann's desire to make the Gospel message relevant to scientific man is in itself admirable. Certainly a greater understanding of the New Testament and a more profound heuristic scholarship in theology and Scripture are always praiseworthy and to be striven for. Moreover, Bultmann's emphasis on the vertical approach to the Lord of the Bible whereby man in his reading of the Sacred Scriptures personally discovers God as God *hic et nunc* and thus finds in this encounter his own authentic existence is acceptable to traditional Christianity. A great asset, too, is Bultmann's effort to preserve the paradoxical aspects of God's mysterious presence, His absolute transcendence yet loving immanence and concern for the affairs of men and the world.

But holy desires cannot be the ultimate criterion of the interpretation of a theology of revelation. Reason guided by living faith must judge the product presented by Bultmann. Unfortunately, both these sources of truth reject Bultmann's theology of revelation as being objectively inaccurate and subjectively arbitrary. Bultmann belittles the historical teachings and deeds of Christ; his theory of scriptural interpretation dilutes both the divine person and historical being of Jesus to the point of suppressing Him as the God-Man and Savior of mankind. On the other hand, he exalts above the Divine Savior a preaching of salvation, a preaching which gets its efficacy in the last analysis from man's own interior decision to accept God. Jesus and the Cross are mere occasions or symbols, not causes of salvation. They merely point; they effect nothing. Thus Baltmann eliminates the objective historical *(historisch)* reality of salvation. Moreover, the whole of Bultmann's theory is founded on a very questionable assertion: that the meaning of the Gospel as traditionally taught cannot existentially win to its allegiance the modern, scientific mind. Bultmann, not being a scientist himself, does not know this to be true, nor has he taken the trouble to demonstrate this assertion as a truth. Moreover, even if it were, *per impossible,* proven to be true that the modern scientific man is psychologically incapable of accepting traditional theology, this criterion for the veracity of the Gospel message would be an irrational, arbitrarily narrow and highly subjective, not to say selective, norm. The truth of the Gospel message will never be attained by polling the scientists. The simple truth is that the study of theology and Scripture is normally beyond the scope of their professional endeavors. Moreover, Christ, in seeking to convince John the Baptist and his followers that He was the true Messiah and teacher of truth, appealed to the relevancy of His message for the masses of the poor, not to its relevancy for the intellectually elite. "The poor have the Gospel preached to them."

Then too, in founding his existential interpretation of the Gospel on a Heideggerian analysis of human existence, Bultmann seems to imply that Jesus came to make men merely tough and honest—not saints. Jesus Himself seems to have been in His highest perfection merely a Heideggerian man of authentic existence way ahead of His time. Jaspers protests this founding of the Gospel message on the desperate conscience of Heidegger's *Dasein* because such a consciousness is neither representative of all men nor does it have universal value in the many men who experience it; such a consciousness is not true of man as man, but simply one form of man's possible experiences. What man universally does experience Bultmann neglects in his theology. The history of mankind testifies that man has inscribed in his depths an insatiable hunger for God, a desire to possess God in a human yet divine Savior through an encounter of reconciliation in faith. This consciousness and hunger hold for scientist as well as for rustics. Indeed the whole New Testament everywhere reveals this hunger for God. St. Paul relates the death and Resurrection of Christ to all men precisely in order to demonstrate their importance for each man's own destiny to physical resurrection and immortal life after the temporal death of this body. Man is not merely destined to death; he is destined to immortal resurrection and transcendent, eternal reunion with God in the really risen Christ. St. Augustine enunciated this eternal human truth in his famous cry to God: "Thou hast made us for Thyself, O Lord, and our hearts are restless until they rest in Thee."

Another unproven assertion in the Bultmannian theology of revelation is the teaching that the Divine Power cannot irrupt into human history with prodigies and miracles because such deeds are incompatible with the scientific conception that the world is ruled by rigorously deterministic, empirical laws. Jaspers asks, "Who gave Bultmann the right to speak in the name of scientific thought?" Moreover, modern science does not claim to have established cosmic determinism as a physically demonstrated law that would inevitably exclude supernatural intrusions into cosmic, human history. Indeed, modern science admits that such meta-empirical problems are beyond the purview of its disciplines. It admits also that it can say nothing either way on this cosmic problem of physical determinism.

Then too, Bultmann's total and radical demythologization of the Gospel message atrophies man's powers of soaring in wonderment to the Transcendent and rejoicing in the mystical. His Heideggerian hermeneutics beget doom and despair in Christians. For when the biblical message is drained of the *"magnalia et mirabilia Dei,"* of the "supernatural interventions and mighty deeds of God" in time on behalf of men, then Christianity as lived, suffered and died for in the two thousand years of its existence is destroyed. And men will never adhere to a Christianity whose message has lost its content and savor. St. Paul warned the early Christians of the black despair that would envelop their spirits if they believed those who were preaching that neither Christ nor the dead had or ever would rise. Apparently this warning was lost on Bultmann in his eagerness to demythologize it. But it bears constant repeating in our day of disbelief and especially as refutation of Bultmannian hermeneutics.

Now if Christ is preached as risen from the dead, how do some among you say that there is no resurrection of the dead? But if there is no resurrection of the dead, neither has Christ risen; and if Christ has not risen, vain then is our preaching, vain too is your faith ... For if the dead do not rise, neither has Christ risen; and if Christ has not risen, vain is your faith, for you are still in your sins ... If with this life only in view we had hoped in Christ, we are of all men the most to be pitied.[3]

3. 1 Cor. 15 : 12–19.

In the final analysis, Bultmann's theology of revelation is a drastic, dismal impoverishment of the Christian Faith. It accomplishes the very thing Bultmann had hoped to avoid, the "shipwreck of Christianity" in the souls of men. Here then is the baffling enigma of Rudolf Bultmann: He was striving to make the preaching of the word of God relevant to twentieth-century man. In order to accomplish this service he drained the Gospel message of every inspiring marvel. He insisted that the adventure of faith, instead of being a cascading irruption downward from the Trinity of Infinite Truth in the Person of the Incarnate Son striving with violently divine love to save desperate man, was rather only man's stoical decision to rise from inauthentic to authentic existence. What a diluted, attenuated adventure the quest for faith became in his thinking! And yet he fully expected this pale stoical ideal to draw men in greater numbers and with stronger bonds than the Christian reality of the crucified, transfigured and gloriously risen Christ! Malevez states that if Bultmann's demythologization is seen finally to be the true meaning of Christianity, then no Christians ever existed before Bultmann's or at least Luther's time. The fact is, he continues, that from the apostolic days of St. Paul Christians always found the essence of their faith in the profession that Jesus Christ, the God-Man, is the very source of Life who died on the Cross and rose from the dead for man's justification and salvation.[4] Bultmann's radical reductionism of the Gospel message leaves him with a theology that is so banal and mediocre that it is incapable of alluring any mind, much less elite minds. By this we mean that as a form of theology and salvation message this teaching will be dismissed. It may well, however, be accepted and has been accepted as an alluring form of humanistic, atheistic rationalism. In this respect, a reading of history should have taught Bultmann that Greek and Roman geniuses had already been to the springs of stoicism in their thirst for authentic existence. He might have recalled that, upon the arrival of apostolic Christianity, millions of noble pagans abandoned stoicism to adhere to the God-Man. After all, they were exchanging the lugubrious

---

4. L. Malevez, S.J., *Le Message Chrétien et le Mythe,* (Brussels: Desclée De Brouwer, 1954), p. 122. N.b. The entire book is an excellent, balanced analysis and refutation of Bultmann's theology of revelation. We are greatly indebted to its treatment in depth of this complex subject.

unnaturalness of stoicism for the transcendent liberty of the Sons of God. In reality, then, it is Bultmann who returns to irrelevant mythology when he expects a Heideggerian stoicism to win the hearts of the masses from the love of the God-Man. A continuing, reflective contrast between true Christianity and Bultmannian Christianity should be enough to dismiss the latter out of hand. Bultmann's faith begets Heideggerian stoics, the faith of the Apostles begets sons of God. Bultmann's Cross is a mere signpost, the Cross of the New Testament is an altar of saving Sacrifice. Bultmann's Resurrection is a verbal, empty symbol of an imaginary conquest of death, the Resurrection of the New Testament is "the first fruits" of man's real conquest of death in the Risen Christ. Bultmann is strangely silent about the intimate nature of the Divine Family, about the rich variety of the divine attributes; all he can say is that God pardons and saves, but there is nothing of the splendor and warmth of the theology of the Trinity and the trinitarian ministrations of the Divine Persons to the sanctification and salvation of man and the universe. Moreover, there is nothing of the grandeur of the theology of the final, eschatological realities of human and world history in Bultmann's compressed hermeneutics. Bultmann's determined anthropocentrism is what blinds his theology to divinely revealed truth, robs it of all wonderful mysteries and denies it sacraments and other sanctifying realities. His theology suffers the cramps arising from frustrating isolationism. For in Bultmann's theology the Church is merely a place where one, as an individual, can hear the preaching of the Word of God and make his private, interior decision for or against the Lord. In reality the Church is simply another profane place, not a temple of worship for the people of God. Indeed listeners in the Church are not a Christian Community; they are individuals accidentally gathered into a crowd. Moreover, the Church's institutions, liturgy and sacraments do not constitute a social sacred service in which the people of God pray and adore together. All Church affiliation, indeed all ecclesiology, is myth and magic for Bultmann. True to its Lutheran origins, Bultmann's theology of revelation rejects holy bonds among men and repeats Luther's protestation that "the entire world is merely profane territory."[5]

5. *Ibid.*, p. 159.

What a starkly cruel pauperization of the New Testament has Bultmann's theology of revelation turned out to be on quiet reflection! It would be only natural to wonder how the masses of the faithful have received it. Has Bultmann really gained the modern mind with his new hermeneutics? Let us listen to the testimony of a Congregational minister, the Rev. Harold O. J. Brown who, as a student and eyewitness of German Christianity, reports on conditions in the German Church today. Writing about the rise of a new, strong traditionalist movement that is gaining a growing and committed following under the Pauline battle cry of "No other Gospel!" the Rev. Dr. Brown observes:

> Modern theology has always professed a concern to make Christianity relevant to the layman, and has encouraged the laity to play a more active role in the Church and in theology. But something seems to have gone wrong. The layman who has not been influenced by radical theology, whose heart is still with the "old time religion," flocks to the "No other Gospel!" movement, giving it a tremendous lay participation. On the other hand, the emancipated laymen, whose religion has been "demythologized" by Bultmann and his cohorts, do not flock to laymen's meetings to spread the enlightenment on a lay level. They just stay at home. Thus a paradox has arisen. Those who have talked most about "making Christianity relevant to twentieth-century man" have few disciples among twentieth-century laymen, because the people they convince give up the church. The Confessional Movement, by contrast, which the radicals have derided for speaking the language of another century, has a strong, committed and growing lay following.[6]

This is not to say that among intellectual circles, especially in the universities, Bultmann's rationalistic hermeneutics is not still quite influential. Its coherent, rational appeal has won the academic mind away from the irrational neo-orthodoxy of Barthian theologians. Brown reports as follows: "The real disciples are being made not by the believing but irrational neo-orthodox, but by the skeptical but rational Bultmann. Today Bultmann's friends and disciples dominate German theological

6. Harold O. J. Brown, "The Struggle for the German Church," *National Review*, April 8, 1969, pp. 334–337 and 349.

education (and exert a tremendous effect on both Protestantism and Catholicism in the United States as well)."[7] That is why we have treated Bultmann at some length in this chapter. His hermeneutics lead straight to death-of-god atheism.

7. *Ibid.*, p. 336.

CHAPTER XII

Tillich:
The God of Contemporaneity

WHEREAS BONHOEFFER WAS REPRESENTED AS REJECT-ing traditional theology as being too "religious" and Bultmann departed from it because it was too "mythological," Tillich breaks with it because it is too "supernaturalist." All three claimed that the modern mind simply cannot accept a Gospel message that is preached in the terminological trappings of the past—as essentialist philosophy, immutable dogma and divine irruptions into human history. Tillich belongs to that liberal school of Protestantism that dissolves dogmas into vague religious experiences. Indeed, he was in the forefront of a liberal protest against Barthian dogmatism. To this very hour Protestant theology is agonizing over the controversies stimulated by the demythologization of Bultmann and the secularization of Tillich. Both are reductionist theologians *par excellence.* Both insist that Christian faith becomes relevant to life only when it is expressed in existentialist terms, though Bultmann alone of the two rivets the Gospel message absolutely to Heideggerian thought forms.

Tillich is proud of being in the theological tradition "of my great teacher Rudolf Bultmann and. . .a product of the nineteenth century, which still taught me when I attended the university of Berlin from 1904 to 1907."[1] Thus, Tillich's theology is existentialist in temperament, deeply concerned with the human experiences in which consciousness of God is discovered. Tillich is convinced that God is not discovered through rational reflection on the cosmos. Discursive reason for him never arrives at God. That is why natural theology is a sterile occupation. There is no dialectical ladder reaching from earth to heaven, from man to God.

On the other hand, Tillich rejects the Barthian teaching that God is found in faith alone. For man has an apologetic hunger to find and feed on God. In the sense that it asks the universe about God, natural theology is asking the right question. But the universe remains mute and the intellect frustrated along this avenue of investigation. As far as Tillich is concerned, the task of theology is one of correlation. Theology must explore man's existential situation and the human questions evoked therein, together with what men as a rule find thinkable and acceptable in this situation. But above all, theology must compare these human questions and their humanly acceptable solutions with the understanding of God contained or implied in the Gospel message. When the individual comprehends that his existential queries are dramatically related to the Christian biblical understanding of God, then, and only then, does he attain existential awareness of God. For consciousness of God, theological comprehension of the human predicament is never anything beyond the existential encounter of individual with God. Rational, discursive, supernatural, historically accurate, object-like awareness of God is simply beyond man's powers. Thus, for Tillich, belief in God is brought down from a level of superior knowledge by the light of faith to the natural level of normal knowledge by concern for moral seriousness. God and faith are the fruit of crisis situations.

But what are the serious concerns of man's life? Man's being and environment are essentially marred by finitude and relativity. Awareness of the fickle existential fragility of human existence wrings from his soul a host of anxiety questions. Why do I exist? Why does anything exist? Why such universal

1. Paul Tillich, *Ultimate Concern* (London: D. Mackenzie Brown, 1965), p. 37.

death, frustration, loss of identity, fraternal hostility? What is
the meaning of a human existence which is so imperfect, so
limited, so destructive? Eventually, reacting under these agonizing conditions, man is forced to ask the last, most serious
question. What is the ultimate ground, the ultimate concern of
my existence? What must I do to become myself, to become a
"New Being?"

In answering this question of Being, of man's most serious
concern, Tillich is determined to eschew any abstractness. It is
true that according to him God is another name for the ground
of man's being. But this does not mean He is the God of human
activity, ideas, formulas or human judgments. Such representations infringe on the transcendence of God; they would
reduce God to the status of an object. Whereas in the experience of ultimate concern man gets beyond subject-object relationships. God cannot be known, as objects can, in scientific
knowledge. God is beyond science in that he is the hidden God,
Deus absconditus, forever meta-empirical. Because He can
never be known as an object of knowledge, God can never be
known as an agent irrupting into history with an incarnate
human nature and performing marvelous deeds or wondrous
miracles. In the realm of ultimate concern one is accepted by
God; the action for man is passive, allowing ultimate concern
to seize him. There is no such action as an active seizure of
truth on the part of man. Man, on that level of experience,
never knows if he has attained the true answers to his anguished questions. He is simply aware that answers have been
given to his ultimate concerns. This awareness of answers received to ultimate questions is very similar to Bultmann's
awareness of the attainment of authentic existence in man's
interior encounter with God. But Tillich calls his awareness the
experience of the "New Being."

Now the New Being is attained in Jesus. But Tillich places
the true message of the New Being not in man's unquestioning
acceptance of the New Testament as the historical Word of God
but in man's acceptance of the symbolic meaning of the historical Jesus who merely manifests in Himself, or is the occasion
for, the manifestation of the New Being in other men. Thus
Tillich, faithful pupil of Bultmann, demonstrates a great skepticism about the historical veracity of the Gospels and insists

that what is important in our experience of the New Being in Jesus is not historical facts in any sense or degree. Once again, as in Bultmann, we find an exclusive stress on the individual's personal existentialist experience as the sole means for getting at the truth of the Gospels. For Tillich distinguishes and separates the revelatory value of the New Testament from its historical value; he minimizes the historicity of the New Testament events and founds his faith on his own arbitrary reinterpretation of these events. He follows his master slavishly in believing it to be possible to separate historical facts from their meanings.

In the last analysis, then, just as for Bultmann so for Tillich, the needs of the modern existentialist mentality verify theological data. Theological truth becomes as relative, fickle and changeable as contemporary man's social needs or individual cravings. On the other hand, however, if history were important, then Christian faith would depend upon it in some serious degree. But, by previous assertion, ultimate concern, alias God, for that is Tillich's new name for God, is meta-historical. It is only by this previous arrangement that God's transcendence can be maintained and faith saved from the probabilities and vagaries of history. It appears, then, that faith, though apparently saved from the fickleness of history, nevertheless now succumbs to the more violent buffetings of psychological crises. Tillich's refusal to permit faith to be born, struggle, survive and mature in the testing events of history and, particularly within the salvation events of the life, death and resurrection of the God-Man, reveals in him a blinding bias against historical objectivity, indeed against all objectivity in man's relations to God. Such historical agnosticism reduces the religious meaning of thousands of years of history to its meaning at this present moment, in this interior incident hidden within the soul. This moment, this event, any moment, any event may embody the encounter of salvation. Again, as in Bultmann, Christ is not the source, nor the beginner and finisher of our faith and salvation; He is merely the symbolic occasion and reminder of how the attainment of our New Being is a real possibility and can become an actuality.

It follows, then, that in the Gospels everything narrated in an objective manner about Jesus Christ is merely symbolic. It is true that symbolical or mythological language does represent man's ultimate concern, for symbols have the power of debouching into vast areas of being beyond themselves. Yet as regards the specifically Christian mythological symbolism, Tillich explains the sacrifice of Jesus the man in this manner. Jesus the man of Nazareth, because He offered Himself on the Cross for others, felt Himself to become and was called by His followers "the Messiah or the Anointed One, the Christ," the one awaited by all nations in which the New Being, divinely healed, would enjoy a world free from the sin of estrangement from oneself, others and God. In answering a question of a student who wanted to know whether the uniqueness of Christ consisted in His role as a center of history or in the symbolic picture of Him presented by the Gospels, Tillich expounded his doctrine on Jesus in these words:

> . . . I refer now to everything we read about Jesus in the Gospels and the epistles of the New Testament. They all contribute to an image. This image, of course, changes in the biblical literature itself, and changes again and again in every century of Christianity. The reality behind it is in no historical case identical with the image. In the New Testament, all the images share one quality in which they are identical: they call Jesus the Christ. In this, all letters and all Gospel stories are identical. And from these are derived many special events, as I would call them, or in terms of literary criticism, "anecdotes." They are not a biography; they are anecdotes that demonstrate something. Something is shown either about Jesus as the Christ or about things which the early groups of followers had to know—how to pray, for instance. The event includes both the fact and the reception. The fact has the power of impressing itself on the disciples in such a way that historical images occur. And these images are very different. If we compare the Mark image and the John image—the image in the first and the fourth Gospels—they are, in many respects and in the whole vision, contradictory. The man who spoke and worked and acted in Mark is not the same as the one who spoke and worked and acted in John. John is a reinterpretation of the life of Jesus in the light of later problems. It is not even so much a biography as the first Gospels. They, at least, use anecdotes with historical backgrounds. John is a theological book, and therefore is best for theology because it answers problems. I very often use it, not because I think that here I have the authentic

words of Jesus—I don't believe there is any authentic word of Jesus in the Fourth Gospel—but because I know that here the meaning of the Christ, the meaning of the fundamental statement, "This is the Christ," is brought out in the light of later problems. And these problems are also our problems. Therefore, I often feel, like Luther, that this is really the chief Gospel, not because it gives us an historical picture, but because it depicts in words the power in this event.[2]

We see, therefore, that Tillich in his determination to accomodate the Gospel message to the "problems of our day" believes he is imitating what John the Evangelist did with the Gospel message for the problems of his day. In desupernaturalizing the New Testament and accomodating its message to man's problematic, existential, modern situation, Tillich drained Christian mysteries of their divine substance, secularizing them all along the line. In his hands, belief in God and Christ, as handed down by thousands of years of Judaeo-Christian written and living tradition, is evacuated of all historical, supernatural substance or content. Man's fall is diluted to mean his creatureliness; sin, the mystery of iniquity, the offense against the infinitely good God is attenuated to mean merely existential estrangement. Moreover, in the words of Mascall, Tillich's assertion that "the grace of God justifies man not only without reference to his merits but even without reference to his faith seems to drive the doctrine of justification beyond the point of paradox to that of absurdity."[3] All the classic, traditional truths—creation, the Fall, Reconciliation, Salvation, the Cross, Resurrection, the Kingdom of God, the Trinity—all of them are mere symbols. They have permanent value and Tillich would hate to part with them. But they must all undergo radical reinterpretation if they are to become acceptable to the modern world.

How Many Gospel Messages Are there in Paul Tillich?

The instrument of profound study, reflection and comparison with historical deeds, documents and living traditions of Revelation is one necessary means for assessing the veracity of a

2. *Ibid.,* pp. 154–155.
3. E. L. Mascall, *The Secularization of Christianity* (New York: Holt, Rinehart and Winston, 1965), p. 14.

Christian theology. Another means, of course, is the constant teaching of the Magisterium of the true Church founded by Christ as "the pillar and ground of truth" and guided by the Holy Spirit to all truth. But Christ did not leave the simple sheep of his flock without a daily, more practical means for distinguishing authentic from inauthentic Christianity. It is the criterion of performance, of the record, of results attained, especially of the metaphysical and moral quality of the results. "A good tree cannot produce bad fruit, neither can a bad tree produce good fruit." On its effects, then, let us seek to answer this question: "What is the secularizing theology of Tillich doing for the faith and religious life of Christians?"

In the Eighth Dialogue of a seminar conducted by Dr. Tillich at the University of California in the spring of 1963 and published, after being read and approved by him, as a book entitled *Ultimate Concern* in London in 1965, student members of the seminar, speaking through a faculty representative, questioned Dr. Tillich as follows:

Professor: Dr. Tillich, are you not a dangerous man? You make paradoxical statements which weaken people's confidence in symbols and liturgies and churches. And you tend to destroy their belief, without giving them anything to replace it. Now you are the most influential theologian of the twentieth century, but are you not primarily an apostle to the intellectuals, speaking in their language? When you broadcast your concepts, do you not harm those people who are unable to comprehend, and will only misapply your ideas?[4]

In answer to this startling and refreshingly frank question, Tillich defends his preaching and writing at great length and with the utmost candor. Here we can only indicate his main arguments, exhorting the reader to enjoy the entire original reply at his leisure. Tillich first sets the historical context of his theological work by comparing his mission to that of his two great contemporaries—Karl Barth and Rudolf Bultmann. Barth courageously fought Nazism through his neo-orthodox Christianity, saving liberal Germanic, indeed all European,

4. Paul Tillich, *Ultimate Concern*, p. 188.

Protestantism from the fate of Nazification or at least of nationalization into a Germanic Christianity. Barth's neo-orthodoxy was triumphant with the defeat of Nazism. But the post-war Christian European intelligentsia were theologically abandoned and slipping alarmingly into secularism and unbelief because they could not accept the overpowering God and Gospel of Barthianism. Both of these neglected the life of the intellect. At this precise moment, Rudolf Bultmann came forward with his famous work on demythologization to save for Christianity those "thinking and doubting people" who could accept his collapsed New Testament message because it stimulated the intellect. The modern intellectual was pleased with a faith received from God and a salvation that consisted in the liberating awareness of authentic existence achieved in Christ But, in the opinion of Tillich, Bultmann had been too radical; he had, by jettisoning Christian symbols and myths, led many Christians into the spiritual wilderness of religious skepticism. Tillich saw himself as the prophet sent to these darkened souls; his mission was to recall them to Christianity through a Gospel message that salvaged symbols and myths but reinterpreted them in a non-literal, modern, existential sense.

Now Tillich admits that his mission as prophet and preacher impaled him on the horns of a dilemma. On the one hand, his work as a prophet-theologian oriented him through his writings to appeal to "those who ask questions" by teaching them the existential, demythologized, collapsed, reinterpreted message of the Gospel. For it was his conviction that the intelligentsia would accept only this and no other Christianity. On the other hand, Tillich's work as pastor-preacher oriented him in his sermons to appeal to "primitive believers" who had no doubts about traditional theology. They would not stomach a demythologized Gospel message. How did Tillich resolve his dilemma? There can be no substitute for his own explanation. He replies:

> *Dr. Tillich:* I presuppose in my theological thinking the entire history of Christian thought up until now, and I consider the attitude of those people who are in doubt or estrangement or opposition to everything ecclesiastical and religious, including Christianity. And I have to speak to them. My work is with those who ask questions, and for

them I am here. For the others, who do not, I have the great problem of tact. Of course, I cannot avoid speaking to them because of a fear of becoming a stumbling block for primitive believers. When I am preaching a sermon—and then I am quite aware of what I am doing—I speak to people who are unshaken in their beliefs and in their acceptance of symbols, in a language which will not undermine their belief. And to those who are actually in a situation of doubt and are even being torn to pieces by it, I hope to speak in such a way that the reasons for their doubts and other stumbling blocks are taken away. On this basis I speak also to a third group, one which has gone through these two stages and is now able again to hear the full power of the message, freed from all difficulties. I can speak to those people, and they are able to understand me, even when I use the old symbols, because they know that I do not mean them in a literal sense.

... I am trying to interpret the Christian message in a new way to them ... I believe that it would be hard for you to find in my sermons any directly negative statements, even against literalism. I simply restrain myself in that situation. For instance, the resurrection stories: I do not criticize in my sermons the highly poetic symbolic story of the empty tomb, although I would so in my theology and have done it in my books. But I speak of what happened to Paul and the other apostles, as Paul describes it in I Corinthians 15. Now that is the preaching method I would recommend for all sermons.[5]

This explanation is most revealing for it indicates clearly that Dr. Tillich, "in trying to interpret the Christian message in a new way for thinking and doubting people," in reality creates a message radically contradictory to the traditionally orthodox Gospel he preaches to "primitive believers." There are, then, two mutually exclusive Gospel messages in Tillich's teachings. On Sundays Tillich is a traditionalist pastor feeding the flock orthodox symbols and doctrines, though for the most part his listeners cannot suspect that their preacher "does not mean them in a literal sense." At other religious services, such as funerals, Tillich again, in order not to disturb the simple faith of the bereaved and their relatives and friends who really believe in a literally physical resurrection of the body because of their belief in the really risen Christ, prays and preaches in

5. *Ibid.*, pp. 191, 193, 194.

an orthodox manner, though, of course, his own religious convictions contradict what he is saying. He tells us that with primitive believers he gives the aid and comfort he is expected to give. In his own words: "In such moments the question of literalism or nonliteralism does not exist, for we have the power of the word . . . I talk with children on the level they can understand."[6]

On the other hand, in theological tracts directed at twentieth-century minded intellectuals, Tillich "undercuts and destroys the primitivism of religious literalism." Again in his own words: "I try to recreate the old realities on another basis."[7] Tillich complains that "primitive believers" are stunted in their historical development of on-going, relevant theology. They still really believe that "the word of God" is just what orthodox theologians of the year 1620 wrote. They think that this is the word of God for all times, although actually it is only the word of the theologians of the year 1620, in Germany and in Holland mostly—only that."[8] Contemporaneity is now advanced and universalized as the new norm and criterion for discovering the valid message of the Gospels. What is historically relevant to modern concerns reveals the content of the word of God. What does the new criterion say of the witnessing of the Apostles who, as men on the scene, sealed with their blood and lives their teachings with regard to the historically objective reality of the salvation events centered in Christ, the Son of God? Tillich, the revolutionist theologian, using the new criterion, cavalierly dismisses the testimony of the Apostles as fantasy. Obviously their supernaturalist scheme of salvation sprang from what these for the most part primitive fishermen imagined happened to Jesus in the violent times of His life and death. Not what Jesus said and did, but what these primitive believers fancied He said and did is narrated in the four Gospels. Such legends of divine irruptions into time and narrations of abnormal events are embarrassing to twentieth-century intellectuals. Obviously the Bible is the source of truth, but only the expurgated edition of the Bible expounded by the radical theologians. Of course, Christians who "in a literalistic atti-

6. *Ibid.*, p. 194.
7. *Ibid.*, p. 192.
8. *Ibid.*, p. 192.

tude" still cling to the visions, myths, symbols and abnormal events narrated by the Apostles, are to be treated with tact and toleration.

This contradictory, dualistic, "one other Gospel" teaching of Tillich defies comment, for it leaves the true believer speechlessly amazed, but the effort must be made for the sake of "thinking and doubting people." One is prone to admire in Tillich his sensitivity for the unshared beliefs and feelings of his primitive listeners. Certainly Tillich's tolerance of their backwardness and patience with their literalness display the prudence and civility of a gentleman. But what must come through as appalling to the man of reason—believer or unbeliever—is that Tillich apparently does not even suspect the sheer inconsistency, not to say dishonesty, of his dual role. He seems unconcerned about the contradictory falsity of at least one of these Gospel messages. Now tolerance and tact are not virtues of the intellect; they are social attitudes, moral virtues if you wish, toward others. But when tolerance and tact are practiced to disguise and deny the truth to others who have a right to it, they then are, in reality, the vices of dishonesty and betrayal. Now, leaving aside the subjective moral consciousness of Tillich, a reasonable man can surely analyze his objective conduct dispassionately.

When writing for intellectuals and revealing what he actually believes, Tillich is certainly behaving honestly, for he is accurately representing his beliefs or lack of them. On the part of the reader, there may be disagreement with the ideas of the writer and the reader will reject those ideas as false. For love of truth, the fundamental virtue of the mind, must of its very nature be intolerant of what it sees as falsity. But intolerance of a writer's false ideas need not proceed to intolerance of his person. It need not flow over into overt, hostile action against the writer. Of course, under certain special circumstances, intellectual intolerance of the false ideas of a person may have to proceed to social intolerance of his person, especially where the person is translating his ideas into actions that are overtly assaulting the common good of society. For example, for a long time the Christian West was intellectually intolerant of the theories of Hitler and yet he went on writing and propagandizing them over the world. But as his teachings were incarnated into a military machine that assaulted all free institutions, the

West was constrained to tolerate the existence of Hitler and his system of thought no longer. Quite reasonably and justly it proceeded to destroy both.

Now this may seem like an academic digression but it is not. Let us look at Tillich's mission as a pastor, his role of preacher to primitive believers. While teaching his Sunday faithful the literal interpretation of the Gospel, Tillich, for all his sensitive feeling for the flock, was *de facto* deceiving the faithful. He was denying them the truth as he believed it and was officially sent to teach it. Hence his civility or tact or prudence in not showing his true convictions was merely a perverted simulacrum of true charity. For true charity, first and foremost, moves men to the mutual sharing of the truth that expands their freedom. Now there were two honest courses open to Tillich the preacher. First, he could have chosen to teach openly what his true convictions about the Gospel message were, risking thereby scandalizing his listeners and being dismissed by them. Because of the scandal to faith it would have caused, this course of action would not have been prudent or socially tactful, but it would have been honest. Second, realizing that he had lost the faith that was adhered to by his listeners and recognizing that as an official preacher he could no longer share what he no longer held, he should have given up his preaching office. He should have refused to pose as if he were still of the religious persuasions of his listeners. This conduct would have been an exercise of both charity and honesty to himself and his congregations.

What can we say about his dualistic role in conducting other religious functions, such as communion or funeral services? For Tillich to justify a performance that simulated adherence to orthodoxy with the words, "In such moments the question of literalism or nonliteralism does not exist, for we have the power of the word," is to my mind one of the most tragic examples of self-delusion through the use of rationalistic, escapist jargon. Let us take the example he uses himself, the preaching and praying of orthodox doctrine at the funeral service. To indicate that the words of the service, "I am the resurrection and life; he who believes in me, though he be dead, shall yet live," do not literally mean that the believer in Christ resting in death before his sorrowing family shall rise again to life like Christ, is to reduce the whole service to a sacrilegious sham and to desecrate the sorrowing faith and hope of the grieving family. Far from "recreating old realities on another basis," as Tillich claims he is doing as he deliteralizes orthodox Christianity, the old reality of a religious funeral service that radiated transcendent meaning, hope and consolation now has no basis in fact at all. For if the basis in fact for the biblical funeral service for Christians—Christ's real resurrection—has all along been merely a basis in fiction, then the traditional burial service itself is as vain, empty and sterile as the fantasy of the resurrection of Christ Himself. Nor is this dismal situation saved by the vacuous assertion "for we have the power of the word." What power has a word that represents no luminous reality outside its mere vocal formulation? If the traditional burial service which is literally and desperately adhered to by the faithful as an augur of real resurrection in their sorrowful confrontation with death is only a performance of *vox et praeterea nihil*—words and nothing more—for Pastor Tillich, then it becomes impossible to understand how Tillich has not lost all Christian faith, since the rock-bottom foundation of all traditional Christianity is the reality of the Resurrection. The suspicion is aroused that Tillich is merely using language to mask an agnostic vacuum. Other theologians have come to a more brutal conclusion, placing Tillich among the nonbelievers. Alasdair Macintyre, in comparing the theological doctrines on God of Bultmann, Robinson and Tillich, writes in his contribution to *The Honest To God Debate:* "Just as Bultmann's view of the New Testament points towards scepticism, so does Tillich's analysis of the doctrine of God. It seems that Dr. Robinson is not alone as a theological atheist."[9] Mascall thinks this judgment against Tillich and Robinson may go too far. Yet he quite perceptively points out that as regards Robinson's thought, "there are trends in his thought which if he followed them out consistently would certainly issue either in atheism or in sheer indifference as to whether God existed or not."[10] It is my opinion that the same assessment can be validly made of Tillich's teachings.

9. Alasdair Macintyre, "God and the Theologians," in *The Honest to God Debate*, ed. by David L. Edwards (Philadelphia: The Westminister Press, 1963), p. 220.
10. E. L. Mascall, *The Secularization of Of Christianity*, Holt, Rinehart and Winston, (New York: 1965), p. 180.

As we saw in the case of the German Church, when treating of Bultmann, démythologized theology is keeping twentieth-century Christians indifferent, stay-at-home agnostics, if not atheists. Now we find that in the American Church, where Tillich's greatest work and influence was accomplished, deliteralized theology leaves the faithful bored and unconcerned—despite the call to ultimate concern—about God and Christianity. In an interview with Dr. Tillich, whom he calls "by far the most notable and original (although not the most comprehensible) articulator of a liberal view of theology," Duncan Norton-Taylor writes:

> Stripped of all else, the question the liberal theologians are asking is the old one that has time and again sundered the Christian Church: Who was Jesus?
> Would the liberals say that Jesus was the Son of God? I inquired tentatively of Professor Tillich. It was a few weeks before his death. He was perched on the edge of a bed in a Manhattan hotel room, where he was waiting for a sculptor who was going to do a bust of him.
> *Tillich:* Both answers to the question—whatever I say—would be wrong. I'm trapped. So I must ask, What do you mean by Son of God? Now (triumphantly) you're trapped. The trap, I see, was that the liberals in rejecting the concept of Christ as the Son of God would be rejecting a metaphor that is useful; but accepting the statement meant taking literally the whole of the Apostles' Creed.[11]

Two weeks before his return to his Creator and Dr. Paul Tillich, famous theologian and scholar, remains obsessed more with preventing himself from being trapped by questions about traditional theology through laying traps for his traditional questioners, than he is about the substantive, liberating sublimity of God's love as revealed in the traditional message of the Gospels. The dedicated Christian reader of this incident cannot help but be saddened by, in the apt words of David Jenkins, "the scandalous poverty" of Tillichian theology, severed as it is from the exhaustless treasuries of theological gold to be found in the vast Scriptural studies of the Churches, the Fathers and Councils of East and West, the great mystics and

11. Duncan Norton-Taylor, "What on Earth is Happening to Protestantism," *Fortune Magazine*, December 1965, pp. 170–231.

saints. Perhaps the serious Christian is irritated even more by
the worldly artfulness with which the revolutionary theologians avoid precisioning and thus sharing their own religious
convictions. Moreover, in America, sincere Christians are
openly registering their protests against a tree of theology that
produces such bad fruit. Norton-Taylor goes on to report that
"the Protestant clergyman is confronted finally from the pews
by people who aren't paying much attention. They aren't because he isn't saying much from the pulpit."[12] In the final analysis, Tillich can be viewed as a modern Titan who conceived the
adventure of faith as a sortie from earth to heaven, an abduc-
tion of God from His throne up there and His incarceration into
human concerns down here. Behold your God is your ultimate
concern, your ground of being, men are being taught. But men
can care less about a God as lifeless, loveless and meaningless
as an immanentized ground of being. For a trapped God can
only have trapped subjects. Tillich himself is the foremost example of this captivity to what is relevant only to the contemporary moment; he is always on the defensive, always parrying
imaginary blows. Men are seeking the God who freely came
down from above in love in order to liberate them from the
shabbiness of the fallen existential condition. The true, the
traditional message of the Gospels once liberated a pagan
world enslaved to the decadent powers of time. Today this message maintains the power to liberate those who have trapped
themselves in large numbers in the existential world of Tillichian agnosticism and scientific atheism.

12. *Ibid.*, p. 231.

CHAPTER XIII

Robinson:

The Depersonalized God

THE BISHOP OF WOOLWICH, JOHN A. T. ROBINSON, IN HIS
controversial book *Honest To God,* published in 1963, states
that the radical theologies of three great contemporary Protestant writers have so moved him that all his writings represent
"his thinking aloud, struggling to think other people's thoughts
after them, yet unable to claim to have understood all that I am
trying to transmit." The three Protestant writers and their
works are: Tillich, *The Shaking Of The Foundations,* Bonhoeffer, *Letters And Papers From Prison* and Bultmann, *New Testament And Mythology.*[1] Four years later, in his book *Exploration Into God,* Robinson reassesses what he did in that
theological bombshell: "But I am coming to believe that the
holding of them together may . . . be the distinctive contribution
of *Honest To God.* And perhaps this is also the characteristically Anglican contribution to the present theological debate—

1. John A. T. Robinson, *Honest To God* (Philadelphia: The Westminister
Press, 1963), pp. 21–24.

to refuse the logical either-or and to attempt a creative synthesis."[2]

What is Robinson trying to harmonize into a creative synthesis? They are two theories of religious significance with opposite consequences. He admits that he was trying to synthesize the ideas of Tillich and those of Bonhoeffer, with the thinking of Bultmann as a sort of bridge between them. Now these former two have their sharp differences. For Tillich all reality was religious, for Bonhoeffer everything was secular; Tillich focused on ultimate concern as God, Bonhoeffer on penultimate questions; Tillich systematized his theology of crisis, Bonhoeffer was an anti-systematizer. Why the effort to whip these opposed men together with such theological wizardry? Because, according to Robinson, these radical theologians have more in common than in dissent, in their novel approaches to the reality of God. How successful has Robinson been in his synthesis?

When one attempts to synthesize opposites while banning the logic of either-or and the exclusiveness of true or false, then, of course, consistency of thinking becomes impossible. Consequently, it is not really surprising that there are revealed in the Bishop of Woolwich's writings not one but two or three Dr. Robinsons. There is the Robinson who would like to remain orthodox, yet lead a "reluctant revolution." There is the Robinson who, in order to "re-locate and re-center the God of out there, up there back in the world and history, would secularize, de-supernaturalize the whole of Christianity, plunging downward into the nature of man and the cosmos to attain a new type of transcendence. Finally, there is the Robinson who, after "clearing the decks" of the false traditional images and conceptions of God, creates his own religion as something better than Christianity with its "God beyond God." Now this last Robinson tells us that he "is prepared to be an agnostic with the agnostics, even an atheist with the atheists." to gain all to this faith.[3] Now the three Robinsons—there are really more, but it is impossible to reveal them all here—move from one theological position to another with such startling dexterity and contradic-

2. John A. T. Robinson, *Exploration With God* (London; SCM Press, 1967), p. 76.
   3. J. A. T. Robinson, *Honest To God*, p. 127.

tory boundings that the reader is treated to a muddled congeries of theologically incoherent positions.

Robinson, in his genuine desire to Christianize the secular has succeeded only in secularizing the Christian. Bultmann had demythologized the Gospels and dissolved their miracles. This was not radical enough for Robinson's tastes. God and miracles must be secularized; that is, explained in a non-religious sense. Transcendence had traditionally meant an adherence of the whole person to the Tri-Personal God dwelling above, beyond, as well as being present to the world. Robinson, following his master Tillich, insists that man must rinse his being absolutely clean of every vestige of traditional, supernatural theology. Even the word "God" will have to be discarded as no longer useful. For God is not a person but "infinite depth;" He is Tillich's "ground of being." Thus a new form of transcendence is formulated to displace the old. Now transcendence is preserved in "the finite world which points beyond itself." But the pertinent question flys from one's lips: "Points to what?" Robinson answers that this is Tillich's great contribution to theology, his feat of detaching transcendence from a projected, supernatural world up there and riveting transcendence to this self-surpassing world down here. But the question remains, since it was not answered but skirted, "Toward what does a self-transcendent world arise?" Robinson's position of immanentism is undermined for it cannot harmonize with the transcendence he so urgently desires. A world that points upward at nothing beyond itself is in reality a world plunged into the void of the Absolute Absurd.

Having immanentized transcendence, Robinson realized he was open to the charge of teaching pantheism. In order to clear himself of this charge, he first sets his own position in relation to the two theories of history that are competing for the adherence of Christians. There is the Teilhardian evolutionary theory that sees the entire universe rushing in expanding progress to a cosmic, collective rendezvous with God in the Omega Point. On the other hand, there is the humanistic dialectic inward, that sees the process of secularization as a dynamic descent away from the illusion of God toward the achievements of a humanity "come of age" in a religionless Christianity. Once again the synthesizing Robinson would harmonize the best in these opposing systems, producing a marriage between inward secularization and the outward evolutionary replacement of traditional Christianity. Such a synthesis would have the great advantage of discarding the dualistic world of traditional theism and integrating reality in natural oneness. Again this synthesis would achieve Tillich's "ecstatic naturalism," i.e., contain God in the depth of a "shot-silk universe," allowing nature and man, together with God, to do anything and create all possible history. Thirdly, this synthesis would impose universal silence on speech and discussion about God that is not pertinent to God's immanent relationships with man and the universe. Fourthly, this synthesis would supress all antithetic exclusivisms between religions. The dividing wall of either-or, true-false, good-evil, yes-no would be demolished among all men. A new essence of Christianity would thus arise across the former, falsifying, trivial demarcations.

Robinson claims that his own synthesis, as the third alternative theory of history, escapes the traps of pantheism. He gives his system the philosophical name of panentheism. Now panentheism rejects pantheism for the same reasons that Christianity rejects it. Pantheism is impersonal, impassive, aesthetic, prone to historical quietism, being unconcerned about pain, evil, injustice or history in any dimension. Its move toward God as being and truth is doomed to the tragedy of personal obliteration. As for his panentheistic synthesis, Robinson claims that it re-centers God as the Great Incognito at the heart of all things, not absorbing them, but revealing Himself in and through all, even in evils, inhumanities and moral corruptions.

For the purpose of providing an incarnate illustration of the sublime secular sainthood achievable through the practice of panentheism in real life, Robinson quotes generously from the ex-communist Rumanian writer Petru Dumitriu's novel *Incognito.* Robinson admits that, in his development to date from his *Honest To God* skepticism about traditional theology, this novel has influenced him as strongly "as any of the more purely theological influences to which I have found myself responding." Here I will summarize the essence of the prolonged passages quoted. The scene represents a prisoner who has been tortured into a dehumanized hulk of humanity, but who saves for himself the meaning of the whole universe by his individual response of love in the very teeth of cosmic and human brutality. The message of human love and goodness that stirs his soul below the piercing screams of his rent body is given as follows:

> This love welling up within me to justify the world by loving and forgiving it, comes from some unknown source that is not me but *thou* . . . It is God! How address him? O Universe? O Heap? O Whole? . . . Dear Father? Dear Comrade? Do I call Lord the air I breathe or the lungs with which I breathe it? God is perfect, yet terrible and evil; He is all things, yet confines himself to none . . . All things, events, persons, faces are the incognitos of God . . . God is composed of volcanoes, cancerous growths and tapeworms . . . That makes me an atheist because I irreverently reduce God to evil as well as to good, to matter as well as to thought? I answer that the hard task of life is to love a world that tortures, to forgive, even bless, it, for this is one of the faces of God, sad and terrifying. God is not found in labelled religions or structured churches; labels are superflous; institutional structures kill. God is found in the fellowship of the secret discipline of love which constitutes the invisible leaven of the Kingdom. The divinity of Christ consists in his deep, intense love of everything   good, evil, perfect, imperfect. Christ is the first of a future mankind wherein a mutation of human hearts will in the end cause the Kingdom of God—the Kingdom, Tao, Agarttha—to descend among men.[4]

Robinson, Anglican bishop whose office it is to defend, explain and propagate the Christian faith, accepts this avowedly non-Christian naturalism, made out of whole cloth, wholeheartedly. He tells us that "comment on it would be an anticlimax." And then he proceeds to praise this "theology of the latent rather than of the manifest Church" as a new "diaphany of the divine," even twisting the words of St. Paul in order to liken it to "the revelation of the glory of God in the face of Jesus Christ." But if Robinson will not comment on this *mélange* of chaotic emotionalism parading as the message of the Kingdom of God, the concerned Christian must. Whereas in *Honest To*

4. J. A. T. Robinson, *Exploration Into God*, (London: SCM Press, 1967), pp. 88–92.

God Robinson expressed his complete indifference to the truth or falsity of traditional theism, here in *Exploration Into God,* he abandons completely any belief in Christianity, using the medium of the novel—a dubious instrument for theological precision—to reduce the traditional content and grandeur of Revelation to the rhetorical rantings of a tortured prisoner who sings an idolatrous hymn to the universe. The verbal denial of pantheism does not save Robinson from trapping himself in the reality. God is everything and everything is God. "It is the ability to take up evil into God and transform it that is the most striking—and shocking—feature of this theology," is his advertisement for allegiance to this, his theology. Of course, the reality is that the Bishop degrades God, identifying Him with evil and immanentizing Him in a brutal world. But even more, that last sentence of his reveals a serious psychological sickness at the heart of the Bishop's thought. He is enamored with the "shocking feature" of this theology. The Bishop has a history of proceeding on his theological itinerary from shock to shock, all of these shocks administered, supposedly as therapeutic measures, to the flock who loves the traditional faith. *Honest To God* shocked the entire Western world and continues to do so by continuing to evacuate Christian content from Christian expression. It is now translated into German as *Gott ist anders* —God Is Different—and imported into East Germany where the Communists are using it as atheist propaganda. "Apparently the East German authorities knew the value of the book better than the bishop himself," reported Congregational minister Harold O. J. Brown, who was on the scene studying the German religious situation.[5]

But in *Exploration Into God* the Bishop goes further than he did in the above-mentioned book in making it easy for people to abandon the historic truths of Christianity. For this blatantly anti-Christian book provides unmistakable evidence of the Bishop's flight from Christianity for those who hesitated before to accept Alasdair Macintyre's vigorous assessment of Robinson's agnosticism, or rather atheism, on the occasion of the appearance of *Honest To God.* At that time Macintyre wrote: "What is striking about Dr. Robinson's book is first and fore-

5. H. O. J. Brown, "The Struggle for the German Church," *National Review,* April 8, 1969, p. 334.

most that he is an atheist . . . The second half of *Honest To God* reveals that the Bishop is a very conservative atheist. He wants an atheist Christology . . ."[6] Well, in *Exploration Into God* the Bishop has attained what he was seeking. Now he is a radical atheist, using Christian language to announce his rejection of Christian faith. Now he explicitly states what he formerly hinted at, that Christianity has been irrevocably replaced by cosmic panentheism—pantheism, the former word now being a philosophical not theological mask and softening of his utter atheism.

What is more, the Bishop advances in his demolition of the reality of God in the second book. God becomes transpersonal, a "divine field" between persons growing in freedom and love. God is a "whole humanity rather than like nature, society or concept." God is Dumitriu's "dense and secret undergrowth which is wholly composed of personal events." Finally, God is Teilhard's "Centre of Centres" in an interlocking web of free spiritual relationship in which the All and the personal are no longer exclusive." And again St. Paul is twisted into serving this muddled pantheism through a misapplication of his prediction of cosmic salvation in Christ.

Any evaluation in depth of Robinson's novel theology will discover that it is an amorphous, grandiose neo-gnosticism. Its style is characterized by a mental bias blind to the hierarchies of being, truth and values. It attempts the impossible; namely, to liquidate all genuine antitheses by fuzzily fusing them. Thus it creates unrealistic constructions because it disregards and contemns given reality. Consequently, Robinson's imagination runs wild, unchecked by the wisdom of experience, reflection or intuition. Utilizing emotional exotic effusions from crisis-novels and pathological poems, the Bishop indulges in exaggerated claims about God and the meaning of Christianity. His hysterical enthusiasm for adapting both to the standards of modern acceptability obliterates the function of his reason, with the tragic consequence that he eschews logical arguments, arbitrarily selects analogical analyses, carelessly ignores scientific, historical sources and oscillates wildly, even artfully, from one contradictory position to another. In the work of Robinson rhapsodizing has replaced reflecting. A mas-

6. *Honest To God Debate*, pp. 215–216.

ter of oversimplification, the Bishop catches many a reader by the superficial plausibility of his theological statements and their specious similarity to traditional dogmas. A little reflection, however, reveals a theological process which evacuates dogma of divine substance and substitutes man-made fictional shadows in its place. Robinson's theology is thus seen to be devaluated currency; indeed his theology is a form of bankruptcy of faith.

In his passionate desire to adapt God to the mentality of progressive, scientific man, Robinson has made an idol of Modernity. He worships at its altar. He has founded the religion of neo-modernism—a religion that has a new God, new theology, new morality, new Gospel, new man, new universe and a new eschatological millenium.

When an orthodox theologian reviews, even cursorily, the doctrinal content of Robinson's capitalized word-constructions or his contorted, visionary hypotheses, a sense of spiritual nausea envelopes his spirit. What poisonous fare is found here in place of the genuine food of divine truth! Let us briefly consider just his theologically reductionist distortion of God, a distortion that destroys the metaphysical nature of God and man as well as sickens the human soul. Robinson sees God as a depersonalized, solely immanentized force or ground of being pervading all reality indifferently. The Bishop's lust for a pancosmic pantheism has blinded him to the ineffable superiority and grandeur of the person. Infinitely inferior to the world of persons is the universe of the impersonal. The world of the personal is an absolutely new, superior, metaphysical and divine dimension of being. Non-personal realities are spiritually asleep; they simply exist, endure existence, unaware of the meaning of being, unawakened to the intelligent, lovable origin and end of all creation. Impersonal realities, bereft as they are of reason and liberty, are destined to be possessed and utilized. A person, on the contrary, is wide-awake to the meaning of being. A person has the unique perfection of possessing himself in thought and love. A divine person, therefore, is perfect awareness of being, i.e., perfect Truth Itself. Moreover, a divine person enjoys perfect possession of himself in perfect liberty and love, i.e. a divine person is Perfect Liberty, Perfect Love.

Now Robinson's God, far from being perfectly free and aware

of being, is caught in cosmic captivity. By calling Him "the God beyond God," Robinson does not liberate his captive God. We have here another example of the use of bombastic, irrational, shock expressions as a substitute for reflection in speech about God. A "God beyond God" is a bloodless, pernicious abstraction, worthy not of adoration but of rejection as a word idol. How infinitely more noble is the orthodox doctrine about God! The Tri-Personal absolute awareness of its Being and absolute Possession of its Persons is in reality the unutterable mystery of the Divine Family. Thus at their plenitude of perfection the Tri-Personal absolute Awareness of Being and absolute Possession of Self are revealed as being tri-social, tri-loving and lovable because they are tri-personal. The perfection of Persons is the very essence of God! What a chasm yawns between the false God of Robinson and the God of Revelation! Robinson's God is a "divine field" between beings that merely keeps them juxtaposed. The Tri-Personal God of Revelation is the Divine Family which invites and raises the human family to conscious, free, interpersonal communion and community through mutual knowledge and love. Robinson's God, drained of all personal perfection, cannot be free, for persons alone enjoy freedom. Robinson's God cannot communicate knowledge or love, for persons alone can share love and expand one another's freedom.

In the last analysis, Robinson's *Exploration into God* is a misnamed enterprise. Had it been named after what it set out to achieve, it would have been called *Degradation of God*. For the whole enterprise dilutes and dissolves the grandeur of God. The book distorts the New Testament message and leads to the decomposition of Christianity. The Robinson theological venture issues out into the deformation of Christianity into a pancosmic monism. A virtuosity in the practice of equivocation is the technique that blurs all the mysteriously sublime differences in the hierarchy of reality and effects this nihilistic monism. A theology that depersonalizes God dehumanizes man. A theology that liquidates realistic antitheses, liquidates liberty. For whenever the contest between truth and falsity, good and evil, natural and supernatural, divine and human is obliterated, man is trapped as a mere moment in a necessarily developing cosmic continuum. In such degrading circumstances man can no longer be challenged as a free person to storm the kingdom of heaven and violently bear it away. The theology of Robinson is therefore an artificial construction of humanistic myths. It can never replace the theology of revelation, that organically maturing relationship between the Divine Family and the human family whereby man freely ascends, through divine sonship in Christ, the God-Man, to the pinnacle of human and divine communion. Robinson's theology, like Feuerbach's—of which he heartily approves—turns out to be just another sterile exercise in anthropological, atheistic humanism.

Because he refuses to listen to the message and realities of the New Testament, because he refuses to imitate the doubting Thomas and to "put his finger into His hands and his hand into His side," because he refuses "to taste and see how sweet" the Lord who really lived in history is, Robinson thought up an esoteric theology out of his own mind, aided by other equally unrealistic rationalizations. He has concocted a hodgepodge of shock-producing, sheer nonsense doctrine that shatters the faith and lives of unwary Christians. His new religion, which is really pantheism dressed in Christian vestments, turns out to be on reflection an old and trite form of atheism. Stripped of its rave notices, its hysterical billings and Christian camouflage, the new Robinsonian religion stands forth naked as an old form of crass naturalism.

CHAPTER XIV

Cox: The Delphic God of the Secular City

IN 1965 DR. HARVEY COX, PROFESSOR OF THEOLOGY
and Culture at Andover Newton Theological School in Massa-
chusetts, dropped one of those book-bombs that explode from
time to time in the world of thought and change the academic-
cultural landscape in a violent and permanent way. Already his
Secular City,[1] a best seller from birth, has gone through eight
printings. Cox is indisputably the most eloquent prophet for
secularization in America, perhaps in the entire West, writing
and preaching today. A Christian cannot ignore his message,
for its very popularity and notoriety are symptomatic of a profound crisis of faith in the soul of the Christian West, a crisis
that is causing a mass movement of the faithful out of the City
of God and into the City of Man. The book is a brutal challenge
to the historical relevance of the Christian way of life for man
"come of age" in modern times. Here we will briefly consider

1. Harvey Cox, *The Secular City* (New York: The Macmillan Company 1965;
paper back, 8th printing, 1966).

its principal theses, underline its assets and evaluate its conclusions.

The preamble to the Coxian creed states that our modern age of science has ushered in a new, revolutionary civilization. The intrinsic characteristic of this new civilization is its dynamic development toward secularization. The creed of secularization itself states that the entire public social life of "man come of age" must be emancipated totally from any further exterior dominance by the harsh, authoritarian commands of metaphysics and religion. Modern man has arrived at humanistic maturity; he is quite capable of forging his own humanized universe unaided by exterior directions. Indeed, he will never again tolerate, much less support, a civilization founded on the twin pillars of a common metaphysics and a common faith. Secularization has finally focused the split vision of man, transferring his sight and energy from the misty horizons of the World beyond to the clear challenges of the World right here. Secularization has sounded the death knell of other-wordly Christianity. It has set itself the goal of refashioning the future of humanity through its program for the complete dedivinization of the temporal.

The Secular City itself is the highest accomplishment of an evolving historical necessity. It began and grew up out of the tribe which was knit together by the bonds of blood and religious myths. Mythological religions impregnated the great events of life—birth, death, marriage, love, war—with their own meanings and directed the entire tribe toward preternatural destinies. However, with the advent of language and currency, the tribe developed upward, becoming the town. In this stage of social evolution diversification of functions, commerce and the work created by advancing science shattered tribal patterns and traditional molds, creating thereby town culture, town religion and town ethics. Town society was the antithesis of the thesis tribal society. The town went on to fashion so highly an industrialized complex that a new synthesis-society, known as "technopolis," came into existence. The Secular City is the apotheosis of this historical dialectical progression. The Secular City is *Technopolis Aeterna*. It is not the Kingdom of God, which is disappearing from public life, back into the hearts of men. But the Secular City opens up new possibilities

for the faith and the Church. Its worldly interests and enterprises bring forth new aspects of the Gospel message that only
awaited our modern era to be discovered. The Bible itself has
always taught secularization, but, since the hour for this message had not yet arrived, the Churches had missed this dimension of the Scriptures.

Cox warns his reader, however, that secularization must not
be confused with secularism. Secularism is the mystique of
laicism; it is a closed, rigid ideology, functioning with all the
narrowness of a new religion. Secularization, on the other
hand, rooted as it is in the Bible, holds that the whole universe
is holy, erasing the distinction between the sacred and profane.
Far from being a rigid, fixed staring vision of the world, secularization is ever new, rushing to keep pace with history's fast-
moving journey toward progressive becoming. In the Secular
City, therefore, truth is not accepted as an eternally fixed and
static body of doctrines, but as the ideas that are relevant to the
present historical moment of development. Reminiscent of the
thinking of the philosophic founder of Pragmatism, the secularist in seeking truth asks the same question that William James
put to himself: "What is the cash value of this idea?" Truth is
ideas that work, get the desired results, move the times ahead.
The same relativized mobility is the criterion for the validity
of an ethical system in the Secular City. There is no absolute
corporate ethical code to which all men must subscribe under
pain of moral degradation and sanction. Ethical and value systems in the Secular City are founded on the latest social consensus. And this is not surprising, but quite normal and to be
expected. For metaphysical relativism naturally leads to moral
relativism, morals being but the practical prolongation of
metaphysical convictions. A sliding metaphysical scale about
the truth of reality begets a sliding moral scale about the goodness of reality as it is incarnated in human conduct.

When he explains the style and spirit of the Secular City, Cox
insists on its pragmatic and profane preoccupations and emphases. These secular virtues are absolutely essential in the
leader who would accomplish worldly goals. The Secular City
prophet and star pragmatic performer who captured the heart
of Harvey Cox was John F. Kennedy. Why was this? Because, in
the eyes of Cox, this leader wasted no time on the borderline,

ultimate questions of truth and religion. Successful performance in getting the day-to-day job done was his yardstick for the truth. And the man was eminently indifferent to any particular religion, even opposing his own fellow Catholics from Pope to peasant from time to time. As for his favorite prophet of the profane, Cox selects Albert Camus as Secular City savior. Camus rejected the Christian God because this God would have men become more interested in the next rather than in this world; he made dreamers rather than doers of men. Moreover, Camus was an atheist in violent revolt, rejecting the Christian God for depriving man of his liberty and responsibility. He never forgave this God, either, for allowing innocent children to suffer so senselessly. Camus held with Proudhon that "God is *the* evil," since He deprives man of his own creative power and prevision. Thus the profane prophet of the Secular City chooses man, despite his failings, in preference to the tyrant God of the Christians.

What about the style of human existence in the Secular City? Paradoxically it becomes progressively atomized and yet progressively collectivized. Technology fragments the unity of the family, swallows up small farmers and artisans, scatters small communities, clogs the cities with displaced millions, seals off intersubjective relationships even among family members and delivers the resultant anonymous human herds to state social engineers who rule with technopolitan computers. Cox calmly accepts this technique of human degradation as the necessary price that must be paid for the advent of the Secular City millenium. After all, he argues, the loss of privacy is balanced by the gain of mobility. And the Bible testifies that a people publicly welded together and constantly on the move can become a great nation, as did the Chosen but wandering People.

What especially concerns the Christian is the nature of the God of the Secular City. And like the other transcendent realities examined in that City of Man, the God of Harvey Cox is ambiguous in the extreme. He is Janus-faced; His deistic countenance faces the European West; His despotic countenance faces the Marxist East. Cox forbids his deistic God from taking part in human affairs. This God of the Enlightenment who has created a perfectible universe must remain a mere spectator as man fashions the cosmos to his own image and likeness. God is not to interfere in human history, not even in the interior consciences of man. This would be despotism. Thus the deistic God of the Secular City is banished from public life. He may not be invoked in civil ceremonies, nor be petitioned for the success of war and the attainment of peace. He is banished even in name from public education; He is not consulted about public morals; He is exiled from human history. In his temporal enterprises to humanize his universe man is to ostracize God even to the extent of maintaining silence about Him, going it alone for fear of losing his humanity if God interfered to help him.

Yet Dr. Cox is in a hurry to bring to completion the erection of his Secular Citadel. But he finds men and their social institutions frustratingly slow to make the changes in doctrine, policies and social structures so absolutely necessary for the achievement of the New Secular Jerusalem. In his estimation, then, some sort of catalyst was needed to speed up the political, socio-historical changes and differentiations required for the creation and celebration of gleaming Technopolis as a reality upon the mountain top. It is in this noble cause that the deistic God of Harvey Cox comes out of celestial retirement to intervene in the temporal affairs of men. Cox calls Him the biblical God, the God who goaded the reluctant Jews on to their rendezvous with the City of Jerusalem. But Cox is careful to explain what he means by biblical; he accepts Van Peursen's, Michalson's and Lehmann's meanings of the term. The first two authors insist that God is the God of History, the last calls Him the God of Politics. Thus Cox's God of social and political change turns out to be none other than the God of History, the God who is the inevitable, immanent, evolutionary process toward the Secular City Summit. Cox's deistic God, formerly ostracized from history, now becomes Cox's Marxist God, the director and catalyst of historical development toward full secularization. For in the Secular City as well as in Marxist cities politics replaces metaphysics as the language of theology. Reflecting on the activist characteristics of Cox's Oriental God, Professor Frederick Wilhelmsen writes:

> This Coxian god is a wild and savage Force bent upon destroying all the icons and statutary thrown up beside the road by Western man on his pilgrimage through time. Cox

commends what he calls "the biblical God" because this god makes his presence known in history by smashing the "idols" of men and by humbling the "spirit of pride." This god is truly a tribal god—a god of the desert, a whirlwind out of the clouds, a god so remote that we must address him not as "Thou" but as "You," as the "You" out there in the darkness, the unknown and unapproachable partner in civilization's destruction. Like all Iconoclasts and Manicheans, the god of Harvey Cox has come riding out of the wastes of the East, determined upon the destruction of Christendom's glories. But this god is not our God, the Triune God of Nicea.[2]

And Cox has a role for the Christian Churches in his Secular City. They are to become instruments in the service of the God who, through politics and social actions, humanizes the world through progressive secularization. They are to abandon any further efforts to sacramentalize or divinize, for in truth such efforts actually desacralized the holy universe. They are to leave the God of personal contemplation and join the god of collective, social activity. The only meaningful future open to Christian Churches is the program of self-secularization, the abandonment of religious universities and their total adherence to politico-social actions and programs calculated to humanize the world.

Secular City—City of Serfdom

In evaluating the thought of Harvey Cox, the reader is impressed by the author's genuine concern for the social betterment of man. Cox treats seriously the important questions of the place and function of God, Christianity, the Churches and the faithful in the modern age of revolutionary, social disintegration. His thought shocks readers and sends them back into reflective seclusion, pondering the ultimate question of God, the question that for philosopher Unamuno eclipsed all other questions: "Is man all alone or not in this universe?" Then too Cox has presented many valid, even brilliant, analyses of social mores, as witness his incisive, condemnatory critique of *Play-*

2. Frederick Wilhelmsen, *Cox's Secular City. . .City Of Night*, a pamphlet published by the Society for the Christian Commonwealth, 422 Washington Bldg. Washington D.C. 20005, 1967.

boy's sexual code. Cox is a seminal thinker, opening avenues of thought that others will follow, refine and organize.

But when one has graciously admitted the talents of Harvey Cox, one must immediately go on to underline the limitations of his teachings. Cox's thesis that all cosmic and human history are inevitably moving toward the apotheosis of secularization is, to say the least, unproven, one-sided and irrationally biased. It suffers from the same voluntaristic reductionism that vitiates the Marxist thesis concerning the fatalistic arrival of the class society. No intelligent, convincing analyses are given explaining why secularization is a reasonable, normal development from tribe through town to technopolis, nor why the desacralization of society is a universal good. Cox seems to revel in making unsubstantiated prophecies, moral judgments, denunciations, commands and even insults. A religious and metaphysical skeptic, Cox, nevertheless, manages to produce a fascinating rationalistic theory of historical progress, a gnosticism that divinizes the temporal, an ethics of social nihilism and a politics of the totalitarian Secular City. Moreover, as Dr. Wilhelmsen has shrewdly observed, there exists in Dr. Cox the Manichean itch for "an excessive dualism: a conscious effort not only to seek distinctions without being, but to force these distinctions into separations and the separations into divorces."[3] God and the world, Church and State, the profane and the holy are forced by Cox into tragic, unnatural, Manichean opposition. Such a reductionist oversimplification of the organically orchestrated complexity of existences into hostile dualisms reveals Cox to be, in Wilhelmsen's view, a kind of Americanized Marx." Wilhelmsen profoundly analyses the disintegrating function of secularization as follows:

> It seems to me that the secularizing spirit, so handsomely articulated by Dr. Cox, is guilty of just this kind of reductionism. First the City of Man and everything found in it is divorced from the City of God. Religion is then interiorized, forbidden expression in the public forum, and the forum is forbidden any traffic with the temple. The fragmenting of life gathers momentum due to the secularists monopoly of demiurgical science. The secularists are eventually able to dissect man into *homo ludens, homo*

3. Frederick Wilhelmsen, *op.cit.*, p. 9.

amans, homo economicus, homo politicus, homo artis-
ticus, etc., severing nerve after nerve of the human spirit
until man finally collapses into the many, having lost the
unity with which he emerged into being from the hand of
God.[4]

But perhaps Harvey Cox's greatest disservice to man is that
he renders revelation and salvation impossible for man. His
Oriental God is a secularizer, while his deistic God is sealed off
from encounter with man through Incarnation, grace, the Sacraments or the gift of divine sonship. Cox does what he accuses
Christianity of having done; he desacralizes man and the universe; he hates the sacraments and liturgies of Christianity and
would wipe them from the face of the earth. In his eyes,
Churches should become departments for social planning
in the Secular City; theology should become politics; liturgy
social action programs; sacraments civic ceremonies. Someone
should have told Dr. Cox that there is nothing new in all this
so-called modern theory and action. Auguste Comte had been
through all this before Dr. Cox, even down to Cox's theory of the
three stages of development from superstitious tribe to scientific Secular City via metaphysical immaturity. Dr. Harvey Cox
and his Secular City is Auguste Comte and his Scientific City
revisited. Where Comte changed theology into sociology and
religion into sociocracy, Cox changes theology into politics and
religion into secularism. The pragmatic City of Harvey Cox
will learn, even as the Scientific City of Comte did before it,
that the ultimate questions of life, death, God, religion, truth,
falsity, freedom, slavery, salvation cannot be solved by natural
human resources. The Secular City is impotent in the face of
these transcendent mysteries. Politics is the science of the
practical, the science of finding adequate policies to solve the
everyday problems of man's temporal enterprise, his art of
self-government. It is very true that many great philosophers
and theologians wrote masterpieces on political matters—
Plato with his *Republic* and *Laws,* Augustine with his *City of*
God, Thomas with his *De Regimine Principis.* But these very
geniuses who honored politics as the highest art of which man
was capable, that of self-government, nevertheless were con-

4. *Ibid.,* pp. 9–10.

vinced that there could be no serious, lasting, just system of self-government except a system founded on the pillars of metaphysical and religious truth. For before man can know or govern himself well, he must make deep researches into the Good, the True, the Beautiful—into God.[5]

In conclusion, then, it can be said that secularized society is isolated society, for secularization cuts man's roots in God. Such a society is in flight downward and inward. For secularization is in essence an apostasy from God, Christ and his Church. To deny that God has come to dwell permanently with man until the end of time and beyond in the everliving events of Christ, His Church, His sacraments, His truth and His grace is to run away from the plenitude of divine-human communion. A secularist society is, therefore, a solipsistic society, condemned by choice to self-inprisonment. When, therefore, Harvey Cox sees in secularization a means toward authentic ecumenism, he tragically misses the metaphysical and divine dimensions of the mystery of apostasy. For it is the sacramental that expands the dimensions of natural beings, lifting them way beyond their natural capacities toward transfiguration in Christ and God. A Secular City purged of every sacred sign points only toward itself and a selfishness that cramps being. Thus, the Secular City which banishes God from man and incarcerates man from God is a City of Serfdom, a city of enforced separation. Such a secularized world must necessarily be heartless, a concentration camp in which are kept the human creatures violently abducted from God. And in order to control the abducted creatures, all remembrances of their love relationships with God will also have to be obliterated. Thus the Secular City is a City that rules by a program of iconoclasm. It secularizes cathedrals, altars, sacred art, sacred books, culturizing them as interesting museums and art objects that recall the superstitious ages of man not yet come of age. It is for this reason that Wilhelmsen calls the Secular City the "City of Night." The Secular City puts out the lights of civilization, the lights of reason and revelation in a program of wild madness that issues in self-inflicted blindness.

Thus, because he refuses to respect the rich complexity of reality, natural and supernatural, because he will not listen to

5. René Marlé, "La Cité Séculière," *Ètudes*, juillet-août, 1966, pp. 120–130.

the diverse needs of the orders of being, because he will not distinguish without divorcing the analogical natures and relations of the different orders of beings and, above all, because he has lost a reverential love and faith in the powers of reason and revelation, Harvey Cox has created the socio-political nightmare known as Technopolis into which he would force the entire human race whether it likes its new city or not. The Christian Church has been founded by the Triune God to be the vessel of salvation for mankind. In determining to destroy her through the process of secularization, Dr. Cox and his Secular City have chosen to become the advance guard of a new barbarism.

Part Four

Gods as Victims of Man

But if God is really dead, and not merely in eclipse because of the weakness of our human vision, then our faith is dead too. What is really to be feared is that the new radicalism will turn out to be an excuse to fall back upon the old liberalism, with its misunderstanding of the Gospel of salvation in Jesus Christ as one of the forms assumed by human religion in its quest for the meaning of life.

God Is Dead: The Anatomy Of A Slogan
Kenneth Hamilton

. . .Concerning the problem of whether there are gods or not, the Pontifex did not know on what he could rely. That is how it was!. . .Do you think that anyone can live that way? One can *live*. . .but one lives as though lost, in a prolonged and mortal anguish. . .The substance of that life is desperation. . .Desperation. . .leads in an early stage to exasperation; and history is filled with exaggerated and extreme phenomena with which man managed to stupefy and inebriate himself.

Man And Crisis
José Ortega y Gasset

I have made my peace with my Maker, much to the dismay of my enlightened friends, who reproach me for this backsliding into the old "superstition," as they like to call my homecoming to God. The entire high clergy of atheism has pronounced its anathema over me, and there are fanatic priestlings of unbelief who would like to span me on the rack that I might revoke my heresies. . .Yes, like the prodigal son, I have returned to God after a long period of tending the swine with the Hegelians.

Werke, II
Heinrich Heine

CHAPTER XV

Vahanian: God's Cultural Pallbearer

WE WILL STUDY IN THIS AND THE NEXT THREE CHAP-
ters the teachings of those new phenomena among men, the
Christian atheists. They proclaim that man can perfectly well
live a full, responsible, mature life without the need of there
being a God. What makes these men so fascinating is that they
are professional Christian theologians who elaborate "death-
of-God" theologies that destroy the very subject of their academic, even pastoral, dedication. One would think that with
God obliterated, the theology of the Son of God would also be
defunct and these unemployed theologians would be turning to
other academic interests to keep themselves profitably engaged. But the very reverse of this expectation is true. Never
have "death-of-God" theologians been busier writing books for
hungry readers or more in demand as lecturers for fascinated
academic audiences. Not only that, but they are also in demand
to address all types of listeners—Christians, atheists, Jews, indeed even the motley millions glued to radio and TV sets. What
can be the secret of their success?

First there is the shock of contradiction. Some statement is proclaimed as a truth which directly contradicts a truth that has been held sacred for centuries. Then there is the fascination of ambiguity. These theologians do not proclaim pure, unadulterated atheism. They are not bold advocates of brazen inconoclasm, nor Church-destroyers, nor Bible-burners. They are iconoclasts of the mind; they are image and idea destroyers. They claim that man's images of God must be jettisoned; these are empty, sterile because the very idea of God is meaningless to the modern mind. Men who still cling to a living, triune God are actually living on old, old memories which are fading into the past, dead, dark ages. There is nothing in modern scientific experience that even begins to correspond to such an outlandish image of God. Believers are invited by the new theologians to come up to the maturity of modern times, drop their old household gods, open their eyes to reality around them and courageously decide to live without God. This coming to terms with Godless reality constitutes authentic human existence.

But on the positive side of the leger, the new radical theologians insist that the loss of God does not entail the loss of Christianity. For in losing God, the modern Christian discovers the full man, Jesus. And in this new discovery Christianity grows as a force that benefits contemporary man. Christian atheists, therefore, perfrom the enlightened task of detaching Jesus from New Testament mythology. They do this by interpreting the New Testament in a Godless manner. For they make a distinction between "Jesus language" and "God language" as they appear in the New Testament. The two are by no means the same and the former is to be prized while the latter is to be purged. Thus the authentic Jesus is revealed and he is found to be calling men of all ages to be his disciples, following him on the hard road of social, moral and experimental progress. In effect, then, what the Godless theologians are trying to do, as they formulate their rosy future, is to preserve something of the Christian tradition while jettisoning other sections of this tradition found to be embarrassing to contemporary man. They admit that they are radical in this procedure, but insist that this process of purification alone will save Christianity as a meaningful and forceful way of life for modern man. As we study each of the four radical theologians treated in these four chapters, we will see how each attempts to justify his reinterpretation of the New Testament and whether, in fact, each does save a meaningful Christianity for mankind, after first divorcing God the Father from Jesus His Son, and then dismissing God as incompatible, even insufferable, to the modern mentality.

And this brings us to another reason for the astonishing success of the Christian atheists' theology. Their "God is dead" movement flatters and sates a deep psychological need in man. It nourishes man's spiritual hunger to be considered "up to date," truly contemporary, avant-gard progressive, hence relevantly meaningful. Every gnostic doctrine invites men into the circle of the elite, thereby preserving man from the horrible experience of spiritual isolation and the loneliness of being left out. Now this radical theology, with its thrilling resonances attuned to the revolutionary spirit of the times, gives men a sense of involvement in the movements of social, cultural, scientific, political and philosophico-theological expansions for human betterment. Any person of spirit and intelligence would want to "get with" such an inspiring movement. And in getting with such a movement enthusiastically, many a person of spirit and intelligence has soared to ecstatic melioristic madness, substituting a secular for sacred, a human for divine way to salvation.

Moreover, this mystique of leveling barriers through revolution, thereby expanding the exercise of liberty, was already vibrant in other contemporary movements which energized through spiritual radiation the "death-of-God" revolution in theology. Kenneth Hamilton perceptively observes that "the new radicalism is the theoretical development of the drive to break down the division between the Church and the world, a drive which has been operating within Christian communities in many places." He goes on, then, to enumerate the astonishing French "worker-priests" experiment in the Catholic Church, the Japanese "no church movement," the American drive to bring the Gospel to Main Street and the return of the Church to the Inner City as examples of this effort to prove that Christianity is not unconcerned about man and his mission in this world. However, the "Death-of-God" movement goes far beyond all these reasonable missions to the world. Capitalizing on the decay of the religious spirit, on the loss of habits and attitudes of piety, on the loss of moral and metaphysical coherence and transcendent direction in a post-Christian age, the radical theologians boldly preach that the establishment of a thoroughly secularized society is the only road to salvation for a world that is spiritually confused, psychologically broken and morally disintegrating into chaotic anonymity.[1]

And what has been the attitude of these prophets for a secularized society toward the protest of orthodox Christians who brand their revolutionary adventures in far-out radicalism as apostasy from God, Christ and Christianity and surrender to a satanized society? They have adamantly, almost obsessively, insisted that traditional Christianity is irrevocably dead. There is no hope of its resurrection. The radicals have accused the traditionalists of repeating dogmatic formulas by rote, almost in magical incantations, formulas that no longer have any meaning for modern man. The traditionalists are callous to the needs of modern man. Moreover, the radicals have also scored the orthodox Christians for their ignorance in not keeping up with the changing times and their fraudulence in not living up to the Christianity they verbally profess. There is no attempt made by the radicals to dulcify their pill of secular profanation for easy consumption by the faithful. Like it or not, Godless Christianity is here to stay. There is a fatalistic finality about their repeated insistence that the only option open to the modern Christian is the following of Christ without the acceptance of God. The only alternative is inauthentic existence, directionless life, a hopeless, loveless absorption into a meaningless world of incommunicable masses. Only the message of the new theological radicalism reveals the mind of Christ for contemporary man. As a matter of cold reality, no other message will be listened to by scientific man. And the essential truth in that message can be expressed in exultant terms as follows: "God is dead! Long live Christ! Long live emancipated man! Long live Godless Christianity!" We will now examine briefly the great, modern representatives of this new, radical, theological message of Godless Christianity. They are: Gabriel Vahanian, Thomas J. J. Altizer, William Hamilton and Paul Van Buren.

1. Kenneth Hamilton, *God Is Dead: The Anatomy of a Slogan* (Grand Rapids, Michigan: William B. Eerdmans Publishing Co. 1966), pp. 20–21.

Gabriel Vahanian: God's Cultural Pallbearer

Gabriel Vahanian was born in 1927 in Marseilles. He studied at the Free Faculty of Protestant Theology in Paris, at the École des Hautes Études of the Sorbonne and at the Theologicial Seminary, Princeton, gaining his licentiate in theology in 1949, his master's degree in theology in 1950 and his doctorate in theology in 1958. He is presently Professor of Religion at Syracuse University. Rudolf Bultmann asserts that Vahanian's *Death of God* is one of the most exciting books he has read in recent years. Written in 1961, the book does not make for smooth reading. It wanders through cultural, political and religious history in order to establish the veracity of the thesis that today man is living in a definitely post-Christian era. In a more recent book, *Wait Without Idols,* Vahanian expresses his great concern over the death of God in literature and theology, especially as they are mutually related. Normally Vahanian writes as an urbane critic of cultural, literary and theological developments. But he can lose his urbanity at times, as when he strikes out at Jacques Maritain and Christopher Dawson in petty disagreement over the medical diagnosis of the dying condition of contemporary Christian culture and civilization. Apparently Maritain and Dawson, as Catholic specialists, had visited and spent long hours studying the patient before Vahanian got around to looking in and they reported that, though presently passing through a serious crisis, Christianity could and would, as it had so often done in previous centuries, recover and regain vigorous health. This report directly contradicted Dr. Vahanian's diagnosis which was that Christianity was already dead. And the Catholic report so irked Dr. Vahanian that, instead of refuting it in a scholarly manner, he lost his composure and accused both Maritain and Dawson, with T. S. Eliot thrown in for good measure, of commiting a fraud on the public. And the fraud consisted in the honest declaration and belief of these men "that Christianity is the loftiest and most spiritual revelation we know and that it has the highest validity."[2] Vahanian himself goes along with Troeltsch, who rejects this thesis for scientific and historical reasons. Well and good. Vahanian is

2. Gabriel Vahanian, *The Death of God* (New York: George Braziller, 1961), p. 158.

entitled to his own conclusions, but he is most unscholarly, uncivil and unconvincing in his name-calling riposte to such great literary men whose achievements far surpass his own. Leaving aside this most uncharacteristic Vahanian lapse into theatrical crying from the pit, we can now turn to a probing of his serious thesis: that "God's death" is everywhere proclaimed as an irreversible fact by the culture, ideals and deeds of our modern post-Christian world.

The cultural fact of our times is that man has lost the sense of any transcendental or supernatural realm of being or existence. All one has to do to judge a society is to examine its practices. And today Christians do not practice their faith. They have abandoned the vision of the world as the theater of God's glory. Instead, they view the world as the theater of the absurd, of misery, of despair. They have substituted an immanentist view of the world for the Christian transcendentalist vision. All human problems are, therefore, approached and solved solely from an immanentist emphasis; all reality is here; there is no hereafter. In such a self-enclosed setting God is simply no longer necessary. Vahanian agrees with Sartre that for modern man God is *de trop,* superfluous. Maybe He exists in Himself, but what difference does that make for modern man? Regardless of whether God is or is not self-existent, His reality as it has been presented through the ages in Biblical and Christian tradition has become today culturally meaningless. Even talking about God is a useless activity, an exercise in futility. T. S. Eliot indicated this secularistic phenomenon when he wrote in his *Christianity And Culture:*

> A society has ceased to be Christian when religious practices have been abandoned, when behaviour ceases to be regulated by reference to Christian principle, and when in effect prosperity in this world for the individual or for the group has become the sole conscious aim. The other point of view which is less readily apprehended, is that a society has not ceased to be Christian until it has become positively something else. It is my contention that we have today a culture which is mainly negative, but which, so far as it is positive, is still Christian. I do not think that it can remain negative, because a negative culture has ceased to be efficient in a world where economic as well as spiritual forces are proving the efficiency of cultures which, even when pagan, are positive; and I believe that the choice

before us is between the formation of a new Christian culture and the acceptance of a pagan one. Both involve radical changes; but I believe that the majority of us, if we could be faced immediately with all the changes which will only be accomplished in several generations, would prefer Christianity.[3]

Vahanian is convinced that man's loss of the sense of transcendence is proof that a culture that was once Christian has ceased to be so because it is being positively informed by an anti-Christian principle—the eternal tendency in man to absolutize and deify his own works and to call the result the religion of Christianity. Thus, one should not be fooled by periodic swells in the masses' interest in religion. These revivals are not signs of a return to authentic Christianity. They are adventures in mere religiosity, "desperate caricatures" of the true Christian faith. And Vahanian, in his theological analysis of current literature and art forms, illustrates the counterfeit Christianity that prevails today from the opening scenes of the film *La Dolce Vita.* There in Rome, the capital of Christendom, a huge statue of Christ, the Savior of mankind, floats suspended from a helicopter over a group of hedonistic sunbathers, prone on the *terrazza* of a plush Italian *palazzo* below, who gape up indifferently and cynically joke about the incongruity of it all. That incongruous scene is a symbol of the sickness of religiosity that infects society. For society for too long has bowed down in worship to the idolatrous gods of cultural religiosity. Now modern man is sick of this idolatry; he is alienated from its hypocrisy; he wants to be forthrightly secular and profane; he wants to affirm himself, to celebrate his world. Hence he no longer has any patience with a Christianity that restricts his thought and liberty, denies him the world and refuses to give itself to him. Culturally and theologically in revolt against Christianity, modern man proclaims that the age of religion has ended.

Of course, adjusting to transitional ages is nothing new to Christianity. In its very inception it had to prove itself to be meaningful to a pagan world whose ideals were the very reverse of its own. Then too, St. Paul had to insist on de-Judaizing the early Church in order to win over the Gentiles. Despite the

3. T. S. Eliot, *Christianity And Culture* (New York: Harcourt Brace and World, Inc., Harvest Book 1949), p. 10.

risk of thereby denying Judaism or falsifying Christianity, the
changes were courageously undertaken and Christianity pros-
pered. Today an even greater chasm separates Christianity
from the modern world. The modern atheistic mentality is utterly opposed to Christianity. Modern day Pauls are calling for
similar accomodations to the needs of the world. They are asking for demythologization (Bultmann), deliteralization (Tillich), de-divinization (Cox) or de-Christianization (Robinson)
of the Gospel in a frenzied attempt to bring together traditional
Christianity and contemporary society in meaningful communion. Vahanian does not consider any of these procedures
radical enough for the attainment of the desired communion.
He writes: "I personally consider that the most radical step
consists not in de-Christianizing the faith but in de-Westerniz-
ing and in de-religionizing Christianity."[4] For no reforms can
come from within the degenerate Christian tradition. If we are
to recover theological significance and depth, if we are to make
the faith live once again in the hearts of modern men, we must
utilize materials, employ approaches and contact organizations outside of and unconnected with traditional Christian
thought. In other words, reformers of the faith must operate
outside the Church, since traditional Christianity is in a dying,
even defunct, state. Vahanian points to the work being done by
literary men in their efforts to purify the faith of religiosity.
Novelists, dramatists, philosophers, movie-directors and non-
religious men of other professions have taken up the task of
iconoclasm. This mission of the destruction of false idols properly belongs to the Church, but the degenerate Church is delinquent in this duty. Post-Christian man thus finds himself
obliged to smash idols, emptying the temple of God of them in
order to ready it for the use of modern man. On the other hand
and more positively, modern man aims at transfiguring life
through the recovery of his own responsible creatureliness in
the face of God's wholly otherness.[5] De-religionizing Christianity renders the faith contemporary without immersing it in
immanentist anthropologies. For this process of reviving the
faith concentrates not on a reconversion of God but on a recon-

    4. Gabriel Vahanian, "Theology and the End of the Age of Religion," *Con-
cilium*, June 1966, Volume 6 Number, 2, p. 51.
    5. Thomas W. Ogletree, *The Death of God Controversy* (Nashville, Tenn.:
Abingdon Press, 1966), p. 24.

version of the moral, social, political and cultural structures and activities of the Church.

Vahanian objects to the dimension of the supernatural in reality which Christian teaching expounds; he claims that this doctrine depreciates the intrinsic worth of creation and of temporal communities. Moreover, this depreciation of the natural and the temporal begets in the depreciator an arrogant spiritual inflation. This insufferable attitude is found in Christian Churches which arrogate for themselves alone an eternal, other-worldly goal of glory. But the absorption of the temporal order into the supernatural violates the independent being and mission of human culture. "Now it is in and through the world," writes Vahanian, "that God's holiness manifests itself. It dwells in the world and no matter whether the world be conceived as profane or religious, it is the world that constitutes the context where faith must assert its secularity and the Church its eschatological reality."[6]

In Vahanian's view, therefore, secularity calls for the Christian's affirmation of faith as a presence in a world that still is endowed with its original goodness. The trouble with Christianity is that it calls men to be saints through a denial of the world. Vahanian agrees with Marx's objection to this Christian challenge: "It is easy to become a saint if one does not want to be a man." The unforgivable sin of Christianity is that it suppresses the manhood of man. Rather than accept such a suppression, modern man opts for religionless Christianity. Post-Christian man refuses to see Christian life as based on a separation from the world. And Vahanian presents post-Christian man's reasoning to this conclusion as follows: "All is grace, therefore God is dead. For if life is meaningless, then there must be no God. But, if it is meaningful . . . it is meaningful by virtue of some kind of immanent grace, therefore God does not exist. If all is grace, then God is dead. Or: All is grace because God is dead."[7]

For post-Christian man, then, true faith is founded on action that attains an eschatological goal within the world and time through socio-cultural structures formed by the world and adhered to by the Church. No longer is faith founded on par-

6. Gabriel Vahanian, "Theology and the End of the Age of Religion," p. 53.
7. Gabriel Vahanian, *The Death of God*, pp. 106–7.

ticipation in structures created by the Church and adhered to by the world. Vahanian has reversed the hierarchic beings, dignities and goals of the world and the Church. Now the world transcends the Church even though this transcendence remains trapped in time. The Church has become the religious, sociological instrument of the world. Now the Church proves her commitment to God by serving the ideals of the world with distinction. Only in this manner may the Christian faith hope to be purified of the dross of religiosity; only thus may a purified Christian faith hope to rescue the world from the profane and save it in religionless Christianity.

The time has come to cease viewing the problem of faith under the aspect of a war between God and man, the world and the Church, believer and unbeliever. This is a deceptive way of posing the problem. Faith should never serve as a justification for any social segregation. Christianity, therefore, should cease identifying itself as a particular, unique, religious cultural and, above all, divine entity. Rather, Christians, imitating St. Paul's example, should be willing to be atheists with atheists in freedom with all men for the sake of God, not in spite of God. This is the new meaning and universality of religionless Christianity. This is the mystique of immanentism, it rejects the opposition between believer and unbeliever. For faith does not separate, rather it affirms "that unbelief waits in ambush for the believer in as much as faith blinds the unbeliever."[8] Men are marked off from each other not as believers and unbelievers, but as being over against God. God is the line of demarcation. What then is the post-Christian man to do, now that he is non-Christian, religionless and Churchless? Vahanian gives his answer in the title of his last book. The post-Christian man must "Wait without Idols." And for what is he to wait? For the eventual breaking in of the Wholly Other—the transcendent God who can never be objectified. Above all, the post-Christian man must never go back to the idolatry of traditional Christianity nor to that "imitation of Christianity" known as religiosity and the caricature of Christianity.

8. Gabriel Vahanian, "Theology and the End of the Age of Religion," p. 55.

Vahanian's Vanishing Vision

In assessing the intellectual horizons of any man we must always remember that each one of us tends to make the limits of his field of vision the limits of all reality. Unfortunately, Vahanian, in his enthusiasm for this world and in his disillusionment with the world of the supernatural has drastically cut back his vision to the temporal, throwing away the infinite horizons of the mythical, the metaphysical and the divine as these have expanded, transfigured and glorified—but never suppressed—the world of man. Vahanian goes about extinguishing the lights in heaven in order to illumine more lights on earth. But if the sun and stars were extinguished, would more light appear on the earth? If the light of the Bible, of the God-Man, of the Church founded by Him and of the millions of scholars and saints who have illumined His message is extinguished, how can that loss ennoble the reality of this world? The dimension of the divine, of the supernatural, in no way minimizes the glory and reality of this world. Vahanian is suffering from a sickness that has afflicted many a noble scholar of our day. They have so focused on the weaknesses of members of Christianity—and no honest man will deny or hide these weaknesses—that they have blinded themselves to the overwhelming evidence of wisdom, goodness, love, self-sacrifice and heroic self-donation of untold millions of Christians living at this very moment, not to mention the glorious history of Christian services to mankind throughout the ages. "Blessed is he who is not scandalized in me," said Christ, who never predicted impeccability for His Chruch but warned His faithful against the false prophets who would arise within it. Because of his antipathy to the failures of some Christians, Vahanian totally negates the infinite accumulation of the Christian treasury of good works, beginning with the divine-human, priceless life and deeds of the God-Man down to the humblest prayer uttered by the sinner in the rear of the Church.

Vahanian has stripped God of his lovable and even human characteristics. God for him is no longer Father, Son, Advocate and Lover of men. Vahanian's God is so totally removed from the affairs of men that it is impossible to contact Him, much less to pray to Him intimately. Vahanian should read the mystics; they would remove the blinders from his eyes and melt the ice in his heart. They would teach him that God is not an absentee landlord who is so sociologically and anthropologically indifferent to mankind that he might as well not exist at all. Vahanian, besides isolating man from God, also isolates man from man, despite his vaunted concern for a cultural revolution as a social event. For in contradiction to the whole familial and social nature of salvation as it is revealed in the Old Testament in the history of the Chosen People and in the New Testament in the history of the Mystical Body of Christ, Vahanian divorces the life of Christian faith from adherence to any known community or people of God. He has atomized Christianity by secularizing it. He advocates religious individualism. His is an individualistic, secularized faith. Now a faith of this kind need not necessarily have any relationship to the transcendent God; it could be an ideal of mere naturalistic culturalism or humanitarianism. Such a faith is no more than an ideal for personal and social betterment. Vahanian thus has reduced true religion to mere diverse manifestations of human cultures. Vahanian is a reductionist theologian; he dilutes the Gospel into becoming a program for cultural betterment.

Throughout all his works, it becomes clear that the doctrines of Vahanian suffer from extreme ambiguity. Precision is not his gift. The word Christianity, for example, is used so fuzzily that one has to read three and four times to try to be fair to the author's thought. For the most part, Vahanian inveighs against Protestant Christianity, but then he switches suddenly to Catholicism, makes no distinctions in doctrines and blankets all Christian sects in his sweeping condemnations. Vahanian raises many questions, answers almost none. Indeed, his forte seems to be to act the iconoclast against false idols, but he is unable to bring back the true God. Vahanian has in effect reduced the Christian God to absolute impotence. So weak has he rendered Him that the God who revealed himself in Christ and the Holy Spirit is represented as never being able to raise up again into vigorous faith the Church He founded in His Son and through the power of His Holy Spirit. For Vahanian informs all mankind—and God for that matter—that post-Christian culture is here to stay. The powers of the Trinity, the graces of Christ's sacrifice and sacraments, the prayers and good deeds of the Communion of the Saints are impotent to renew the face of the earth in a revival of Christian civilization and sanctification. In his attempt to prove that the God of Christianity negates all religious systems, metaphysical, religious or cultural, Vahanian tries to prove too much. In effect, he proves nothing and remains repeating over and over again in an almost compulsive incantation that Christianity is dead, dead, dead. He never demonstrates why he believes what he believes nor why what he believes is fated to remain forever. Vahanian welcomes the demise of traditional Crhistianity with an almost morose pleasure; he celebrates its burial and with the sword of his pen stands guard over its sealed tomb lest the imposter rise again. He is dogmatically sure Christianity is dead but there gnaws at his spirit the fear of its resurrection. With the impostor dead and buried, Vahanian calls for a new program for faith. He writes: "What is needed is not so much a theological reformation as a cultural revolution. . .Western culture, the paraphernalia of faith in God, is at last expiring. . .Accordingly, the transfiguration of culture is the most urgent task of the present day. But this is a cultural task; it cannot be the result of any revival. To this task we are all obliged. It is the cultural obligation of post-Christian man, be he theologian or not, Christian or not."[9] In the final analysis, it appears to me that Vahanian with religious fervor puts his faith no longer in Christianity or the God of Christianity but in a self-contained, humanistic, religionless naturalism which he represents as the new, worldly, historical transcendentalism.[10]

9. Gabriel Vahanian, *"Beyond the Death of God,* article in *The Meaning of the Death of God, Protestant, Jewish and Catholic Scholars Explore Atheistic Theology,* ed. Bernard Murchland (New York: Random House, a Vintage Book, 1967), p. 11.
10. Robert Adolfo, O.S.A., "Is God Dead," article in *The Meaning of the Death of God,* p. 88.

CHAPTER XVI

Altizer:
Mortician of a Mystic God

VAHANIAN'S THEOLOGICAL REFLECTIONS SEEM THE acme of urbane analysis when compared to the prophetic visions of Thomas J. J. Altizer. Moving from right to left—from Vahanian through Cox, Hamilton, Altizer to Van Buren—we discover a continuum of Death-of-God theologians which divides into "soft" and "hard" radicals. Hamilton, himself a "hard" radical, gives us this distinction. Vahanian and Cox are "soft" radical theologicans for they use the "death of God" phrase with quotations around one or both of the nouns. Hamilton, Altizer and Van Buren are "hard" radical theologians for they drop all qualifications and state simply that God is dead, if indeed He ever existed.[1]

Dr. Thomas J. J. Altizer, an Episcopal layman, formerly Professor of Bible and Religion at Emory University, not only gets rid of God in his theological activities but also elaborates

1. William Hamilton, "The Shape of a Radical Theology," *The Christian Century*, LXXXII, October 6, 1965, p. 1220.

and presents a religious world-view of his own undertaken from the very inception of his theological adventures. He has been described as a "profane mystic" or "apocalyptic prophet" writing "pure poetry" which is "beautiful" but "unintelligible" theology.[2] Hamilton himself has described his fellow "hard" radical theologian as being "mystical, spiritual and apocalyptic . . . all élan, wildness, excessive generalization, brimming with colorful, flamboyant and emotive language."[3] Yet despite the roar of agitation and exaggeration in the Altizian apocalypse, a rather consistent, though unacceptable, theological message comes forth from the storm. It has to be considered seriously for its genuine Christian elements, refuted vigorously for its theological nihilism and rejected out of hand for the goal it would attain—an inhuman, chaotic, illusory humanism—Nietzche's horrifying eternal recurrence.

Altizer's new, religious world-vision arises from his disturbed conviction that a life of authentic Christian faith is no longer possible in the Church of traditional theology. The traditional message is irrelevant to the tenor of the times and the thinking of contemporary man. Yet since the Christian Church insists on teaching traditional theology without regard to its lack of impact on current thought, it must be accused of engaging in a form of irrational faithlessness. It is scarcely surprising, therefore, that the reaction to this traditional stubbornness has been a revolt against the Chruch, its dogmas and morals. At first the revolt took the form of indifference to the traditional teachings and practices of the Church. Today an aggressive assertion that God and the Christian era are dead and buried has succeeded to that indifference. Altizer testifies to this change thus:

> If there is one clear portal to the twentieth century, it is a passage through the death of God, the collapse of any meaning or reality lying beyond the newly discovered radical immanence of modern man, an immanence dissolving even the memory or the shadow of transcendence.[4]

2. Thomas W. Ogletree, *The Death of God Controversey*, Abingdon Press (New York: 1966), p. 75.

3. William Hamilton and Thomas J. J. Altizer, *Radical Theology And The Death Of God* (New York: The Bobbs—Merrill Co. Inc., 1966). pp. 31–32.

4. Thomas J. J. Altizer, *The Gosple of Christian Atheism*, (Philadelphia: Westminster Press, 1966), p. 22.

Out of this cultural situation which links the death of God with the demise of faith in transcendence, Altizer moves to confront the new theological situation. He is convinced that both these deaths ought to be the principal themes of the new Christian theology. Now it is his conviction that the Christian situation will be bettered only from a perspective on the Gospel message which arises and is pursued from outside Christianity. Altizer, therefore, proposes to study the Christian faith through its comparison with other world religions. Only through a comparative religion course of study will Christian faith be rediscovered and reinvigorated. The darkness and chaos of our era have amply demonstrated that the God of traditional transcendence and the Christ of the Gospels are both dead. Modern man will just have to open his eyes, come to terms with the harsh reality of the day and seek both God and Christ only in the events happening in the world of today. This means, of course, the heart-rending break with thousands of years of traditional faith; it demands self-severance from the Church as the Mystical Body of Christ and people of God; it calls for a break with the Biblical idea of divine authority. All this entails the danger of plunging oneself into theological nihilism, the madness of atheism and captivity to collectivized tyranny. Altizer foresees and fears these dangers. But he insists that true faith is always tested through the risks it undergoes. Moreover, the revival of true religious consciousness can only be achieved from the tomb of the dead God. For when the door of a transcendent religious vision is slammed shut, horizons to secularized religious consciousness dawn with infinite expansiveness. Out of the ashes of religious traditionalism, religious secularism will arise, Religious secularism is the womb that will give birth to a new contemporary community of revived Christian faith.

Altizer has thus committed himself to an impossible task. He intends to found a secularized Christianity by severing his roots from Scripture, Christian tradition, the Primitive Church, the Church of contemporary witnessing and from all traditional credal and sacramental professions of faith. How does Altizer propose to perform this impossible task? He proposes to break all ancient molds and to dissolve all ancient Christian institutions. For example, he announced the coming of a new community of faith in which a new Word will arise. In it the isolation and segregation imposed by the traditional Church will be overcome. The canon of revelation, considered as completed and closed by the traditional Church, will be reopened to reveal the new, secular revelations contained in the Gospel which are meaningful for modern times. Moreover, the narrow human walls of the Church, restricted as they are to the baptized, will be knocked down in order to admit and embrace as a true Christian any person, baptized or not, who lives an authentic human existence. Holy Scripture will be reinterpreted to make clear the secular significance of Revelation. The creation of this daring new vision of Christian faith will achieve the triumph of secularism over traditionalism, that is, the triumph of man over decadent Christianity.

The Death of God: A Suicide

According to Altizer, Nietzsche was wrong on one very important point. Man has not killed God, heroic as that deed might have been. God died by His own hand. The death was an act, or rather a process, of divine suicide. While comparing Oriental Mysticism with Biblical Eschatology, Altizer found that the fundamental idea of Hinduism, Buddhism, Christianity, indeed of all religions, centered on the ultimate identity of the Nothing and the All. Religion is merely the dialectic between these two, breaking forth into the synthesis of advancing faith. True, the movements of the Oriental and the Christian religious consciousnesses travel in diametrically opposite directions. For Oriental Mysticism is a radical rejection of the world whose actualities are seen as illusory, substanceless shadows. Among the Orientals "the fallen" are those living immersed in the concrete. The sacred are those who recover the ultimate, unfallen Totality of Being—the eternal, quiet, inactive Totality of all being. In comparison with the kaleidoscopic variety and concreteness of the world's actualities, the Totality of Being must be called Nothingness, the primordial Non-Being. And paradoxically this Non-Being, this Oriental ultimate Reality, can be spiritually recovered only by men who sever themselves from the transitory realities of this concrete world and lose themselves in the eternal, peaceful, anonymity of the Totality of Nothingness. Thus Oriental mystics move up from immanence in the real world, out of concrete consciousness, away from thought, volition, sensation, back from the achievement of personality toward the transcendent dissolution of their very persons into the Totality of the Supreme Non-Being. And this self-annihilation is accomplished in a dialectical manner, i.e., through an affirmation of the world that negates and radically transforms it. The profane, its separateness, its individuality, its consciousness are all annulled in order to affirm the Totality of the Sacred Non-Being. It is only through such a dialectic that the essential identity of the profane world with the Sacred Totality is disclosed. Only thus does negation achieve affirmation. By negating the profane world the Oriental Mystic plunges into the self-annihilating sea of the Sacred.

Continuing his speculative exploration into the nature of the dialectic between the All and the Nothing as this is revealed in Christianity, Altizer finds that the Incarnation, the central event of Christian faith, propels man in a direction diametrically opposed to that of Oriental Mysticism. Here the drama of history consists in the movement of the supreme All downward. The Sacred, the Transcendent descends into the profane, the concrete, the transitory. Here the Creator is seeking his creatures; in Oriental Mysticism the creatures are seeking their Supreme All. The advent of the Divine Word orients man toward process, history, change, activity, eschatological destiny. Here consciousness is heightened, intensified and the drama of personal commitment and decision is of tragic importance. Here there is no movement backward, no escape to a peaceful, prior Reality untainted by time. The Incarnation is the realization of the highest intensity and intimacy of participation in the adventure of faith, of salvation, of humanization. Christians, thus, do not accept the Oriental vision of retirement into quietism and self-annihilation. Their Supreme Being is not a static, world-rejecting ultimate Reality. Christians rather affirm the advent of the Sacred Reality into time, into human flesh. Even at this moment this Sacred Being is in the process of achieving His own and His fellow men's sacred destiny in history. This Sacred Reality is God as revealed in Jesus Christ, the Incarnate Word.

As might have been surmised by this time, the principle that pervades and moves the Altizian theory of religion as a world process is expressed as the "coincidence of opposites" *(coincidentia oppositorum)*. Micea Eliade, in his studies of ancient religions, impressed Altizer with the working of this principle at the heart of all religions. It demonstrated so well the dialectical conflict between the sacred and the profane. Thus for Altizer the latest and most perfect synthesis of this principle is the following: The sacred will be recovered in this broken world, where God has died by His own hand, only through the welcoming and full application to all strata of human and cosmic existence of the process of secularization in the modern world. Therefore, the full meaning of the dialectic is realized when the opposition between the sacred and the profane is resolved in the "coincidence of the opposites." In Christianity the ultimate between the two is achieved in the death of God, when God annihilated His transcendence and Himself through His incarnation, immersion in time and the historical, immanent rejection of his total Otherness. In a generous act of self-sacrificing love in behalf of His creatures, God has gladly destroyed His transcendent, divine nature, plunging into secular, profane flesh. Spirit has moved into flesh and flesh into spirit. Both spirit and flesh are now immanently transfigured in a new unity, the unity of "Word and History." Whereas formerly Altizer saw the death of God as a cultural fact, now he sees it as a perfectly willed and planned process of the formerly transcendent God. Through the Incarnation of His Word and His Word's determined choice of His own death on the Cross, God has annihilated Himself. What has finally happened today is that cultural, social and philosophical, but above all, theological atheists have come to realize that the divine suicidal event was initiated at the moment of the Incarnation. Moreover, contrary to traditional Christianity's teaching, there is no return through resurrection from this death of transcendence. And traditional Christianity's attempts to celebrate a resurrectional and ascensional recovery of transcendence are but a self-deception of enormously cruel proportions foredoomed to lead men to despair and social suicide.

Altizer expands and completes his theory of the secular world process as the triumph of immanence over transcendence, profaneness over sacredness, man over God by an appeal to three men whom he accepts as authentic prophets of

that secular Christianity which has displaced forever ecclesiastical Christianity. His radical Christian heroes are
Blake, Hegel and Nietzsche. Hegel contributed to the Altizian
vision the goal of the union of spirit and flesh and the dialectical method for achieving this union. Hegel's negations succeed
in accomplishing the death of God, the incarnation of Spirit
and the identification of God with Jesus the man. It is in the
dialectic of contradiction that the Trinity and transcendence
are annihilated. In this dialectic divinity descends to Jesus and
through Jesus to humanity. Man now has a new and final
rebirth of the Christian Word. The new Word is the ever recurring reality of further Incarnations which continually negate
previous manifestations of the Word in order that the Word
may become flesh anew in each new secular event. William
Blake, the English mystical poet, confirms the Hegelian-
Altizian vision of Christianity. To the "kenotic" Christology
which emphasizes the emptying of divinity process accomplished in Jesus, Blake adds the identification of the now total
immanent God with Christ. "God *is* Jesus." God is now so fully
poured out into creatures that he no longer exists as the Other,
the Person, the All. This divine self-annihilation is an act of
supreme love and grace. Christians alone can realize the enormity of this self-oblation of God on behalf of His creation. The
God who was formerly transcendent and wholly Other has now
been transformed into the forward movement immanent in the
process of history. God has now become Nietzsche's Nay-saying
to the supernatural world and Yea-saying to the human world.
Through the Hegelian dialectic, the Blakian identification of
divine and human, the Nietzschean revolt against the Divine
Transcendence and choice of the human, Altizer announces the
death of God and the liberation of the profane cosmos from the
jealous God of Judaism and the rigorous God of Christian predestinationism. Such a God of traditional Christianity can only
be viewed today by modern man as a Satan who would restrict
the creative activity of all men or as an Anti-Christ who, unlike
Jesus who liberates man, would impose on mankind the enslavement of dread, chaos and death.

Following through with the logic of a "kenotic"—divinity-
emptying—Christology, Altizer develops a revolutionary interpretation of Christ's presence in the contemporary world.

Christian faith can no longer be bound to the events of the past. For all previous manifestations of Christ have been negated, indeed, surpassed in the dialectical process of the immanent secularization and profanization through the absorption of the divine in the world. Today Jesus Christ is no longer to be adhered to as the Divine Word of God. For God is now dead and no longer has a Word. Today Jesus Christ meets each man in the events of on-going history. Jesus Christ, his own ever present Word, has negated all former expressions of faith in Himself. As ever present in a forward-moving process, Jesus Christ has moved history and mankind through the narrows of the death of God and has opened up the vast sea of secularization to their faith. Thus today Christian faith consists primarily in the celebration of the death of God. Both Nietzsche and Blake saw Jesus as the abolition of all distance between God and man. Blake spoke of Jesus as the great affirmer of life who by his very death created a universal family of Man, a community of love and brotherhood. Thus Jesus is no longer the Son of God of traditional Christianity. He is the center of the universal family of man. Any modern appreciation of the presence of Jesus in history must now be a humanity-centered vision of a man in whom there was no resentment, no denial of the world, no "alien" God. Altizer writes on this point:

> True, our history has progressively but decisively dissolved every sign and image of the Christ who was once present in the Church. Yet the name of Jesus can continue to embody the innermost reality of faith if it can make concretely present the total union of God and man, even if that union should finally obliterate the God of a former faith. As the God who *is* Jesus becomes ever more deeply incarnate in the body of humanity, he loses every semblance of his former visage, until he appears wherever there is energy and life.[5]

But in order to emphasize and make permanent Christ's ongoing "process-presences" in the world, Altizer had recourse to the abhorrent Nietzschean idea of the Eternal Recurrence. This doctrine demands the eternal repetition of all events in an endless cycle of existence and non-existence, of life, death,

5. *Ibid.,* pp. 74–75.

resurrection—a revolving, monotonous wheel of fate which goes in no direction, has no meaning and reduces cosmic and vital processes to sheer chaotic flux. In the face of this circle of absurdity and captivity the reality of Eternal Recurrence drives man to an agonized "Nay-saying" to life and the world. On the other hand, man's "Yea-saying" is for flight into the oblivion of the primordial Totality. But Nietzsche challenges man to do the very opposite and heroic deed to the natural deed he would perform. Man will only truly affirm his love for life when he says "Yes!" to the horrors of Eternal Recurrence, when he *wills* Eternal Recurrence, when he calls it back with the words: "This is how it was! This is how I want it forever!" Thus the Nietzschean man wills each moment in all its concreteness, especially the present moment, for only thus can he prove his love for life. Joy in the Eternal Recurrence is the proof that man accepts life with all its ambiguities, tragedies and absurdities. Thus those alone are truly redeemed who can dance, like Zarathustra, in joy over the Eternal Recurrence.

Altizer accepts Nietzsche's challenge and interprets his saying, "Being begins in every Now," as a truth which manifests that the center of life is not elsewhere, not in the past, not in the future, not in certain events of the Old and New Testaments, but everywhere and "eternity" is in every Now. Thus in meeting the on-going Christ in each present moment man enters into eternal life. Each present secular moment and event reveals the sacred at the heart of the profane. Time, process and space transform present moments into the plentitude of the sacred. Altizer's new profession of faith becomes, "I believe in Christ present in this moment as the center of life here and now and nowhere else. Because of this belief I love the world, I embrace its tragedy, its absurdity as an epiphany of the body of Christ."[6]

Christian faith today believes, therefore, that God is dead, that he has been absorbed into the fullness of the life-process of the world. The true Christian, the one living his faith according to Altizer, is now identified with the true Nietzschean, with Zarathustra. For both are forever pledging themselves in a "Yea-saying" to life, the world and Eternal Recurrence as they meet the Jesus immanent in the presently occurring events.

6. *Ibid.*, pp. 155–156.

Every moment the new Christian embraces each new epiphany of the immanent Christ. The true Christian is wedded to the flux of existence; this process is his destiny, his joy, his reward. The true Christian professes his faith in Jesus Christ, the Word-process who is continually negating his past and creating new, even contradictory, expressions of himself. Here, then, is the religion of Altizer. It is a religion which totally rejects traditional Christianity. It is a religion with a total adherence and allegiance to the cult of newness. Let us now attempt to evaluate it in the light of objective historical thought and of revelation.

Assessment of Altizian Atheism

Altizer's Christian atheism is sometimes described as an *original* form of Christian faith. This new faith aims at revealing a third mission in the presence of God—or to be more exact, an endlessly new coming of Christ in a world completely desacralized. The new presence of the Christ-Spirit is a process given essentially in each instant, in *our* present, *our* time, *our* existence. Christian faith, therefore, no longer consists in adherence to Divine Persons but in apprehensions of the Divine Process. In a moment we will assess this new faith's claim to originality. For the present, however, we can assert that many of the emphases of Altizian atheism needed reinvestigation and restatement. Among them there is the Altizian challenge for the concrete expression of an authentic Christian faith committed to the service of contemporary man. Another contribution is the insight that would pursue the study of the way in which different cultures mold and develop the message of revelation. Of special significance for modern times is Altizer's emphasis on investigating the social nature of the Incarnation. In Gabriel Marcel the renewal of the study of the mystery of the Incarnation had, long before Altizer, led to an inspiring and fruitful development of a philosophy of communion and a theology of community. Through his deep reflections on the mystery of the Incarnation, Marcel has plumbed the heart of the sacred in man and the world in a far more inspiring way than has Altizer. One wonders if a reading of Marcel might not have spared Altizer the horrible mistake of confusing the sacred

with Nietzsche's Eternal Recurrence. Another plus in Altizer's
radical theology is his rejection of the false, Calvinist notion of
God as the totally "alien" Other, unconcerned about the development of man and his world, who from all eternity predes-
tines souls to hell or heaven, not according to the just deserts
of their morally free conduct but according to divine whim.
Altizer is to be praised, too, for reaffirming in a novel but arrest-
ing way a Christian truth emphasized by St. Paul: "Now is the
acceptable time; now is the time of salvation; today if you hear
his voice, harden not your hearts." The insight that salvific
faith transcends specific times, places, circumstances and endures forever in an adherence to God through Christ is a much-
needed modern reaffirmation of God's ardent desire to save all
men. True, Altizer erroneously formulates this truth, destroying the whole, vigorous continuity of the enduring social life of
the faith in the human family which is reborn and consecrated
to the family of God through Baptism and Holy Communion.
There is a coldness to sacraments in Altizian atheism. Despite
these few Christian elements, Altizer's religion is emptied of
grace.

On a balanced review, therefore, of the whole system, Altizer's Christian atheism is seen to be anything but original. It
is an eclectic theological patchwork drawn from a variety of
incoherent systems and presented as the new theology for our
age. It is gnosticism dressed in modern clothing. Many of its
elements can be traced back to the times of the early Fathers
of the Church. Altizer's mystical approach is really his gnosti-
cal approach to God. St. John the Evangelist was already refuting this gnosticism in his Gospel. Gnosticism also originally
claimed to be modern, authentic Christianity. It maintained
that the teachings of the Gospel had to be interpreted and ac-
comodated to the ideas sacred and acceptable to the Graeco-
Roman religious consciousness. For Philo, Jesus was the
demi-urge, not God. He was the Spirit-Word who captured the
intellectual elite through the infusion of a secret, loftier learning than that possessed by ordinary Christians. Thus belief in
this creaturely semi-God was not to be equated with the crass
belief of primitive Christians in the Divinity of Jesus, the Son
of God. The Word was God's cosmic emanation, a creaturely
go-between with a mission to the truly elite among men. In his

system Altizer performs a marriage between the Gnostic "ae-ons" and the process of historical evolution. This gives his Christ-Process-Spirit an up-to-date, fashionable appeal to the nouveau elite. Yet fundamentally, whether it is Hegel's dialec-tically evolving Spirit, or Altizer's immanently dying God, the Divine remains a Sacred Reality emptying itself as it moves through the cosmos and incarnates itself deeper and deeper in matter and flesh. As for the Gnostics, so also Altizian salvation consists in liberation from ignorance, chance, petrification and in insertion into the stream of dynamic change and process through the secret knowledge available to the enlightened. Gnostics always break clean from Christian tradition; they are apostates from orthodoxy; their faith is a philosophy. Gnostics have no theological roots. Together with the Gnostics of old Altizer cuts himself off from the theological traditions and wit-nessing to the true faith, in order to construct an eclectic theo-logical mélange of his own.

In emptying the Incarnation of its Tri-Personal significance and reducing it to a mere process, Altizer destroys the human personal relationship of faith, hope and love in the Divine Per-sons who remain eternally God after the Incarnation of the Son through whom they have now become God "who has pitched his tent among men in order to live with men and save them." Men cannot profess faith, hope or love in a process, for it is the nature of a process, depersonalized as it is, to invade and subju-gate its victims. The Incarnation is an I-Thou, God-Man, God-Me intimate event of love. "He loved me and delivered himself up for me," exclaimed St. Paul in a bewildering cry of gratitude to the Son of God. Moreover, the Incarnation is an event of history that endures throughout time, not merely discontinu-ously at each instant. St. Paul celebrates the constancy and permanence of the Christ of history, "Jesus Christ yesterday, today and the same forever." Today's presence of Christ in time, in His Church, in the souls of men does not empty either past history or the on-going process of the present or the es-chatological approach of the future of the meaning of the mes-sage He brought and taught in the days of His earthly existence. The Son of God who had come is the same who is present until the consummation of the world and the same who is to come again in power and glory at the end of time. Altizer's obsession to destroy the meaning of the past history of salvation seems to arise from a blind cult of modernity. He forgets that to be human means to be endowed essentially with memory. "As often as you do this," said Christ to his Apostles at the last supper, "you will do it in memory of me." Altizer fails to see that love means to live in and with the memories of the beloved. Moreover, to be strong in faith and hope means to live with adherence to the Person in whom we have placed our faith and hope, even though the visible absence of the beloved might be the occasion for our doubting or despairing in His continued existence and love for us. In times of trial and temptation, loss of memory can lead to loss of faith, hope and love. Indeed, in such times, loss of memory may lead to loss of selfhood. To attempt to live outside the vital current of a tradition of faith, hope and love is to attempt to live without the essential elements needed for spiritual life; it is to attempt to live a living death. This existence ends by becoming a chaotic wandering among unrelated novelties; it is a rootless, rudderless existence. For after all, the past need not be the enemy of the present nor a threat to the future. The Incarnation of God's Son is the decree of love from all eternity that gives transcendent, sublime meaning to the whole of time, space and history within and beyond the confines of the created universe.

In professing that each new epiphany of Christ negates all previous affirmations of the Word, Altizer is asking men to put their faith in a meaningless succession of passing moments. If the Word-of-the-present-moment is entirely different from the Word-of-the-past-moment and will be followed the next instant by another totally different Word, then both the identity of the Word and the identity of the believer are destroyed in the impossibility of establishing a conscious, meaningful, permanent relationship between them. The future is destroyed; there is no hope possible for the establishment of the Kingdom of God. A succession of moments in energy and life adds up to epiphanies of No One, Nobody and Nonsense. It boggles the human intellect and nauseates the human heart to require men to put their faith and love in meaningless exuberant energy and life, both of which, as blind forces, can and have already, become absolutes for madmen who have used and adored them as idols. Nietzsche's Will for Power is the exact opposite of Christ's Will for Grace. The former destroys meaning, love, joy, communion and makes divine salvation impossible, for it absolutizes the lust for a Satanic domination of mankind. Nietzsche's Will for Power leads man onto the road of metaphysical nihilism and dumps him into the pit of moral madness. On the other hand, Christ's Will for Grace embraces fallen man, restores his identity, sanctifies and endows him with a plentitude of intelligence and liberty in a process that divinizes his humanity and leads him into the ecstasy of a beatific, Trinitarian communion. Here is an infinitely higher life, a divine energy that achieves the fullness of meaning, beatific inter-communion of the divine-human families.

In his interpretation of the Scriptures Altizer is guilty of a glaring oversight. He never adverts to the convenants of love and fidelity which God has made with man. Both to His Chosen People of the Old Israel and to His Son's Christian People of the New Jerusalem God pledges His love and fidelity. And He never fails them, though they often are unfaithful to Him. "If we are faithless, he remains faithful, for he cannot disown himself." Therefore, by negating divine transcendence and imprisoning God in an on-going historical process from which He is no longer distinguishable, Altizer not only celebrates the death of God but also the impossibility of God's remaining faithful to His people through the convenants He swore to keep with them. In Altizer's religion the sacred is no longer possible, for the All-Holy One is annihilated. And Altizer wants it this way, for he attacks Christian attempts to regain transcendence and the Sacred through the Resurrection and Ascension of Christ to the Father as myths of irresponsible, infantile, primitive men. The truth of the matter is, of course, that the very nature of transcendence consists in God's freedom and power to be present wherever He wills to work without ever being confined to that work or place or time. Indeed, even man shares this divine gift of transcendence to some degree, for no matter how limited his nature, his position, his performance, nevertheless, as a free and intelligent image of God, man can always aspire to go up higher, to perform better, to surpass, through spiritual achievements, the limitations of flesh, time and circumstances. Man's reach for the moon and his plunge to the floor of the oceans are but physical expressions of his metaphysical hunger to embrace the heart of reality in his embrace of the Divinity. The Incarnation of the Son of God has raised man's metaphysical hunger for transcendence to the power of divine infinity.

Perhaps the most despairing aspect of Altizer's rejection of man's divine-human adventure in transcendence is his abject acceptance of Nietzsche's Eternal Recurrence. Acceptance of the *status quo* exactly as it is and forever implies that the man of Christian atheism has no ideals for the service and betterment of his fellow man. With regard to programs for removing injustices, alleviating tragedies, sanctifying and ennobling society, he is forever uninterested and unemployed. His new faith demands that he say Yes to all as it is. It is the will of the fates that things be so. And he has made the will of Eternal Recurrence his own will. In this position of spiritual prostration before Eternal Recurrence, the whole glorious Christian vision and mission for the ethical and sacramental transformation of man in Christ is extinguished and forgotten forever.

When he reviews the journey taken by his radical theology, Altizer is honest in admitting that he has traveled a long distance away from traditional Christianity. He admits he has abandoned the Church as the Church continues to understand herself, the prolongation of the Incarnate Son of God in history until the end of time. He no longer sees the Church as Christ represented her in His appearance to St. Paul on the road to Damascus: "Saul, Saul, why are you persecuting me?" And Paul said, "Who art thou, Lord?" And he said, "I am Jesus, whom you are persecuting." Having destroyed the personal identity of Jesus and the social identity of the Church for the sake of his up-to-date process-Word and process-believer, Altizer gladly admits his apostasy from the continuity of the Mystical Body of Christ. But he insists that this apostasy to his new perspectives of faith is a form of fidelity to the new and true meaning of the Gospel message for modern man. On closer analysis, we find that we have an interesting dilemma in Altizer's profession of a new faith. On the one hand, Altizer upraided traditional Christianity for being irrelevant to modern man because it continually regressed to a pre-incarnate form of the Word, to a Transcendent God, to a dualism of flesh and spirit, profane and sacred, natural and supernatural. Altizer today heralds the good news that his Christian atheism has liberated man from these heremetically sealed dogmatic dualisms through the deaths of God, transcendence and a restrictive, particularized Church. Now if regression is a grevious theological fault, how is it that Altizer invites the modern Christian to regress to Gnostic mysticism and Hegelian idealism and to put his faith in these old, discarded dogmatic systems? How is it that Altizer finds pre-Christian monism more Christian than Christian dualism? One wonders whether, in the last analysis, Altizer's feverish theology announcing, "God is dead" differs significantly from Plutarch's terrible cry, "Great Pan is dead!" Have they not both slain a mystic false God? A man-made God?

CHAPTER XVII

Hamilton:
Orestean Assassin of God

WILLIAM HAMILTON GLORIES IN THE TITLE OF "NEW radical Protestant theologian." As such he is defiant in his revolt against his early Christian faith and training, both of which he rejects as having been hopelessly out-of-date and ill-suited to prepare him for the thrilling contemporary world. In the beginning, as a divinity student at Union Theological Seminary, New York, Hamilton was a neo-orthodox, Barthian Christian. Indeed, in his first book, *The New Essence Of Christianity,* published in 1961, Hamilton had not yet become a radical theologian. In that work Hamilton clearly upholds the existence of God and affirms the Resurrection of Jesus "as an ordinary event," even though he cautiously relegates this affirmation to a footnote.[1]

In an article published in *The Christian Scholar* in 1963 and entitled "Daring to be the Enemy of God," Hamilton tried hard

1. William Hamilton, *The New Essence Of Christianity* (New York: Association Press, 1961), p. 55.

to rescue Mozart's Don Giovanni for heaven by applying Kierkegaard's dialectic of leaps from aesthetic through ethical to religious maturity. In the eyes of Hamilton Don Giovanni seemed to typify the ambiguous state of current Protestant theologians, neither damned nor saved, but detained permanently in limbo. As for himself, Hamilton was thoroughly dissatisfied with the state of theology and refused to be detained anywhere. He was on an urgent quest "to see if there is anybody out there."[2] In an essay, which proved to be largely biographical, "Thursday's Child," Hamilton came to some startling conclusions about the condition of contemporary theologians and gave an even more amazing exhortation as to what Christians should do about this situation.

> ... The theologian today and tomorrow is a man without faith, without hope, with only the present, with only love to guide him. I propose that we should not only acknowledge, but will this faithlessness. What does it mean to say that the theologian in America is a man without faith? Is he a man without God? ... He has his doctrine of God, several of them no doubt, and all correct ... He really doesn't believe in God, or that there is a God, or that God exists. . . Something has happened. At the center of his thoughts and meditations is a void, a disappearance, an absence... Does the theologian go to church? The answer is "no." He may, in the past, have concealed this "no" from himself by escaping into church work, speaking to church groups, preaching at church or college, slaking his thirst for worship and word in more protected communities. But now he is facing up to this banal answer to the banal question, and he wills to say "no" openly.[3]

In 1965 in an interview with Ved Mehta, Hamilton revealed his rapid development from neo-orthodox to radical theologian. "I am beginning to feel," he said, "that the time has come for me to put up or shut up, for me to be an in or an out."[4] But it was in 1966 that Hamilton finally decided to become a "hard" radical theologian, heralding the literal death of God and iden-

---

2. William Hamilton, "The Shape of a Radical Theology," *Christian Century,* LXXXII, October 6, 1965, p. 1220.

3. Thomas J. J. Altizer and William Hamilton, *op. cit.,* pp. 87–88.

4. Ved Mehta, *The New Theologian,* (New York: Harper and Row, 1966). Also in *The New Yorker,* November 13, 20, 27, 1965.

tifying himself with a *new radical theology* as the only contemporary movement capable of saving man from neo-
orthodoxy's "alienation" by plunging him into an "up-to-date
theology of social involvement."

Hamilton's charges against Barthian neo-orthodoxy were
many and serious. The Barthian God is utterly beyond the grasp
of human reason, totally transcendent in all aspects. This dire
God rules a world of tragedy and existential pessimism. He is
the God of that broken-down "good old world of middle-of-the-
road ecumenical neo-orthodoxy." To be sure, neo-orthodoxy
started out well, as a revolt against liberal theology's arrogant
assurance that God could be kept in its own coterie of conformism. Neo-orthodoxy, before and after the World War II years,
brought visionary man back to the harsh realities of earth and
heaven. It preached once again the God of moral holiness who
punishes wickedness and shows Himself in the events of history as the remunerator of the good and the avenger of the
wicked. For this God of holiness, truth and consequences went
together; there was no escape from moral wickedness. Thus
neo-orthodoxy reminded man that his greatest tragedy was to
choose to become God's enemy through choice of sin. Neo-
orthodoxy called for absolute, blind faith in God for the power
to achieve righteousness. Liberal self-reliance was a myth exploded by the horrors of two World Wars. Nevertheless, in
Hamilton's eyes, neo-orthodoxy, through constant protest
against the modern world, hardened into a narrow, pessimistic
theology. It despaired of any good from the world, from science,
from technology or from natural man. It thus fell hopelessly
behind the times. Hamilton accused neo-orthodoxy of creating
"men skilled in avoiding unprofitable" commitments, careful
about risks, very wise in seeing how not to make fools of themselves."[5] In a word, neo-orthodoxy had become the new complacent, established religion and suffered from the lack of vision
and spiritual sclerosis of any establishment. Its selfish pessimism had no appeal for men in a world where the new battle
cry that moved millions was "social revolution," no longer
"spiritual alienation." And Hamilton belonged to the new generation; he could no longer tolerate the restrictive, out-of-date
pessimism of neo-orthodoxy. By temperament an optimist,

5. Thomas J. J. Altizer and William Hamilton, *op. cit.*, p. 158.

Hamilton was enthusiastic about all things modern, secular and human. Hamilton says "yes" to a world full of new forms of technology, of the mass media, of great scientific projects like space conquests and lunar landings. His new theology exudes technological optimism; it is totally involved in all that happens, accepts change instantaneously, trusts the world, the future and drives for a world beyond culture, beyond civilization, beyond tragedy.

In his break with Barthianism and in his thrilling vision of the future, Hamilton was aided by his encounter with Bonhoeffer. He enthusiastically accepted Bonhoeffer's insights about the role of God, religion and the Church in relationship to man's noble mission to humanize the world. With Bonhoeffer he rejected a traditional God who comes to man as his needs-fulfiller or problem-solver. Augustine was wrong. Men's hearts are not necessarily restless until they rest in such a God. The empirical fact is that modern theologians have not been able to find or locate any religious *a priori,* or part of self or part of human experience that needs God. "There is no God-shaped blank within man."[6] Moreover, the biblical God abandoned man even as man clung desperately to Him on the precipice of faith or despair. What is more, however, is that in today's world, which moves rapidly from the sacred to the secular, from the cloister to the world, God is superfluous; He is simply not needed. "My Protestant has no God, has no faith in God, and affirms both the death of God and the death of all forms of theism. Even so he is not primarily a man of negation, for if there is a movement away from God and religion, there is a more important movement into, for, toward the world, worldly life and the neighbor as the bearer of the worldly Jesus."[7] God is thus, at best, demoted to being merely one of the possible alternatives in the radically pluralistic, cultural milieu of contemporary man.

Once again reflecting Bonhoeffer, Hamilton rejects the traditional God because modern man has come of age and no longer needs Him. Modern man can now put his trust in the world as the fulfiller of his needs, the solver of his problems. Is there any meaning possible in God? asks Hamilton. Perhaps we can find

6. *Ibid.,* p. 40.
7. *Ibid.,* p. 37.

a meaning by taking the non-discarded part of a famous distinction made by St. Augustine. That distinction is between the useful and joyful aspects of a being, its *uti* and *frui*. We have rejected the God who is there to be used. That God is dead. Yet almost nostalgically Hamilton opts for the God whom perhaps one may someday enjoy. He writes:

> If God is not needed, if it is to the world and not to God that we repair for our needs and problems, then perhaps we may come to see that He is to be enjoyed and delighted in ... Our waiting for God, our godlessness, is partly a search for a language and style by which we might be enabled to stand before Him once again, delighting in His presence.[8]

At the beginning of his career as a theologian while he was under the powerful influence of Albert Camus, the problem that most tried Hamilton's faith in the existence of God was the problem of suffering, not the thrilling call of a scientific age. Once he became a radical theologian, Hamilton rejected the Christian God for being impotent to prevent the suffering of innocent children. Appeals to reasons of faith which see God drawing higher good out of physical evil no longer ring true to modern man who wants honest, forthright answers. The suffering of the innocent which revealed the feebleness of God led Hamilton to observe that man cannot live as a Christian for long without coming eventually to acknowledge the loss of God.

Another area of Hamilton's theological vision which Bonhoeffer influenced most drastically is his view of the nature and role of the Christian Church in the religious life of man. Like Bonhoeffer, Hamilton frankly admits that he is alienated from the Church. Indeed, if he does not completely despair of any good coming from the Christian Church, he scarcely hopes for any help at all from it. He examines the Church under three viewpoints, rejects the first two and accepts the third, which so dilutes the Christian Church that she is no longer recognizable as the community founded in Christ. Looked at traditionally as the community of God's people, endowed with the marks of oneness, holiness, catholicity and apostolicity, Hamilton finds this Church useful as a participator in ecumenical dialogue. Yet he negates even this small usefulness of the Church when,

8. *Ibid.*, p. 41.

commenting on the breakdown of organized religion in American life, he says that we are well beyond the time when ecumenical dialogues or denominational merges can be expected to arrest this breakdown. Secondly, the Church can be viewed as being found wherever the Word of God is preached and the sacraments are administered. Hamilton finds this communal body very beneficial to his calling as a teacher of theology. But since religion is no longer necessary for a mankind moving from the cloister and temple to the world, so also there is no longer any need for a Church peddling a full-blown, useless theology. Finally, the only notion of the Church which Hamilton finds religiously significant and acceptable is the one which holds that the Church is found wherever Christ is being formed among men in the world, even if there are no sacramental ties in this formation.

As Ogletree shrewdly observes, "For Hamilton . . . the movement from the Church to the world has usually meant a movement 'out of the Church.' "[9] Hamilton himself says that "the theologian of today and tomorrow is neither despairing nor hopeful about the Church. He is simply not interested. He no longer has the energy or the concern to answer ecclesiastical questions about what the Church must do to revitalize itself."[10] Hamilton has become a theologian of the world, isolated from every confessional denomination; he is a Christian according to his own standards of what a Christian should be in the contemporary world—one who works in the world through a community of concerned citizens, not for God or religion or eternal purposes, but for civil rights causes, in wars against poverty, crusades against war and in other such purely humanitarian movements.

Though he would detach the individual Christian from membership in any particularized Church, Hamilton does so for noble and positive reasons. It is true that Hamilton represents the modern Godless Christian as waiting, somewhat passively, in silence and prayer, for the possible advent of the God in whom one can rejoice, even if one cannot have faith or hope in Him. Nevertheless, this prayerful waiting is not to be totally

9. Thomas W. Ogletree, *The Death Of God Controversy* (New York: Abingdon Press, 1966), p. 36.

10. Thomas J. J. Altizer and William Hamilton, *Radical Theology And The Death Of God,* p. 88.

passive. Meantime there is positive work to be accomplished. The Godless Christian must achieve new discipleship with Jesus. This is accomplished when the religionless, Godless Christian binds himself to Jesus, not as to an object or ground of faith, nor as though adhering to a person, but as standing in a place, the place of Jesus. This new Christian who has lost faith and hope, nevertheless, is called upon to maintain love by imitating the example of Jesus Christ. Jesus took His place in the world, alongside His neighbor, in favor of His neighbor. The new Christian is in a very real sense the *"lieu-tenant"* of Jesus. Even more precisely, the new Christian has the responsible task of unmasking, of demasking the Jesus who is hidden in all human events that take place in and for the world. He has the noble vocation of becoming Jesus to the world and to his neighbor. This vocation is to be achieved at the heart of concrete existence, for example, in the fight for civil rights, social justice, the alleviation of human misery and all such humane endeavors.

For the theologian who courageously takes up the tasks of this new discipleship with Jesus, the reward is great. He becomes a man of maturity. He grows up from the fearful, hesitant indecision of the traditionally cramped Christian to the fearless, decisive, clear man of secular, optimistic action. He moves beyond the anguished quest for selfish salvation to the heroic duties of humanizing a world. Using literary heroes to illustrate this graduation from grimness to greatness, Hamilton says that the new Christian theologian advances from an Oedipus to an Orestes, from a Hamlet to a Prospero stature. Unfortunately, in laboring to find secular saints in the classic world upon whom he could model his own creation, the godless theologian, Hamilton deformed the god-fearing giants of Sophocles, Aeschylus and Shakespeare out of all harmony with the heroic originals of these master-dramatists. With this in mind, the reader should view the following Orestean theology as a zealous Hamiltonian attempt to justify the founding of a society of godless, churchless theologians.

Oedipus and Hamlet are both torn with inner anguish over the identity of their fathers, their filial relationship to authority and their duty to avenge crimes committed against them. Oedipus, driven by the fates, unknowingly kills his father;

Hamlet kills his father's assassin. But both these figures are solitary, sin-obsessed, God-cringing theological weaklings. They are types which represent the demeaning posturings of traditional Christians with their excessive fear of sin, wailings before God and beggings for reconciliation. The time has come for an end to such theological solitariness and bowing and scraping before a traditionally tyrant God and traditionally authoritarian Church. The literary figures whose example can lead the new theologians out of the morass of traditional servitude are Orestes and Prospero. Orestes boldly, even joyously, kills his mother, thus cleansing the world of her infidelity. He has no qualms of conscience, no fear of the gods; he exults in doing his duty. Prospero, for his part, gladly abjures all mysteries, magic and theisms, embracing a religionless, atheistic world. So too the new theologians must joyously destroy their faithless mother, traditional Christianity. With an Orestean theology they must gladly proclaim the death of God, dissolving man's preoccupation with sin, faith, hope, salvation and personal security. For Orestean theology centers on man for man's sake and for the sake of man's world. Moreover, the new theologians, in imitation of Prospero, must dare to let God, the temple, sacraments, dogmas, mystery and the sacred go with joy. They must run back to their dukedoms of this world, assuming the princely duties of fostering their secular cities toward post-Christian, post-cultural, post-civilized milleniums where Jesus is truly found and served in the neighbor.

This is what it means to be a new, Christian theologian, come of age. It means to have gone beyond the quest for personal salvation from sin. It means standing confidently, optimistically "in a world, in the city, with both the needy neighbor and the enemy."[11] The new Christian theologian has inverted the traditional order that existed between God and the neighbor. Hamilton writes: "We move to our neighbor, to the city and to the world out of a sense of the loss of God."[12] No longer is God the center of human history, of prayer, of human endeavor. The man Jesus has moved to the center as focus of these activities and in him, man, our neighbor.

11. *Ibid.*, p. 48.
12. *Ibid.*, p. 48.

Reflections on Hamilton's Radical Atheism

How can we analyze Hamilton's revolt against traditional Christianity and his venture into a theology of radical atheism? First, we must notice that there is a fairly frenetic tonality to Hamilton's style of thought and expression. He began with the theology of a faith difficult to maintain before the onslaughts of a savage yet paradoxically marvelous and scientifically expanding world. On the testimony of his own highly personal, confessional writings, his faith was revealed as tottering, unsteady, obscure and transported into a sort of continual flux. It was a faith of impartial simplicity and progressive gropings, characterized, above all, by refreshing candor and intellectual honesty, as it moved from neo-orthodoxy to neo-atheism. He presented his thought in ardent spurts of personal narration and reflection, leaving behind undeveloped, uncoordinated "theological fragments."

Now thinking in autobiographical fragments does liberate one for the expression of highly subjective theological prepossessions unconnected with any confessional allegiance. Thus a feeling of irresponsibility for what is said is engendered in the theologian of fragments; he is uncommitted to any specific faith or faithful. On the other hand, cut off from a living, coherent tradition of organic orthodoxy, the go-it-alone theologian is bound to fall into the pit of theological reductionism where he usually ends up a hopeless captive of his own contradictory constructions. This is exactly what has happened to Hamilton. His incoherent fragments of theology have frustrated his serious readers and sent off Hamilton himself frantically trying to keep up with the most recent passing theological (sociological?) passions. In this critique three theological theses prominent in Hamilton's recent work will be reviewed: the "death of God," the universal ethical commitment of man and the nature of the new discipleship to Jesus.

One of the greatest snares of personalistic, fragmentary thinking is the penchant for the thinker to declare as universally true what he personally experiences and wants to be true. On the question of the death of God, Hamilton, it seems to me, has fallen into this voluntaristic trap. He has experienced the loss of God as a needs-fulfiller and problem-solver. Many other contemporary Christians have had this same experience. Therefore God is dead in our times for all men. The universal conclusion is scarcely warranted, even after we have granted the premises. The conclusion is thus seen to be an irrational, voluntaristic imposition on objective reality. But perhaps Hamilton was speaking of the death of God only metaphorically? He makes his position very clear on this point.

> We have insisted all along that "death of God" must not be taken as symbolic rhetoric for something else. There really is a sense of not-having, of not-believing, of having lost, not just the idols or the gods of religion, but God himself, and this is an experience that is not peculiar to a neurotic few, nor is it private or inward. Death of God is a public event in our history.[13]

Let us for the sake of further discussion grant Hamilton the truth that God is dead in our history. "What then shall we God-less Christians do?" we ask this radical theologian. And the answer? Simply to wait in reverent prayer and selfless social action for the neighbor, hoping for the return of the dead God who may reappear to be enjoyed. But what religious meaning can there be in waiting prayerfully for the return of a defunct God? Hamilton answers: "Waiting here refers to the whole experience I have called the death of God, including the attack on religion and the search for a means by which God, not needed, may be enjoyed."[14]

The intrinsic metaphysical contradiction and psychological impossibility in Hamilton's exhortatory teaching is fully realized when we recall that this same teacher has already insisted that man is incapable of receiving God with any of his powers. "There is no God-shaped blank within man" means, if it means anything, that there is no capacity for receiving God in man. Moreover, had not Hamilton already taught us that "the breakdown of the religious *a priori* means that there is no way, ontological, cultural or psychological, to locate a part of the self or a part of human experience that needs God"? Now we are exhorted to wait and pray for a God we could never ontologically know or psychologically adhere to even if He returned!

13. *Ibid.*, pp. 46–47.
14. *Ibid.*, p. 46.

And we are also further advised to enjoy this God should He return. But the religious activity of joy in a person is also a metaphysical and psychological impossibility. For joy in someone is the fruit of previous knowledge, faith, hope, love and communion with that someone. Yet the Godless Christian is incapable of knowledge, faith or hope in God. Nevertheless, he is exhorted to rejoice without the absolutely necessary pre-essentials for the experience of joy. How all this is possible is perhaps the deepest mystery of Hamiltonian theological fragmentations. Moreover, although Hamilton has displayed an intense dislike and unwillingness to live with and reflect upon orthodox mysteries, he has cheerily come to terms with such bewildering dogmas of his own creation.

From an insistence on theologizing in isolation from the Bible, tradition and the Church, the last of which St. Paul calls "the pillar and ground of truth," Hamilton trapped himself in "God-talk" that was simply irrational. Again irrevocably cutting himself off from his traditional and historical roots, Hamilton challenges man, as a morally committed individual, to give himself in love and freedom for his neighbor in the center of this world's struggles for civil and social betterment. Salvation is now identified with social, economic and political progress. This is another voluntaristic, immanentist corruption of the transcendent truth expressed in the Gospels by Christ as the Son of God. "This is eternal life, that they may know Thee, Eternal Father, and Jesus Christ whom Thou hast sent." Hamilton advances a Gnostic interpretation of Christian salvation. He replaces eternal life with an historic, future, civil, political and cultural millenarianism. He subsumes moral good and evil, sin and holiness, damnation and salvation under the different contemporary, evolutionary stages of scientific and social progress. In such a Gnostic human commitment to worldly, responsible, developmental progress, there is really no place for original sin, no need for a Redeemer, no call for a Christ on the Cross in a blood-letting redemption. And as for the myths of resurrection, ascension and eternal personal glorification or damnation, these can be rejected as dreams and fears of primitive, infantile man. Today man come of age has no need for the comforts or fears of these theological fantasies. Man needs only himself; he will be saved solely by the goodness of his fellow man.

Once again isolation from living traditional truth had led Hamilton into the land of theological enchantment. His vision of *homo homini salvator,* man the sole savior of his fellow man, is totally unrealistic. Realistic man is fallen man, torn between good and evil, preoccupied with his own selfish interests, competing violently with his fellow man for whatever he can snatch from him. If men rise at times to the heights of self-effacing love and sacrifice, it is because of the presence of some divine, redemptive person whose transcendent love and example of self-donation inspires fallen man to rise beyond self-seeking to the stance of self-giving. The naiveté of Hamilton's optimism concerning man's social goodness to his fellow man as the sole source of human salvation has been exploded recently by the escalation in violence, race riots and bloody revolutions in precisely those countries where more was being done than ever before—legally, economically, educationally and socially—for the advancement of civil rights and overall social betterment. In denying God, Hamilton has effectively denied the divine dimension of man. Hence his ethics of escalating social welfare is incapable of attaining even man's social salvation. For man's social salvation is an important, though inferior part, of his theological salvation. Ethical social advancement, cut off from man's theological and religious advancement, can very easily succeed in merely exacerbating man's terrestrial appetites to the irrational degree where, uncontrolled by his spiritual vision, they erupt in a resentful, ugly, revolutionary state of greedy madness. Hamilton's radical atheism in denying man the food of God, the food of transcendence, drives him into moral madness.

Finally we treat of Hamilton's decision to establish Jesus as the central person in his radical theology. Now Hamilton admits that this Jesus is not divine, not the Son of God; Jesus no longer is the locus of God's revelation. And Hamilton even anticipates the obvious, unavoidable challenge to this position. If Jesus is not God, "Why have you chosen Jesus as the object of your obedience?" He replies that his sole reason is his free decision to do so. Here again we have a sort of Sartrean voluntarism that imposes meaning on reality solely by subjective fiat. Hamilton asserts his option thus:

Jesus is the one to whom I repair, the one before whom I
stand, the one whose way with others is also to be my way
because there is something there, in his words, his life, his
way with others, his death, that I do not find elsewhere. I
am drawn, and I have given my allegiance.[15]

An unconditional loyalty given to one human hero rather
than to another doesn't explain but only states a particular
allegiance. The choice in itself remains meaningless. Why not
Socrates instead of Jesus? Socrates also gave his life freely in
defence of his moral principles. Unless Jesus can be adhered to
as being unconditionally more than mere man, as being divine,
it makes no sense to exhort all men to give themselves to their
neighbor the way Jesus did. Indeed Jesus Himself appealed to
man's total allegiance expressly because of His divine origin.
"He who sees me sees the Father; he who receives me receives
Him who sent me; he who denies me before men, him will I
deny before my Father in heaven." Hamilton has chosen to
ignore the overwhelming New Testament evidence that Jesus
called for total allegiance to Himself because he was God. Because he had chosen the death of God, Hamilton also had to
evacuate the divine in Jesus. He had to reduce Jesus to the
status of a mere man; good, but no longer able to call for the
total allegiance that only the Infinitely Holy One could reasonably call for.

It is hardly surprising, therefore, to find that Hamilton's
Jesus is not the Jesus of the Gospels. Hamilton gives Jesus the
function of being next to the neighbor, in the neighbor in love,
without ever disturbing the neighbor over his addiction to
moral good or evil, his acceptance or rejection of the Father, his
openness to or rejection of the truth. This sentimental, humanitarian Jesus is a sacrilegious caricature of the Jesus Christ who
is the Truth in Person. The Jesus of the Gospels parted with His
friends, with the religious authorities, with His chosen people,
with the Roman law, with His very life rather than deny the
truth of His revelation or change in one iota His Father's plan
for the salvation of the world. Hamilton's fragments destroy
this Jesus.

15. William Hamilton, "The Shape of Radical Theology," *Christian Century*,
LXXXII, October 6, 1965, p. 1221.

Moreover, true Christianity teaches that before the human person can find Jesus in his neighbor, he must first encounter Jesus as Jesus is in Himself. In every man's encounter with Jesus, there must eventually come the test that came to Peter. "Who do you say that I am?" When a person replies with Peter, "Thou art the Christ, the Son of the Living God," he has found the true Son of God. For he has entered into communion with the true Jesus, a communion founded on the basis of revealed truth. Once a person has found and established Jesus as the God-Man in his own heart, then, and only then, can a fruitful search for Jesus in the neighbor be undertaken. Hamilton makes the fatal mistake of placing the finding of Christ in my neighbor above the level of my direct communion with Christ in faith, hope and love. Jesus has already warned His disciples of this illusion of being able to save themselves and others without prior communion with Himself. "Without me you can do nothing; unless the branch remains in the vine, it remains alone; every branch that is cut off, withers, dries up and is cast into the fire."

In effect, then, Hamilton has given man an impossible mission—the socio-ethical salvation of the world through the imitation of a Jesus who never existed. This superficial, secular crusade is a cruel hoax and reveals Hamilton's abysmal loss both of the significance of man and of the divine romance with man. For it is only in the intimate I-Thou communion of Jesus Christ, Son of God, with each person that the family of the Triune God saves the family of mankind. Only in the sociality of the Mystical Body of Christ is the human person saved. Before a man can radiate Christ to his neighbor, he must have the infinitely Holy Christ abiding permanently within himself. The tragedy of Hamilton's fragment is that from irresponsible "God-talk" about the death of God he has produced illusory "Jesus-talk" about the socio-ethical salvation of man.

CHAPTER XVIII

Van Buren: Annihilator of a Linguistic Deity

WE HAVE SEEN THAT WILLIAM HAMILTON, DESPITE the ardor of his official rejection of God, remained at heart an incurable neo-orthodox theologian. For even as the corpse of the *uti*—useful—God was being buried, a prayerful Hamilton kept peering into the wings of the future for the appearance of the *frui*—delightful—God who might come to dispel the darkness enveloping the stage of human existence. No such ambiguous inconsistency troubles the lucid soul of Paul Van Buren. A clinically cool diagnostician of linguistic malignancies, Dr. Van Buren admitted to Ved Mehta in a recent interview: "I don't pray. I just reflect on things."[1]

As a fledgling reflector, Van Buren did his theology under Karl Barth, taking his doctorate at Basel and producing a very orthodox thesis on Calvin's doctrine of Reconciliation. Then he discovered linguistic philosophy in the *Philosophical Investigations* of the later Wittgenstein and the writings of the whole

1. Ved Mehta, *The New Theologian.*

British school of linguistic analysts. After subjecting his neo-orthodoxy to the light of linguistic criticism, Van Buren, ever the seeker of greater clarity and precision, rejected Barthianism completely and wrote his *Secular Meaning of the Gospel*, the book which, he tells his readers, "represented an important step in a personal struggle to overcome my own theological past."[2] As to the progress of his theological thought since the publication of this book in 1963, we must be content to speculate in wonder as to how really radical Van Buren has become, tantalized by his statement to Mehta: "What I am thinking now is a lot more radical than what I said in my book."[3]

As a professor, he has moved from a teaching post at a theological seminary to one in a secular university, convinced, with Hamilton, that religion must move out of the cloister into the world. His move symbolizes the shift of his theological emphasis from Church to city affairs, from ecclesiastical to cultural significance. He has chosen the community of scholarship over the community of faith. In his mind there can be no return to traditional theology; the scientific, empirical attitude is here to stay; nostalgic traditional regressions only alienate secular Christians and isolate the Church. Today secular Christianity has a completely new mission; it must foster a radically secularist vision in its faithful. Van Buren is quite blunt about this matter as is evidenced by his totally secularist interpretation of the Gospel message. He is not in the least interested in making converts to Christianity. He wants to make secular and non-secular Christians radically more secular. His basic dogma is that, in order to be an up-to-date Christian, a Christian in the truest sense of the word, the faithful must let that mind be in them which is in the twentieth century empiricist. And what is the caliber of that mind? It is characterized by the qualities of clarity, hard-headedness and honesty. It concentrates on all the reality there is, the realities of this world. Thus, it is incapable of finding "any empirical linguistic anchorage" for the traditionalist's visions of transcendent beings—God and his supernatural satelites. If they are to catch up with the dynamic, prevailing outlook and enjoy a profitable rapport with contem-

2. Van Burean, "Theology in the Context of Culture," *The Christian Century*, LXXXII, April 7, 1965, p. 429.
3. Ved Mehta, *op. cit.*

porary, cultural, technologized society, the Christian Churches will have to undergo a major metamorphosis. They will have to abandon dedication to apologetics and evangelism. In place of that sterile mission, they will have to foster in their members a Godless, secularist, intellectualist vision of man and his surrounding world.

As it has for other modern radical theologians, Bonhoeffer's religionless Christianity served as the bridge over which Van Buren traveled from traditional to atheistic theology. Van Buren expresses admiration for Bonhoeffer, the theologian who refused to retreat from a world "come of age" and had the courage to begin a "nonreligious interpretation of biblical concepts."[4] Indeed, Van Buren was inspired to answer the question posed by Bonhoeffer but which he himself could not answer because of his untimely death at the hands of the Nazis: "How can the Christian who is himself a secular man understand his faith in a secular way?"[5] Although he rejected Bonhoeffer's separation of religion from the Christian faith and used a method in answering his question "far removed from Bonhoeffer's thought," Van Buren, nevertheless, felt that he remained true to his mentor's theologically pioneering spirit. True, Bonhoeffer never arrived at a Christian atheism, but then he never had the time to develop the inevitable conclusions arising from his theological adventure in secularization. Van Buren makes use of his mentor's great initial thrust into the world and arrives at a consistent "Christian Atheism." For him, as we shall see, God is dead in the very real sense that modern empirical thinking can find no place for the idea of a transcendent Being in any of its enterprises. An idea that answers to no empirical reality has to be discarded, for it is meaningless. Such is the sad status of the word "God." Man is not obliged to play impossibly irrational language games. Why then keep in current coinage a meaningless word that represents a nonexistent Being? Yet there are some profitable and truth-attaining language games and Van Buren excels in playing the analytical language game which dissolves the image of God. And Nelson expresses the effect of Van Buren's work thus:

4. Paul M. Van Buren, *The Secular Meaning of the Gospel* (New York: The Macmillan Company, 1966), pp. 1–2.
5. *Ibid.*, p. 2.

So God has been edged out of the world, nor has he suffered death as a historical event. He seems to be like Julian Huxley's depiction of the deity: "the last fading smile of a Cosmic Cheshire Cat." The Cosmic Cat is gone, the smile fades, the vacuum alone remains.[6]

The Language Game in Which God Dies

In the critique he undertook of the idea of God, Van Buren proceeded in the same manner as the "logical postivists" who established for themselves "a principle of verification" that would determine the truth or falsity of human statements. According to this principle, only those propositions have meaning which can be verified in empirical experience. Of course, other statements involving formal definitions of concepts and operative in the relationships between these concepts are also meaningful. Of such a nature are mathematical and logical statements. Thus, a proposition is meaningful in a factual sense if we can empirically identify, expose and analyze observations which constitute evidence of its truth or falsity. All other propositions, apart from purely formal ones, are meaningless. When this principle of verification is applied to Christian theology, and especially to statements about God, we must conclude that the term "God" is meaningless, for no experimental facts give evidence of its truth or falsity.

However, to this principle of verification as enunciated by the logical positivists, Van Buren has seen fit to add a distinction of his own between cognitive and noncognitive propositions, thereby expanding the types of verification. Now cognitive propositions are about existing data and say something about reality independently of the speaker's own attitudes or feelings. Public, objective evidence can verify these statements. On the contrary, noncognitive statements are not about reality as such but about a given way of looking at reality. These propositions propose a point of view which is subjective and define a practical meaning which can be verified in an entirely new and subjective way. Since personal stances are so predominant in such statements, one viewpoint on life cannot be proved objectively on empirical data to be true or false, good

6. J. Robert Nelson, "Deicide, Theothanasia, or What Do You Mean?" in *The Meaning of the Death of God* (New York: Vintage books, 1967), p. 198.

or bad in comparison with another viewpoint. For the meaning-fulness of noncognitive propositions arises from the conduct of the speaker of these propositions. If the speaker's behavior is in consistent harmony with his statements, then his point of view is verified in his own life. If his behavior is consistently in contradiction to his statements, then his statements can be taken as false. In summary, the test of truth in noncognitive statements consists in whether a person practices what he preaches.

When applied to the word "God," Van Buren's expanded position on the principle of verification has annihilating effects. Certainly assertions about God are not subject to objective empirical proof. Consequently, such statements tell us nothing about reality in the empirical world. It must be, therefore, that the word "God" belongs in noncognitive statements, those, that is, that express a particular subjective outlook on life. But even in noncognitive statements the word "God" is most misleading, for it seems to be compatible with anything and everything the human attitude or viewpoint wants it to mean. This is precisely the sad status of neo-orthodoxy's affirmations concerning a transcendent and wholly other God. Moreover, existential statements about God, such as those of Bultmann and Ogden, force God to undergo "death by a thousand qualifications." The same is true of Whitehead's process-philosophy terminology about the Deity. Literally and unqualifiedly, then, the word "God" is useless, dead. For the sake of clarity, the word "God" should be dropped. Once such a useless expression is removed, man can then analyze more profitably and creatively his own subjective attitudes and viewpoints. In Van Buren's thought this means that statements about God are really to be translated into statements about man. God-talk is really man-talk. In his interview with Mehta, Van Buren said: "I am trying to argue that it (Christianity) is fundamentally about man, that its language about God is one way—a dated way, among a number of ways—of saying what it is Christianity wants to say about man and human life and human history."[7]

Now the translation of God-talk into man-talk should not stop with its application to the reality of the Supreme Being. It must be carried further, particularly in reference to the message of

7. Paul Van Buren, Interview with Mehta, *op. cit.*, p. 153.

the Gospels, to the central figure of those Gospels, Jesus of Nazareth, and to the central truth of those Gospels, the narration of the Resurrection. Indeed, Van Buren is willing to stake the truth or falsity of his secular translation of the Gospels on the ability of his secular interpretation of the language connected with Easter to withstand the criticism of the theologians. He writes:

> One of the ways in which the New Testament writers speak about Jesus is in divine and quasi-divine terms—Son of God, and what have you. . . What I am trying to do is to understand the Bible on a naturalistic or humanistic level, to find out how the references to the absolute and the supernatural are used in expressing on a human level the understanding and convictions that the New Testament writers had about their world. For by using these large cosmological terms in speaking about this particular happening, this event—the history of Jesus—they were saying the most that they could say about this man. If a man in the first century had wanted to say of a certain person that he had given him an insight into what human life was all about, he would have almost normally said, "That man is divine."[8]

In effect, what Van Buren maintains by his analytical method is that the essential significance of Christianity can be distilled from the Gospels and presented to modern Christians without any reference needed to the word "God." For Christianity is fundamentally about man, not God. Christianity is about a style of human existence, about human viewpoints, attitudes, dispositions and moral behavior. What makes Van Buren's theological humanism so plausible is the partial truth this oversimplified view of the Gospels contains. It is true that God, as the abstract, Pure-Act Supreme Being has not entered human history and thus never becomes as such the object of faith and love. But the God of the Gospels is the God-Man. And in the words of Karl Barth, this Incarnate God is the God who is "for man," who pitched his tent among men, became their teacher, pastor, physician and partner in a covenant of mutual self-donation. It follows, in a very true sense, therefore, that since the coming of the Son of God, all statements about God are inextricably bound

8. *Ibid.*, p. 148.

up with statements about man. This unique essential together-
ness between God and man achieved in the Incarnation and
consummated in the salvation history of Jesus is eternally indissoluble. Where Van Buren makes his great theological blunder is not in linking God-statements with man-statements, but
in doing this in order to reductively obliterate the meaning and
reality of any God-statement. He would divorce God from man
by contending that man exists alone in this universe, without
any God. In his opinion, there is no evidence of any dimension
of reality in the Gospels that testifies to the presence of a
"more" than man in human history. All that can be found in the
Gospels is a naturalistic, humanistic Christianity. Naturally, if
this Van Buren doctrine is true, then Christianity has lost its
raison d'être; it no longer has any meaning, serves no purpose
and should be dispensed with altogether.

In his *Secular Meaning Of The Gospel,* Van Buren attempts
to reduce the entire orthodox Christian message of the Gospels
to a network of noncognitive propositions. Thus traditional
Christian theology doesn't really need God, nor a Divine Risen
Christ, nor a Virgin Birth, nor miracles, nor a supernatural
destiny for man. For none of these assertions can be objectively
verified as real events of history that took place in the empirical world. Rather, all these myths are merely a subjective viewpoint, a way of looking at man and his situation. All these
myths have evolved out of the subjective prepossessions of a
particular historical community, the Christian community. If
one expects to appreciate the special character of this community, one must study the history of the man Jesus. Moreover,
even though this history is full of many difficulties, nevertheless it adequately supplies man with the lineaments of the real
Jesus and assures him of solid theological conclusions on the
nature of Christianity. Now Van Buren's picture of Jesus is,
humanly speaking, very appealing. Jesus is an amazingly free
man, immune from the world's sollicitations and involve-
ments, disentangled from religious rigidities and rituals, se-
renely unclouded by fear or anxiety and, most inspiring of all,
always available to his neighbor, eager to subject himself in
service for others.

Now a man of such noble character will be expected to have
an extraordinary influence upon his fellowmen. This was emi-

nently true in the case of Jesus. For Van Buren the reality of what Jesus meant to the Christian Community is the crucial question for any version of Christian theology. And certainly Van Buren's interpretation of the meaning of Jesus to the Christian Community reveals his ingenuity at developing his own brand of secular, humanistic Christianity.

> Jesus of Nazareth was a free man in his own life, who attracted followers and created enemies according to the dynamics of personality and in a manner comparable to the effect of other liberated persons in history upon people about them. He died as a result of the threat that such a free man poses for insecure and bound men. His disciples were left no less insecure and frightened. Two days later, Peter, and then other disciples, had an experience of which Jesus was the sense-content. They experienced a discernment-situation in which Jesus the free man whom they had known, themselves, and indeed the whole world, were seen in a quite new way. From that moment, the disciples began to possess something of the freedom of Jesus. His freedom began to be "contagious." For the disciples, therefore, the story of Jesus could not be told simply as the story of a free man who died. Because of the new way in which the disciples saw him and because of what had happened to them, the story had to include the event of Easter. In telling the story of Jesus of Nazareth, therefore, they told it as the story of the free man who had set them free. This was the story which they proclaimed as the Gospel for all men.[9]

It is clear that Van Buren teaches that the secular meaning of the resurrection of Jesus from the dead was merely that Jesus' followers found themselves caught up in the freedom of Jesus himself. Within that freedom these disciples themselves became free men, courageously free to face even death without fear. Thus the Easter event is not at all a marvelous deed of God that happened to Jesus. Jesus did not rise from the dead; he is presently no different than the unnumbered millions of other dead. But something did happen to the followers of Jesus. In their minds faith arose now for the first time in Jesus. There were no Christians before this psychological Easter-seizure of the souls of the disciples of Jesus.

9. Paul M. Van Buren, *The Secular Meaning Of The Gospel,* p. 134.

> According to the New Testament, Christian faith first arose in connection with the event of Easter and afterwards in the context of the proclamation of that event . . . Easter was the turning-point in the way the disciples looked at and spoke of Jesus; from that time they saw him and spoke of him in a new way . . . The one of whom the disciples spoke in a new way beginning on Easter was the man whom they had known by the name of Jesus, a man of Nazareth whose brothers, sisters and parents were known.[10]

When he attempts to explain why the disciples and later the Christians looked on Jesus not only as a man risen physically from the dead but also as their Lord and God, Van Buren again makes use of the metaphor of "contagion." Christians adhere to Jesus as their Lord and God through a commitment to live the freedom they have discovered in him through the event of Easter. Whereas before the Easter event, the disciples were frightened and cowardly, now they courageously imitate the life of freedom and generous self-sacrifice they have discovered in Jesus. Modern orthodox Christians take their allegiance to the divinity and lordship of Jesus from the psychological Easter-seizure experienced by the first disciples. Quite clearly, then, Christian theology, which Van Buren has already reduced to purely subjective adventures, is now reduced further to being merely subjective ethics. The new secular Christianity consists, therefore, in man's acceptance of the challenge to live for his neighbor after the example of Jesus. But what is so exclusive about Jesus that men should imitate his self-sacrifice for the neighbor? Others, like Socrates, have freely given themselves for the neighbor. Why not make them the supreme model for ethical imitation? Van Buren admits the truth of this objection, but places the uniqueness of Jesus in the fact that Jesus is a free man who set other men free. Because of his role as liberator in the Christian Community, which no other man can share, Christians have always and must always imitate Jesus as their supreme model. Of course, when Christians so exalt their model that they call him God of God, Light of Light, very God of very God, they are merely being over-enthusiastic toward the man Jesus who has liberated them. In reality, how-

10. *Ibid.*, pp. 116, 117.

ever, Christians understand man, his life of dignity and freedom, his history, the destiny of the world, indeed of the whole
creation, to be the beneficiaries of the "contagious freedom of
Jesus."[11]

In summary, then, for Van Buren, Christian theology is not
founded on truth-revealing cosmological or metaphysical principles. Nor is it founded on marvelous events of history which
can be empirically verified, despite the contrary claim of traditional Christians. No, Christian theology, and the faith springing from it, is merely a special human perspective upon man.
The traditional Christian faith constitutes merely a particular
point of view regarding the human condition and destiny. This
point of view is founded on no empirically existing God; it does
not arise from any supernatural intrusion of the Supreme Being into history. There have taken place no marvelous miracles
that testify to the eternal, other-worldly destiny of man. No,
this particular vision of man arises from the excessive enthusiasm of Jesus' disciples who were profoundly changed through
their experience of "the contagious freedom" of their master.
On the other hand, the modern secular Christian who rejects
all supernaturalism, nevertheless chooses to participate in the
self-sacrificing freedom of the man Jesus. As for traditional
Christians who imitate the self-donating freedom of Jesus,
when they confess Jesus to be their Lord and God, all they are
really doing is proclaiming their own commitment to the man
Jesus and to his generous secular way of life. When they do this,
modern Christians unavoidably invite other men to share their
vision of Jesus, the world, themselves and their neighbors.
Thus, when it has become completely concerned with man and
no longer with God, Christian theology finally becomes meaningful and profitable to man come of age.

Diagnosis of Van Buren's Linguistic Atheism

In any serious effort to evaluate Van Burens' annihilation of
God and secularization of the Gospel message, the attention
must first focus on the ideals and attitudes of Van Buren himself. As do all the other radical theologians, so too Van Buren
admits to an intense enthusiasm about everything modern and

11. *Ibid.*, pp. 137, 139.

scientific. His first approach to any theological proposition is not, therefore, one which asks whether the statement is true, nor whether it reflects the goodness and beauty of God and Christ as these are revealed in the Bible, nor whether the particular proposition has any intrinsic value. Rather, the predominant psychological attitude is one of subjective pragmatism. "Is this theological proposition new? If new, is it up-to-date? If up-to-date, will it suit modern man and find acceptance in a challenging, audacious, progressive technologized age?" If the answer to all these questions is affirmative, then the theological proposition advanced has "cash value," that is, in Van Buren's eyes, it is true. Thus, truth is a category imposed on theological statements from outside, both from the surrounding world of modernity and from the psychological prepossessions of the radical Christian atheists who both form and conform to that world.

The "cash value" norm is applied to God to determine whether he should be kept or let go. Now, since God is obviously inoperative in our age and since science is performing whatever functions God used to perform, then God is dead; He no longer fits in anywhere. Van Buren and his theologically radical cohorts are thus seen to be captives of the current craze for trends and ideas that are "alive and in the contemporary air." Aside from a spiritual revulsion at the immature, crude vulgarization exhibited by this "cash value" attitude towards transcendent truth, one is appalled at how supposedly intelligent men can seriously adhere to doctrines which are already proving to be as fickle and short-lived as the popular fashionableness that puffs them. The radical theologians have lost the sense of reverential wonderment that man should experience in the presence of the eternal, unchanging, noble attractiveness of truth. "What does a man's spirit hunger more ardently for than truth?" exclaimed the great St. Augustine. If Van Buren and his radical confreres could only regain that reverential wonderment and spiritual hunger for eternal, objective truth which is enthroned in its plentitude in the Triune God, then, perhaps, they would also appreciate the humor of Mark Twain's announcement when applied to the eternally living God: "The reports of my death are greatly exaggerated." And while on the subject of humor, that inimitably witty genius,

Chesterton, wrote some incisive words about the immaturity of those who take their truth from the contemporary clock.

> An imbecile habit has arisen in modern controversy of saying that such and such a creed can be held in one age but cannot be held in another. Some dogma, we are told, was credible in the twelfth century, but is not credible in the twentieth. You might as well say that a certain philosophy can be believed on Mondays, but cannot be believed on Tuesdays. You might as well say of a view of the cosmos that it was suitable to half-past four. What a man can believe depends upon his philosophy, not upon the clock or the century. If a man believes in unalterable natural law, he cannot believe in any miracle in any age.[12]

So much for the psychological perspective of Van Buren, who admits his own bias in behalf of "certain empirical attitudes ... for a deep interest in questions of human life this side of the 'beyond' ... and confesses to a corresponding lack of interest in ... the great metaphysical questions."[13]

Given Van Buren's "frankly autobiographical" bias in favor of secularism and against traditional theology, what can be said of his method of reducing God-statements to man-statements with the result of eliminating both the being and the word "God?" His basic epistemological principle seems valid enough; namely, that assertions compatible with anything and everything say nothing. Moreover, as applied to irrational neo-orthodoxy, existentialism and the theology of process-philosophy this principle does expose many meaningless assertions made by Protestant theologians. But when applied to the orthodox idea of God, to the New Testament and the history of Jesus of Nazareth, this principle of analysis is utterly sterile for attaining truth in these matters. It fails so miserably that we will show how Van Buren, following his own principle, has been led to some very startling non-sensical conclusions. We will show how he has fallen into the very subjectivism to which, in his opinion, traditional Christians have become hopeless victims.

Contrary to Van Buren's assertion, the Christian affirmation of the existence of God is not a "blik," that is, a fundamental

12. G. K. Chesterton, *Orthodoxy* (New York: Doubleday, Image Books, 1959), pp. 74–75.
13. Paul M. Van Buren, *The Secular Meaning Of The Gospel*, pp. xiii–xiv.

attitude or orientation or commitment to see a being in a certain way, even though empirical reality cannot verify this being or view of the being. Christians find God in the realm of the empirical; for them a universe of beings, beauty, truth, order convinces their reason about the existence of its Author. Through faith, however, Christians know that God entered human history in the person of Jesus Christ who infallibly proved Himself to be God by an overwhelming number of wondrous deeds and signs, culminating in His physical resurrection from the dead. There is nothing exclusively subjectivistic about this knowledge. Certainly this unique God of the Christian cannot be asserted to be compatible with anything and everything. He is the God of Abraham, Isaac, Joseph, of the Old and New Testaments, unique in nature, powers and transcendent ways of acting. As for the New Testament truth that God was in Jesus, St. Paul relates his own witness and the eye-witnessing of over five hundred others who saw, touched, ate and drank with the risen Lord. Indeed so empirically certain is St. Paul of the physical, bodily resurrection of Jesus, his Lord and God, that he bases the life of his mission and of Christianity on the empirical historicity of this event. "If Christ has not risen, then our preaching is in vain and your faith is in vain." The early Christians gladly subjected their beliefs to concrete empirical tests; there was nothing blind or esoteric about their faith, grounded as it was on historical facticity.

For example, how would Van Buren explain the initial, hard-headed, empirical "blik" of Thomas the doubting apostle? Here was a man who withstood the first-hand testimony of the other disciples who were his friends. And he put down some very concrete empirical conditions before he would even consider accepting the resurrection of Jesus of Nazareth. "Unless I see in his hands the print of the nails, and put my finger into the place of the nails, and put my hand into his side, I will not believe." Such empirical demands ought to satisfy even the modern, scientifically oriented Van Buren. When, after eight days, Jesus meets literally each empirical demand of the empirical Thomas, that saintly empiricist cries out to his risen Lord, "My Lord and my God!" In all truth can Thomas be said to be expressing on the second occasion a particular view of life or has something really tremendous, affecting his whole life empirically, taken place before his eyes so that factual evidence of the resurrection of Jesus has removed his doubts forever? Once again applying Van Buren's epistemological principle of analysis, the claim of Christians that Christ rose from the dead is not a statement that is compatible with anything or everything and therefore meaningless. The resurrection of Jesus is the most unique event in all history and applies solely to His experience.

Yet despite the overwhelming evidence for its veracity, Van Buren insists that the material given by the Evangelists on the Resurrection was "not intended to be documentary evidence of historical or biographical facts. It was a story in the service of the Easter kerygma."[14] Mascall, commenting on Van Buren's interpretation of the Easter event and on the intentions which Van Buren has inserted into those early witnesses from a position some two thousand years after them, writes:

> Van Buren may, of course, for reasons of his own maintain that this material is not reliable documentary evidence of the historical or biographical facts, but to say that it was not *intended* to be such is to fly in the face of such plain statements as the opening words of St. Luke's Gospel. And to suggest that the primitive Church deliberately embroidered the simple human life of Jesus with a mass of mythical and largely miraculous material in order to convince either itself or outsiders of the authenticity of a purely psychological "Easter experience" is to attribute to the first generation of Christians a degree of conscious sophistication for which there is really no evidence.[15]

We owe it to the sharp observation of Dr. Warwick Montgomery that Van Buren's so-called plausible analytical interpretation of the Gospel is exposed as being a judgment compatible with anything and everything and therefore proving nothing. No matter what incident is taken from the Gospels to disprove Van Buren's interpretation, Van Buren will always dismiss each episode as simply indicating how powerful the "discernment situation" or "blik", creating a new, subjective outlook in the souls of the disciples, really was. Even the Thomas episode

14. *Ibid.*, p. 118.
15. E. L. Mascall, *The Secularization of Christianity* (New York: Holt, Rinehard and Winston, 1966), p. 74.

used above can be dismissed in such a way. The powerful statement of Peter: "For we were not following fictitious tales when we made known to you the power and coming of Our Lord Jesus Christ, but we have been eye-witnesses of this grandeur," can also be laughed off in this way. Dr. Montgomery goes on to illustrate the irrationality of Van Buren's linguistic tactic by using apt analogies from non-religious happenings. Here is one of those apt illustrations.

> Or suppose I were to say: "My wife studied art history and enjoys painting," and you commented: "You really love her, don't you?" "Well, yes," I would say, "but she *does* have artistic interests. Here are her transcripts representing art courses she's taken, here are paintings she's done, and ..." At which point you interrupt with a sweep of the hand: "Come, come, no need to bother with that; I can recognize true love when I see it!" My composure would be retained with great difficulty, since I would find it impossible under the circumstances to get across a genuinely factual point.[16]

What Van Buren is telling modern, come-of-age man is that his viewpoint, that of secular empiricism or empirical secularism, if you prefer, is the only authentic way of interpreting the Gospels. Even though he is forced to admit that the disciples of Jesus looked upon their own experience of Easter in a far more objective and simpler way, nevertheless Van Buren insists on forcing his "blik," his "categorical commitments," upon their experience through the uncritical use of linguistic empiricism. We have seen that in his secularist reconstruction of the Gospel events Van Buren has been "hoist by his own petard." For his reductionist translation of the empirical language of the Gospels whereby he reinterprets the divine, historical events of the Incarnation and the Resurrection into non-cognitive, subjectivistic statements of the primitive Christians only reveals his own non-cognitive, artificial, irrational, biased viewpoint against these same historical events. Throughout his work, Van Buren is almost never critical where the empirical and secular

16. John Warwick Montgomery, "A Philosophical-Theological Critique of the Death of God Movement," in *The Meaning Of The Death Of God* (New York: Vintage Books, 1967), pp. 51–52. This splendid article has helped this study on the radical theologians immensely.

are concerned. But once let the supernatural become the subject of inquiry and he loses all semblance of empirical objectivity. Then he discovers in the Gospels, in Jesus, in traditional Christianity whatever he wants to find there. "The idea of the empirical intervention of a supernatural 'God' in the world of men has been ruled out by the influence of modern science on our thinking," he tells us.[17] Notice, Van Buren does not say science has proved God to be impossible. He does say that "the influence of modern science on our thinking" has ruled out the intervention of a supernatural "God" for him. This is an expression of a personal psychological reaction and attitude in Paul Van Buren; it is his viewpoint, his "blik." Apparently, then, it is not a love for linguistic accuracy, nor a dedication to science, but a capitulation to the thrilling secularist environment directed by scientific technology that led Van Buren to annihilate God and evacuate the Gospels of all supernatural meaning. And Mascall reminds us that Van Buren caved in to the secularist, atheistic atmosphere despite the fact that he could have so easily encountered large amounts of serious writing in recent years that stress the harmony that can exist between science and theology, writing which shows "no tendency to abandon the traditional doctrines of Christian theology."

When we analyze his use of the linguistic weapon for the accomplishment of his reductionist crimes, we discover that Van Buren was not even faithful to Wittgenstein's principles. His classification of propositions into cognitive and non-cognitive in order to suppress the use of the word "God" falsified Wittgenstein's honest concern to accent and describe the multiplicity of linguistic forms. Both Ogeltree and Montgomery take issue with Van Buren for misrepresenting the genuine contributions of Wittgenstein to the study of the "Language games." Montgomery takes issue with Van Buren for changing the meanings of certain language games in an arbitrary way to suit his own purposes. In his eyes, Van Buren's unwarranted reduction of the Gospels to the structure of psychological subjectivism has landed Van Buren in the pit of artificial nonsensicality. Ogletree takes issue with Van Buren's interpretation of theological statements. He insists, in opposition to Van Buren, that theological statements can be understood as saying

17. Paul M. Van Buren, *The Secular Meaning Of The Gospel* p. 100.

something objectively true about the nature of reality. And since this is so, it follows that the word "God" is not necessarily misleading, nor can it be reduced simply to subjective attitudes and viewpoints. In attempting to prove too much, therefore, Van Buren has proved nothing. God, the divinity of Jesus, His bodily resurrection and the transcendence of the Gospel message are as alive today as they ever were. Van Buren has merely revealed his own inadequate, narrowed viewpoint, his personal "blik" against God and the supernatural.

In conclusion, we should take notice of the pertinent similarities among the radical theologians. Why have they all chosen man in preference to God? Interestingly enough, each of these theologians was at one time in his life under the weighty influence of Barthian neo-orthodoxy. And each revolted against this influence. Why? Alasdair MacIntyre gives an incisive explanation:

> We can see the harsh dilemma of a would-be contemporary theology. The theologians begin from orthodoxy, but the orthodoxy which has learnt from Kierkegaard and Barth becomes too easily a closed circle, in which believer speaks only to believer, in which all human content is concealed. Turning aside from this arid in-group theology, the most perceptive theologians wish to translate what they have to say to an atheistic world. But they are doomed to one of two failures. Either they succeed in their translation: in which case what they find themselves saying has been transformed into the atheism of their hearers. Or they fail in their translation: in which case no one hears what they have to say but themselves.[18]

So the radical theologians were suffering intellectual suffocation within the rigidly closed circle of neo-orthodoxy. For neo-orthodoxy refused to identify the Word of God with any human intellectual mission. Faith is a pure gift of God, totally transcending any human comprehension. But if human reason cannot grasp the Word of God in any accurate way, then the Scriptures, like any other human writings, might easily be fallible. Perhaps Christ is after all only a limited man like other men and his emptying of himself did not involve the putting off

18. Alasdair MacIntyre, "God and the Theologians," *Encounter*, London, XXI, September 1963, p. 7.

of his divine glory. Certainly, intellectually alive men of this world will not want to be kept in the straight jacket of an irrational orthodoxy which demands equally irrational religious and ethical commitments. The God of Karl Barth and Soren Kierkegaard is so utterly beyond human reason that he becomes for the faithful the Wholly Other. Intellectual rebels, within and outside the Church, will reject such a God as tyrant, unrealistic, non-existent. Hence they will develop first a demythologized God, then a deliteralized God, then a depersonalized God and finally a dead God. For in the last analysis, modern man in order to attain his mature manhood will have to destroy a God who frustrates his highest powers and who, above all, insults his intellect. Yet somehow the nostalgia for Christianity demands that Godless man remain a Christian. And so a program of theological theory and ethical practice is developed by the radical theologians. It is the program aimed at producing religionless, atheistic Christians dedicated, like the man Jesus, to the service of their neighbor. It is the program of Christian Atheism.

We have attempted to trace briefly the steps in this process-theology, following it from static, self-enclosed orthodoxy to open, dynamically evolving, secularist atheism. Theologians have come a long way in a short time. In the life time of Bultmann, they have traveled from demythologization to decide. Yet we have seen that the reductionist assertions made about God and the Gospels by the radical theologians are so compatible with anything and everything that they leave man with a meaningless message and mission. They exhort man to study a Godless theology, put his faith in a secular, social Jesus, practice a religionless Christianity, adhere to Christian Atheism and replace a defunct God with divinized Man.

CHAPTER XIX

The Idolatrous Heart of Godless Humanism

IN THE PRECEDING CHAPTERS WE HAVE DEVOTED OUR research to demonstrating that the great modern apostles for atheism, each with his own style and genius, have equated their espousal of atheism with their adventure to achieve man's mental emancipation and personal liberation from the tyranny of a Deity who imposed upon mankind from above the shackles of crystalloid creeds and moral dictates. Each atheism explored claims to have liberated man by exposing, and thereby dissolving, the religious myth which was conceived, born, developed and maintained through the exploitation of mankind's infancy and adolescence. In attempting to control the superstitious fears that were spawned in the darkness of his infantile ignorance, man created the God of religion in whom he could take refuge from the overwhelming tragedies of daily life. Thus, God and His transcendent world of beings became man's "security blanket," his "opium" according to Marx, the anodyne that made this life barely bearable in time on the promise of the "pie-in-the-sky" awaiting him as a reward in the next. This was how God and religion all started, in the days of man's infancy and adolescence.

Today, however, man has come of age. The era of superstition has been superceded by the era of science. Twentieth-century man is the creation of a long series of happy—and some very unhappy—happenings, nearly all of them apparently salutary revolutions. Galileo and Canon Copernicus liberated astronomy and the earth from the static cosmology of Ptolemy and Aristotle when they demonstrate that the earth, along with its sister planets, moved around the sun, changing its positional relationship to the heavenly bodies from instant to instant. The French Revolution violently changed the confessional State into the laicized State; the Romantic movement shifted man's social focus from being centered on God to a concentration on nature and man. Science and technology presented man with the key to a total control of his physical environment. Darwin exploded the theory of the direct creation of man by God, making man's appearance as a being the inevitable result of a long chain of evolutionary development of the entire universe, which is still projecting itself into the future. Even Cardinal Newman's *Development Of Christian Doctrine* introduced the dynamics of change into the traditional dogmas of the apparently changeless Catholic Church. The American Revolution liberated the New World from the bonds of the Old and opened up a whole new continent. In this seminal revolution can be seen the beginning of the dissolution of the colonial empires of the great European powers, a dissolution which in our day has occasioned the rise of a host of newly created nations. The eruptions of change in the world of politics as the result of two World Wars have established today two giant hegemonies sparring in collateral localized wars while preparing for a final international showdown. Social earthquakes have rocked the worlds of workers, students, races and religions. Is it any wonder, then, that twentieth-century man sees himself as essentially an activist, the product of progressive process, involved with ardent passion to his last atom and idea in the cult of change?

Not satisfied with changing his cosmology, science, society, politics, economics and art, twentieth-century man decided to make the most radical change of all. He decided to change his God. He discarded the transcendent Deity for the ever-present deity of man. Twentieth-century man's divine adventure is no longer the Absolute Thou of transcendence. His adventure is the creature Thou, contemporary man. But when confronted with the assertion that the Transcendent Deity became immanent in the God-Man Jesus Christ, twentieth-century man proceeded to change Jesus radically. Jesus is no longer the God-Man. Jesus is the "man for others," but, note well, Jesus is only man, not God and not God-Man, certainly not God in the sense that he is one of the Divine Persons in the Triune Godhead which is absolutely Transcendent. Such a Triune God is, for the enlightened twentieth-century man, pure fiction.

In an age of supreme optimism about progressive change, when man has conquered gravity, broken through his own atmosphere captured the moon and is already taking close-up photos of other planets prior to landing there also, it is hardly surprising that he has made a religious cult, an idolatry, a fanatical liturgy of evolutionary development. His new God is the Future Progress of Man. And he has put his fervent, total, blind faith in that God. Twentieth-century man is passionately in love with the God of Change, which he has identified with the God of Future Progress. He is viscerally violent against established, orderly, permanent things; his appetite for the new is insatiable. He revels in the contradictory because the clash between contradictories assures him of the experience of change, of the experience of progress in the ensuing chaos and confusion. And this fierce mania for change at any cost has captured the minds of many of mankind's leaders—scientists, philosophers, theologians, statesmen, educators, clergymen and artists—men, who instead of swallowing all changes as good and healthy, should be rationally sifting constructive from destructive change and leading the people to accept only the new that organically invigorates what is permanent in the old. But many of these leaders are themselves enthused about the deification of evolutionary man.

Dr. Edmund R. Leach, prominent anthropologist and provost of King's College at Cambridge, exilarated by man's triumph over science and superstition, is refreshingly frank about man's present position and role in the worlds of science, religion and morals. In an article modestly entitled "We Scientists Have the Right to Play God," he writes:

> The scientist can now play God in his role as wonder-worker, but can he—and should he—also play God as moral arbiter? . . . There can be no source for these moral judgments except the scientist himself. In traditional religion, morality was held to derive from God, but God was only credited with the authority to establish and enforce moral laws because He was also credited with supernatural powers of creation and destruction. Those powers have now been usurped by man, and he must take on the moral responsibility that goes with them.[1]

In explaining why man had to usurp those divine powers of creation and destruction and why man must accept the responsibility of making and enforcing his own moral rules, Dr. Leach relies on the famous Feuerbachian thesis which states that God, after all, was only a projection into the beyond of fearful, ignorant man's best qualities. Dr. Leach cleverly exposes the human functions attributed to that mythical Deity. God as creator sets the cosmological clock ticking; as lawgiver He promulgates the moral code; as judge He imposes sanctions on criminals; as "trickster" He arbitrarily interferes in human affairs, testing and gathering His own clique of the righteous as He segregates them from the wicked; as mediator He judges and saves sinners. Dr. Leach concludes:

> These attributes of God are by definition "superhuman," but they are nevertheless qualities of an essentially human kind, The God of Judeo-Christianity is, in all His aspects, whether creator, judge, trickster or mediator, quite explicitly anthropomorphic, and the converse is equally true: There is necessarily something godlike about every human being . . . But unless we teach those of the next generation that they can afford to be atheists only if they assume the moral responsibilities of God, the prospects for the human race are decidedly bleak.[2]

1. Edmund R. Leach, "We Scientists Have the Right to Play God," *The Saturday Evening Post*, NY., November 16, 1968, p. 16.
2. *Ibid.*, pp. 16, 20.

Surely the humanist atheist's ability to dissolve human bleakness in the future should be easily documented by his success in dispelling today the gloom of his contemporary fellows. For, by definition, humanists are depicited as saviors of humanity at large as well as apostles of the individual's personal and social freedoms. Therefore we seek in the record the degree of atheist man's humanity to his fellow man. Has Almighty Man's love and service to his fellow man excelled that of the Almighty God whom he has displaced? We expect atheist man's performance to answer two questions: First, have atheist humans emancipated and expanded the mind of man? Second, have atheist humanists enlarged the exercise and enjoyment of man's personal freedoms?

Atheist Humanists and the Mind of Man

Has atheistic humanism expanded the intellectual freedom of man? The compelling weight of historical evidence forces us to answer No. In so far as atheistic humanism is professedly busy suppressing the religious visions and convictions of mankind, it is the enemy of intellectual religious liberty. For atheism is inherently opposed to any religious thinking that historically and rationally fosters faith in God. The logic of the atheist's denial of God's objective existence leads him to ridicule God's existence in the hearts of believers. Of course, many humanist atheists will claim that their opposition to religious vision is restricted only to the realm of intellectual controversy where they feel it their duty to persuade believers to part with this non-existent mythical Being. As a matter of reality, however, the atheist intellectual, and above all the atheist professor, while undermining the religious vision of their fellow men, are in effect attempting a drastic shortening of the intellectual horizons of man. They put blinders on man and limit his power to pierce reality with his metaphysical and intuitional vision. They cut back man's vision to a time-space-matter narrowness. They work to close off all human openings, drives, hungers, projections in intellectual adventures toward Absolute Transcendence. For they deny both the existence of an absolute Being beyond man and the presence of a permanent appetite in man for the achievement of communion with that Absolute Being. Thus, it becomes ludicrous to listen to the humanist atheist protesting his tolerance of believers in the dictum of Voltaire: "I heartily disagree with what you say, but will defend to the death your right to say it." This is pleasant but empty rhetoric. For, like Voltaire, atheistic humanists revel in destroying the faith of believers, thereby effectively paralyzing both the capacity and the right of many for personal investigation into doctrine and meaningful participation in the free exercise of religion.

At a time when man's achievements in spatial transcendence have sent him soaring to the breath-taking horizon of the moon, at a time when his simultaneous presence on earth and moon so broaden his vision that for the first time in history man could both ecstatically rejoice over the full splendor of his earth and awesomely shiver over the barren desolateness of his moon, one wonders how atheistic humanists can maintain their zeal in denying the very possibility of spiritual transcendence. Why do they continue to close their minds and refuse to suspect—if not yet see—that man's triumphs in spatial transcendence to a new presence on other planets are but magnificent witnesses to his inner, insatiable, spiritual soarings toward a transfigured presence with Other Persons? Since they pride themselves on being open-minded, intellectual atheists ought at least to investigate the possibility of the existence of spiritual transcendence and relationship with the thrilling transcendence of science. In this respect believers in God enjoy far greater intellectual vision than their atheist brothers. For the believer in God accepts the vision of science and harmoniously raises it, through free, intellectually creative activity in the science of theology, to the infinite degree of inexhaustible wonderment. Whereas the atheist, terrorized by intellectual insecurity, refuses to soar beyond the space-time-matter horizon. His metaphysical agnosticism and skepticism leads him to deny man's capacity to ascend from science and the limited freedom of *praxis* in daily life to higher truth or fuller freedom—to the very plenitude of Truth and Freedom.

Nevertheless, atheists are never sure, no matter how vocally certain they sound, about God's non-existence. They are constantly haunted by the fear that they have not really banished

forever either the presence or power of the Absolute One by
their scientific feats or dogmatic fulminations. The fact that so
many millions still believe in God, including many scientific
geniuses of impressive achievements, is a canker of insecurity
gnawing at their hearts. Thus, the overlords of atheism seize
and propagandize every startling event that seems to foster
their deed of deicide. Apparently comrade Gagarin had specific
orders to see if God were hiding in outer space. Atheist scientists on earth had already demonstrated that he did not exist in
matter or motion or the earth's atmosphere. It would be one of
the tasks of fellow atheist Gagarin to check on God in outer
space. Astronaut Gagarin's report to Chief Atheist Khrushchev
was a foregone conclusion. We can imagine his scientific message: "Comrade Khrushchev, there is no sign of The Enemy in
outer space. By night I checked every beam of light, every twin-
kle that pierced that ocean of darkness. By day the pitiless sun
uncovered the entire heavens. He is not to be found anywhere
out there, nowhere in the unfolding, receding infinity of skies."
A jubilant Khrushchev announced this news to the world as if
it were a new scientific fact.

The amused believer is reminded here of the similar response of the atheist surgeon who, upon opening up his patient,
complained that he did not find the human soul. Such statements by atheistic scientists are exercises in cynical ridicule.
Far from being scientific, they substitute the reaction of ridicule for the reflection of reason in the hope of destroying the
reality of religion. Of course, what should be obvious to any
honestly intelligent man, believer or unbeliever, is that such
pseudo-scientific reports present a version of God tailored to
the mental capacity of a child; the atheist creators of this non-
God then make their own mythical creation the object of their
frivolous attack.

The most eloquent counter-attack to such babble of atheists
in our days was the lunar liturgy, the prayers of the American
astronauts. In awe and reverence—virtues forgotten by atheists
—they sang the glory of God as they sailed over the cold moon.
In a voyage of half a million miles through spatial silence they
discovered God. In that silent, awesome sanctuary they experienced the mighty, ineffable, exquisitely gentle presence of
God. They saw Him everywhere—in the blinding brilliance of
the sun, the colorful sparkling gem of the earth, the prehistoric

ruggedness of the moon, the infernal blackness of the infinite interstellar spatial seas. Indeed, they heard Him in the very thunderous sacred silence of space and in the hushed rhythm of the circling spheres. To a world-wide audience of hundreds of millions, outside atheistically dominated countries where this lunar liturgy was banned, astronauts Anders, Lovell and Borman celebrated God's creation of heaven, earth, light, day, night, the seas, lands and all forms of life. And with God they agreed enthusiastically that "it was good!" In awe, reverence and filial love they told the whole world what they experienced. Good? That was the understatement of the centuries. It was fantastic, stupenduous, magnificent, sublime! Across the centuries they echoed the ecstatic exclamation of the Psalmist: "The heavens proclaim the glory of God and the firmament announces the work of his hands." Some quarter of a million miles away on the good earth, atheists who heard these prayers ground their teeth in desperation. So He is there too? Apparently there is no escape from God!

But perhaps the atheistic humanists who are adamantly opposed to religious thinking and practice do not suffocate man's liberty in other fields of intellectual endeavor? Surely their visceral hostility to theological and religious thought is restricted to this area of their peculiar prejudice. First, let us observe with pragmatic boldness some significant actions of the leaders of the citadels of Organized Atheism to find an empirical answer to our question. Mao, the high priest of Organized Atheism in China, announced some years ago an intellectual Spring with the proclamation: "Let a hundred flowers bloom!" Encouraged, many literary, political, scientific and cultural scholars felt free to expose, each in his own genre, what was wrong with "the great leap forward" and to suggest how the movement could be improved. No sooner had these flowers reared their varied colorful heads than they were decapitated. The intellectual Spring had been a ruse to uncover the seeds of intellectual sedition which the tyrannical overlords were quite sure were hidden in the soil of their Garden of Atheism. Not long after this cultural emancipation from dangerously creative ideas, the Red Guards flourished out of the soil in which were buried the Red Flowers. The whole world knows how effectively the Red Guards reduced the intellectual, creatively free activity of China to zero. In the jungle they created every-

one was too busy either killing someone else or fleeing madly
to stay alive. There was neither time, nor concern, nor the
conditions to work at the adventure of expanding the intellectual accomplishments of the soul of China.

But perhaps greater intellectual freedom blooms in the Garden of Russian Atheism? Well, let us listen to the latest witness
from that paradise and then consider some recent events of
history. The answer to this question, I assure you, will not be
muddled. In an interview given to the press in London and
recorded on European TV as well as printed verbatim in Italy's
TV Radiocorriere for September 14–20, 1969, Anatol Kuznetsov,
famous Russian novelist whose works have sold more than
seven million copies in Russian alone, told the world why he
abandoned his native land and all the privileges he enjoyed as
a member of the Writers' Union of the Soviet Union:

> I fled; I am settled here in London because all these privi-
> leges—the apartment in the city, the home in the country,
> the automobile, the secretary—count for absolutely noth-
> ing in comparison with what is the sole purpose of my life:
> to write, to write what I please, to write with freedom. In
> Russia I could have all these privileges only by compro-
> mising my conscience: I wrote only what I was ordered to
> write from above . . . Consequently, I wrote against my
> conscience . . . Had I remained there I would have gone
> mad, perhaps even committed suicide . . . In the twenty-
> five years that they published my writings not one of my
> works was printed the way I had written it; they were
> published with their heads reversed and . . . therefore, I
> have decided to reject them all . . . For that reason what-
> ever has been published—the seven million copies in Rus-
> sian and the incalculable number of other copies
> translated into more than forty languages—I renounce
> them all; I reject them all . . . They are not my works; they
> are something I see as far removed from myself . . . I will
> reprint everything here in London, without the cuts or
> manipulations made in Russia.[3]

The bloody Hungarian Revolution in 1956 was touched off
quite spontaneously when the young generation of communist
university students sought some greater freedom of choice in
the academic curriculum. One rather reasonable petition was

---

3. Anatol Kuznetsov, "Ora Posso Vivere" ("Now I can Live"), interviewed by
Alberto Michelini, *TV Radiocorriere,* September 14–20, 1969, pp. 15–16.

the study of their own language and literature and the greater use of the Hungarian language in the giving of lectures. Because freedom is contagious, the initial success in this field led to greater demands for freedom of the press, radio and political preference. The atheist overlords could not tolerate these normal freedoms. In the frightful bloodshed they inflicted to stifle the voice of freedom twenty-thousand Hungarians were mowed down with tanks and Comrade Khrushchev executed newly elected Imre Nagy and General Pal Meter with whom he had met, ostensibly to form a compromise that would give the Hungarians the greater freedoms they claimed. From the sacred, inviolable chambers of international protocol the Premier and his General went to prison and death in one of the most barbarous crimes of the times.

The monstrous mentality of organized atheism demands the total submission and even perversion of the creative powers of man. The Kuznetsov interview is only *the most* recent reminder among thousands of previous reminders that the words of Valeriy Tarsis are still true today. Addressing Western writers in general and Steinbeck in particular on the subject of their naive belief that Soviet writers were free to write as they pleased, Tarsis wrote in his book *Ward 7:* "Had he (Steinbeck) been born a Soviet citizen, he could never have published a line —he would more likely have been killed under Stalin or have shared the fate of Almazov today. (No offense meant, Mr. Steinbeck! A mental hospital is the only place for an honest writer in Russia nowadays!)"[4] Writer Tarsis was actually committed to a mental hospital and fellow-writer Andrei Sinyavsky to five years at hard labor for expressing ideas against tyranny and aspirations for greater liberty. In the cities of organized atheism control of the human mind is almost total. Education is a monopoly of the Party; so are the media of communication, which are completely censored. Every art, science, congress, concert, athletic activity, indeed every public activity is programmed with one-directional determinism—toward propagandizing whatever fosters the coming of the classless, godless society. In the history of mankind there has never been a more completely tyrannical control of human minds than that

---

4. Valeriy Tarsis, *Ward 7* (New York: E. P. Dutton & Co., 1965). Quoted in the Special Edition of *National Review,* "50 Years of Soviet Communism", October 31, 1967, p. 1185.

achieved today by the inquisition of organized militant atheism wherever it has come to power. Organized conspiratorial atheism has brought to consummate perfection the inhuman arts of propaganda, brain washing and the forced self-accusations of pre-desired crimes which were never committed by the "enemies of the State" confessing them.

But perhaps it can be objected that the suppression of intellectual freedom in the countries of organized atheism is due not so much to their atheism as to their political totalitarianism. After all, there are many atheists—even some atheist organizations like the Humanists—in the West who at least verbally oppose the organized atheist inquisition against academic freedom and even fight legal battles for greater individual freedom. We happily admit that this is true. But we will have to demonstrate that, according to their metaphysical concept of man, such atheists are acting illogically when they oppose the tyranny of their fellow-atheists. On their own principles they should logically and eventually become tyrants themselves if, of course, they remain atheists. We hasten to add that we are not against this pragmatic illogicality and we encourage atheists in the West to continue to defend freedom no matter how long they remain atheists. But we fear, from studying events developing in America today, that many of these atheists have discovered, whether by force of events or by reflection makes no difference, their illogicality and, instead of giving up their atheism, have given up their illogical promotion of human freedom. Their false metaphysics of man has finally pulled their overt actions into logical line and they have become, like their confreres in the East, atheistic tyrants. Why are we forced to maintain this unhappy conclusion? To find the answer let us consider the radical opposition between the atheist and Christian understanding of the nature of man and draw the inevitable conclusions. Then, let us check the record to see if Western atheists are really defending the freedom of man, his truly *human* freedom.

Atheist Man Versus Christian Man

The metaphysical nature of freedom will be radically different according to the diverse answers given to this prior and absolutely fundamental question: Who is this being, man, whose freedom we are discussing? What is the metaphysical make-up of this being the boundaries of whose freedom we are attempting to chart and even expand? Before we can begin to define man's liberty as a freedom *from* any external restraints or even as a freedom *for* such and such goals under such and such circumstances, it is absolutely essential to know man in a metaphysically accurate way. Knowing the objective reality about man's substantive being means that we come to know accurately his origin, orientation and final destiny. Now on the self-evident principle that a being normally acts according to the dynamic orientation of its nature, powers and appetites we can conclude that man will be expected to exercise his freedom according to the metaphysical make-up of his being to which he adheres with intellectual and emotional intensity.

Now on a careful examination of the claims that the liberal Western atheist makes for man—we use the word *liberal* here in its original sense as indicating one who truly fosters or hopes to foster greater personal liberty—we discover that the Western atheist is championing a concept of man which is radically opposed to man as he exists both in natural and revelational reality. Considered under the light of natural reason, man is totally a creature down to the inner metaphysical roots of his being and up to the heights of the plenitude of his perfections. Thus he is totally dependent always on a Supreme Being and always partially dependent on other beings for his existence, powers and activities. As creature man is intrinsically limited in existence, powers and achievements; thus, his thinking and willing will always be limited, however great their marvelous expansion. When we consider man under the light of revelation, we find that the Christian view of man accepts the findings of reason and adds the contributions of revelation. Man in Christ is raised above his merely natural powers to a quasi-divine state of organic life and development. True, he never ceases to remain fully a creature, but now his nature, powers and activities are lifted to a higher life and perfection through transformation in Christ. His destiny becomes the direct vision of the Godhead after death on condition that he freely accepts God as revealed in His Son Christ and does the will of God as revealed by Christ during his temporal life of trial. Within this metaphysical and revelational concept of man, man's liberty is seen to be founded in the liberty of God, with its exercise limited both by man's own reason and the divine plan for the salvation of man through the achievement of holiness which is adherence to God. Thus, for the Christian, man's freedom consists negatively in a freedom *from* any external restraints that would prevent his reasonable and sacramental development toward God. Positively his freedom consists in the right to perform all reasonable and sanctifying actions that will bring him to the direct vision of God in eternity. It must carefully be noticed that man's freedom is always limited; it is always subordinate to right reason and the revealed Will of God. Now let us study the atheist's concept of man and human freedom.

Man is, for the atheist, totally independent of God, for God does not exist at all. Man is the end product, the highest result of a universe in evolution. A collection of atoms, product of matter in evolutionary progress, man should not be regarded as a creature, for he generates thought and volition on his own. Since the movement producing him is eternal, man himself is eternal. He is thus the author of himself, his own absolute. He creates his own culture, values, customs, laws and morals. He can do this because he is endowed with absolute liberty of thought and freedom of action. Thus man alone defines his own origin, orientation and destiny. And he defines these entirely within the horizon of this material world and life which are the only universe and life that are real. Thus man's freedom is absolutely limitless, for subordination to its own decisions is no subordination at all. Man is thus free *from* whatever he decides must not restrain his liberty; he is free *for* whatever he decides he wants to do. Man is a law, the only law, unto himself.

Now it should be clear that the nature of the freedom defended by the atheist is radically opposed to the nature of the freedom defended by the Christian. The origin, scope and destiny of such radically opposed freedoms should logically bring them into intellectual and even physical conflict. Let us now try to clarify the practical conflict that exists between the athetistic and Christian ideas of human freedom.

Absolute Humanism Road to Absolute Despotism

When the atheist, against the vast evidence of the world in which God's "visible attributes are clearly seen," decides against possessing the knowledge of God, he simultaneously arrogates to himself the mission of persuading others to embrace his atheism. The mysterious psychological explanation of this drive to win converts to atheism is that this drive is but the passionate dimension of the atheist's decision against God. His denial of God is simultaneously his assertion of himself as being above God. His rejection of God is his projection of himself into the place formerly held by God. The metaphysical mystery profoundly explaining the psychological hostility of the atheist toward God is to be sought in a fundamental law of all reality. That law can be stated thus: No being can be neutral to the Source of all being. Being either witnesses to or denies the Source of all being; being either accepts or rejects the Source of all being. This law is clearly observed in inanimate nature where all beings obey, testify to and glorify their Creator in a manner determined by the fixed laws of the universe. But this law is even more profoundly and dramatically true of intelligent beings whose neutrality toward God is made impossible by the exercise of an intellect that hungers for infinite knowledge and a freedom that aspires to transcendent power. "He who is not with me," says Jesus, "is against me. And he who does not gather with me, scatters." In confrontation with God no intelligent being can remain static. By a metaphysically natural drive its hunger for transcendence is oriented toward Supreme Being. But because of its gift of freedom an intelligent being may deflect its drive for the divine away from God.

In this mysterious ability to direct himself in a free manner lies man's challenge to give himself to or withhold himself from God, his challenge to love or hate God. But the decision to love or hate God does not remain statically within the lover or hater, for, like love, hatred is also diffusive of itself. And just as love of God creates a community of lovers of God so too hatred of God moves to create a community of haters of God. Both love and hate drive to incarnate themselves in the beings of others. For love and hate are dynamic metaphysically relational realities. We can only love or hate the other or all those connected with the other. Thus, the true lover of God becomes an apostle for God; he shares his certitude, faith and love of God with those he aims to win to God. On the contrary, the real hater of God becomes an apostolic adversary of God; he radiates his doubt, denial and resentment of God to those he wants to win to atheism. There is therefore, a profound, metaphysical, logical and anti-social drive in every form of open or hidden atheism. Atheists beget atheists just as saints beget saints, just as men of God beget men of God, and devils beget devils.

It would be a mistake to think that atheists neglect the mind of man; they do make what seems like a valid appeal to the reason of their fellow men. In reality, however, upon closer analysis this appeal to reason is seen to be counterfeit; it is nothing more than a massive propaganda assault upon the mind intended to swamp the light of reason with its intensive passion. Not the compelling force of evidence but the compulsive force of passion pressed into the service of half-truths and downright falsehoods is ceaselessly employed to fashion conformity and unanimity of mind in favor of atheism. Conceived in the initial falsehood that God cannot exist because His being would threaten man's being, His knowledge negate man's mind, His freedom erase man's liberty, atheism is born and advances through an aggression against the mind of man of an army of arbitrary falsehoods. We need only the witness of Sacred Scripture to demonstrate this truth.

Satan, the father of lies, corrupted himself and legions of good spirits on the lie that he and they could become God. That lie begot hatred of God in these spirits and this hatred drove them to attempt the dethronement of God and the faithful angels. Their assault against both was a miserable failure. Christ told his apostles that "I saw Satan like lightning falling from heaven." And St. Peter relates that he saw the evil spirits "being drawn by infernal ropes into the pit of hell." The attempt to rule heaven without God ended in enslavement in hell without rule, heaven or God. On the other hand, the faithful spirits won both heaven and the direct presence of God. "For to serve God is to reign."

The historical demonstration of this truth continued in the drama of man's fall. Satan knew that God loved man and destined him for Himself. Because God loved man Satan hated him. He therefore attacked and corrupted mankind in its head in order to strike at God and all God loved. Once again the tactic was the tyranny of the lie, seduction through suasive propaganda: "You will be like God, knowing good and evil." Man fell from an exalted innocence and a freedom immune from the infinite assaults of wickedness into the confining pit of sin. The same lesson is horrifyingly clear throughout all sacred and profane history: Whoever strikes against God strikes down himself. The atheist denying God degrades himself. The atheist exalting himself above God sinks below the level of animate and inanimate beings. Liberation from God is enslavement in creatures. Absolute humanism is the sure road to absolute despotism. Denial of God as truth begets the imprisonment of man in the self-imposed darkness of his own myths. Flight from total dependence on God guarantees for man the utter loss of his freedom in a brutal enslavement either to sheer anarchy or to the tyrant who must eventually arise to impose upon the chaos of limitless human liberty the artificial, inhuman order of the concentration camp. We will only profoundly appreciate the satanic nature of atheism when we realize that denial of God is not merely an indifferent Nay-saying to God, but a kind of blasphemous joy at hating God and a thrilling decision to unite men in a community of enduring hate for the purpose of banishing God from the hearts of men.

Now the liberal atheists of the West know that the wanton exercise of limitless freedom can only lead to social chaos. This, of course, they do not want. Yet, since they cannot appeal to a benevolently Divine Source of absolute moral values in order to persuade their fellow men to exercise their freedom reasonably, the atheists must rely on external pressures to attain a human expression of freedom that respects the rights and liberty of all. Such artificial, external controls on the exercise of human liberty consist in man-made laws, customs and fashions. In effect the majority opinion of men prevailing at present alone restricts the scope of liberty. But history demonstrates that such artificial controls maintain a rather tenuous hold on the passions and despotic arbitrariness of man. Moral values founded solely on such exterior artificial standards are founded on the shifting sand of popular opinion, subject to the winds of change at any moment. Moreover, morality by majority preference alone is a two-edged sword. It may be constructive or destructive of man and society. The sexual morality popular in the cities of Sodom and Gomorrah brought them to utter destruction. The racial morality popular in Nazi Germany aimed at the extermination of the Jews. Any morality that depends on the whims of the masses, the spirit of the times, the instability of circumstances and the accidents of place is always a threat to freedom, often actually suppressing it. For, as happens often in times of decay, when all things are in disarray, there exists in this doctrine of moral relativism no eternally valid tribunal functioning beyond the tempests of time and immune from the temptations of tyrants, to which atheists can appeal for an absolutely just defense of their rights. The initial tragedy of the atheists takes place in the area of truth. They deny God as absolute Being and Goodness and they divinize man. Trapped in this false metaphysics, they becomes victims of philosophic relativism. Self-enslavement in the field of morals is an exorable brutal consequence of metaphysical self-enslavement in falsity. Once again "hoist by their own petard," this time in the sphere of moral relativism, atheists are helpless in trying to guarantee mankind his truly human goals of justice, truth, peace, prosperity, security or freedom. For just as absolute truth in the Being of God is the ultimate rampart against the rampant pretensions of false ideologies, so too, absolute justice in that same God is the last court of appeals for curtailing the rampant crime of wanton freedom. In a morality that appeals to the absolute Justice of God, men, for the sake of their fellow men, will witness with their lives to a truth and justice they know exists as eternally incorruptible and which will certainly prevail, even though it may presently be crushed under the heel of the tyrant. Whereas in a morality founded on metaphysical relativism, the tyranny of the totalitarian state, of the crowd bent on crime, of the pressure of prevailing propaganda and popular decadence will be opposed by no rationally sustained resistance of atheists. We need only analyze some recent tragic history. The apathy in the West before the utterly absurd absolutist dogmas—not to mention the massive heinous crimes—of Nazism, Fascism and Communism must be attributed to the West's retreat from adherence to God by faith and reason. On the part of believers, metaphysical and moral relativism weakened their attachment to God and produced in them a startling tolerance of incredible myths and an unnatural insensitivity to monstrous crimes. On the art of agnostics, sceptics and atheists, where their anti-theism did not produce an actual alliance with the criminals in power, it nevertheless rendered their protests puny and meaningless, since it was known that, at least in doctrine, they were themselves advocates of absolutist humanism, albeit of a more moderate type. Even today their inability to resist effectively the assaults of red absolutism indirectly aids the cause of this tyranny, if only by aiding the myth that this tyranny is invincible. Atheists have yet to learn the lesson so brilliantly taught by Dostoevsky through a character in one of his novels. Schigalev brutally lives out to its bitter consequences the doctrine of absolute revolution promoted in Nechaev's nefarious book, *Catechism For Revolution.* At the end of his odious accomplishments Schigalev makes the following confession: "After starting out from unlimited freedom I arrive at unlimited despotism."[5] When man becomes God, history testifies that then millions of men become imprisoned slaves, terrified automatons and murdered corpses. Society, in the words of Gabriel Marcel, becomes a "termite colony."

Atheist Humanism: Cancer in Community Life

When man becomes his own absolute center, then God becomes his hell, because God sets limits to man's greatness. But once having attained autoerotic sovereignty, a monstrous metamorphosis takes place in atheist man. He begins to feed on his own fellow men, for they now are his hell, threatening to rob him of his freedom. When God is rejected because he is seen as man's hell, then man, whom God loves, suffers the same fate and for the same reason. There is a frightening resemblance between the atheist humanist as a cell of society and a malignantly cancerous cell in the human body. Both cells have thrown off any service of subordination to the health of the communities in which they thrive. They act and grow according to their own uncontrolled ravenous appetites feeding parasitically on the whole organism. As runaway cells they

5. Georg Siegmund, *God On Trial,* p. 420.

invade and destroy every healthy cell in the body until they extinguish life and speed to completion the total disintegration of the unity of the body. Atheist humanism is a psychic cancer. It shares two major characteristics with physical cancer. Both these human cancers arise from the arbitrary rebellion of a subordinate cell against the established social harmony of the whole. Secondly, both these cancerous rebellions are metastatic and messianic in their aggression to the death against organism and community.

Earlier we indicated that atheist humanism in cutting man off from communion with God also isolates him from his fellow man. St. Paul indicates why these twin evils strike humanity together. Reminding the Roman Christians of those pagans who refused to accept the true God, he wrote: "As they have resolved against possessing the knowledge of God, God has given them up to a reprobate sense . . . so that they do what is not fitting, being filled with all iniquity . . ." He then goes on to enumerate a litany of heinous, unnatural vices which man, abandoned by God to the wantonness of his stubborn fallen nature, gladly, even proudly commits. He tells us that those practicing these crimes are deserving of death. And history records that nations, empires, the vast power of Rome itself sank into oblivion, destroyed by self-indulgent immorality.

This reprobate sense which moves atheists to "applaud others doing the same wicked deeds they themselves do," is the fire of cancer that is consuming modern nations. The late C. E. M. Joad, an atheist who returned to God through an exchange of a series of letters with Sir Arnold Lunn wrote in his book, *The Present And Future Of Religion:*

> Religious belief is rapidly and palpably on the decline. Young people in particular are either indifferent to religion or hostile to it. For the first time in history there is coming to maturity a generation of men and women who have no religion, and who feel no need for one. They are content to ignore it . . . Also they are very unhappy. And the suicide rate is abnormally high.[6]

Moreover, this reprobate sense has created a spirit of fear and suspicion which is saturating society. The bad fruit of this

6. Sir Arnold Lunn and Garth Lean, *The New Morlity* (London: Blandford Press, Revised and Enlarged edition, 1967), Quoted by Sir. Arnold Lunn on p. 25.

spirit is everywhere to be seen—contention, violence and dissolute sexual decadence. There is a mania abroad for plays, movies, magazines and T.V. shows based totally on cruelty, violence and sexual perversion. Part of the explanation for this unchecked indulgence in cruelty, morbidity and perversion is due to liberal atheists who, pressing ahead with their false ideas of freedom, come to the defence of man's unreasonable expressions of free love, free violence, free looting of property, free drugs, freedom to subvert society or to drop out of all social responsibility. Thus, such men have succeeded through the courts in attaining legal approval for many types of immoral conduct—divorce as a relief from marriage, abortion as a liberation from the unwanted child, contraceptive services as a protection against pregnancy, homosexuality for consenting adults. Moreover, the permissive program of these moral storm troopers calls for legalized euthanasia, artificial insemination, the free use of "soft" drugs and many other bills that would legalize other immoralities. These advocates of legalized immorality have attacked some of the most basic natural rights of man. Their influence on the judicial thinking of the courts has been most effective. For example, judicial "twistifications" of such previously well-defined notions as "establishment of religion" and obscenity have led to United States Supreme Court decisions which violate the rights of conscience of the majority in the name of imaginary freedom for the minority. To argue legally from the clear constitutional law of "no state religion" to the incredible position of "no voluntary prayer may be said by children in public schools." is to degrade the majesty of law by pressing it into the service of one's hostility to God and religion. Father Costanzo, S.J., Professor of Political Science and Constitutional Law at Fordham University, writes that such interpreting of the First Amendment "is not only wild and absurd reasoning but is also contrary to American legal and natural history, and in direct contradiction of the history of education in American schools, public as well as private."[7]

Moreover, the nature, purpose and limitations of freedom of expression in the communications media and the press have been so irrationally defined and expanded by the emotional, sophistical arguments of the legalistic storm troopers with

7. Rev. Joseph F. Costanzo, S.J., "Religion in Public School Education," *Thought*, Fordham University Press, N.Y., Vol. XXXI, No. 121, pp. 18–19.

atheistic proclivities that it has now become all but impossible
for the Court to recognize obscenity and thus practically impossible to convict anyone of the crime of obscenity. Meanwhile,
a deluge of patently pornographic poison floods the public market and, to the frustrating dismay of angry parents and citizens,
corrupts the morals of the nation. Writing from New York on
May 2, 1968, English correspondent Mr. Ian Brodie indicated
why America was fast deteriorating from a puritan to a pagan
society:

> The keys to this personality change are a number of Su-
> preme Court decisions which virtually outlaw censorship
> and decree that obscenity is not illegal . . . It is a curious
> irony that the Supreme Court, dedicated to preserving the
> freedom which is the foundation of American life, has
> confused it with license. In doing so it has given its seal of
> approval to the sick society which will undermine the
> United States from within.[8]

Leavening the social anarchy escalating in the sick society of
the West are the moral licenses advocated by some prominent
intellectual atheists. Mathematician Bertrand Russell, who
held that "the whole conception of God is a conception derived
from ancient Oriental despotisms . . . quite unworthy of men,"[9]
also defended sexual promiscuity, going so far as to advise
wives to be as unfaithful as husbands. His biographer, Alan
Wood, writes about Russell's ideas on marriage morals and pre-
marital sex thus:

> Russell noted that marital infidelity was traditionally
> greater among husbands than wives . . . it seemed that, to
> make all things square, wives should be as unfaithful as
> husbands. He suggested that marriage should not be re-
> garded as excluding outside sexual relations; and that hus-
> bands, instead of restraining their inclinations in this
> regard, should confine themselves to restraining any jeal-
> ousy at similar infidelities by their wives . . . It was un-
> desirable, he said, that either a man or a woman should
> enter upon the serious business of a marriage intended to

---

8. Sir Arnold Lunn and Garth Lean, *Christian Counter-Attack*, (London:
Blandford Press, 1969), pp. 50–51.
9. Bertrand Russell, *Why I Am Not A Christian* (London: Unwin Books),
1967, p. 26.

lead to children without having had previous sexual intercourse; and this view, though still controversial, became
widely accepted in many countries.[10]

It is scarcely surprising that Mr. Wood concludes that "more
than anyone else he changed the outlook on sex morality of a
whole new generation."[11]

Dr. Joseph Fletcher, Professor of Ethics at the Episcopal Theological Seminary, Cambridge, Mass., says that good morals all
depend on the situation. He tells us that there are situations
when the last six commandments of God, *"any* or *all of them,"*
which normally forbid murder, adultery, stealing, false witnessing and covetousness, may have to be broken by the morally good man who will act from the motive of tender love, the
motive that makes all human acts good. "Not every pre-marital
sex relationship or theft or fornication or conspiracy to destroy
a lawfully constituted government is evil." "Every man must
decide for himself according to his own estimate of conditions:
and no one can decide for him or impugn the decision to which
he comes."[12] Here is secular atheistic humanism in a clear,
pure state, for it assumes in each individual the divine preroga-
tives to act as totally as one wills concerning the ways of men.

Herbert Marcuse, philosopher and now fast-fading idol of the
radical Left because "he is unduly suspicious of sexual freedom," nevertheless did not disappoint his student worshipers in
the beginning of his oracular career when he advocated the
free use of drugs as an excellent expression of total protest and
freedom. Sir Julian Huxley, scientist-humanist-atheist, for
whom non-scientifically proven evolution is nevertheless *de
fide,* is on public record for the future improvement of the
human race through the use of wide-scale compulsory artificial
insemination. The generic intelligence of the race can be raised
by a process of eugenic selection. But in practice how does one
encourage geniuses and bright people to have more children,
especially in an age obsessed with preventing children from
coming along to life? The matter should not be left to the pri-

10. Alan Wood, *Bertrand Russell: The Passionate Sceptic* (London: Unwin
Books, 1957), pp. 149–152.
11. *Ibid.,* p. 146.
12. Joseph Fletcher, *Situation Ethics* (Philadelphia: Westminster Press,
1966), p. 74.

vate decisions of the more intelligent, otherwise the needed psychosocial evolution will never develop rapidly enough. Therefore, eugenics, aided by the coercive power of the government, "will eventually have to have recourse to methods like multiple artificial insemination by preferred donors of high genetic quality."[13]

Dr. Harvey Cox, Professor of Church and Society at Harvard University, advocates a new allegiance of religious fervor, not to the City of God but to the Secular City. Man's devotion to this new church is to be expressed through the practice of the virtures of profanity and pragmatism. In the Coxian lexicon profanity defines and celebrates man's escape from the temple while promoting a human life guided by the norms of religionless morality. Self-achieved salvation is man's destiny here and here alone. Pragmatism emphasizes the "come of age" secularist's program for salvation. It consists in performing great historical acts of political and social reform. Only through the spirit of profanity and the performance of pragmatism will man escape from the tyranny of God and the hypocrisy of Christian moralism, pietism and legalism. The God in the Secular City is Almighty Man.

Thus because of the novel interpretations of leading influential intellectuals, many of whom are robust atheists while others, supposedly Christian, are in reality thin theologians afflicted with a fever for atheism, the sick society of the West is dying of an overdose of freedom. The essential freedom of man consists in freedom from God. Freedom for truth consists in freedom for man-made truth not for transcendent truth. Freedom of religion is interpreted to be freedom from religion. Freedom of self-expression is identified with feedom from any restraint at all in man's personal and social life. As a result, the falsity is fostered in the minds of millions that any legitimately established power or authority is the natural mortal enemy of man. God, Church, family, State, traditional dogma, morality, law and even all institutions established for the common good of man: congress, schools, courts, capital, labor—the whole system is represented as being rotten and ripe for revolutionary burning. In a word, atheistic humanism tends to rot every natu-

13. Sir. Arnold Lunn and Garth Lean. *The Cult Of Softness*, (London: Blandford Press, 1969), p. 65.

ral and social differentiation into an opposition of resentment, hate and violence. The "affectless society," that is loveless society, soon degenerates into the jungle of inflamed litigation and overt violent crime. For where atheistic humanism flourishes there exists a general flight from reason and revelation and that society which St. Paul described in his letter to the Romans is once again realized as a monstrous reality—a society in the throes of its own self-inflicted fevers, dying violently by its own hand because it has lived lustfully by its own will "without affection, without fidelity, without mercy."

Conclusion: The Agony of Godless Humanism

Atheists have introduced a mythical war, a hostile contradiction at the heart of the metaphysical-religious-moral-legal continuum of sacredly ordered being. For them God is the enemy of man; the divine-natural-moral-law morality is the enemy of political, social and civic society; positive civic and federal laws are artificial barriers calculated to maintain social injustice and prevent needed reform. Thus the atheist humanist, when he uses philosophic and religious relativism to deny God, shatters the complementary harmony that exists in the metaphysical-religious-moral continuum established by the all-wise Creator. But this work of demolition does not stop here. For the atheist is thorough, if nothing else. Now using the battering ram of legal positivism, he levels the wall of unity that maintains the religious-moral-legal continuum of tranquillity. The atheist humanist is a total wrecker; he aims at destroying those four towers of strength set up by God and maintained by God-fearing men for the establishment, protection and development of man's life as an adventure toward God in which the spiritual always takes the primacy over the material. In denying the tri-une God the atheist would also smash that coherent trinity of reality—God, man and religious morality—established to bring man personal peace, social order and divine sanctity. The atheist violently divorces God from man, man from religious morals and religious morals from positive law, thereby creating three abysmal spiritual vacuums in the life of man in the vain hope of setting man totally free. In reality he traps himself in his own net of despotism.

The theistic vacuum inevitably leads to the religious-moral vacuum and these two eventually lead to the legal vacuum. Almighty Man, swollen with arrogance, rushes in to fill the theistic vacuum left by the deposed Deity. Licentious hedonism —eventually in the form of violently idolatrized sex—usurps the vacant throne of the absolute divine natural-law morality. Finally, anarchism snatches the reins of lawlessness and, drunk with the power of limitless freedom, drives the herds of men through total chaos to totalitarian despotism. Thus do extremes meet and total human freedom identifies itself with total human slavery. Such is the brutal, logical, metaphysical-historical dialectic of atheistic humanism. Via violent revolutionary rationalism, nations have traveled the route from atheistic confessionalism to laicism to totalitarian Caesarism. The France that fell under the despotic power of Napoleonic Caesarism is a classic example. In our own day, deluding seven million Cubans with the atheistic cry of hope, *"Humanismo es nostra vida,"*—"Humanism is our way,"—atheist Fidel Castro has led a formerly free nation into moral, economic destitution and the termite slavery of communistic Caesarism. "In a universe without God," wrote Andre Malraux, "life is absurd."[14] And we add, violently brutal, for when man is his own God, heads roll and blood flows copiously on the altar of man's satanic pride and insatiable lust for power over his fellow man.

Even within its own house of organized atheism, godless humanism will not tolerate any expansion of freedom of expression or action among its sons of atheism. We have already considered the classic case of China. The most recent historical proof of this intransigence to human liberty even for the sons of atheism is the example of Czechoslovakia. In the late summer of 1968 a veritable Pentecost of liberating winds was set in motion for the nation by those sons of the Party, Dubcek and Smrkowsky; the citizens were heartened with a hope for new freedom. The Stalinist tyrant, Novotny, was deposed; political measures liberalizing the communications media were promulgated; the economy was loosened a bit from the grip of socialism. Dialogue with free Europe and the whole West began to flourish. Atheist humanists in the free world were enthusias-

14. Julian Critchley, "André Malraux: A Profile", *The Times Saturday Review*, November 18, 1967, Quoted in *Christian Counter-Attack*, p. 70.

tically comparing the humane communism of Russia and Europe with that brutal brand in power in China. They saw fresh hope for the world in the mellowing, the liberalization taking place in the atheistic humanism in Czechoslovakia. They predicted another Yugoslavia; that is, another nation enjoying political, economic, cultural sovereignty yet remaining within the atheistic humanist hegemony. Here was proof that atheistic humanism, even in its political incarnation, did encourage human freedom.

Suddenly the political and spiritual winds changed. A harsh freeze set in from the north. That sound from heaven did not come from the violent blowing of the liberating Spirit; it came from invading war planes. Those tongues of fire that parted darkness from dawn were not the polyglot gift of life-giving dialogue; they were the tongues of tanks, the gun fire that silenced the tongues of national freedom in fear and death. The new course to freedom was barricaded; the iron curtain was reinforced with the inner military curtain of occupation. At the moment of this writing the purge of the heretics from freedom is in full swing; thousands are disappearing into prisons and labor camps. Already the leaders for the reforms fostering freedom are politically destroyed. Dubcek was expelled from the Praesidium of the Communist Party and sent to a quasi-exile as Ambassador to Turkey. Smrkowsky is expelled from political life altogether. Moreover, the process of their spiritual degradation grinds on relentlessly, directed by Quislings empowered to obliterate all local voices for freedom. Press, radio and television are again throttled, echoing only slogans of the purging Party. Once again atheist humanists of the West are in a state of shock at the brutal methods of their fellow atheists. But once again they refuse to draw the metaphysical conclusions or apply the pragmatic rule of evil fruit evil tree.

They refuse to see that atheistic ideology gives birth to the cult of inhuman cruelty. Nicholas Berdyaev, who suffered at the hands of Russian atheism, called this religion of secularism "an inverted theocracy." And history continually witnesses to the truth of this description. When Stalin died at the end of a reign of terror, purges and blood, Mr. Khrushchev, emotionally shaken by the record of this human monster, denounced in his famous de-Stalinization report to the Party, the divinization of the Party leader which had given Stalin absolute control over the whole U.S.S.R. Khrushchev complained that the cult of the leader developed by Stalin had a religious and supernatural quality about it that made him into a god:

> It is intolerable and foreign to the spirit of Marxism-Leninism to exalt a person and to make him a superman endowed with supernatural qualities equal to a God. Such a man is supposed to know everything, to think for the whole world, to do everything and to be infallible.[15]

Khrushchev was wrong in one important point. For the facts of history show that the cult of divinizing the Party leader is not at all foreign to the spirit of Marxism-Leninism, but indeed natural to it. As Gaston Fessard reminds us, the divinizing cult of the leader of the Party began the day after Lenin's death when all his collaborators canonized him, embalmed him, established and created his tomb as a shrine for atheist pilgrims. In demanding and exacting divine homage, Stalin acted in the name of Leninism, liquidating, even as Lenin did, all his enemies, acting always as one equal to a god. Moreover, divinization inevitably overtook Khruschev himself. Acting as one equal to a god he conducted purges of his own at his home. Abroad he chrushed the Hungarian revolution for freedom, killing some twenty thousand with tank fire. Again in the international sphere he threatened the whole world with atomic war over communist Cuba which he saved for Castroite slavery. This is the same Mr. Khrushchev who was in tears as he narrated the nightmarish cruelties of his former god, Stalin. What had happened to his protest against the cult of personality? Slowly, inexorably, under the pressure of atheistic ideology and in the continuous struggle to suppress the human spirit

15. Gaston Fessard, "The Theological Structure of Marxist Atheism," *Concilium*, Burns & Oates, London, June 1966, p. 10. Early in October 1969, twenty years after his rise to power, a liturgy honoring Mao in China flashed across the TV screens of the world. In cadenced unison millions of the faithful, regimented at his feet, chanted hymns of praise. Together they projected arms skyward, the Vangel of Mao's thoughts in their hands. Cameras caught the religious delirium in the eyes; sound-tracks recorded the fervor of screeching voices. Posters, full of savage slogans, depicted comrades crushing heretical heads. Above it all on his massive altar, divine Mao smiled his Oriental smile. Never have I seen human divinization and human degradation coincide so perfectly in so ghastly an atheistic liturgy.

which is forever striving to break the bonds of enslavement, throw down its oppressors and transcend into the space of human freedom, the Party leader evolves from atheist humanist to despot God. Like a divinized Nero fearful of losing his power to other gods, he does not hesitate to commit crimes that once shocked him in his predecessor god. Now, himself habituated to crime, he liquidated foes, friends, even family. Now it all seems to easy, so natural, to hurl divine thunderbolts. And he justifies the most heinous deeds as acts of dutiful fidelity to that future God who is coming through the historical evolution of the proletariat—the God of the classless society. True, his atheist comrades removed Khrushchev from power before he could become totally habituated to or invincibly established on the throne of his divinity. Nevertheless, in this church of organized atheism the divinizing cult of the party leader cannot be eradicated; it is the logical, inevitable fruit of man's madness to displace the true God. Whether the tyrant human god is divined through the cult of one person or of that secularized trinity, the troika, makes no difference. The leader atheist or the troika of atheists or the Party of atheists or even the Union of Socialist Republics of Atheism, can as it suits the purposes of the Party each be magnified into the Divine Being. For, under the pain of commiting social suicide, some form of cult of human divinity must be maintained. For without such a cult the ideology of atheism must surely collapse, since the cult constitutes the basis of its power.

Atheism is an idolatry which worships that strange God—absolute Man. There is in the nature of atheism a metaphysical connection between its arrogant assumption of divinity and its self-indulgence in egocentric absolutism. For just as the child, spoiled on the excessive love of its parents, turns upon and attacks them with irrational cruelty, so too the atheist, spoiled on the excessive flattery of humanists proclaiming him god, turns on mankind and brutally victimizes it. At the mysterious depths of moral wickedness, self-indulgence in absolutism and boundless cruelty join forces in an allied effort to destroy god and man. The fact is that humanism without God has not succeeded in humanizing man; it has succeeded in driving man insane and putting him to work wrecking the world and his own great civilization. Chesterton was convinced that when man

denied God, he would not believe in nothing, but he would believe in anything. He would, moreover, not do nothing, but as
a fanatic he would do anything, even wreck this world out of
hatred of the nonexistent other. Chesterton wrote:

> There are men who will ruin themselves and ruin their
> civilization if they may ruin also this old fantastic tale.
> This is the last and most astounding fact about this faith;
> that its enemies will use any weapon against it, the sword
> that cuts their own fingers, and the firebrands that burn
> their own homes . . . He (the atheist fanatic) sacrifices the
> very existence of humanity to the non-existence of God.
> He offers his victims not to the altar, but merely to assert
> the idleness of the altar and the emptiness of the throne.
> He is ready to ruin even that primary ethic by which all
> things live, for his strange and eternal vengeance upon
> some one who never lived at all.[16]

Some forty-three years ago, in 1926, Oswald Spengler, like a
prophet of old called in to advise a king of Israel about God's
wrath on a faithless nation, wrote, as a salutary warning to the
Western Nations, a diagnosis of the disease that was slowly but
surely destroying them.

> You are dying. I see in you all the characteristic stigma of
> decay. I can prove that your great wealth and your great
> poverty, your capitalism and your socialism, your wars
> and your revolutions, your atheism and your pessimism
> and your cynicism, your immorality, your broken-down
> marriages, your birth-control, that is bleeding you from
> the bottom and killing you off at the top in your brains—
> can prove to you that these were characteristic marks of
> the dying ages of ancient states—Alexandria and Greece
> and neurotic Rome.[17]

In conclusion, then, the overwhelming weight of past and
present historical evidence demonstrates that anthropologist
Dr. Edmund R. Leach is tragically mistaken when he claims
that "it has become useless to appeal to God against the Devil;
the scientist must be the sole source of his morality . . . Man

16. Mr G. K. Chesterton, *Orthodoxy*, pp. 238–139.
17. Oswald Spengler, *Decline Of The West* (London: Allen & Unwin, 1932),
p. 000

must assume the moral responsibilities of God."[18] For, throughout this study of the many faces of that strange god, Almighty Man, we have seen that man, in attempting to do precisely that —be an atheist and his own God—has only succeeded in establishing an inhuman humanism, a political and religiously perverted atheism which violently forces him and that third of the world where this atheism is the official religion into total bondage to the father of lies and the unnatural perversions that lead on to nihilism. Idol-perverted through the worship of itself, atheistic humanism practices the licentious liturgy of feeding its Man-God idol on man-god victims, a sort of divine-human cannibalism. The adventure of atheism is seen, in the last analysis, to be that unfathomable iniquity which attacks the very roots of reality, divorcing things, persons, societies from God and organizing them into a militant Kingdom of hate that ceaselessly and sacrilegiously assaults the sanctity of God and the dignity of men.

Lenin, that arch-atheist who assessed Christianity as The Enemy to be destroyed, expressed a profound truth in these words: "Our revolution will never succeed until the myth of God is removed from the mind of man." He certainly had a clear, total grasp of the messianic drama being fought out through the ages. *Deus delendus est.* "God must be destroyed" is the battle cry of militant atheists. In the last fifty to sixty years these atheists have attained much success. They have turned back the great Christian missionary armies from China, Africa and other foreign lands. China seems completely conquered by militant atheism. Russia, Eastern Europe and now Cuba, formerly Christian, are now part of that third of the world under the rule of organized atheism. Bad as this defeat is for the forces of belief, Christianity now seems to be in full retreat also in the West. In Europe and America the disintegration of Protestant theology—dogma and morals—before the onslaughts of secularism has led to the disintegration of the Protestant Churches. Europe and America are now highly desacralized areas of the world. Finally, the Catholic Church, infected with the "new modernism," is being interiorly torn

18. Dr. Edmund R. Leach, "We Scientists Have the Right to Play God," *The Saturday Evening Post*, November 16, 1968, p. 20.

asunder by "a spirit of corrosive criticism that has become fashionable in certain sections of Catholic life," according to the testimony of Pope Paul VI himself. What is alarming about this criticism is that it attacks not only policies of churchmen in the Church, but above all casts doubt on the veracity of many long-established dogmas and morals. It is a crisis of authority and of faith. It thus appears that the missionaries of atheism are successfully creating a world culture founded on the dogma that God is dead.

What can believers do to reclaim the world for the true God? First, believers must become as clear-headed about the nature of the struggle as Lenin was. Their battle cry must be: *Atheismus delendus est:* (Atheism must be destroyed). Second, and more important, believers must become as effectively militant against the enemies of God as the Chosen People and the early Christians were against the idolators of their times. Today there is need of militant believers. The counter-attack the children of light will have to mount must be double-pronged. They must articulately dispel the darkness created by the propagandists for atheism, using doctrine and history—facts and results —to unveil the utter insubstantiality and hypocrisy of the atheist cause. Moreover, and above all, believers must witness by bold deeds of *moral rectitude* to the majesty and holiness of the transcendent God and Christ. Their good works must shine before men, lifting them from the seduction of humanism to the glorification of man in the Father. What is needed is "salted" not sentimental, infectious not infected believers and Christians. Like the Psalmist and prophets of old, like John the baptist and Christ Himself, believers must challenge and condemn the current, popular, heretical nostrums of atheist humanism, preferring to be "with God" than "with it in the world," even if in imitation of the prophets, the Baptist and Christ, their stand for God should cost them the scourge of persecution and loss of life. For the conflict between atheism and belief in God ought never to be reduced to a non-decisional dialogue between intellectual opponents, nor to a choice between war and peace, but only to a choice between victory and defeat. The believer must work to kill the error of atheism so as to share, through persuasion, with the atheist whom he loves, the joy of possessing God as truth and Love. Moreover, a victorious faith in God must prepare the militant believer to pay joyfully the sacrifices of victory, even as a victorious Christ first willingly endured the sacrifice of the cross.

The ideals and zeals of the men studied, however inadequately, in this work demonstrate a profound fact about man: The most urgent need in man is his metaphysical hunger for communion with a personal God. Man cannot, and hence will not, remain neutral to the mystery of a personal Divine Presence. For this personal Divine Presence alone gives adequate meaning and mission to his life. This truth was long ago testified to by God Himself in the company of Moses on Mt. Thabor. Commissioned to sculpt into stone the most important commandments by which man could live meaningfully and holily, Moses failed to write the following commandment: "Thou shall not be an atheist." Instead his first commandment read: "I am the Lord thy God . . . Thou shalt not have strange gods before me." It was as if Moses had written: "Atheists are not godless men; they are men addicted to false gods." Thus, the battle of love to which the Christian is honorably called today is the struggle to liberate his atheist neighbors from enthrallment to false gods and to help these neighbors find the True God. And in order to fulfill this noble mission the Christian may never forget that the escape from the dungeons of the false gods to the mountain of the True God demands a persevering, courageous journey through the desert of self-sacrifice.

Bibliography

Allen, George and Unwin, *I Believe,* A Symposium (London: Unwin Books, 1965).

Altizer, Thomas, *The Gospel of Christian Atheism* (Philadelphia: Westminster, 1966).

Balthasar, Hans Urs von, *The God Question and Modern Man* (London: Seabury, 1967).

Bannan, John F., *The Philosophy of Merleau-Ponty* (New York: Harcourt, Brace & World, 1967).

Barrett, William, *Irrational Man* (New York: Doubleday Anchor, 1962).

——, *What Is Existentialism?* (New York: Grove Press, 1964).

Barth, Karl, *God Here and Now* (London: Routledge and Kegan Paul, 1964).

——, *The Word of God and the Word of Man* (New York: Harper Torchbooks, 1957).

Baum, Gregory, editor, *The Future of Belief Debate* (New York: Herder and Herder, 1967).

Blamires, Harry, *The Christian Mind* (London: S.P.C.K., 1966).

Bochenski, I. M., *Contemporary European Philosophy* (Berkeley: University of California Press, 1966).

Bonhoeffer, Dietrich, *Letters and Papers from Prison,* edited by Eberhard Bethge, translated by Reginald H. Fuller (New York: Macmillan, 1953).

——, *Life Together* (London: SCM Press, 1965).

——, *No Rusty Swords* (New York: Harper & Row, 1965).

Borne, Étienne, *Atheism* (New York: Hawthorn Publishers, 1961).

Bosanquet, Mary, *The Life and Death of Dietrich Bonhoeffer* (London: Hodder & Stoughton, 1968).

Brinton, Crane, *The Anatomy of Revolution* (New York: Vintage Books, 1952).

——, *The Jacobins* (New York: Macmillan, 1930).

——, *Nietzsche* (New York: Harper Torchbooks, 1965).

Brown, Harold, O. J., *The Protest of a Troubled Protestant* (New Rochelle, N.Y.: Arlington House, 1969).

Bultmann, Rudolf and Jaspers, Karl, *Myth and Christianity* (New York: Noonday, 1958).

————, *New Testament and Mythology* in *Kerygma and Myth,* 2 vols. (New York: Harper Torchbooks, 1961).

Burkle, Howard, R., *The Non-Existence of God* (New York: Herder and Herder, 1969).

Calvez, Jean-Yves, *La Pensée de Karl Marx* (Paris: Editions du Seuil, 1956).

Camus, Albert, *Cross Purpose* (London: Penguin, 1965).

————, *The Myth of Sisyphus,* translated by Justin O'Brien (New York: Vintage Books, 1965).

————, *The Plague,* translated by Stuart Gilbert (London: Penguin, 1967).

————, *The Fall,* translated by Justin O'Brien (New York: Alfred A. Knopf, 1965).

————, *The Rebel* (New York: Alfred A. Knopf, 1966).

Caute, David, editor, *Essential Writings of Karl Marx* (London: Panther, 1967).

Chesterton, G. K., *Orthodoxy* (New York: Doubleday, 1959).

Ciszek, Walter J., *With God in Russia* (New York: Doubleday Image, 1964).

Comisión Interprovincial Española, *Decreto sobre ateismo* (Madrid: 1966).

Comte, Auguste, *Cours de philosophie positive,* Vol. I (Paris: Société Positiviste, 1892-94).

————, *Système de politique positive* (Paris: Société Positiviste, 1912).

————, *Catéchisme positiviste* (Paris: [Réédition] Garnier, 1909).

Copleston, Frederick, *History of Philosophy,* Vols. 7 and 8, Parts I and II (New York: Doubleday Image, 1965, 1966).

————, *Contemporary Philosophy* (London: Burns & Oates, 1965).

Costanzo, Joseph F., *The Academy and the City* (Cork: Cork University Press, 1961).

————, *Academic Freedom and the Intellectual* (Cork: Cork University Press, 1960).

————, *This Nation Under God* (New York: Herder and Herder, 1964).

Cox, Harvey, *The Secular City* (New York: Macmillan, 1965).

Cullmann, Oscar, *Christ and Time* (London: SCM Press, 1962).

Daniélou, Jean, *God and the Ways of Knowing* (Cleveland: World Publishing, 1965).

————, *Lord of History* (Chicago: Regnery, 1958).

D'Arcy, Martin, *Communism and Christianity* (New York: Penguin, 1956).

De Beauvoir, Simone, *The Ethics of Ambiguity* (New York: Citadel Press, 1967).

D'Holbach, P. T., *Christianity Unveiled,* translated by Robertson and Gowan (New York: Columbian Press, 1795).

de Lubac, Henri, *Atheisme et sens de l'homme* (Paris: Éditions du Cerf, 1968).

———, *The Drama of Atheist Humanism* (Cleveland: World Publishing, 1965).

Denton, David E., *The Philosophy of Albert Camus* (Boston: Prime Publishers, 1967).

Derrick, Christopher, *Trimming the Ark* (New York: P. J. Kennedy & Sons, 1967).

Desan, Wilfrid, *The Tragic Finale* (New York: Harper Torchbooks, 1960).

De Waelhens, A., *Une Philosophie de l'ambiguité: L'existentialisme de Maurice Merleau-Ponty* (Louvain: 1951).

Dewart, Leslie, *The Future of Belief* (New York: Herder and Herder, 1966).

Dirscherl, Denis, editor, *Speaking of God* (Milwaukee: Bruce, 1967).

Dostoevsky, Feodor, *The Brothers Karamazov* (New York: Modern Library, 1950).

———, *The Grand Inquisitor* (London: E. Matthews & Marrot, 1930).

———, *The Idiot* (London: Penguin, 1955).

———, *The Devils (The Possessed),* translated by David Magarshark (London: Penguin, 1953).

Dumas, Georges, *Psychologie des deux messies positivistes: Saint Simon et Auguste Comte* (Paris: Alcan, 1905).

Edwards, David L., *The Honest to God Debate* (Philadelphia: Westminster, 1963).

Eliot, T. S. *Christianity and Culture* (New York: Harcourt, Brace & World, 1949).

Fabro, Cornelio, *God in Exile: Modern Atheism* (Westminster, Md.: Newman Press, 1968).

Feuer, Lewis S., ed., *Marx & Engels: Basic Writings* (New York: Doubleday, 1959).

Feuerbach, Ludwig, *The Essence of Christianity,* translated by George Eliot (New York: Harper Torchbooks, 1957).

Fletcher, Joseph, *Situation Ethics* (Philadelphia: Westminster, 1966).

Ortega y Gasset, José, *Man and Crisis* (London: George Allen & Unwin, 1958).

———, *The Revolt of the Masses* (London: Unwin Books, 1963).

Gilson, Étienne, *Christianity and Philosophy* (New York: Sheed and Ward, 1939).

———, *God and Philosophy* (New Haven: Yale University Press, 1941).

———, *Les Tribulations de Sophie* (Paris: J. Vrin, 1967).

Girardi, Giulio, *L'ateismo contemporaneo,* Direttore (Torino: Società Editrice Internazionale, Vol. 2, 1967).

Girardi, Giulio, *L'atheisme dans la vie et la culture contemporaines,* Tome I, Vol. 1; Tome 1, Vol. 2 (Paris: Desclée & Cie, 1967, 1968).

Hamilton, William, *The New Essence of Christianity* (New York: Association Press, 1961).

Hazard, P., *European Thought in the Eighteenth Century* (New Haven: Yale University Press, 1954).

————, *The European Mind* (London: Hollis and Carter, 1953).

Hebblethwaite, Peter, *The Council Fathers and Atheism* (New York: Paulist Press, 1966).

Heidegger, Martin, *Being and Time,* translated by John Macquarrie and Edward Robinson (Oxford: Basil Blackwell, 1967).

————, *Existence and Being* (London: Vision Press, 1968).

————, "Letter on Humanism," in *Philosophy in the Twentieth Century* (New York: Random House, 1962).

Herberg, Will, *Four Existentialist Theologians* (New York: Doubleday, 1958).

Hick, John, *The Existence of God* (New York: Macmillan, 1964).

Hildebrand, Dietrich von, *Christian Ethics* (New York: David McKay Co., 1953).

————, *Graven Images* (New York: David McKay Co., 1957).

————, *The New Tower of Babel* (New York: P. J. Kennedy & Sons, 1953).

————, *Trojan Horse in the City of God* (Chicago: Franciscan Herald Press, 1967).

Hoyle, Fred, *The Nature of the Universe* (London: Penguin, 1965).

Jaspers, Karl, *Nietzsche and Christianity,* translated by E. B. Ashton (Chicago: Regnery, 1961).

————, *Reason and Existence* (New York: Noonday Press, 1955).

Jenkins, Daniel, *Believing in God* (London: Carey Kingsgate Press, 1965).

Jenkins, David E., *Guide to the Debate About God* (Philadelphia: Westminster, 1966).

Jolivet, Régis, *The God of Reason* (New York: Hawthorn Publishers, 1958).

Kaufmann, Walter, trans., *The Portable Nietzsche* (New York: Viking Press, 1967).

————, *Nietzsche: Philosopher, Psychologist, Antichrist* (Cleveland: World Publishing, 1966).

Knox, Ronald, A., *Enthusiasm* (Oxford: Clarendon Press, 1950).

Kwant, Remy C., *The Phenomenological Philosophy of Merleau-Ponty* (Pittsburgh: Duquesne University Press, 1963).

Lacroix, Jean, *The Meaning of Modern Atheism,* translated by Garrett Barden (New York: Macmillan, 1965).

Lean, Garth, *Brave Men Choose* (London: Blandford Press, 1961).

———, *John Wesley, Anglican* (London: Blandford Press, 1964).

Lenin, V. I., *Selected Works* (New York: International Publishers, Vol. IX, 1943).

Luijpen, William A., *Phenomenology and Atheism* (Pittsburgh: Duquesne University Press, 1964).

———, *Existential Phenomenology* (Pittsburgh: Duquesne University Press, 1960).

———, *Phenomenology and Metaphysics* (Pittsburgh: Duquesne University Press, 1965).

Lunn, Arnold and Lean, Garth, *Christian Counter-Attack* (London: Blandford Press, 1969).

———, and Lean, Garth, *The New Morality,* rev. ed. (London: Blandford Press, 1967).

———, and Lean, Garth, *The Cult of Softness* (London: Blandford Press, 1969).

Lyons, Eugene, *Workers' Paradise Lost* (New York: Funk & Wagnalls, 1967).

Macquarrie, John, *An Existentialist Theology* (New York: Harper Torchbooks, 1965).

———, *Martin Heidegger,* (London: Lutterworth Press, 1968).

Malevez, L., *Le Message Chrétien et le mythe* (Brussels: Desclée de Brouwer, 1954).

Malik, Charles, *War and Peace* (New York: National Committee for a Free Europe, 1950).

Marcel, Gabriel, *The Philosophy of Existence* (New York: Citadel, 1968).

Maritain, Jacques, *Moral Philosophy* (London: Geoffrey Bles, 1964).

Marlé, René, *Bonhoeffer: The Man and His Work* (New York: Newman Press, 1968).

———, *Bultmann et l'interprétation du Nouveau Testament* (Paris: Aubier, 1955).

Marty, Martin B., *Varieties of Unbelief* (New York: Doubleday Anchor, 1966).

———, *The Holy Family* (London: Lawrence & Wishart, 1956).

Mascall, E. L., *He Who Is* (London: Libra Books, 1966).

———, *The Christian Universe* (London: Darton, Longman & Todd, 1966).

———, *The Secularization of Christianity* (New York: Holt, Rinehart and Winston, 1965).

Mehta, Ved M., *The New Theologian* (New York: Harper & Row, 1966).

Mendel, Arthur, editor, *Essential Works of Marx* (New York: Bantam, 1965).

Merleau-Ponty, Maurice, *Éloge de la Philosophie* (Paris: Gallimard, 1960).

———, *Phénoménologie de la perception* (Paris: Gallimard, 1945).

———, *Sens et Non-Sens* (Paris: Nagel, 1966).

———, *Humanisme et Terreur* (Paris: Gallimard, 1947).

Mill, John Stuart, *Auguste Comte and Positivism* (Ann Arbor, Michigan: University of Michigan Press, 1961).

Mineka, Francis E., ed., *Collected Works of John Stuart Mill* (Toronto: Toronto University Press, Vol XIII, 1963).

Molnar, Thomas, *Sartre: Ideologue of Our Time* (New York: Funk & Wagnalls, 1968).

———, *Utopia: The Perennial Heresy* (New York: Sheed and Ward, 1967).

Murchland, Bernard, editor, *The Meaning of the Death of God* (New York: Random House, 1967).

Murray, John Courtney, *The Problem of God* (New Haven: Yale University Press, 1964).

Niebuhr, Reinhold, *Faith and History* (New York: Charles Scribner's Sons, 1949).

Nietzsche, Friedrich, *The Antichrist* (New York: Viking Press, 1954).

———, *The Gay Science* (New York: Viking Press, 1954).

———, *Unpublished Letters* (London: Peter Owen, 1960).

———, *The Birth of Tragedy* (New York: Doubleday, 1956).

———, *The Genealogy of Morals* (New York: Doubleday, 1967).

———, *Beyond Good and Evil* (Chicago: Henry Regnery, 1966).

———, *Joyful Wisdom* (New York: Macmillan, 1910).

Ogletree, Thomas W., *The Death of God Controversy* (Nashville: Abingdon, 1966).

O'Meara, Thomas and Weisser, Donald, *Rudolf Bultmann in Catholic Thought* (New York: Herder and Herder, 1968).

Pascal, Blaise, *Pensées,* edited by Brunschvicg (London: Penguin, 1966).

Picard, Max, *Hitler in Ourselves* (Hinsdale, Ill.: Regnery, 1947).

Pope Pius XI, Encyclical *on Atheistic Communism* ("Divini Redemptoris." 1937) (New York: The America Press, 1937).

Rahner, Karl, ed., *The Pastoral Approach to Atheism* (New York: Paulist, 1967).

Ramsey, Paul, *Nine Modern Moralists* (Englewood Cliffs: Prentice Hall, 1962).

Ravines, Eudocio, *The Yenan Way* (New York: Charles Scribner's Sons, 1951).

Richard, Robert L., *Secularization Theology* (New York: Herder and Herder, 1967).

Roberts, David E., *Existentialism and Religious Belief,* Galaxy Books (New York: Oxford University Press, 1959).

Robinson, John A. T., *Honest to God* (Philadelphia: Westminster, 1963).

——, *Exploration into God* (London: SCM Press, 1967).

Russell, Bertrand, *Why I Am Not a Christian* (London: Unwin Books, 1967).

Sartre, Jean-Paul, *Literary and Philosophical Essays* (New York: Collier, 1962).

——, *Existentialism and Humanism,* translated by Philip Mairet (London: Methuen & Co., 1966).

——, *The Reprieve,* translated by Eric Sutton (London: Penguin, 1966).

——, *The Words,* translated by Irene Clephane (London: Penguin, 1967).

——, *Being and Nothingness,* translated by Hazel E. Barnes (London: Methuen & Co., 1966).

——, *The Devil and the Good Lord, and Two Other Plays,* translated by Kitty Black (New York: Vintage, 1962).

——, *No Exit and Three Other Plays,* translated by Stuart Gilbert (New York: Vintage, 1963).

——, *Iron in the Soul* (London: Penguin, 1967).

——, *The Age of Reason* (London: Penguin, 1967).

——, *The Chips Are Down* (Boston: Prime Publishers, 1965).

——, *What Is Literature?* (London: University Paperbacks, 1967).

Sciacca, Michele Federico, *Philosophical Trends in the Contemporary World* (Notre Dame, Indiana: University of Notre Dame Press, 1964).

Siegmund, Georg, *God on Trial,* translated by Elinor Castendyk Briefs (New York: Desclée & Company, 1967).

——, *Belief in God and Mental Health* (New York: Desclée & Co., 1965).

Sontag, Frederick, *The Crisis of Faith* (New York: Doubleday, 1969).

Spengler, Oswald, *The Decline of the West* (London: Allen & Unwin, 1932).

Thonnard, F. J., *Précis d'histoire de la philosophie* (Paris: Desclée & Cie, 1966).

Tillich, Paul, *Ultimate Concern* (London: D. Mackenzie Brown, 1965).

——, *The Shaking Of The Foundations* (London: Penguin, 1966).

——, *The Eternal Now* (London: SCM Press, 1963).

——, *The Courage To Be* (New Haven: Yale University Press, 1965).

Tresmontant, Claude, *Comment se pose Aujourd'hui le problème de l'existence de Dieu* (Paris: Éditions du Seuil, 1966).

———, *Les Idées maîtresses de la métaphysique chrétienne* (Paris: Éditions du Seuil, 1962).

Università Gregoriana, Conferenze: *Psicologia dell'Ateismo* (Rome: 1967).

Vahanian, Gabriel, *The Death of God* (New York: George Braziller, 1961).

Van Buren, Paul M., *The Secular Meaning of the Gospel* (New York: Macmillan, 1966).

Versényi, Laszlo, *Heidegger: Being and Truth* (New Haven: Yale University Press, 1965).

Villaseñor, José Sánchez, *Ortega y Gasset: Existentialist* (Chicago: Regnery, 1949).

Voegelin, Eric, *The New Science of Politics* (Chicago: University of Chicago Press, 1952).

Wetter, Gustav, S.J., *Le Materialisme dialectique* (Brussels: Desclée de Brouwer, 1962).

———, *Fondamenti della Filosofia Marxista* (Milano: Fabbri, 1966).

——— and Leonhard, Wolfgang, *L'Ideologie sovietique contemporaine* (Paris: Payot, 1965).

Wilhelmsen, Frederick, *Cox's Secular City: City of Night* (Washington D.C.: Society For the Christian Commonwealth, 1967).

Wood, Alan, *Bertrand Russell: The Passionate Sceptic* (London: Unwin Books, 1957).

Woodyard, David O., *Living Without God Before God* (Philadelphia: Westminster, 1968).

Index